**Eastern
Africa
Series**

A POLITICAL ECOLOGY OF KENYA'S MAU FOREST

A Political Ecology of Kenya's Mau Forest

The Land, the Trees, and the People

LISA ELENA FUCHS

JAMES CURREY

Published in association with the French Institute for
Research in Africa

IFRA Nairobi

Institut Français de Recherche en Afrique
French Institute for Research in Africa

James Currey
is an imprint of
Boydell & Brewer Ltd
www.jamescurrey.com

and of
Boydell & Brewer Inc.
www.boydellandbrewer.com

First published 2023
Paperback edition 2026

The publisher has no responsibility for the continued existence or accuracy of
URLs for external or third-party internet websites referred
to in this book, and does not guarantee that any content on such
websites is, or will remain, accurate or appropriate

Our Authorised Representative for product safety in the EU is
Easy Access System Europe – Mustamäe tee 50, 10621 Tallinn, Estonia,
gpsr.requests@easproject.com

British Library Cataloguing in Publication Data

A catalogue record for this book is available from The British Library

ISBN 978-1-84701-347-7 (James Currey hardback)
ISBN 978-1-84701-355-2 (James Currey paperback)

For my mum
Who gave everything
So I could be

Contents

Illustrations

Maps

Figures

Tables

Full credit details are provided in the captions to the images in the text.
The author and publisher are grateful to all the institutions and individuals for permission to reproduce the materials in which they hold
copyright. Every effort has been made to trace the copyright holders;
apologies are offered for any omission, and the publisher will be pleased
to add any necessary acknowledgement in subsequent editions.

Abbreviations

AFD	French Development Agency
AP	Administration Police Service of Kenya
CBFM	Community-based forest management
CBNRM	Community-based natural resource management
CBO	Community-based organisation
CDE	Centre for Development and Environment (University of Bern)
CDTF	Community Development Trust Fund, joint initiative of the Government of Kenya and the European Union (established in 1996)
CEO	Chief executive officer
CF	Community forestry
CFA	Community forest association
CIG	'Common interest group' in the context of the World Bank's KAPAP project
CITES	Convention on the International Trade in Endangered Species of Wild Flora and Fauna (1973)
CWG	'Common working group' in the context of the World Bank's KAPAP project
DC	District Commissioner of the Government of Kenya
DFO	District Forest Officer of the Ministry of Forestry of Kenya
EMCA	The Environmental Management and Co-ordination Act of Kenya (1999)
ENSDA	Ewaso Nyiro South Development Authority
FAN	Forest Action Network (NGO)
FAO	Food and Agricultural Organization of the United Nations

FCLIP	Forest Conservation and Livelihood Improvement Project
GBM	Green Belt Movement (NGO)
GEF	Global Environment Facility, controlled by UNEP and the EU (since 1991)
GIS	Geographic information system
GoK	Government of Kenya (in references)
ICRAF	World Agroforestry (an international NGO)
ICS	Interim Coordinating Secretariat for the Mau Restoration (2009–2012/13)
ID	Identification document
IDP	Internally displaced person
IEBC	Independent Electoral and Boundaries Commission (since 2011)
IFRA	French Research Institute in Africa
ILO	International Labour Organization
ITPA	Indian Transfer of Property Act (1882)
IUCN	World Conservation Union (an international NGO)
JICA	Japan International Cooperation Agency
KAPAP	Kenya Agricultural Productivity and Agro-Business Project, second phase (KAPP II) of KAPP, implemented from 2009 to 2015
KAPP	Kenya Agricultural Productivity Project, a two-phased, 11-year programme funded by the World Bank. The second phase (KAPP II) is referred to as KAPAP
KAPSLM	Kenya Agricultural Production and Sustainable Land Management Project funded by the World Bank, as part of KAPP
KES	Kenya Shilling, currency in Kenya ($1 = roughly KES 100 at the time of the research)
KFS	Kenya Forest Service, parastatal organisation in charge of forest management in Kenya (since 2007)
KFWG	Kenya Forest Working Group
KJAS	Kenya Joint Assistance Strategy, an attempt to stream-line and coordinate foreign aid between the Kenyan Government and seventeen development partners (2007–2012)

KTBH	Kenya Top Bar Hive
KWS	Kenya Wildlife Service, parastatal organisation in charge of wildlife management in Kenya (since 1989)
KWTA	Kenya Water Towers Agency (since 2012/13)
M&E	Monitoring and evaluation
MaCoDev	Mariashoni Community Development group (CBO)
MCA	Member of Community Assembly, the local representative elected at ward level
MEFoCo	Mau East Forest Conservancy Forum, also called Forest Conservation Committee or the 'Forum' (CBO)
MoW	Ministry of Water, governmental Ministry of Kenya
MP	Member of Parliament
NACOFA	National Association of CFAs (NGO)
NARC	National Rainbow Coalition, a political party that was in power from 2002 to 2005
Necofa	Network for Eco-farming in Africa (NGO)
Nema	National Environmental Management Authority (since 2002)
NGO	Non-governmental organisation
NLC	National Land Commission of Kenya (since 2012)
NRC	Norwegian Refugee Council (NGO)
NTFPs	Non-timber forest products
ODM	Orange Democratic Movement, political party in Kenya (since 2005)
OPAT	Ogiek Peoples Ancestral Territories Atlas, publication produced by the NGO ERMIS Africa in 2011
OWC	Ogiek Welfare Council (CBO)
PAO	Protected area outreach
PELIS	Plantation establishment and livelihood improvement scheme, established by 2005 Forest Act
PES	Payment for environmental/ecosystem services
PEV	Post-election violence (typically reference is made to the 2007/2008 crisis in Kenya)
PFM	Participatory forest management

REDD	United Nations Programme on Reducing Emissions from Deforestation and Forest Degradation
REDD+	United Nations Programme on Reducing Emissions from Deforestation and Forest Degradation in developing countries, and the role of conservation, sustainable management of forests, and enhancement of forest carbon stocks in developing countries
RLA	Registered Land Act (1963)
SFM	Sustainable forest management
SIDA	Swedish Development Agency
SMP	Strategic management plan
TEK	Traditional ecological knowledge
TMA	Timber Manufacturers Association (CBO)
UNEP	United Nations Environment Programme
UNEP-WCMC	UN Environment World Conservation Monitoring Centre (in references)
USA	United States of America
USAID	United States Agency for International Development
WRUA	Water resource user association

Glossary

'Backshwara' is a practice that involves cutting single trees and carrying them on one's back, typically to sawmills. Since the spelling of the term is unclear, it is used in quotes.

Brundtland Report is how the 1987 report of the World Commission on the Environment and Development (WCED) is frequently referred to. The Report coined the terms sustainable development and precautionary principle, concepts that have since become the leitmotif for environmental policies worldwide.

Comply is a timber company. Alongside Raiply and Timsales, Comply is one of the three major commercial players in the timber and wood-producing industry in Kenya. All three belong to the Rai Group of companies.

Debe (Swahili) is a twenty-litre bucket that is typically used in rural Kenya to trade honey and other agricultural goods and food items, including cooking fat, flour, and milk.

'Dorobo' a derogatory term derived from the Maasai term *'Il Torobbo'*, designating people without cattle. The contentious term is commonly used to refer to forest dwellers who might or might not be part of the traditional hunter-and-gatherer Ogiek community.

Gunia (Swahili) is a bag or sack typically made from woven plastic fibre that is used to measure, transport and store agricultural goods. One *gunia* of maize typically weighs about 90kgs, while a *gunia* of potatoes usually weighs about 120kg.

'In-migrants' is an expression with which the Ogiek in the Eastern Mau sometimes refer to the non-Ogiek living in the forest. Other common terms are 'foreigners' or 'newcomers' in English, and *'wageni'* (guests) in Swahili. That term usually designates persons who have settled in the Mau Forest since the mid-1990s and mainly belong to the broader Kalenjin community, including Kipsigis, Tugen, and Nandi. Sometimes, members of the Kamba, Kisii, or other communities are included as well. Due to the somewhat derogatory connotation of the term, it is used in quotes.

Kalenjin is an ethnic grouping of eight culturally and linguistically related groups, sometimes referred to as 'tribes'. These groups include the Kipsigis, Tugen, and Nandi. They are designated as Highland Nilotes. Their common identity was not professed until a Nandi radio presenter proposed to unite all Nandi speakers under the term Kalenjin in the 1940s.

Kikuyu also called Gikuyu or Agikuyu are a Bantu-speaking ethnic grouping who traditionally live in the central highlands near Mount Kenya. The Kikuyu are the largest ethnic group in Kenya.

Konoito refers to a particular traditional Ogiek socio-spatial unit. Before the spatial reorganisation enforced by the colonial government, the Mau Forest used to be subdivided into forest tracts, main lineage territories called *konoito*. Each clan was given its own *konoito*, which typically spanned different altitudes and eco-climatic zones, within which clan members had land-use rights. Other sources spell the term *gonoitweeg*.

Koret refers to a family transect unit within a *konoito* clan territory. A *koret* could range from one to ten square miles, and ran parallel to the overall clan territory lines, thus allowing for transhumance through the different eco-climatic zones from the highlands to the lowlands.

Maasai is an ethnic grouping considered indigenous to East Africa. The Maasai are a Nilotic semi-nomadic people living across Kenya and Tanzania.

'Mgeni' (Swahili) means 'guest' and is the singular of *'wageni'*, the Swahili expression commonly used among the Ogiek in the Eastern Mau to refer to non-Ogiek forest dwellers. See description for 'in-migrants'.

'Miti ya mungu' (Swahili) means God's trees and is an expression used among the Ogiek to refer to indigenous trees. Other common terms include *'miti kienyeji'* (indigenous trees) or *'miti ya zamani'* (erstwhile trees), and *'miti ya dawa'* (medicinal trees).

'Miti ya wazungu' (Swahili) means white people's trees and an expression used among the Ogiek to refer to exotic or non-indigenous trees. Other related terms include *'miti ya kisasa'* (modern trees), *'miti ya serikali'* (the Government's trees), or *'miti ya biashara'* (trees for business).

Ndung'u Report is the 2004 Report of the Commission of Inquiry into the Illegal/Irregular Allocation of Public Land. The Commission was commonly known as the 'Ndung'u Commission', named after its chairperson Paul Ndung'u. The Report uncovered connections between inadequate land law systems, land distribution, and corruption. Its recommendations were fundamental for Kenya's land reforms, including for forest land.

Njonjo Report   is the 2002 Report of the Commission of Inquiry into Land Law Systems. The 'Njonjo Commission', named after its chairperson and then-Attorney General Charles Mugane Njonjo, was established in 1999. The acclaimed Report proposed a framework for a new land policy ahead of the 2002 general elections that eventually led to Kenya's democratic transition. The Report later became known as one of the first key events in Kenya's land reforms.

Ogiek   is a traditional hunter-and-gatherer community that is officially recognised as the indigenous community of the Mau Forest. The wider Ogiek community is composed of twelve different sub-groups, or sub-tribes. Three of these twelve sub-groups traditionally lived in the Eastern Mau, namely the Tyepkwereg, Morisionig and Kipchorng'woneg. Those three sub-groups encompass twenty-one clans. The Ogiek language is a Kalenjin language of the Southern Nilotic group. While the Ogiek are counted as part of the wider Kalenjin community, their association is contested by members of other Kalenjin groups and academics alike.

Shamba (Swahili)   refers to a field, plot or a family farm in Kenya. The '*shamba*' system is a forest land-use system that was first introduced by the colonial government, later regulated through the 1968 Forest Act, and then discontinued in the late 1980s. Under the *shamba* system, foresters could allocate plots in government forest plantations to individual farmers. These farmers were allowed to cultivate the land in exchange for taking care of the tree seedlings until they grew to a specific size. The system, in principle, allowed to effectively combine forest production and livelihood requirements. A revamped version of the *shamba* system was introduced through the 2005 Forests Act in the shape of PELIS, the 'plantation establishment and livelihood improvement scheme'.

Small- and medium-scale sawmillers   or simply 'sawmillers' refers to smaller players in the timber industry apart from the 'big three' commercial timber companies. These sawmillers are represented by the Timber Manufacturers Association.

Timsales   is a timber company. Alongside Comply and Raiply, Timsales is one of the three major commercial players in the Kenyan timber and wood-producing industry. All three belong to the Rai Group of companies. While Raiply and Comply operated primarily in the western parts of the Mau Forest and at a smaller scale in the western parts of the Eastern Mau, Timsales operated at a significant scale in the Kiptunga Forest in the Eastern Mau, which is part of the broader Mariashoni area. Timsales' main factory is in Elburgon, the transit town at the edge of the Eastern Mau approximately 10 km from Mariashoni Centre, the small trading centre from where this research was conducted.

'Wageni' (Swahili)   means 'guests' and is the plural of *'mgeni'*. See descriptions for *'mgeni'* and 'in-migrants'.

Waki Report   is the commonly used name of the 2008 Report of the Commission of Inquiry into the Post-Election Violence (CIPEV) that investigated the post-election violence crisis that engulfed Kenya after the 2007 general elections.

Acknowledgements

I am grateful for the support of many, whose guidance, patience, and trust have contributed tremendously to my ability to bring this work to fruition.

I am greatly indebted to Professor Dr Bernard Calas, Professor of Geography at Bordeaux III University and former Director at the French Research Institute in Africa (IFRA), Nairobi, who encouraged me to pursue my interest in the political ecology of environmental and forest management in Kenya. I thank the consecutive directors of IFRA, especially Dr Marie-Aude Fouéré, and the British Institute in Eastern Africa (BIEA), as well as the BIEA-IFRA research associates crew. The financial support of both, alongside the German Academic Exchange Service's (DAAD), have allowed me to undertake this exciting project.

I am grateful for the interest, support, and numerous conversations with various individuals from the Government, non-government, university, and the press, who have advised me along the way, especially Francis ole Nkako, Director General of the Kenya Water Towers Agency (KWTA), Professor James B. Kung'u, Dean of the School of Environmental Studies at Kenyatta University, Rudolf Makhanu, former National coordinator of the Kenya Forest Working Group (KFWG), Samuel Karanja Muhunyu, Country Coordinator of the Network for Eco-farming (Necofa) Kenya, and George Sayagie, journalist at the *Daily Nation*.

My research in the Mau Forest would not have been possible without my fantastic research assistants Lynette Cheruiyot and Ibrahim Mwangi. It was also enabled by numerous administrative and political representatives in Mariashoni and the wider Eastern Mau. I am particularly grateful for the support received from Joseph K. Towett, famous Ogiek leader from Mariashoni, head of the Ogiek Welfare Council (OWC), and chairman of the Ogiek Council of Elders established by the Interim Coordinating Secretariat for the Mau Rehabilitation (ICS). Furthermore, most of my work is built on the reflections and deep insights gained from the hundreds of conversations with the residents of Mariashoni throughout the fifteen months I spent in the area. I am deeply grateful.

I sincerely appreciate the support and guidance received from my academic supervisors Professor Dr Michael Bollig, Professor at the Institute for Social and Cultural Anthropology and Vice-Speaker for the Global South Studies Centre Cologne at the University of Cologne, and Dr Martin Skrydstrup, Associate Professor of Globalisation & Sustainability at the Department of Management, Society and Communication of the Copenhagen Business School. I am also greatly indebted to my consecutive supervisors at World Agroforestry (ICRAF), Dr Henry Neufeldt and Dr Fergus Sinclair, and my team members Levi Orero, Lucy Njuguna, Lang'at Kipkorir and Fabio Ricci particularly, alongside the invaluable support of many other colleagues and friends in Kenya and beyond.

My profound thanks go to my family, especially my parents and sisters. Beyond raising me to be an independent, perseverant, and optimistic person, your support and care have allowed me to keep things together throughout the years of hard work on this study. Last, I want to thank my partner John, and my baby Ayla, who might not yet fully grasp the wonder she has ignited in me since coming into this world. You are the beginning and the end of everything. I am because you are, in anticipation, in hindsight, and the present. Always.

Introduction

'Imagine if trees gave off Wifi signals, we would be planting so many trees and we'd probably save the planet too. Too bad they only produce the oxygen we breathe'. While the origin of the quote that circulated the internet in the early 2000s is unclear, the adoption and use of the slogan by influential environmental organisations, including the World Wide Fund for Nature (WWF) and Action Against Hunger,[1] questions society's collective approaches to complex matters. The quote itself and its popularisation through environmental organisations make manifest that there is a growing sense of concern about environmental topics, specifically climate change. However, it also shows that, despite increased awareness, we give too little attention to the urgency of doing something about it. The quote further alludes to the potential power of individuals coming together to preserve important public goods through collective action successfully. It recognises and places responsibility in the hands of each of us and thus individualises the duty of environmental care. However, in doing so, it also crucially neglects the structural role played by various actors and components at the system level, for instance, governments, industries, and even the very nature of the economic world order. Yet, major environmental crises of our time call for reconceptualisations at this systemic level and hence require much more than individual behaviour change.

The interconnectedness of these local and global dynamics of cause and consequence, and roles and responsibilities of various actors, is the focus of this book on the scramble for Kenya's Mau Forest. It is based on empirical findings resulting from research undertaken in the Mariashoni settlement area within the Eastern Mau Forest between 2011 and 2013. The Mau Forest's massive degradation and destruction were acknowledged when the area became a major agricultural frontier in the 1990s, following years of commercial timber extraction and conversion of indigenous forests into forest plantations. Until then, the Mau Forest was commonly profiled as the most important closed-canopy forest in Kenya and the wider East African region due to its numerous

---

1   See 'If trees gave off Wifi signals' Greenpeace illustration or Action contre la Faim (ACF) illustration on Pininterest.com (accessed 6 August 2017).

economic, environmental, and social roles. Under the considerable influence of both national and international conservation actors, the Kenyan government set out to reverse land and forest degradation in the Mau Forest in 2008. In response to the public outcry over the Mau Forest destruction, a Special Task Force was mandated in July 2008 to advise the Government on how to best 'Save the Mau'. Its objective was to propose pathways to address ecological and social issues underlying the destruction (GoK, 2009d, 2009e). The 'crisis' and 'emergency' discourses employed at the time considerably influenced the design, implementation and outcomes of the consecutive forest rehabilitation and restoration policies and programmes. Despite the prominence of the Mau Forest crisis, in the years following the deployment of the governmental Mau Forest Task Force and the publication of its acclaimed and detailed report in March 2009, and countless appeals from prominent people, from then-Prime Minister Raila Odinga to famous singer Iddi Achieng,[2] the degradation, destruction, and depletion of Mau Forest have continued unabatedly regardless of the rehabilitation programme. Identifying and analysing the drivers of this environmental crisis is thus critical to understanding how the factors underpinning it might be addressed.

Through a micro-level analysis of the supposed '"environmental" crisis'[3] witnessed in the Eastern Mau Forest, this book addresses the issue of the politicisation of global environmental crises. It analyses roles and responsibilities in both the forest's destruction and its rehabilitation. It does so by looking at systemic and agent-based drivers over various time frames, retracing the colonial legacy and exploring post-Independence policies and practices. The Mau Forest is also a space of intense contestation and competition over the 'sovereignty of definition',[4] leading to multiple claims of legitimacy: *which* forest, and

---

[2]   Iddi Achieng released a song called 'Ni Yako Ni Yetu (Save the Mau)', which translates as 'It is Yours; It is Ours (Save the Mau) in 2012, see e.g., www. youtube.com/watch?v=Km8Q1NYWUpE (published 26 May 2013, accessed 10 March 2017).

[3]   'Environmental crisis' is put in quotes since the crisis witnessed in the Mau Forest is deconstructed as a political, economic, and socio-cultural crisis beyond the somewhat simplifying *environmental* crisis label throughout this study. To improve readability, these quotes are dropped in the remaining text. However, mention of the Mau crisis in terms of environmental crisis is sometimes qualified as 'supposed' or 'alleged' in line with this interpretation and argument. Furthermore, while the term crisis is used frequently in this study, its usage is mainly conditioned by the fact that relevant authorities and actors branded the Mau situation as a crisis – rather than by the author identifying it as such.

[4]   Sovereignty of definition (translated from the German term *Definitionshoheit*) means having the power to define which meaning specific terms or events have, or ought to have according to the person/group in power.

whose? *What kinds* of forest and land use, and *by whom*? *What types* of destruction, caused *by whom*? While 'the Mau is a forest complex with a lot of complexities' [1/002],[5] its significance is such that identifying and addressing both the drivers of forest degradation and the dynamics that have prevented its rehabilitation should be one such matter that unites collective action and consciousness across scales to increase chances to 'Save the Mau' after all.

The scramble for the Mau Forest

The Mau Forest is Kenya's biggest closed-canopy montane forest ecosystem and the thus biggest of the country's five major water towers or montanes,[6] alongside Mt Elgon, the Cherangany Hills, the Aberdares, and Mt Kenya. While a forest, or a woodland, in general, can be defined as 'land under natural or planted stands of trees whether productive or not, and includes land from which forests have been cleared, but that will be reforested in the foreseeable future' (FAO, 1991, ix), a quantifiable definition includes 'land spanning more than 0.5 hectares with trees higher than 5 metres and a canopy cover of more than 10 per cent, or trees able to reach these thresholds in situ' (FAO, 2012, p. 3). A montane forest or water tower, according to the Kenyan government's official definition, is 'an area that acts as a receptacle for rainwater and that stores water in the aquifers underneath it and gradually releases the water to the springs and springs emanating from it' (Republic of Kenya, 2012b). It extends over 416,543 ha, or 4,165 km², in the fertile Rift Valley region and is roughly located between Nakuru to the east, Narok to the south, Kericho to the west and ldoret to the north (see Map 1). Administratively, the forest was composed of twenty-two blocks, most of which were protected through gazettement as forest reserves in 1932 (GoK, 2009e). Of these twenty-two forest blocks, twenty-one were forest reserves under the authority of the Government as they are located on Public Land, previously called Government Land. The block located furthest south, the Maasai Mau Forest, has a special status as it stands on Trust Land, now Community Land, and is thus considered a community forest reserve. It is administered by the Narok County Council (GoK, 2009b, 2009d, 2009e, 2010b, 2010c).

With over twenty rivers originating in its midst, the Mau Forest is a critical ecological resource for the country and the entire East African region. The Complex forms the upper catchment of almost all main

[5]   Over 250 interviews were conducted to feed this study. These interviews are referenced in brackets in the text, and an overview is provided in Appendix 2.
[6]   UNEP and others use the terms 'montane forest' and 'water tower' interchangeably in the Kenyan context (UNEP, 2012, Abstract).

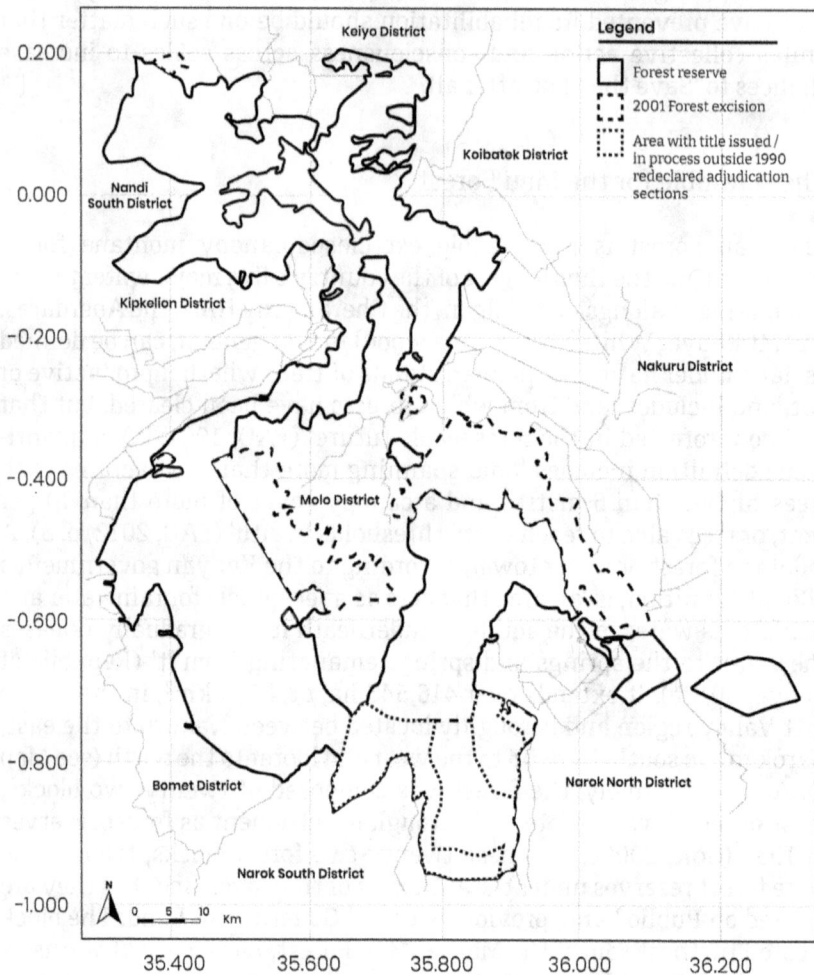

Map 1   Mau Forest Complex Map.

Source: Adapted from KFS, 2009. Note: The officially recognised map of the
Mau Forest Complex highlights two particular types of territories: 1) 67,000 ha
of forest land excised in the South-Western and Eastern Mau in 2001 indicated
with dash line, and 2) areas in the Maasai Mau for which land titles were issued
indicated with square dot line.

rivers west of the Rift Valley, feeding into five significant lakes in the region. Three of these lakes are of direct cross-boundary importance, namely Lake Victoria which is part of the wider Nile River Basin, Lake Turkana that borders Ethiopia, and Lake Natron that borders Tanzania. Many ecosystems depend on the Mau Forest, notably the famous Serengeti National Park, which forms one large ecosystem with Kenya's Maasai Mara. They together are the site of the 'Great Migration' of wildebeests and zebras, recognised as one of the Wonders of the World. Various other major conservation areas are significantly impacted by the Mau Forest, which hold a variety of protected wildlife, biodiversity, scenic landscapes, and recognised Important Bird Areas. These designated wetlands meet the Criteria for identifying Wetlands of International Importance, so-called Ramsar Sites, and are the only remnant of the Guineo-Congolian forest ecosystem in Kenya (UNEP, KFS, & KFWG, 2005).

The Mau Forest is crucial for its ecological functions, for its climate, biodiversity and water, as well as socio-economically, since it creates optimal conditions for tea production, one of Kenya's export products and thus foreign currency earners, on which 430,000 persons depend directly in the area surrounding the Mau Forest alone (GoK, 2009b, 2009d; UNEP et al., 2005). The wider beneficiaries of the Mau Forest are estimated at several million. According to the United Nations Environment Programme (UNEP), three million people live in the sub-locations crossed by the major rivers whose upper catchments are formed by the Mau Forest (UNEP et al., 2005; UNEP, 2008). Another expert said that ten million people, a quarter of the Kenyan population, depend on Mau Forest [1/019], while another estimated that the Mau ecosystem supports a third of the country's population [1/021]. The Mau Forest is also recognised as the ancestral homeland of the Ogiek community,[7] one of the only officially recognised indigenous hunter-gatherer groups in Kenya (GoK, 2009d, 2009e).

The forest's unprecedented degradation and destruction

The Mau Forest experienced substantial environmental impacts and transformations. Deforestation and degradation of the Mau Forest severely increased from the mid-1990s. The clearance of 107,707 ha,

---

[7] Though their use is controversial in academic circles, in Kenya, the terms 'tribe', 'ethnic group' or 'community' are frequently used. They refer to the idea that every Kenyan belongs to a smaller group of citizens, bound by some form of common or local place of origin. In this book, all three terms are used interchangeably, following a common practice in Kenya, without further theoretical specification. Furthermore, throughout the text, the common English spelling of the names of these communities is used without taking sides in conceptual or ideological conflicts associated with different types of spelling.

more than a quarter of the total Forest Complex, between the 1970s and the 2000s critically impacted the ecological balance of the areas surrounding the Forest, of the country, and of the entire East African region (GoK, 2009e). The significant forest excisions of 2001 alone led to the loss of 67,000 ha of forest land, predominantly in the Mau Forest (UNEP, 2008). Forest excisions in the Eastern and South-Western Mau in 2001 alone accounted for 35,301 ha and 22,797 ha, respectively, representing 54.3% and 27.3% of these forests. Since the summit of the Mau escarpment is located within the excised zones in the Eastern Mau, the 2001 excision literally affected the 'top' of the Mau Forest. Based on satellite imagery (Landsat Multispectral Scanner and Enhanced Thematic Mapper images), as well as insights into changes in forest boundaries, authors of the (2008) UNEP report further estimate the loss of dense vegetation cover between 1973 and 2003 in the Eastern Mau at 36,780 ha, representing 49% of its total dense vegetation cover, 15,820 ha of which was inside the forest reserve boundaries and 20,960 ha outside them. Forest excisions in these areas, by 2009, had further-more led to the in-migration of approximately 15,000 and 13,000 house-holds, respectively, accounting together for 28,000 settler households in these two vast areas. The UNEP (2008) report further estimated that 2,400 households had illegally encroached into the Maasai Mau Forest. Loss of forest cover between 1986 and 2003 in the Maasai Mau was estimated at 20,330 ha in total, 3,382 ha within the forest boundaries and 16,948 ha outside of the boundaries, representing 30% of the forest inside and outside the official boundaries of Maasai Mau Forest. Because of changes in forest status, vegetation cover, and strong in-migration, the Eastern, South-Western and Maasai Mau Forest blocks were consid-ered particularly affected and vulnerable to continuous environmental destruction (UNEP, 2008).

Deforestation can be defined as 'conversion of forest to other land use or the permanent reduction of the tree canopy cover below the minimum 10 per cent threshold' (FAO, 2012, p. 5), typically measured as the annual decline in forest and woodland coverage, relative to the figure for the previous year. The term excludes areas in which trees are harvested as part of cyclic and hence sustainable forest resource production activities and only concerns the total loss of forest cover. Beyond total loss, other forms of degradation that are often less visible pose severe threats to forests, including the Mau Forest (Nyangena, 2008). Degradation can generally be classified into threats to habitats and threats to species. The former include habitat loss, habitat fragmen-tation, habitat disturbance, uncontrolled logging, increasing rates of fire, overharvesting of fuelwood and overgrazing of sensitive habitats. In contrast, the latter includes species extinction, loss of species range, and competition by invasive species (Bongers & Tennigkeit, 2010).

Deforestation has manifold consequences. One of its most important and immediate effects is a reduction in water levels in nearby rivers and water catchment areas. The loss of vegetation cover in the Mau Forest led to essential reductions in groundwater levels and river water levels, rendering some of the rivers seasonal (UNEP, 2008). The reduction of river water levels was the main negative impact in the Mau region, which was often attributed to climate change. Over the first decade of the 2000s, reduced water levels were mainly experienced outside of the Mau Forest, especially in Nakuru town, that had to cope with reduced water accessibility and decreasing numbers of flamingos, one of the biggest attractions of the Nakuru National Park [1/002]. Owners of the vast tea plantations, primarily located in the western parts of the Mau Forest, complained about erratic rains that endangered their harvest [1/021].[8] Other consequences were the destruction of habitat for wildlife and conservation areas, as well as a deterioration of living conditions for people who depend on the forest directly or indirectly, including forest-dwelling and forest-adjacent communities.

According to UNEP estimates, and based on figures concerning deforestation and timber and fuelwood volumes from 2000 to 2010, the deforestation rate in Kenya was 5,000 ha/year by 2010, equivalent to a cash revenue of KES 1.36 billion ($13.62 million). At the same time, the cumulative negative effect of deforestation on the economy, through a reduction of regulating services, was estimated at KES 3.65 billion ($36.52 million) per year by 2010 and thus 2.8 times the cash revenue of deforestation. This reduction was mainly attributed to changes in river flows with significant adverse effects on agricultural production, hydropower generation, inland fish production, and human health through a decrease in high-quality potable water and an increase in diseases. The loss in above-ground carbon storage potential due to deforestation alone was estimated at KES 341 million ($3.41 million) in 2010. Further, taking the secondary multiplier effects into account, the total negative impact of deforestation in 2010 was estimated at KES 5.8 billion ($58 million) for 2010 and thus 4.2 times higher than the cash revenue from deforestation (UNEP, 2012).

Concerning general forest trends, a Food and Agricultural Organization of the United Nations (FAO) (2007) report indicates that the world average and the African average of forest area primarily designated for production purposes stands at around 30% of total land use. The report further states that the area designated for production reduced at a constant rate of about 300,000 ha per year in eastern Africa alone, while wood removed from forests increased from ca. 185 to ca. 320 million m^3 per year between 1990 and 2005, despite the supply from

8   See also: Editorial, 'Reclaim the Mau or we are doomed', *Daily Nation*, 2 April 2009.

forest plantations being limited. This indicates that deforestation of natural forests has increased (Bongers & Tennigkeit, 2010). Globally, forest cover remained constant at around 30% of total land use by 2010, while the African average reduced to about 20% (FAO, 2016). The 2016 FAO report also chronicles a net forest loss of 7 million ha in tropical countries from 2000–2010, particularly in low-income countries, and indicates that most of the loss occurred in natural forests (FAO, 2016). According to the 'Global Forest Resources Assessment 2015', the global forest area reduced by 3.1%, and hence by 129 million ha between 1990 and 2015, to less than 4 billion ha, indicating that deforestation remains a 'matter of deep concern' despite a slowing annual deforestation rate from an average of 7.3 million ha in the 1990s (FAO, 2016). While the FAO uses various techniques to reduce errors in estimations, the Global Forest Resources Assessment (FRA) figures for Kenya have changed so drastically over the last years that none of these figures is explicitly cited here. Official government figures also vary considerably from the FAO figures. By the 1990s, 12% of the land was supposedly covered by closed-canopy forests, which reduced to roughly 1.5%, or 3.5 million ha, in the late 2000s (Standing & Gachanja, 2014). Despite uncertainty attached to these figures, the forest cover reduction trends that are reported globally match trends observed in the Mau Forest.

The Mau Forest Rehabilitation Programme

The Kenyan government started addressing the massive destruction affecting the Mau Forest in 2008 after being approached by a UNEP-led coalition of external actors. Forest conservation, and the conservation of the Mau Forest specifically, had been of high priority to then-UNEP Director Christian Lambrechts for several years.[9] In that vein, Lambrechts collaborated with a coalition of interested individuals from various government and non-government organisations[10] to prepare a compelling petition to the Government. In response, the first flights to

[9]   Lambrechts had by then authored and co-authored various documents documenting the state of Kenya's forests, and particularly the Mau Forest, including (ENSDA, UNEP, KFWG, & KWS, 2005; UNEP, ENSDA, KFWG, KWS, & RSRS, 2006).

[10]   Core partners were the Kenya Forests Working Group (KFWG), a small but powerful NGO; the Ewaso Ngiro South Development Authority (ENSDA), a state corporation established in 1989 to support livelihood development in several counties touched by the Mau Forest, including Narok and Nakuru; alongside the Kenya Wildlife Service (KWS), the parastatal responsible for wildlife management; and the Department of Resource Surveys and Remote Sensing (DRSRS), at the time part of the Ministry of Environment and Natural Resources. Public forums further helped to mobilise other powerful players, including representatives from tea companies whose farms surrounded the Mau Forest.

assess the deforestation in the Mau Forest Complex were undertaken with significant government and non-government stakeholders on 27 May 2008 (GoK, 2009b). Shortly after that, the petition containing aerial surveys of the water towers that clearly illustrated the extent of destruction that had been taking place was presented to the Kenyan government, including the Kenya Forest Service (KFS) and the Ministry of Water (MoW). The aerial surveys were used to illustrate the extent of the destruction and thus appeal to the Government to address the situation urgently [1/030]. In response to the sense of urgency created, a major ministerial conference was held on the Mau Forest, which endorsed the establishment of a Mau Task Force on 15 July 2008. Raila Odinga, then Prime Minister, mandated a Special Task Force on 21 July 2008 to advise the Government on steps and possibilities to 'Save the Mau'. The membership was devised to 'ensure fair representation of primary stakeholders, including government institutions, affected communities and non-governmental organizations'[11] (GoK, 2009e, p. 20). The Mau Task Force submitted its final report to the Government on 21 March 2009, approved by Cabinet on 30 July 2009 and adopted by Parliament on 15 September 2009 as a framework for the Mau Forest Rehabilitation Programme (GoK, 2009b).

Instead of a comprehensive root cause analysis, the 'Report of the Prime Minister's Task Force on the conservation of the Mau Forest Complex' (2009e) only mentions the presumed causes of the 'Mau crisis' in passing, and with slightly changing formulations: 'irregular and ill-planned settlements, as well as ... uncontrolled and illegal forest resource extraction and conversion to agricultural production' (p. 6), 'encroachment, excisions and illegal forest resources extraction' (p. 9), and 'encroachment, ill-planned and irregular settlements, as well as illegal forest resources extraction' (p. 9). Further details about these alleged causes are only mentioned once: 'The degradation is attributed to political interference, weak law enforcement and management capacities of mandated institutions, high dependence on the forests by the communities and inadequate governance systems' (p. 22).

The text hence implicitly alludes to two root causes. First, the destruction of the Mau Forest was blamed on the forest dwellers who had supposedly encroached on the Mau Forest. Furthermore, their natural resource use had presumably exacerbated the forest's carrying capacity, and their need for food led to the unsustainable conversion

---

[11] The Task Force was composed of 29 members, including two women, and led by chairman Professor Fredrick Owino. The secretariat included Christian Lambrechts (at the time UNEP Director), Julius Kipngetich (at the time KWS CEO), David Mbugua (at the time KFS Director), and Francis ole Nkako (at the time Managing Director of the Uaso Nyiro South Development Authority) (see more details of GoK, 2009e in Annex I).

of forest to agricultural land. Because of the sheer number of settlers, due to their presumed poverty, and because they supposedly considered forests as 'open-access' resources without well-defined property rights and hence freely exploitable by all, the Mau Forest's degradation was represented as an almost linear and thus predictable process.[12] The association of supposedly poor communities with adverse environmental outcomes is commonly conceptualised as the Poverty-Environment Nexus (Martin, 2005; Nunan, 2015). In that vein, the Task Force Report states that 'extensive encroachment have [sic.] also taken place, leading to the destruction of some 29,000 hectares of indigenous forest' (GoK, 2009e, p. 22). Citing a different figure, authors of *The Star* newspaper claimed in 2017 that 'the more than 30,000 settlers had over the years cut down trees, destroying over 100,000 hectares of Kenya's most important forest'.[13] This analysis is in line with the FAO (2016) Status of the World's Forests reports that prominently analyse factors contributing to forest loss on a global scale. These factors are grouped into three categories: agriculture-related, wood and forest-related, or social and governance-related. The top factors in each of these categories are agriculture and shifting cultivation (58%), encroachment and land grabbing (50%), and livestock grazing (33%) for the first category; need for forest products including fuelwood (50%), decreasing forest resources (25%), insecure tenure of forest land (25%), and unsustainable harvesting rates (25%) for the second category; as well as population growth (42%), settlements and industrial development (42%), and increasing poverty (33%) for the third category (FAO, 2016). Similarly, the World Resources Institute et al. (2007) attribute the loss of Kenya's primary forest to subsistence activities and agricultural expansion.

The second root cause mentioned in the Task Force Report (2009e) is 'institutional failure', which supposedly conditioned over-extraction of forest resources and land-use change from forest to agricultural land, leading to forest loss. In that vein, the Report states that 'ill-planned settlements endorsed by the Government have been the main causes of the loss of forestland in the Mau Forests Complex' (GoK, 2009e, p. 22). The Task Force experts invoked institutional failure leading to ill-planned forest landscapes characterised by weak law enforcement and management capacities, and even political interference (GoK, 2009d, 2009e, 2010c). Despite this recognition, public discussions centred mainly on populist explanation patterns that blamed forest-dwelling

---

[12] See: Morgan, J., 'Kenya's heart stops pumping', *BBC News*, 29 September 2009; Wallis, D., 'Kenya evicts squatters from vital Mau Forest', *Reuters*, 19 November 2009; Editorial, 'Rid the Mau of squatters', *Daily Nation*, 25 August 2014; Kemei, K., 'MP wants Mau settlers evicted next month', *The Standard*, 27 December 2010.

[13] Murimi, J. and Muchangi, J., 'Mau Forest depletion at the root of worsening droughts and conflicts', *The Star*, 20 March 2017.

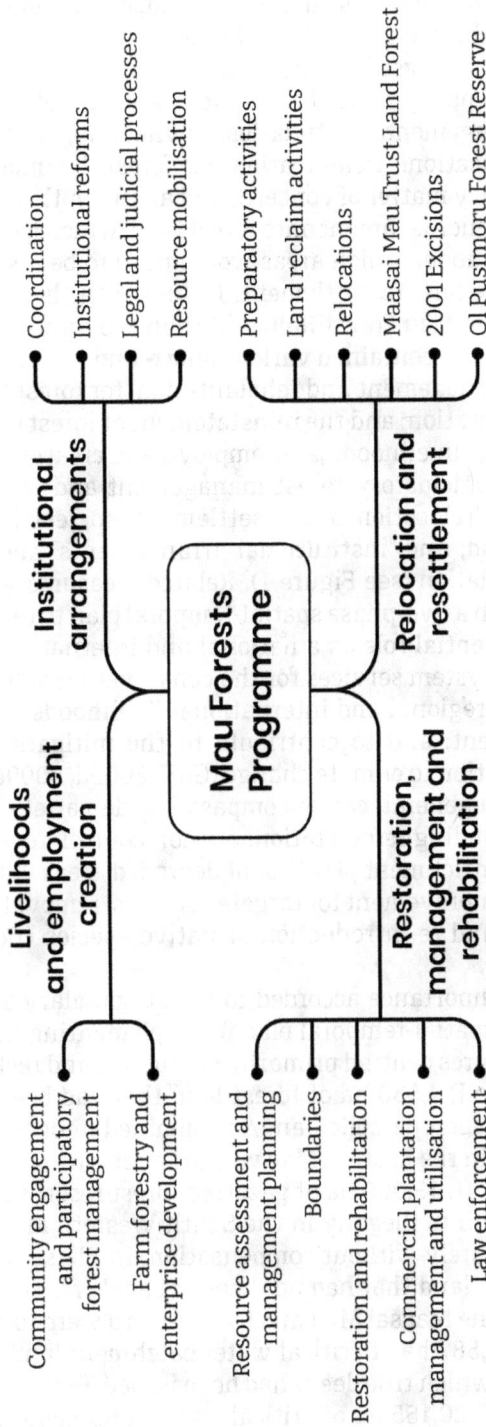

Figure 1 Visual representation of the components and sub-components of the Mau Forest Rehabilitation Programme.

Source: GoK, 2010c, p. 5.

and forest-adjacent communities on the one hand, or individual actions of greedy land grabbers on the other, largely without taking more complex, structural, and systemic causes into account.

The Task Force Report proposed a way forward by addressing four core aspects: management, boundaries, ownership, and restoration/resource-mobilisation. Demarcation of forest boundaries was addressed as a primary matter of concern, and an in-depth assessment was carried out into encroachment onto forest land, which led to specific recommendations about which areas would need to be restored and which areas could be left for settlement. In line with the Task Force Report's guidance, the Mau Forest Rehabilitation Programme included four components, which contained various short- and long-term measures: 'restoration, management and rehabilitation' for forest boundary solidification, reforestation, and the reinstatement of forest production provisions and sites; 'livelihoods and employment creation' through the promotion of participatory forest management and on-farm forestry development; 'relocation and resettlement' to reclaim illegally excised forest land; and 'institutional arrangements' and reforms for improved coordination (see Figure 1). Related measures were to be implemented through a five-phase spatial-temporal plan to re-establish the Mau Forest's essential role as a national and international watershed; to provide ecosystem services for the conservation of biodiversity; to support local, regional and international livelihoods; to sustain economic development; and to contribute to the mitigation of and allowance for adaptation to climate change (GoK, 2009d, 2009e, 2010c). Forest restoration, in general, can encompass a wide variety of intentional activities, including reforestation, erosion control, revegetation of disturbed areas, enrichment planting of degraded areas with valuable species, habitat improvement for targeted species, removal of exotic non-native species and re-introduction of native species (Bongers & Tennigkeit, 2010).

In line with the importance accorded to forest boundary solidification, the five-phase spatial-temporal plan for implementing the identified short-term measures centred primarily on Public Land reclamation (see Map 2). In Phase I, 4,530 ha of forest land that had been excised in 2001 but had not been parcelled and/or remained unoccupied near the Mau escarpment in the Eastern Mau was to be returned with immediate effect. In Phase II, 19,000 ha of gazetted forest reserve land that had been encroached into illegally in the South-Western Mau were to be recovered immediately without compensation. In Phase III, 23,300 ha of protected forest land that had not been set aside for settlements at any point within the Maasai Mau and Ol Pusimoru were to be recovered. In Phase IV, 61,587 ha of critical water catchment land that had been excised and for which title deeds had been issued were to be recovered. And in Phase V, 20,155 ha of critical water catchment land that had been partly adjudicated, but was still gazetted, was to be recovered (GoK, 2009c).

Timelines, steps and procedures, including measures to deal with formal and informal landowners and compensation modes, were outlined in detail in various reports and presentations (e.g., GoK, 2009b, 2009c, 2009d, 2009e, 2010c). According to the plan, forest dwellers were to leave the areas within these 'critical water catchments', and settlements were to be disbanded. This included settlements resulting from presumed encroachment and those that previous administrations had illegally established. The plan also provided for fencing of most threatened forest areas to allow for natural regeneration and assisted reforestation. According to the plan, land title deeds for plots within the defined areas were to be returned, and their validity was declared expired. Compensation for land losses was only considered for third-party purchasers and not those to whom the lands were initially, and often illegally, allocated. According to the initial plan, the only ones allowed to remain in the Forest were members of the Ogiek community. However, the Ogiek were to be resettled from the upstream areas to ecologically less sensitive downstream areas. These measures were to be accompanied by sensitisation and tree-planting activities (GoK, 2009c, 2009d, 2009e, 2010c). While Phase I and II were to be completed before the end of 2009 (GoK, 2009a), the Task Force foresaw extended time frames for Phases III, IV, and V (GoK, 2010d).

The implementation of the 'Save the Mau' initiative was to be coordinated and supervised by an Interim Coordinating Secretariat for the Mau Restoration (ICS), comprising five staff members representing Government, private sector, and non-governmental organisations. The ICS was to be homed in the Ministry of the Prime Minister and was officially established on 4 September 2009 (GoK, 2009b). After its six-month term, the ICS was to dissolve into the yet-to-be-created Mau Forests Complex Authority. Enforcement of set rules and boundaries on the ground was to be ensured by a joint enforcement unit comprising the KFS, the Kenya Wildlife Service (KWS), the Administration Police (AP) and the Narok County Council (NCC) (GoK, 2009e).

Beyond the five-phase plan, and in line with the long-term measures proposed by the Task Force Report, a more holistic approach to the Mau Forest's management was to be adopted. The latter was to provide exceptional protection of water catchment areas and biodiversity hotspots and supersede the prevailing forestry-based perspective and philosophy, which had focused on timber and wood production rather than on ecosystem conservation. The same effort defined four biodiversity spots within the Complex (GoK, 2009d, 2009e, 2010c).

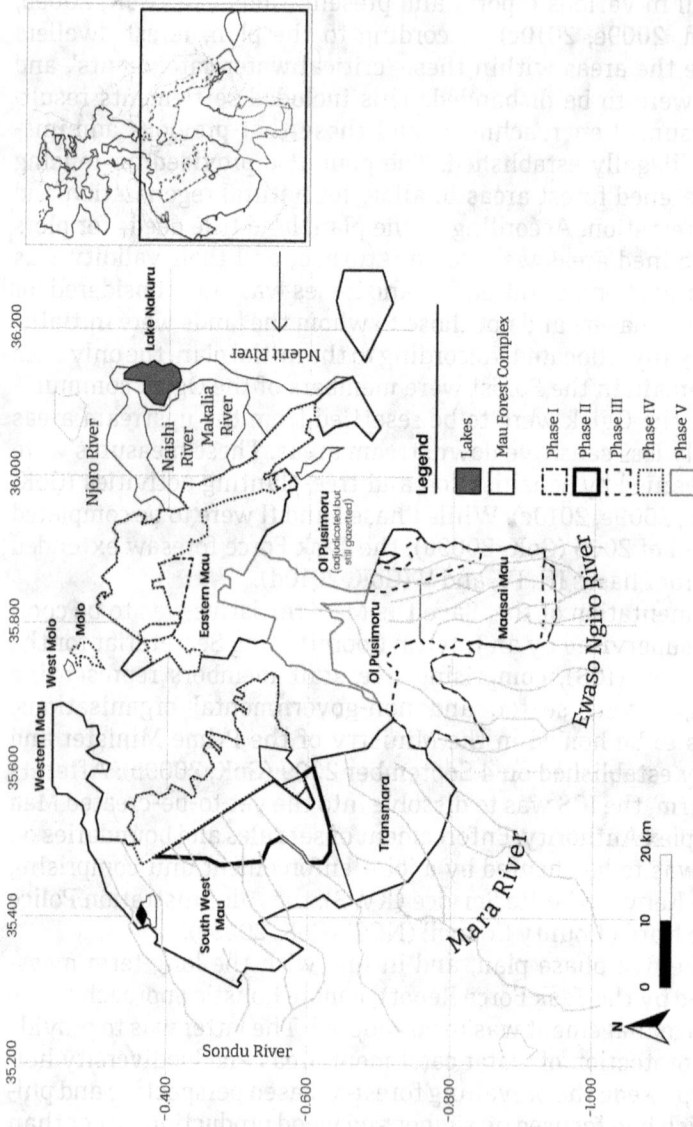

Map 2 The five spatial zones of the 'Save the Mau' programme in the lower half of the Mau Forest.

Source: Adapted from GoK, 2009c. Note: Phases I to V are represented through different line types: 1) Phase I is indicated with dash dot, 2) Phase II with thick solid, 3) Phase III with dash, 4) Phase IV with dash dot, and 5) Phase V with lighter solid.

Early successes and failure in rehabilitation

Despite the momentum witnessed in 2008 and 2009, the Task Force met various obstacles from the onset. Challenges occurred already during the demarcation exercise since there were no clear records about where the forest boundaries, and thus the border between protected forest and settlement areas, were supposed to be. The Task Force initially attempted to differentiate between encroached forest areas and 'originally allowed' settlement schemes. Since early post-colonial times, the Government had created the latter by converting former White Highlands that had been occupied by Europeans under colonial rule into Government and later Public Land. While the Government mostly parcelled and sold the land to individual buyers, a few settlements were also created to settle communities that had become landless (Kameri-Mbote, 2009; Klopp & Lumumba, 2016). The Task Force soon learned that their distinction did not match the realities on the ground because forest dwellers, in many instances, held title deeds for what, according to the Task Force definition, should have been forest land. It became increasingly apparent that the consecutive authorities had de- and relocated the forest boundaries multiple times and that there was no clear yardstick by which the boundaries should or could have been defined. This also translated into different maps containing different boundaries, both for external and internal borders. Consequently, since the Task Force had to define boundaries, it sometimes fixed them in a way that led to conflicts between the Task Force Secretariat and the forest-dwelling communities [1/002]. According to a high official of the ICS, who was chairing the Task Force's boundaries team, the ICS finally decided to use the 1932 map that the colonial government had developed for the initial gazettement of the Mau Forest as the 'original' forest map against which changes were recorded [1/267]. No official reason for settling on this rather than another map was provided, apart from the fact that it was the map that the colonial government had used to define the initial legal protection status of the Mau Forest. The five-phase spatial-temporal plan was also devised based on these boundaries (see Map 2).

The implementation of the five-phase plan was faced with further challenges. Initial progress was achieved, and Phase I was implemented without significant hindrances, which might mainly be attributed to the fact that none of the to-be-recovered areas in the Eastern Mau was officially settled. Tides, however, turned as soon as the plan to 'Save the Mau' entered Phase II, which was to be implemented in late 2009 in the South-Western Mau. The area had been densely settled, and recovery of the forest land, in the first place, meant displacing the settlers. In the process, all national and some international media outlets shared images of violent evictions.[14] Whereas the 'Save the Mau' campaign was given exceptional media attention, and most of the population ostensibly backed the Government's plans in the beginning, this support reduced considerably during the eviction of forest dwellers during the year 2010. Consequently, various actors started using the human tragedy facing the evictees to reject the Government's ambitious plans to 'Save the Mau' altogether. Negative attitudes among Kenyans increased when eleven camps for internally displaced persons (IDPs) were opened along the re-established forest boundary in the South-West Mau, propelling dwellers into deplorable humanitarian conditions (Landesa, 2011). Since the wider Rift Valley area had regularly experienced a violent displacement of residents in election years in the previous twenty years, the Government lost considerable support for its rehabilitation agenda. The basic assumption, while planning to evacuate settlers from the designated forest areas, had been that forest dwellers would return to where they had come from. However, this idea soon proved inconsistent, since first, 'their "come from" is not easy to locate in a long history of displacement' [1/002]. Furthermore, 'going back' to what might be described as the place of origin of most of these settlers was complicated because the original pre-colonial settlements of the members of the Kipsigis community in question, for instance, became Crown Lands and thus farmland for the colonialists and were later transformed into the vast tea estates [1/002]. Most of those that were to be evicted hence did not have anywhere to 'go back' to. In Phase III, executing officers were met with open hostility, and violent confrontations ensued. The initial forest land recovery plan was halted at that moment, in early 2010, and not further pursued [1/040].

After the initial halt of the five-phase forest restoration plan in 2010, the 'Saving the Mau' became increasingly politicised, with different actors attempting to frame the campaign against the Mau Forest restoration as a defence of the settlers' human rights. Most importantly, the Mau case was taken up by the coalition Government's main opposition and political inheritors of the former Kenyan government that had illegally subdivided and allocated the land in the Mau Forest.[15] In doing so, they attempted to propose a counter-narrative to the one popularised by a coalition of forest dwellers, political supporters, as well as national and international non-governmental organisations (NGOs) that framed the forest's initial conversion to settlements and the allocation of plots to

[14] See also: 'Mau Forest evictions' photo series on the *Daily Nation* website; Wallis, D., 'Kenya evicts squatters from vital Mau Forest', *Reuters*, 19 November 2009; Rice, X., 'Kenya evicts thousands of forest squatters in attempt to save Rift valley', *The Guardian*, 18 November 2009; Morgan, J., 'Kenya's heart stops pumping', *BBC News*, 29 September 2009.
[15] See also: Munyeki, J., 'Rift Valley MPs oppose phase three Mau evictions', *The Standard*, 27 March 2010.

individuals from non-forest-dwelling communities in 1997 as a human rights offence. Attempting to change the narrative and to benefit from defending the rights of 'the ordinary people', they pursued a 'strategy of "human shield" [in which] big men use the destiny of small peasants, whenever criticism arises, to defend their land' [1/002]. The political sabotage of the restoration agenda equally employed strategies of confusion and excessive demand, for instance, by inciting ordinary citizens to 'flood' the IDP camps in which the persons displaced from the forest settled after their eviction and effectively overwhelmed the agencies that were supposedly responsible for them. The difficulty of determining who was a 'genuine' Mau evictee and who was not, and who should, therefore, be taken care of and eventually compensated or not majorly contributed to the failure of the 'Save the Mau' programme [1/002]. Confronted with a deadlock situation, no significant changes to the status quo of the 'Save the Mau' initiative or attempts to restructure activities were made by any state organs between late 2010 or early 2011 and 2013 [1/040]. The politicisation of the Mau Forest rehabilitation rose steeply in the run-up to the March 2013 General Elections, which overshadowed the willingness of political leaders to take on risks of further pushing the Mau agenda [1/040]. Indeed, this agenda was one of the hot political issues during the election campaigns, and the election of either candidate was directly equated with support or opposition to the rehabilitation of Mau Forest and thus with the decision whether or not rehabilitation would continue (Fuchs, 2014).[16] As expected, the Mau restoration agenda slowly disintegrated after the victory of the coalition that had been opposed to its implementation, and activities related to its rehabilitation remained vastly below the ambitious plans initially formulated in the 2009 Task Force Report.[17]

Progress achieved by April 2013 included [1/040]:

1) Phase I: 4,530 ha of land recovered, and Phase I completed.[18]

2) Phase II: 19,000 ha of land recovered, and settlers evacuated. To complement Phase II, the Agricultural Development Cooperation recovered 1,250 ha next to the Mau Forest.

[16] The representation of Uhuru Kenyatta as being opposed to the forest restoration was mainly informed by his association with William Ruto who had been a plain-spoken opponent of evictions in the Mau Forest. Kenyatta refrained from taking a clear stand on matters involving forest conservation while positioning his government as pro-settler (see, for instance, Kirui, K., 'Mau Forest land caveat will soon be lifted, Tunai promises', *The Star*, 17 August 2016). Beyond that, his family was rumoured to hold shares in the timber-producing companies that operated in the Mau Forest [1/005, 1/008, 5/233].

[17] See also: Murimi, J. and Muchangi, J., 'Mau Forest depletion at the root of worsening droughts and conflicts', *The Star*, 20 March 2017.

[18] 2,950 ha of this excised but not parcelled land was supposedly recovered in the wider Mariashoni area (GoK, 2009a).

3) Phase III: 20,600 ha to be recovered and people to be evicted were profiled, but budget allocation was pending. Parts of the money allocated went into resettlement of evictees of Phase II.

4) Phase IV: Need for a study to differentiate 'critical water catchment areas' from where people would be evacuated. Plan to compensate settlers and promote 'prescribed farming', including agroforestry and bamboo farming, in non-critical areas. The prescribed farming should be informed by the 'Green Kenya Initiative' implemented under the Prime Minister's office, and that was later inherited by the Kenya Water Towers Agency (KWTA), in which strong livelihood-centred programmes were implemented within a 5 km radius of water catchment areas, including a focus on renewable energy; (fruit) tree planting; sustainable land productivity improvement; and bio enterprises, including honey, milk, and mushrooms.

5) Phase V: Roughly 20,155 ha to be recovered according to a study undertaken by ProMara, which also recommended environmental easement strategies, *Private Land* property rights and promoted agroforestry. Payment for Ecosystem Services (PES) schemes were to be implemented in the Maasai areas since the Maasai community was traditionally a non-farming community and might not be convinced of the benefits that can be drawn from agroforestry projects.

Initially, the ICS had planned for a largely exclusionist intervention in the Mau Forest, in line with traditional approaches to environmental conservation in Kenya. However, the experiences and challenges faced by the ICS since the beginning of the forest rehabilitation activities manifested some of the difficulty of implementing such exclusionist policies. Despite forest rehabilitation successes witnessed in the areas from which forest dwellers had been evicted, in which natural regeneration supposedly was 'very strong' [1/022, 1/040], the ICS shifted focus from a mitigation-centred approach focusing on land recovery and natural forest regeneration to a more integrated approach, combining mitigation and adaptation strategies, after widespread and political opposition to the approach increased. However, activities or progress on the ground were limited. Towards the end of 2013, a group of concerned Ogiek elders, who had supported the 'Save the Mau' initiative, complained about the 'poor Mau revival pace'. They also accused the Jubilee administration of being 'reluctant to complete the job' in an open letter addressed to State House. The chairman of the Ogiek Council of Elders wrote that 'numerous interventions have been proposed to stem the destruction, but it will not happen without the goodwill of the two leaders (President and his deputy)'.[19]

[19] Sayagie, G./Okeyo, V., 'Ogiek elders complain of poor Mau revival pace', *Daily Nation*, 2 October 2013, p. 22.

The urgent need to understand and address the Mau Forest crisis

The rapid failure of the Mau Forest Rehabilitation Programme empha-sises the urgency of investigating and understanding the crisis' root causes and dynamics. Interestingly, the dynamics driving the crisis in the Mau Forest have remained largely disregarded in theory and empirical research. Explanation patterns in government documentation treating the Mau crisis, including the Task Force Report, remained partial and insufficiently informed of the Mau Forest Rehabilitation Programme.

What we know and what we need to know

The perhaps best-known paper about the Mau Forest is Klopp and Sang's (2011) 'Maps, Power, and the Destruction of the Mau Forest in Kenya' published in the *Georgetown Journal of International Affairs*. They argue that the Mau Forest struggle is profoundly related to the power relations that influence the creation, control, and use of forest data, especially maps. They describe maps as human creations rather than objective reflections of a supposed reality that reflect the interests of those who make them. Their purpose is control over land, and maps are tools for this aim, especially in land appropriation processes. They also discuss the profound consequences on people's rights and livelihoods, especially the indigenous Ogiek people. Land in the Eastern Mau is also addressed by Musembi and Kameri-Mbote's (2013) paper 'Mobility, Marginality and Tenure Transformation in Kenya: Explorations of Community Property Rights in Law and Practice' published in *Nomadic Peoples*. The authors interrogate the importance and effects of the seminal official recognition of community land rights through Kenya's 2010 Constitu-tion based on 'ethnicity, culture or similar community of interest' in the Ogiek community. They specifically analyse community concepts and their relations to national and local resource rights discourses in the context of rapidly changing tenure, land use, and tension between individual and communal tenure.

Treating the ecological importance of the Mau Forest, Mutugi and Kiiru published 'Biodiversity, Local Resource, Natural Heritage, Regional Concern, and Global Impact: The Case of Mau Forest, Kenya' in the *European Scientific Journal* in 2015. They discuss the environmental, social, and economic losses incurred over the previous twenty years due to the estimated destruction of 2,000 km² of forest in the Mau. They specifi-cally invoke biodiversity reduction, drastically reduced water levels in the many rivers emanating from the forest, and economic losses in agri-culture, tourism, and the energy sector. Langat, Maranga, Aboud, and Cheboiwo (2016) from the Kenya Forestry Research Institute (KEFRI) studied the 'Role of Forest Resources to Local Livelihoods' in the East Mau Forest Ecosystem in a paper published in the *International Journal of Forestry Research*. They argue that, despite unsustainable land-use change, forest degradation, and biodiversity loss witnessed in the Mau Forest, little empirical data exist on the role of forest resources on forest livelihoods. Their quantitative study showed that forest income from wood, timber, and non-timber forest products (NTFPs) was significant to interviewed households, contributing about one-third of their total income. They found that poorer households depended more on forest resources while richer households derived higher forest income.

Chaudhry (2015) published her study, 'The Impact of Climate Change on Human Security: The case of the Mau Forest Complex' in *Development*. She examines climate-change-induced human security implications among the Mau Complex's forest-dwelling and adjacent communities. Based largely on secondary literature and government policy review, she argues that frequent droughts and heavy rains add pressure on land, water, and pastures, endangering economic, food, health, environmental, political, personal, and communal security. She also calls for a comprehensive policy response to climate change.

In the field of environmental education, Ronoh published 'Contextualising historical and socio-anthropological literature on indigenous education in enhancing environmental conservation: case of Ogiek of Mau Forest, Kenya' in the *European Journal of Alternative Education Studies* in 2016. His critical analysis of secondary literature focused on understanding the influence of indigenous learning and training included in Ogiek initiation rites on sustainable environmental conservation. He also analysed the influence of colonial and post-colonial governments on the traditional 'gender-based' indigenous education system of environmental management and the integration of traditional ecological knowledge in modern environmental management strategies. The author claims that the Ogiek have maintained, adapted, expanded and successfully integrated their knowledge in externally engineered environmental conservation strategies despite the immense pressure of modernisation, for instance through changes in land tenure and forest policies, forest encroachment by other ethnic groups, colonial annexation of the forest, the transformation of the production system towards agro-pastoral livelihoods, systematic deforestation, the creation of new settlement schemes, etc.

Apart from the published academic work, a small number of university research projects have treated the Mau Forest. Environmental management in the Eastern Mau is addressed by Spruyt's (2011) MA thesis from Gent University, 'Changing Concepts of Nature and Conservation Regarding Eastern Mau Forest' through a case study of the Mariashoni Ogiek. She proposes an ethnographic study to shed light on the human aspects of conservation, specifically on community members' understanding of environmental changes, conservation programmes, and their adaptation strategies. She finds that the Ogiek in the Eastern Mau differentiate their self-representation temporarily between 'Now' and 'Then', modernity and tradition. Nonetheless, she argues that the Ogiek continue to have a distinctive worldview that connects man and nature, opposing the Western assumption of a dichotomy between both. She also discerns a 'flexible and multidisciplinary approach of Ogiek ecological knowledge' (Spruyt, 2011, p. 105) that should inform other conservation policies and the Mau Forest Rehabilitation Programme. She concludes that, despite changes in Ogiek lives and livelihoods, they continue to preserve the environment and should be central partners in the fight to 'Save the Mau'.

Bore (2014) submitted her MA thesis entitled 'A Struggle between Livelihoods and Forest Conservation: A case of Mau Forest in Kenya' to the Institute of Development Studies of the University of Nairobi. She conducted a household survey in Tinet in Kericho County along the South-West Mau to analyse the dilemma forest-dwelling communities face in ensuring their livelihoods while conserving the environment. She finds considerable dependence on forest products among households, tension between the need to access and use forest resources, and the Government's formal forest laws and regulations hindering this access. She also calls for forest conservation policies that emphasise equity, which recognise resource-dependent communities as valuable partners in sustainably protecting and conserving the forest.

The politics of the Mau Forest are treated in Soi's (2015) MA study, 'Politics and Conservation of the Mau Forest' from the Department of Political Science and Public Administration, University of Nairobi. His study, based on research conducted in Kiptororo Location in the South-Western Mau, intends to contribute to both policy and science. He invokes political ecology to investigate his hypotheses that politics were involved in the destruction of the Mau and that there is political interest in conserving the Mau Forest. He finds that politicians used loopholes in existing legislation to advance tribal/community land interests. He further recommends harmonising all environmental and forest conservation regulations, sensitising citizens and politicians on the importance of forests, and involving both in decision-making processes.

The dissertation of PhD candidate Kweyu (2015) from the Wangari Maathai Institute for Peace and Environmental Studies from the University of Nairobi addresses 'Linking the social and the spatial in forest-related conflicts' through a case study of the Eastern Mau Forest Adjacent Communities. He investigates the sources of conflict in the Eastern Mau, with particular focus on the role of beliefs, values, and attitudes of different parties to conflicts. He finds that conflicts form an ethnic identity pattern, some of which occur in the context of resources (pasture and land), while others are related to national elections rather than resource competition. He further asserts that conflicts in forestry are likely to escalate at the intersection of identity and spatial-geographical factors. He concludes and recommends integrating traditional conflict-resolution mechanisms and mediation into the peacebuilding processes in potential conflict zones. His study was implemented as part of the STAKE (Stabilizing Kenya through Resolving Forest Related Conflicts) project.

Further, in the conflict-resolution field, Oruya-Oginga (2015) addresses 'Environmental Diplomacy and Conflict Resolution' through a case study of the Mau Forest in her MA thesis from the Institute of Diplomacy and International Studies at the University of Nairobi. She examines environmental awareness and the role of environmental diplomacy. She finds that there is a need to demarcate legal boundaries, assess critical water areas, and issue land title deeds. She also recommends establishing community forest associations (CFAs) and other integrated and participatory approaches to conflict resolution and dispute settlement to further environmental diplomacy and conservation.

Apart from the published and unpublished academic works, a few studies produced by members of the Ogiek Welfare Council (OWC), a community-based association whose objectives are to advance the diverse interests of the Ogiek community, discuss land matters in the Eastern Mau, including Towett's (2004) 'Ogiek Land Cases and Historical Injustices 1902–2004. Vol. 1' and Sang's (2003) study 'The Ogiek in Mau Forest' published by the Forest People's Programme, as well as Kamau's (2000) book 'The Ogiek: The Ongoing Destruction of a Minority Tribe in Kenya. An In-depth Report'.

Other scientific literature about the Mau Forest is limited to anthropological studies of the Ogiek, the indigenous hunter-gatherer community whose ancestral lands lie within the wider Mau Forest. Outstanding among these are Hobley (1903), Huntingford since the 1920s (1929; 1931; 1942; 1951, 1955), and, since the 1970s, Blackburn (1970, 1974, 1986), Kratz (1980, 1993, 1996, 1999), and van Zwanenberg (1976). Beyond these classical anthropological studies, the more recent transformations of contemporary Ogiek societies have not been addressed in the scientific literature. There is one notable exception: 'The Ogiek Peoples Ancestral Territories Atlas' (OPAT), which ERMIS Africa jointly produced with the Eastern and Southern Africa Partnership Programme (ESAPP) and the Centre for Development and Environment (CDE) from the University of Bern, Switzerland, that was first published in Kenya in A3 format in 2011 (Muchemi & Ehrensperger, 2011).

However, despite several studies about the Mau Forest having been published, these publications are largely inconsequential to understanding the complexity of the environmental crisis of the Mau Forest. Furthermore, these contributions and their conclusions remain mostly sectoral and narrow, sometimes biased and somewhat naïve, and often abstract and general.

Using a political ecology lens to analyse complex environmental crises

Considering the limitations in the available literature about environmental management in the Eastern Mau and the limited guidance on suitable theoretical approaches and considerations for this book, matters related to natural resource management extracted from relevant empirical studies about similar environmental crises inform and guide this research. Striving for a holistic and comprehensive approach, research approaches from within the spectrum of the political ecology school of thought propose relevant frameworks. Political ecology suggests ways of seeing, analysing, and interpreting situations in which environmental change occurs. The broader conceptual framework for this study is derived from these specific ways of looking at environmental crises.

The origins and disciplinary locations of political ecology are multiple. Bryant and Bailey (1997) argue that political ecology, particularly regarding the Global South, developed slowly given evolutions in other fields, especially in cultural ecology and radical development geography, and in line with real-life challenges to previous approaches to the analysis of environmental crises in the early 1970s.[20] Other related fields are ecological economics, environmental economics, environmental history, environmental management, environmental politics, environmental sociology, global ecology, and human ecology. Political ecology is thus straddling various main disciplines, including anthropology, political sciences, economics, history, sociology, and geography.

Eric Wolf's paper 'Ownership and Political Ecology', published in *Anthropological Quarterly* (1972), is considered one of the founding papers in which a political ecology perspective was applied to studying an environmental issue. The field, however, only developed more boldly in the mid-1980s, with publications of Watts (1983), Blaikie (1985), Bunker (1985), and Hecht (1985), which sought to counter works that were previously associated with the political ecology terminology, including by Ehrlich (1968), Hardin (1968), Heilbroner (1974), and Ophuls (1977). The latter were particularly criticised for their contribution to the spread of neo-Malthusian ecological 'crisis' discourses, which, in their various variations and forms, were based on Thomas Malthus' famous 1798 publication in which he argues that human population growth would outrun the growth of food production because the former supposedly grew exponentially, while the latter grew arithmetically (Diamond, 2005). According to these discourses, population growth in the Global South and consumption levels in the Global North

---

[20] Due to the pertinence of Bryant and Bailey's analysis of the history of the field, this section is mainly based on their 1997 publication. Indications about important publications are also drawn from the same. Additions and completions are referenced.

would lead to an imminent social and environmental catastrophe unless a strong state-enforced 'limits to growth' (Bryant & Bailey, 1997, p. 10).

A separate strand that contributed to the emergence of the field of political ecology with a primary focus on the Global South emerged out of work on environmental topics in anthropology during the 1960s and 1970s, which eventually adopted the labels of cultural ecology or ecological anthropology. Research undertaken within these disciplines by Bennett (1976), Hardesty (1977), Orlove (1980), and Ellen (1982), for instance, predominantly analysed the relations between culture and environmental management practices. These works, however, represented human-environment interactions as largely apolitical.

It was not until the mid-1980s that a few researchers, including Hecht (1985), Little and Horowitz (1987), and Bassett (1988), started combining anthropological and political-economic structural analyses, leading to the emergence of political ecology as a research field. In the late 1970s and early 1980s, many political ecologists resorted to neo-Marxism, explaining local environmental conflicts mainly through class relations, and surplus extraction linked to global capitalist production. This strand included authors like Cliffe and Moorsom (1979), Hedlund (1979), and O'Brien (1985). Their works were criticised for treating most other influences, apart from capital and class, as a 'black box'. Considering that critique, the second wave of political-ecological works emerged in the late 1980s based on a broader range of theoretical sources and conceptual thinking. The precursors of that more holistic strand of political ecology were Blaikie and Brookfield (1987), Hecht and Cockburn (1989), and Guha (1989). Their studies attracted others, many of whom became defining names for the field, including Peluso (1992), Neumann (1992), and Watts and Peet (1993). The latter works focused their attention on providing a more complex and comprehensive understanding of how power relations influence and mediate human-environment interactions. The third phase of political ecology then drew on poststructuralist and discourse-theoretical concepts and methodologies. Works that influenced the theoretical developments associated with that phase include Said (1978), Bhabha (1994), and Escobar (1995), while authors such as Fairhead and Leach (1995), Fortmann (1995), Jewitt (1995), or Peet and Watts (1996) provided empirical studies that analysed the paths of influence of knowledge and power in mediating political-ecological situations.

Criticising the third phase of political-ecological work as being overly poststructuralist and focusing too much on the politics of locality, Bryant and Bailey (1997) argue that, in times of globalisation, political-ecological analyses require two elements to be appropriate for the study of environmental crises. Political ecology focusing on the Global South must develop 'rigorous analyses which link local level production processes and decision-making with the larger political economy to explain these different experiences' (Bassett, 1988, p. 469), on the one hand, while retaining room for contingency and flexibility in explanation on the other hand. Consequently, environmental problems in the Global South[21] are not primarily the result of a policy or market failure but driven by broader political and economic dynamics, which might be associated with the overall capitalist market system, but also with state promotion of environmentally destructive economic activities, or the ruling classes' interest in political power, national security, or personal enrichment, among others. The logical consequence of the first underlying understanding is that, by definition, there cannot be a 'quick-fix' technical policy solution to environmental problems defined by deep-rooted complexities. The second fundamental understanding is thus that complex environmental crises require far-reaching changes to political and economic processes at local, regional, and global scales if a shift in the status quo is to be achieved.

Political ecology, at its core, 'highlights the interwoven character of the discursive, material, social and cultural dimensions of the human-environment relation' (Escobar, 1999, p. 2), and hence of social change, environment, and development. By emphasising and analysing asymmetrical power relations among and between different social actors in their competition for access, use, and control of natural resources, political ecology approaches and concepts connect the work of anthropologists, geographers, political scientists, and sociologists (Vaccaro, Beltran, & Paquet, 2013). Furthermore, the approach is suitable for the analysis of environmental crises, since a 'transdisciplinary approach is needed, where human systems and ecological systems are seen as one system with numerous feedbacks across scales in time and space' (Folke, 1996, p. 371). Adams and Hutton (2007) specifically suggest using a political ecology perspective to analyse the nexus between the ecological, economic and social pillars of conservation to gain insights into the purpose, the power dynamics, and the costs of conservation. Researchers investigating the determinants of 'environmental conflicts' furthermore argue that the close linkage of economic, political, and environmental variables contributing to an environmental conflict requires holistic approaches that pay close attention to the interaction of these variables (Hauge & Ellingsen, 1998). Political ecology generally attributes environmental changes to the interdependence and interaction of political, socio-economic and ecological processes (Bassett & Crummey, 2003). More constructivist works emphasise the role of socialised perceptions, and hence culture, in understandings and representations of

---

[21] In view of constructivist, post-structuralist, capitalism-critical and other debates, the terms 'Global South', rather than 'Third World' or 'developing countries', as well as the 'Global North', rather than the 'First World' or 'developed countries' are used throughout the text.

the world and the specific (environmental) set-up (Little, 2003). Timura (2001) resumés the same succinctly:

> (N)atural resources and perceptions of resource scarcity are inextricably entwined within social, political, and economic structures as well as socialized understandings of the world [rendering it necessary] to pay explicit attention to the changing understandings that those involved in conflict have of natural resources, and of their changing (or perhaps unchanging) positions within their economic, political, and cultural worlds [and hence] how a community's position within the larger political sphere and economy may affect its members' understandings of the resources, the dispute, and the range of options available to them to resolve it. (p. 111)

Political ecology analyses seemingly align with complexity-embracing approaches that gained popularity in development discourse and practice, notably the three pillars concept, which defines sustainable development at the intersection between ecological, economic, and social well-being. The concept was popularised through the 1987 World Commission on Environment and Development Report, more commonly referred to as the 'Brundtland Report' and further consolidated by the 1992 United Nations 'Earth' Summit held in Rio de Janeiro (Guyer & Richards, 1996; Okidi, Kameri-Mbote, & Akech, 2008; Wamukoya & Ludeki, 2003). Apart from the initial three-pillared model, various other visual representations of the three sustainability components surfaced, including a Venn diagram with three interconnected circles, as well as a diagram containing three concentric circles, with the economic component being the inner circle, the social component being the middle, and environmental component being the outer circle. While each has its merits, all representations are highly anthropocentric, compartmentalised, and lack completeness and continuity (Lozano, 2008). The sustainable development concept itself engendered important philosophical and conceptual debates, for instance, by Bosselmann (2008), who conceptualises sustainability through the image of the Temple of Life. In this 'temple', ecological integrity is the foundation, economic welfare and social welfare are the two pillars, and cultural identity is the roof, which arguably 'surely is more sustainable than three pillars lacking fundament and roof' (p. 321). He argues that the Temple of Life embodies what he calls 'ecological rationality' rather than economic rationality and that it hence represents a step away from the anthropocentrism of the initial sustainable development models. Considering such critiques, several institutions started considering culture as a 'fourth pillar' (Hawkes, 2001), while a political dimension remained conspicuously absent. Given persistent criticism, some institutions adopted the 'Circles of Sustainability' model as an updated version of the three-pillar model of sustainable development. The circle is divided into four domains, namely ecology, economics, politics, and culture, each subdivided into seven subdomains. Each of these twenty-eight criteria was to be assessed with the help of a nine-point scale. The model was first presented at the Rio+20 Summit in 2012 and has since been adopted conceptually and as an evaluation method by various organisations (James, 2015). The 'circles' model certainly represents a more sophisticated approach to analysing sustainable development, with explicit inclusion of political factors, including organisation and governance, law and justice, communication and movement, representation and negotiation, security and accord, dialogue and reconciliation, as well as ethics and accountability. However, like any other model that seeks to be comprehensive by compounding a multitude of variables into pre-set categories and then to assess these quantitatively, the concept is not easy to manoeuvre, and analyses are not easily replicable. Altogether, numerous political ecologists doubt the pertinence of the paradigm and claim that it cannot address intensifying environmental problems (Bryant & Bailey, 1997).

Altogether, political ecology is a response to environmental analysis approaches that are either entirely apolitical or attribute only relative importance to political dynamics and instead attribute a fundamental role to politics in both the perpetuation of political-ecological conflicts and in defining solutions to environmental crises. Hence, the political ecology school places the analysis of power structures at the centre of the study (Bryant & Bailey, 1997; Hulme, 2009). In doing so, it postulates that 'every "environmental" struggle is, at its foundations, a struggle among interests about power' and hence that 'every environmental story is a story about power' (Weiner, 2005, p. 409). Fundamentally, political ecology defines environmental and ecological conditions in a given context as a result of social and political processes (Adams & Hutton, 2007). Therefore, environmental crises can be understood as situations in which 'the status quo is an outcome of political interests and struggles' (Bryant & Bailey, 1997, p. 5).

A conceptual framework for applying a political ecology lens

Analysing the nature and the implications of various aspects of 'politicised environments' is at the core of political ecology analyses. This is based on the fundamental assumption that environmental problems can neither be understood nor solved in isolation from the political, economic, and social contexts within which they are created. Various approaches can be taken in analysing environmental crises, or specific aspects of these crises, in political ecology research. These approaches are not mutually exclusive, and most authors combine different ones in their research.[22] According to Bryant and Bailey (1997), the first approach is to apply a political ecology lens to analyse a specific environmental problem or a set of problems such as soil erosion, deforestation, water pollution, or land degradation. One of the works associated with this first approach is Blaikie's (1985) analysis of the political ecology of soil erosion, which highlighted the importance of a hierarchy of interlinked social, political, and economic forces operating at local, regional, and global scales. The second approach is to concentrate on a specific concept related to political-ecological questions and to understand the dynamics between different concepts and actors in pursuing various interests, and, ultimately, the outcome of the interaction of these concepts and the physical environment. Analyses that fall under that second approach explored, for instance, the effects of the 'dominant discourse of scientific forestry' or the 'sustainable development paradigm'. A third approach relates political-ecological analyses with socio-economic characteristics such as class, ethnicity, and gender. Then a fourth approach is more actor-oriented and studies the interests, characteristics, and actions of different types of actors within a given environmental crisis setting.[23] This last approach englobes an analysis of the agency that individual and institutional actors possess, alongside an analysis of their narratives with the help of which they describe and explain what is happening (Liverman, 2015). Bryant and Bailey (1997) also differentiate between three different temporalities that can be considered in political-ecological analyses, notably the everyday, episodic, and systemic time frames, which differ in terms of physical changes, the rate of impact, the nature of the human impact, the political response and critical concepts.

Despite differences in the ways the political ecology lens can be applied to the study of empirical cases, a few underlying assumptions typically guide the analysis of situations of environmental stress. In line with the conceptualisation of a 'politicised environment', the first assumption is that costs and benefits that come with environmental change are unequally distributed among different actors. The second assumption is that this unequal distribution interacts with existing social and economic inequalities, either reinforcing or reducing them, and that environmental change affects the political and social status quo. The third assumption then is that the social, political, and eco-

[22] Due to the pertinence of Bryant and Bailey's summary of various political-ecological approaches, this brief introductory section is mainly based on their 1997 publication. Additions and completions are referenced.
[23] Bryant and Bailey define a fifth approach that examines political-ecological analyses within a specific geographical context. It does, however, not seem relevant to propose these region-based analyses as a different approach since all political-ecological studies are context-based, whether located within wider regions or not.

nomic implications of environmental change also alter the powers of different actors, notably affecting the ability of actors to control or resist others. Overall, 'power is thus ... a key concept in efforts to specify the topography of a politicised environment' (Bryant & Bailey, 1997, p. 39). While a multitude of conceptualisations of various dimensions of power has been brought forward, particularly in the field of political sciences, many political ecologists define the concept 'in relation to the ability of an actor to control their own interaction with the environment and the interaction of other actors with the environment. It is above all "the control that one party has over the environment of another party"' (Bryant & Bailey, 1997, p. 39). This conceptualisation is largely in line with Weber's (1922) 'power over' concept. The 'politicised environment' hence centres on unequal power relations and how these interact with the physical characteristics of the natural resources in question (Khan, 2013).

According to Bryant and Bailey (1997), the analysis of the effects of power can involve different sets of questions. The three main questions concern (a) the various ways and forms in which actors seek control over the environment of other actors, (b) the translation and manifestation of these power relations in the physical environment, and (c) critically, the agency of the less powerful actors to resist the more powerful ones. The most fundamental and direct way in which actors can exert power over the environment of another actor is by controlling their access to that environment and its resources, including land and forests. Another way in which power is exerted is by controlling where activities that potentially harm the health of the environment and human beings are carried out. A third way an actor can exert control over another actor's environment is by controlling the societal prioritisation of environmental projects and problems. The latter includes questions of priority setting in terms of geographical space in which activities are carried out, as well as about the very nature of such activities. One pertinent example mentioned by Bryant and Bailey (1997) concerns the provisions of support for plantation forestry in the name of engaging in 'green' activities, which points towards the underlying premise that private businesses pursuing forest production purportedly are essential drivers in the fight against deforestation. The interests and ideas of powerful actors are far-reaching, they say, since their influence is reflected in multiple spheres, including a favourable regulatory regime and the provision of state subsidies for supposedly sustainable forest plantation development, independently from the fact that those who are 'local' and other grassroots actors typically oppose such technocratic and capitalist approaches to reforestation and often attempt to get support for alternative community forestry projects. The last way control is exerted over others' environment is through discourse, particularly by framing what is supposedly environmentally friendly and thus legitimate and what is not. Power, here, is a matter of 'winning the battle of ideas' about what constitutes legitimate use of the environment and its resources. Concerning the plantation forestry example, Bryant and Bailey (1997) explain that

> states have not been content merely to exert physical control over designated forests at the expense of other actors, but have also sought to justify this move in terms of 'ecologically bad' practices of the latter (i.e. the 'destructive' shifting cultivator) compared with the 'ecologically good' practices of the state ... by controlling what J. Scott (1990) terms the 'public transcript' – that is, the 'socially accepted' version of events represented in public documents, legal political ideologies, ... and so on. Through control of the public transcript, actors seek to render 'natural' the triumph of their partisan interests on a society-wide basis. (pp. 41–2)

The second set of questions concerning the influence of power on the environment can be read in the physical environment itself. The manifestation of power relations in the physical environment, and in environmental crises particularly, can be 'read' as the results of these power relations. The priority setting of the influential actors is thus 'translated' in the physical environment. While the figuration of a given environment 'encodes' social consequences, including exclusion and dispossession by conferring different opportunities for environmental access and decision-making power (Weiner, 2005), these 'codes' can also be read 'in reverse' in the environment.

Lastly, the question of subjugated actors' agency explores patterns of resistance. Resistance can take various forms, from open confrontation to silent opposition. In line with Scott's (1985) work on the 'weapons of the weak', the less powerful often avoid attracting attention to their opposition by employing 'everyday forms of resistance'. Such acts can take various forms of resistance to the rules and regulations imposed by more powerful actors, and sometimes lead to defiance of the norms and objectives underlying these rules. Examples include forest clearance for food crop cultivation in protected forests, poaching of big game in wildlife parks or the cultivation of 'forbidden' crops, which translate into an attempt to assert a presumed right to shape the landscape against the structures enforced by more powerful actors. In the context of the forestry example, community mapping exercises that define the extent of community or ancestral forests can be understood as contestation over the legitimate definition of the environment. In other cases, powerful actors 'provide an opportunity' for less powerful actors to resist since pursuing the former's interests is diametrically opposed to the latter's interests. In response to activities imposed on their landscape, the latter can, for instance, sabotage activities pursued by the powerful actors. The less powerful actors are the 'locals' who dispose of more intricate knowledge of the area, notably local environmental knowledge. Despite controlling the physical realities of the environment, powerful actors often seek to legitimise their control by shaping the 'public script', or the officially recognised discourse about a given (environmental) situation. This is particularly true for state actors, who typically seek to legitimise their control over other actors' environments by invoking the fact that they hold a 'stewardship' role, which confers a responsibility to create and preserve the 'common good'. Other influential actors legitimise their actions in the name of creating employment. Their quest for legitimacy is, however, potentially endangered by counter-narratives of the subjugated, whose 'hidden transcripts' potentially endanger the 'official story' of a given situation. Hence, the seemingly less powerful actors can influence public perception if they successfully attract criticism to the powerful actors' activities, leading to the wider population's opinion becoming unfavourable and their activities being publicly represented as 'illegitimate'. This can have important and potentially far-reaching political and economic consequences. New communication media have increased the opportunities for subjugated groups and individuals to access the limelight and attract attention to their 'hidden transcripts', illustrating that social relations and positions are fluid and that while 'power influences the topography of a politicised environment ... the relative position of actors can never be adduced exclusively from material considerations' (Bryant & Bailey, 1997, p. 46). The power concept, in these analyses, is in line with Arendt's (1970) 'power with' concept.

Adams and Hutton (2007) propose focusing the analysis of the 'politicised environment' of an environmental crisis on the relationship between people and nature, matters of rights and access to land and natural resources, the role of the state and various other powerful actors or ideas, including scientific or other narratives and understandings of nature. Weiner (2005) suggests asking who controls access to resources and amenities, what the trade-offs are, who is expected to bear the risks and costs, who believes that they will benefit, who controls the range of choices that are made available to the public as it takes significant decisions, what are the conditions of these choices and who takes them, what outcomes are projected by 'experts', how are the expected risks and benefits represented, and how will social structures and relationships change because of specific choices. Munro (2003) further recommends questioning why resource-management strategies, implemented by an apparently 'strong' state with effective agricultural agencies, have been relatively unsuccessful, what this persistent problem reveals about relationships between the state, rural resource users, and nature, and what appropriate resource-management policies should look like.

Given the complexity of the Mau crisis, a holistic but flexible conceptual framework was used for the study underlying this book. Consequently, the scramble for the Mau Forest is analysed in the light of the 'politicised environment' of natural resource management in Kenya in general and forest and land governance specifically, in line with a somewhat general conceptual framework for political ecology analyses of environmental crises (see Figure 2). It encompasses features such as post-coloniality in environmental thinking and practice, the exercise of power and the workings of political will at various scales, neo-colonialism and neo-patrimonialism in land and forest use and management, and the shifting use of ethnonationalism for political benefits and control.

From local to global: Forest degradation and rehabilitation in Mariashoni, Eastern Mau Forest

This book endeavours to fill the gap in understanding the Mau Forest crisis, which was identified both in the literature and in conservation practice, by proposing a holistic and innovative approach to analysing why forest degradation and destruction in the Mau Forest were not addressed and dealt with successfully. With more than 400,000 ha, the Mau Forest is vast and, due to differences in local history, experiences, and land rights regimes, different parts of the forest have different stories. This research is deliberately context-specific to be relevant and acknowledge the complexity of the scramble for the Mau. It concentrates on perspectives and representations in the wider Mariashoni area in the Eastern Mau Forest alone.[24] The Eastern Mau Forest case study provides insights into the complex circumstances in which so-called environmental crises materialise and are perpetuated, allowing informed assumptions about issues affecting the wider forest. Doing so can also contribute to understanding the potential of proposed solutions to address the crisis.

Since the Eastern Mau is one of the areas most affected by forest degradation and destruction, the research underlying this book was primarily conducted in Mariashoni Location, Molo Sub-County, Nakuru County, located in the Eastern Mau Forest, which is situated in the eastern parts of the Mau Forest and encompasses eight forest stations, namely Sururu, Likia, Teret, Nessuit, Elburgon, Mariashoni, Kiptunga, and Baraget. The area of the Eastern Mau Forest, according to officially

---

[24] The mention of perspectives and representations in the text does not mean that a full-fledged discourse analysis was undertaken. However, it emphasises the fact that the data used for this study are self-reported interview data. Qualitative interviews do not allow verifying whether expressed observations and opinions are factually aligned or congruent with the interviewed persons' perceptions or thoughts. Their verbal contributions are hence classified as perspectives or representations rather than thoughts, opinions, or convictions. When potential opinions are mentioned, they are typically introduced as someone 'expressing the opinion' rather than 'having an opinion'.

Figure 2 General conceptual framework for political ecology analyses of environmental 'crises'.

Source: Author composition based on various referenced sources.

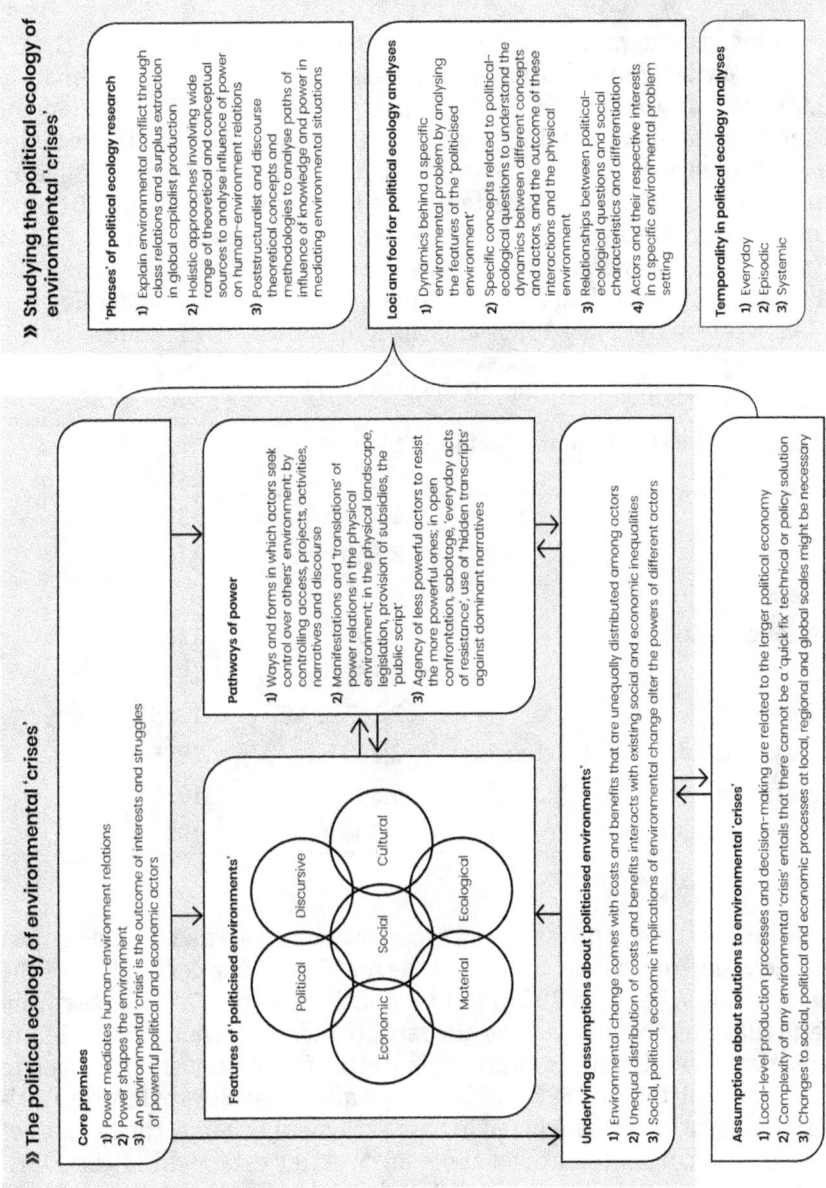

» **The political ecology of environmental 'crises'**

Core premises

1) Power mediates human–environment relations
2) Power shapes the environment
3) An environmental 'crisis' is the outcome of interests and struggles of powerful political and economic actors

Features of 'politicised environments'

Political · Discursive · Cultural
Economic · Social · Ecological
· Material

Pathways of power

1) Ways and forms in which actors seek control over others' environment; by controlling access, projects, activities, narratives and discourse

2) Manifestations and 'translations' of power relations in the physical landscape; in the physical environment; the provision of subsidies, legislation, provision of subsidies, the 'public script'

3) Agency of less powerful actors to resist the more powerful ones; in open confrontation, sabotage, 'everyday acts of resistance', use of 'hidden transcripts' against dominant narratives

Underlying assumptions about 'politicised environments'

1) Environmental change comes with costs and benefits that are unequally distributed among actors
2) Unequal distribution of costs and benefits interacts with existing social and economic inequalities
3) Social, political, economic implications of environmental change alter the powers of different actors

Assumptions about solutions to environmental 'crises'

1) Local-level production processes and decision-making are related to the larger political economy
2) Complexity of any environmental 'crisis' entails that there cannot be a 'quick fix' technical or policy solution
3) Changes to social, political and economic processes at local, regional and global scales might be necessary

» **Studying the political ecology of environmental 'crises'**

'Phases' of political ecology research

1) Explain environmental conflict through class relations and surplus extraction in global capitalist production

2) Holistic approaches involving wide range of theoretical and conceptual sources to analyse influence of power on human–environment relations

3) Poststructuralist and discourse theoretical concepts and methodologies to analyse paths of influence of knowledge and power in mediating environmental situations

Loci and foci for political ecology analyses

1) Dynamics behind a specific environmental problem by analysing the features of the 'politicised environment'

2) Specific concepts related to political-ecological questions to understand the dynamics between different concepts and actors, and the outcome of these interactions and the physical environment

3) Relationships between political-ecological questions and social characteristics and differentiation

4) Actors and their respective interests in a specific environmental problem setting

Temporality in political ecology analyses

1) Everyday
2) Episodic
3) Systemic

recognised borders, covers about 65,000 ha (ENSDA et al., 2005; UNEP, 2008). Mariashoni Location encompassed an area of approximately 9,000 ha, of which 8,300 ha were part of the Mariashoni settlement scheme established and declared in 1997 (GoK, 2009e). To formally establish various settlement schemes in the Eastern Mau (see Table 1), more than 35,000 ha of gazetted forest land were excised in 2001, representing a net forest loss of the same size. Conversely, almost half of Eastern Mau's dense vegetation cover was lost between 1973 and 2003 alone, and several thousand households moved into the wider Eastern Mau between the early 1990s and the mid-2000s (UNEP, 2008).

Table 1   Settlement schemes in the Eastern Mau Forest.

Name of the settlement scheme	Size	Year of initial establishment
Sigotik	1,812 ha	1994
Baraget	2,800 ha	n/a
Nessuit	4,740 ha	n/a
Ngongongeri	4,100 ha	1996
Sururu	5,852 ha	1994
Teret	2,117 ha	1995
Likia (including Likia Extension)	2,290 ha	1995
Mariashoni	8,300 ha	1996
Kapsita (Elburgon)	3,300 ha	1997

Source: GoK, 2009e, pp. 36–7.

While a mixture of primary and secondary forests[25] had occupied most of the wider Mariashoni area until the mid-1990s, the declaration of the settlement scheme in 1997 led to a quasi-total removal of trees from land that was demarcated and allocated to individual households. Many observers noted that the cypress plantation forest almost reached up to Elburgon until 1996–1997 [5/233]. Since more than 80% of land in Mariashoni Location was included in the settlement scheme, the net loss of forest was calculated at the same 80%. After establishing the Mariashoni settlement scheme in 1997, which led to the demarcation of land and the privatisation of individual plots of forest land, most commonly five-acre pieces of land at a time, Mariashoni Centre changed rapidly. The subdivision of land led to individualisation in land use and often to the

[25] Primary forest is original, 'virgin', 'natural' forest; secondary forest is planted: it can be monocropped plantations (e.g. pine, cypress) or mixed, nature-imitating forests. The core difference is that primary forest is the original forest that grows somewhere and secondary forest is human-made forest.

establishment of homesteads and private small-scale farms, commonly referred to as *shambas*, at the expense of trees and shrubs. Even though individual trees and small forest patches had remained standing within the settlement scheme, these lost their status as forests and thereby their protection by law. Consequently, primary and secondary forests were reduced, wild herbs, fruits, and nuts were reduced, bees and other wild animals withdrew, and the overall environment was transformed considerably. With the transformation in the natural environment and the spatial organisation of the area came an adaptation of the forest dwellers' lifestyles and practices [3/063].

The Eastern Mau Forest is said to have always been the 'national habitat' of the Ogiek (Towett, 2004).[26] The Ogiek are considered forest-based hunters and gatherers who traditionally lived in different forest areas in western Kenya and northern Tanzania. Most of the remaining members of the various Ogiek communities were found within the Mau Forest Complex and the Mt Elgon Forest areas (Muchemi & Ehrensperger, 2011). They are arguably the largest remaining hunter-gatherer group in Kenya (Ohenjo, 2003). Apart from the Ogiek, members of many other communities, locally often referred to as *'wageni'* (guests) when speaking in Swahili, or 'foreigners' and 'newcomers' when speaking in English, lived in Mariashoni. Most of them were from other Kalenjin communities, predominantly from the Kipsigis, Tugen, and Nandi communities, alongside several members of the Kisii, Luo, Kamba, and Kikuyu communities. While members of the Kikuyu community had settled in parts of the Eastern Mau as forest workers since colonial times, the members of most other communities only started arriving in the Eastern Mau in the late 1990s. The area had witnessed in- and out-migration of different groups of people throughout history, often related to broader political dynamics, including the politics of land, which engendered politics of belonging and exclusion, and contributed significantly to politically instigated and land-related clashes between different communities. Various political events are particularly noteworthy, including the coup attempt on President Moi in 1982 that contributed to his regime becoming increasingly authoritarian, as well as the push for political reform and the reinstallation of multipartyism in the 1990s that eventually led to the democratic transition in 2002. Apart from the regular residents, a large group of persons travelled in and out of the forest daily. These were mainly traders and persons working with large-scale timber companies, as well as small

---

[26] While most of the early anthropological and a few current studies spell Ogiek with a 'k' instead of the 'g', and hence Okiek, I consistently spell Ogiek with the at present more common 'g'. Furthermore, even though the official singular of 'Ogiek' is 'Ogiot', the term Ogiek is used here to refer to members of the community in singular and plural, as is commonly done.

and medium-scale sawmills, mostly Kikuyu, who typically hailed from the nearby towns including Elburgon, Njoro, and Nakuru.

The primary research underlying this book combined in-depth literature and archive study with on- and off-site field research in the sense of a multi-sited ethnography. In terms of methods, in line with most contemporary social science studies (Cresswell et al., 2003; Johnson & Onwuegbuzie, 2004; Teddlie & Tashakkori, 2009), a flexible mixed-methods approach including mainly qualitative and fewer complementary quantitative methods was used. Due to the sensitivity of the topic at the time of the research, in the context of rumours about possible forest conservation-related evictions and hopes for compensation, the methods needed to be adapted regularly and methodologically. Ethically, the research was guided by the 'do no harm' clause, for instance, included in the American Anthropological Association's Code of Ethics.[27] Epistemologically, the research required critical reflexivity and a constant questioning of situationality and positionality, ensuring awareness of and avoiding bias in both data collection and interpretation as much as possible (Alvesson & Skoldberg, 2009; Bourdieu & Wacquant, 1992; Brewer, 2000; Clifford & Marcus, 1986; England, 1994; Geertz, 1973; Gouldner, 1970; Gregory et al. 2009; Kaufman, 2013; D'Silva et al., 2016). Methods and entire approaches were adapted throughout the 15-month-long field work in a continuous effort to make the residents feel safe to interact with us, and thus to increase the likelihood of collecting valid, high-quality, and comprehensive data.

Mariashoni Location encompassed three sub-locations, namely Kitiro, Kiptunga, and Mariashoni. A former fourth sub-location, Ndoswa, was upgraded to form a separate location in 2010. The field research in Mariashoni itself concentrated mainly on an area within a radius of approximately 3 km around Mariashoni Shopping Centre, located at -0.36649, 35.82486 at an altitude of ca. 2,670 MAMSL (see Map 3) in Kitiro sub-location.

---

[27] Article one states: 'A primary ethical obligation shared by anthropologists is to do no harm. It is imperative that, before any anthropological work be undertaken ... each researcher thinks through the possible ways that the research might cause harm. Among the most serious harms that anthropologists should seek to avoid are harm to dignity, and to bodily and material well-being, especially when research is conducted among vulnerable populations. Anthropologists should not only avoid causing direct and immediate harm but also should weigh carefully the potential consequences and inadvertent impacts of their work ... Anthropological work must similarly reflect deliberate and thoughtful consideration of potential unintended consequences and long-term impacts on individuals, communities, identities, tangible and intangible heritage and environments. (American Anthropological Association, 2012, p. 4)'.

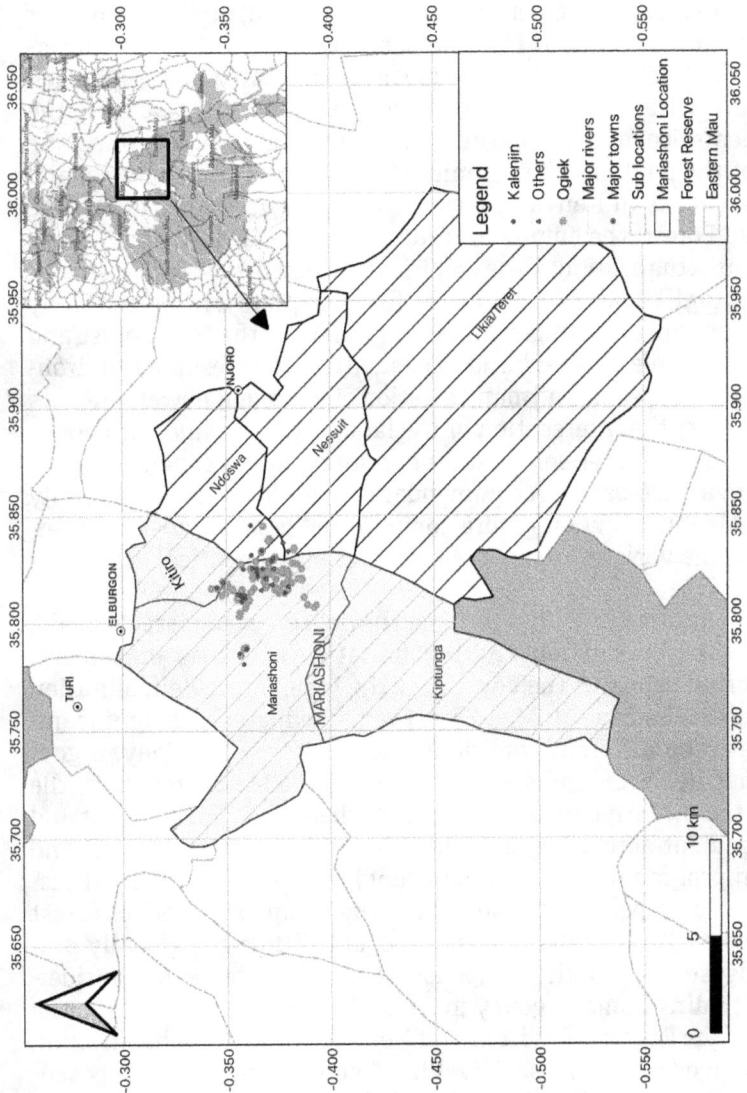

Map 3 Interviewed households in Mariashoni in the Eastern Mau Forest.

Source: Author composition using QGIS based on GIS data collected during structured interviews.
Note: The indicated ethnicity of respondents is based on self-identification in the survey, where 'Kalenjin' includes all Kalenjin sub-groups apart from the Ogiek.

Analysing the political ecology of the Mau Forest crisis

Following a broad political ecology approach, this book is structured in chapters that align with the four main lines of inquiry that were engaged: (1) The politics of conservation aid; (2) The commercial forestry industry; (3) The political economy of land; (4) The politics of belonging and exclusion at the intersection of the politics of conservation aid, extractive forestry monopolies, and land patronage. Each of these empirical chapters is organised in four sub-chapters: the general theoretical background and literature review related to specific features of the politicised environment of land, natural resource, and forest governance in Kenya; the contextual background as applicable for the Mau Forest; the empirical results from the Eastern Mau Forest; and the contextualisation of the empirical results in view of the general and contextual backgrounds. These four chapters are preceded by this Introduction, outlining the challenges facing the Mau Forest and approaches to 'Save the Mau', and problematises the presumed environmental crises as a result and manifestation of divergent power interests and relations at the intersection of the land, the trees, and the people. The book's last chapter comprises a summary, and a conclusion that proposes evidence-based recommendations for how to realistically 'Save the Mau' in view of a more complex and comprehensive understanding of the various interrelated features of the political ecology of the Mau crisis.

The main argument of Chapter 1, on the politics of conservation aid, is that forest conservation and rehabilitation activities implemented by external actors in the context of the Mau Forest Rehabilitation Programme in the Eastern Mau Forest remained largely insignificant. Caught between different traditions and priorities, the Kenyan government had neglected forest conservation in the Mau Forest until the advent of the initiative to 'Save the Mau'. Thereafter, government and non-government actors implemented climate change mitigation and adaptation programmes that were strongly inspired by external discourses and approaches without taking the complex drivers of forest degradation and non-protection into account. While the globally promoted ecosystems thinking emphasised the importance of considering and including human agency in natural resource conservation, the influence of the Poverty-Environment Nexus led to forest rehabilitation being conceived of in terms of livelihood enhancement for supposedly poor forest dwellers by supporting their engagement in agricultural 'best practices'. However, the nexus lodged the responsibility for both destruction and rehabilitation with ordinary people and targeted behaviour change on their farms within the forest – while portraying both as predominantly apolitical processes. The implemented projects furthermore focused solely on easily accessible areas and people in the

Eastern Mau, leading to local bias and elite capture of both livelihood and community participation initiatives. Faced with headwind from state forest management authorities, the promoted community forestry vehicle, the CFA, had no stake in forest management, benefit- or power-sharing. In remaining state forest areas, a traditional 'fences and fines' approach superseded the more holistic forest management approach proposed by Mau Forest Rehabilitation Programme. The only activities tied to 'Save the Mau' in these areas were heavily mediatised tree-planting drives that involved the planting of seedlings of contextually unsuitable tree species whose management was neglected; most of the seedlings died.

Chapter 2, on commercial forestry industry, analyses the Kenyan government's priority setting at the intersection of its developer and steward roles. The main argument is that, despite the conservation rhetoric, commercial forest production by politically connected large-scale timber companies remained the primary priority and use of the Mau Forest. Consequently, forest management continued being geared towards forest production rather than conservation. The timber companies kept operating during the logging ban, effective from 1999 to 2011, and after it was revoked. The 'Save the Mau' initiative was hence faced with the Government's prioritisation of its developer role. Instead of saving the ailing forest from further destruction, the 12-year-long logging ban had a further perverse effect on forest cover and forest health in the Eastern Mau since the small sawmillers, henceforth excluded from state forests, turned to any trees found on-farm within the settlement schemes. Parallel to continuous forest plantation exploitation, the small sawmillers hence deforested the 'private' land holdings. They thereby also normalised forest destruction and exploitation and fostered benefit-centred mindsets among forest dwellers.

Chapter 3 focuses on the importance of the land below the trees. The main argument of this chapter is that the political economy of land is a major contributor to the failure of the rehabilitation enterprise in the Mau Forest overall, and specifically in the Eastern Mau Forest. Allocation and distribution of fertile forest land had been used increasingly to reward and maintain political loyalty since the early 1990s, benefiting both 'big men' and ordinary Kenyans, although mainly from communities whose support then-President Daniel arap Moi courted. The Ogiek were mostly excluded from these land redistribution exercises in the Eastern Mau, and a first schism appeared in the local Ogiek community between those who wanted to access small-scale land holdings, and those who opposed them because such land use denied and disrupted their traditional socio-spatial organisation. Despite obtaining an injunction, and hence a legal halt to further forest conversion in the Eastern Mau, land continued being parcelled and sold or leased out. The emerging land market pitted many groups of people against each other and led to a normalisation of land subdivision, land-use change, and to a generalised sense of land insecurity, which had a far-reaching impact on the health of the land within the settlement schemes. Many Ogiek engaged in both the land market within the settlement scheme and converted forest land outside of the settlement boundaries to de facto farmland, typically in line with a narrative that emphasised their exclusion, disempowerment, and marginalisation.

The main argument of Chapter 4, on the politics of belonging and exclusion, is that the dynamic making of identities contributed strongly to the environmental crisis. Specifically, since 'identity' considerably influenced access to and use of land and natural resources, the construction of identity between 'self' and 'other' among different individuals and groups of people considerably shaped their interaction with their environments. First, the local Ogiek differentiated between several groups of *wageni* or 'in-migrants' based on various criteria, including duration of stay and ostensible willingness to integrate into the local community. Beyond that, the intersection of experiences related to the arrival of thousands of *wageni* since the early 1990s – the Ogiek being largely dispossessed of the land that they used to considered as theirs, the near-total deforestation of the settlement scheme and the subdivision and individual allocation of lands that had previously been community-owned – rendered Ogiek livelihoods in the area very vulnerable, and contributed strongly to the Ogiek blaming these most recent arrivals for the Mau crisis. Beyond forcing the Ogiek to adapt to their new socio-spatial realities, this in-migration, together with increased sedentarisation and formal education, as well as exposure to farming lifestyles and to the financial benefits of forest commodification, also led to a further schism within the local Ogiek community. Consequently, the Ogiek community was deeply divided between those who emphasised their hunter-gatherer heritage and claim to a sole legitimate presence in and use of the Eastern Mau and those whose objectives focused primarily on living a good life in material terms. This schism mainly manifested along generational lines, and numerous Ogiek youths actively engaged in forest destruction. While their overall impact might have been small, the societal change these youths engendered and portrayed created doubts about the Ogiek community's legitimacy in claiming that they should be respected as the 'guardians of the forest'. The mutual accusation between Ogiek and *wageni* groups for their supposed contribution to forest degradation prevented the community from elaborating a joint vision and action plan about how to indeed 'Save the Mau'.

The Politics of Conservation Aid:
The Development State and 'Saving the Mau'

The initiative to 'Save the Mau' brought various conservation aid actors to the Mau Forest, both governmental and non-governmental. The initiative can be understood in the context of a global rise in green governmentality, which included various international environmental agreements, including the 1992 Convention on Biological Diversity (CBD), the 1973 Convention on the International Trade in Endangered Species of Wild Flora and Fauna (CITES), the 1979 Convention on the Conservation of Migratory Species of Wild Animals (CMS), the 1994 Convention to Combat Desertification (CCD), the 1992 Framework Convention on Climate Change (UNFCCC), Agenda 21, the 1994 International Tropical Timber Agreement (ITTA), the 1997 Kyoto Protocol, the 1987 Montreal Protocol on Substances that Deplete the Ozone Layer, the 1971 Ramsar Convention on Wetlands of International Importance, alongside many others (Bongers & Tennigkeit, 2010; Johnson, 1976; Meyer et al., 1997; Okidi, 2008; Okidi et al., 2008). Conservation aid to Kenya progressively increased, which bore significant conservation efforts, including for the Mau Forest. Some of the conservation activities implemented were directly related to the Mau Forest Rehabilitation Programme. While NGOs had previously engaged with forest-dwelling and adjacent communities, these interactions were primarily focused on land rather than environmental issues. With the branding of the 'Mau crisis' as an environmental crisis, the politics of conservation aid arrived in the Mau Forest.

The politicised environment: Environmental conservation and management concepts and practice

In Kenya, forest management and conservation are embedded in and influenced by the broader environmental conservation, land use, and land-management history. Contemporary forest conservation policies and practices are a legacy of general environmental management policies and should be understood in their historical context.

The colonial legacy in conservation narratives and practices

During the colonial period, environmental stress was explained by a 'single story', a kind of 'master narrative'. This colonial legacy defined the trajectory of environmental policy and practice in Kenya, which influenced the multiple attempts and failed approaches to conserving the country's spectacular environments.

Institutionalised and centralised environmental management in Kenya, as in most African countries, was established under the colonial governments in the early 20th century. Most of these governments organised natural resource management in four branches, dividing wildlife, forestry, fisheries, and agriculture in pursuit of 'governmentality' (Foucault, 1991), which demanded rational forms of management of resources and populations through administrative apparatuses of the state, based on expert knowledge (Escobar, 1999). While wildlife became the core concern of environmental conservation, forestry, fisheries, and agriculture were primarily approached regarding production and resource exploitation (Bongers & Tennigkeit, 2010). Both tendencies were rooted in European colonialism, European conceptualisations and ideals of scenic African landscapes and nature, and colonialists' habitus (Adams, 2001; Constantin, 1994; McCann, 1999; Murphree, 2000; Neumann, 1998; Ville, 1998).[1]

In Kenya, environmental conservation thinking was closely linked to the history of British colonisation. The arrival of the first colonialists in the late 1880s and the presence of 'abundant nature' and wildlife contributed to the solid establishment of hunting as part of the colonialists' habitus. Due to its popularity, hunting was effectively regulated from as early as 1897 to protect 'natural beauty' and stop wildlife extinction through uncontrolled hunting. The narrative involving a presumed 'degradation of the African Eden' underlay the inception of conservation enterprises in Kenya, as in the wider African context (McCann, 1999). State-enforced protection of wildlife and natural resources thus started with the beginning of the colonial enterprise in Kenya (Taylor, 2001). From the onset, conservation policies contributed to the exclusion of Africans from what the scientific explorer Sir Henry Hamilton Johnston, in 1884, described as '*le plus extraordinaire terrain de chasse du monde*' (the most extraordinary hunting grounds in the world) (Ville, 1998, p. 234), in the light of the common assumption that the Africans were responsible for supposed environmental degradation because of their presumed contribution to deforestation, overstocking, cultivation of slopes, over-cultivation, and increases in the cultivated area among others (McCann, 1999). In the 1920s, the colonial administration further tightened these regulations by creating dedicated game

[1]   The entire section is largely shaped by these texts. Precisions and complementary sources are referenced.

reserves and by imposing hunting quotas for white hunters to generate supplementary income for the colonial administration while rendering trophy hunting and ivory exploitation more lucrative. Consequently, African hunting and settling within these reserves became prohibited. Overall, the 1930s seem to have been fundamental in 'setting a story of degradation and prescribing the world public's image of what African landscapes should look like. Subsequent efforts at conservation often were attempts by human agents to freeze the landscape's dynamism and achieve a scene that conforms to prevailing ideas about Africa's "natural" state' (McCann, 1999, p. 75).

Then, in the late 1940s and 1950s, a significant ideological and spatial-organisational shift took place in the conceptualisation and concretisation of conservation policies, from preserving wildlife for Euro-American trophy hunting to creating national parks where animals were to live as protected species in their natural habitats. After World War II, these became the 'keystone institutions of environmental conservation' (O'Neill, 1996, p. 521), inviolable sanctuaries in which all human activity was forbidden. Within the following twenty years, the country's biggest and most important national parks were created, including Nairobi (1946), Tsavo (1948), Amboseli (1974, after having been gazetted as National Reserve in 1948), Mount Kenya (1949), Aberdare (1951), and Nakuru (1968) (UNEP-WCMC, 2014). The establishment of these formal conservation institutions in Kenya followed trends in Western Europe and the USA, where national parks were created from the late 19th century, most emblematically the Yellowstone National Park in 1872. In the United Kingdom, the first small natural reserves were created in the 1880s, although legislation for creating nature parks and reserves was only adopted in the 1940s. This legislation emerged in the post-war period, in which discourses of the conservationists' lobby, mainly composed of scientific 'experts' and international NGOs, as well as the white hunters' lobby, forestry and wildlife bureaucrats and environmental 'romantics' began to converge (Compagnon, 2000). The creation of national parks and game reserves became a vehicle for a broader colonial redefinition of space and land (Collett, 1987). Forests, specifically, were protected through two statutes, either by being part of the land belonging to a given national park or reserve or through gazettement, which provided for state protection of a designated forest. To be effective, according to relevant legislation in force, an official announcement of a gazettement intention had to be published in a state gazette or the Official Journal. Once gazetted, human activity became restricted in these forest areas, subjected to strict regulation, and only permitted to the holders of specific permits, in line with rules on land use in national parks (Ville, 1998). The colonial government set up most of the gazetted forest reserves between the early 1900s and 1963 (Standing & Gachanja, 2014).

Socio-spatial reorganisation in forests and other environments went hand in hand with establishing a uniform discourse on environmental management. This discourse that Adams and Hulme (2001) label the 'narrative of fortress conservation' (p. 10) focused mainly on three issues. First, the threat of extinction of wildlife and nature; second, the humans as the destroyers; and third, protectionist conservation as salvation. These three elements became the foundation of what Murphree (2000) describes as the first of four phases of environmental management in Africa: conservation *against* the population. This discourse was underpinned by pseudo-*scientific* arguments, which helped rationalise aesthetic and economic motives. The necessity of conserving what was depicted as the last stances of 'paradise', natural beauty and 'wilderness' threatened with extinction, was emphasised. This necessity to preserve African landscapes was mainly derived from the perception that 'this is the way Africa should look' (statement made by a British expatriate ecologist serving as an official of an influential international conservation organisation, cited in Neumann, 1998, p. 1). This discourse further accentuated the representation of human activity, even humanity, as the chief destroyer of nature, thereby implying that local indigenous populations were archaic and backward, and responsible for land degradation through deforestation and erosion and thus incapable of managing their own natural resources. Expulsion and exclusion of the local population from protected areas were consequently the only option to save the 'wilderness', defining exclusion as the historical foundation of conservation (Brown, 2003). In previously created game reserves, shooting animals had already become an exclusive right for white hunters who paid for their licences. The national park policies then led to the complete eviction of local community members. According to Neumann (1998), 'it is not enough to physically remove human agency and occupation from the landscape, it must be completely purged from history' (p. 30), and in doing so 'parks help to ... not only deny the Other their history but also create a new history in which the Other literally has no place' (p. 31).

In line with the attempt to control these spaces, the same spaces needed to be closed (Neumann, 1998) and local people and their hunting, farming, firewood collecting, logging, and settling were controlled through the enforcement of a 'fences and fines approach' (Adams & Hulme, 2001, p. 10) with 'hard edges' protected by armed rangers and fences (Barrow, Gichohi, & Infield, 2001). Fences, according to philosopher Razac (2000), barbed wire fences in particular are instruments that serve the political management of space by preventing unmeant intrusions. Whereas they primarily mark a polarisation between a threatening 'exterior' and a protected hence safeguarded 'interior', the locality of security and insecurity might be on one side of the fence or the other, with the separating fence deciding over inclusion or exclusion. The scientifically justified conservation discourse insisted on excluding the local population from protected areas while providing revenue for the colonial administration through the lucrative exploitation of ivory and trophy hunting. This controversy is accurately reflected in the title of Steinhart's (2006) publication *Black Poachers, White Hunters: A Social History of Hunting in Colonial Kenya*. In the same vein, forest management, in line with other colonial forestry projects, was primarily concerned with rational and science-based 'sustained-yield forest management [that] was inescapably based on a denigration of allegedly 'inefficient' folk uses of the forest ... to justify enclosures and removals' (Weiner, 2005, p. 413).

After Independence, Kenya, like many African countries, largely maintained the colonial conservation policies of exclusion in place, and continuity between environmental policies of colonial and post-Independence administrations was clear (Bassett & Crummey, 2003; Bongers & Tennigkeit, 2010; Thenya, Wandago, Nahama, & Gachanja, 2008). This resulted in a situation in which *'les décisions coloniales s'inscrivent durablement dans le paysage contemporain'* (colonial decisions have drawn permanent lines in the contemporary landscape) (Calas, 1998, p. 37). It was not until the late 1970s, with the enactment of a total hunting ban in 1977, a ban on trade in animal products in 1978, and the establishment of a new focus on photo tourism, that the characteristics and purpose of national parks changed. Banning hunting and trade of animal products followed the rationale of conserving nature as an asset for tourism, which had become a key sector of the country's economy. At the same time, exclusion of local communities as a central element of conservation undertakings remained the guiding principle, with stricter policies contributing to further criminalisation of local practices of subsistence hunting from 1989 henceforth. Since then, beyond human interference in protected areas, all hunting activities have been criminalised, discursively and, as with any offence, became henceforth punishable by law (Steinhart, 2006).

In line with the overall political ecology concept that 'every environmental story is a story about power' (Weiner, 2005, p. 409), the dominance of the colonial power over all aspects of the territory, including its environment, served as a symbolic representation of the presumed superiority of the national park policies' initiators. According to Constantin (1994), there was a historical link between environmental politics and domination enterprises that did not disappear with the end of colonial times and that appreciation of the landscape was equalled with an 'elevated sensibility' that only the educated 'proper' bourgeois could produce. Struggle over class identity and cultural values, in the African context at the time, mainly over racial identity, were at the heart of national park policies. In that sense, the 'national parks movement witnessed a convergence of ideas about landscape appreciation, social identity and nature protection' (Neumann, 1998, p. 24), rendering national parks the 'dreamwork of imperialism' (Neumann, 1998, p. 17).

Ecologically, the effective enclosure of delimited territories in many instances contributed to spatial confinement and an overall reduction of the accessible territory for the animals, leading to a destruction of habitat, an interruption of migratory routes due to human installations, as well as to an augmentation of total animal numbers within the protected areas. The intensification of tourism in some parks also led to partial ecological degradation (Calas, 1998). Outside of Kenya, various studies found that biodiversity had effectively declined within the most restrictive parts of protected areas (O'Neill, 1996) and that centralised conservation efforts, in general, had failed (Gibson & Koontz, 1998). At the same time, forest depletion and destruction within gazetted forest reserves in Kenya that were managed along similar 'fences and fines' principles peaked in the 1990s (Mugo, Nyandiga, & Gachanja, 2010; Njeru, 2012; Standing & Gachanja, 2014).

The advent of green governmentality and polycentrality in environmental governance

Having witnessed the failure of 'fences and fines' approaches in protecting the country's environment, the Kenyan government gradually changed its approach to environmental management and embraced various forms of community inclusion in conservation in the 1990s (Adams, 2001; Barrow et al., 2001; Barrow & Murphree, 2001; Compagnon, 2000; Connan, 2007; Hulme & Murphree, 2001b; Ville, 1998). The evolution of 'scientifically' supported and socially accepted conservation approaches away from coercive to more inclusive models was, once again, strongly influenced by changes in international discourses that started to openly question the sustainability of the 'fortress conservation' approaches during the same period (Duffy, 1997).

While the colonial superpowers had driven the influence of external conceptualisations of nature and conservation with the support of selected organisations and lobby groups, this external influence changed shape in the post-colonial world. Indeed, natural resource management and governance slowly became subject to international environmental law, leading to increasing international standardisation of modes, approaches, and the terminology employed in environmental conservation matters. Since the early 1970s, this external influence has been streamlined and consolidated into transnationally and multilaterally agreed upon environmental management principles and practices (Bongers & Tennigkeit, 2010; Johnson, 1976; Mackey, 2008; Meyer et al. 1997; O'Neill, 1996). Before then, no general international law principles were comprehensively concerned with the 'ecological system of the world' (Johnson, 1976, p. 55). After that, international attention to environmental crises and their management increased steadily, particularly in the context of rising awareness of the potential impact of human influence on the world's environments and the climate. The rise of multilateralism in environmental management can hence directly be related to the 'discovery' of anthropogenic climate change, which emerged as a significant public policy issue by the mid-to-late 1980s (Hulme, 2009). At the same time, the rise of international environmental law marked a turning point in the conceptualisation of humankind: 'The concept of man as master of the Earth is now being replaced by the concept of man as "Custodian of the Earth"' (Johnson, 1976, p. 55).

Crucial for this evolution were the 1972 Meadows Report 'The Limits to Growth' and the 1972 UN Conference on the Human Environment in Stockholm, the first-ever global conference with the specific objective of addressing environmental protection (Okidi, 2008), and the Conference's Declaration containing twenty-six general principles relating to the protection of nature by addressing the relationship between conservation and development. These were followed by the creation of the UN Environment Programme (UNEP), headquartered in Nairobi, Kenya, in the same year (Johnson, 1976). Several events and documents have since contributed to shaping the rise of a world environmental regime, understood as 'a partially integrated collection of world-level organizations, understandings, and assumptions that specify the relationship of human society to nature' (Meyer et al., 1997, p. 623). After the publication of the influential 1987 Brundtland Report, the concepts of sustainable development and the related precautionary principle gained prominence and became the international leitmotif for environmental policies (Guyer & Richards, 1996; Okidi et al., 2008) and 'buzzword(s) for global change in environmental governance' (Wamukoya & Ludeki, 2003, p. iv). The sustainable development idea that promotes the dual objective 'to meet the needs and aspirations of the present, without compromising the ability to meet those of the future' (World Commission on Environment and Development, 1987, p. 43) provides a framework for integrating environmental policies and development strategies (Hulme, 2009). These concepts entered the vocabulary and discourse of relevant conservation actors, and their objectives became part of all environmental laws and regulations. After the Brundtland Report, several international agreements consolidated an international environmental regime. Beyond the overall 'sustainable development' terminology, alongside the 'precautionary principle', multiple other terms were promoted through these reports and became part of the general environmental discourse.

Gradually, adaptation became the new development paradigm (Hulme, 2009) following the near-universal acknowledgement that climate change is 'real' (Weisser, Doevenspeck, Müller-Mahn, & Bollig,

2011). This shift in the development discourse and practice entailed a turning away from the primary focus on controlling the emission of various greenhouse gases responsible for much of the anthropogenic climate change (mitigation). Instead, the building and enhancement of adaptive capacity and resilience to climate change and variability became a priority, with a focus on individual and communal behaviour change. A new livelihoods-centred approach to natural resource management emerged as well: The pursuit of environmental easement in and around crucial natural resources, often through payment for ecosystem services (PES) schemes. These were often supported by 'green' climate funds, predominantly through the Global Environment Facility (GEF), or specific mitigation and/or adaptation finance mechanisms, including Reducing Emissions from Deforestation and Forest Degradation programmes (REDD and REDD+). Environmental easement became a trendy way of compensating private landowners for entering legally binding arrangements with an easement holder, through which landowner agreed to restrict their land use and grant the easement holder various rights to enforce restrictions to achieve conservation goals (Bray, 2016; Michael, 2003; Parker, 2004). In the wake of these developments, some authors argue that the consolidation of an international environmental regime also brought about a 'neoliberal conservation' phase, in which nature became commodified (Vaccaro et al., 2013) through the establishment of 'green economies' (Nakhooda, Caravani, Bird, & Schalatek, 2011). Such approaches were solidified and streamlined by overall globalisation and through a steep increase in 'environmental' funds (Kull, Ibrahim, & Meredith, 2006).

Despite the emergence of an international environmental regime and the manifestation of new conservation organisations and institutions, state parties continued to have to negotiate and enact the rules and concepts included in these international treaties through national legislation because there is no supra-order in the community of states allowing execution of international law through a supra-state organ (Johnson, 1976). Karen Bäckstrand conceptualised these instances of global environmental governance in terms of 'green governmentality', which takes the form of a centralised and bureaucratised multilateral negotiation system that places the nation-state at the centre of the Government arrangements (Bäckstrand & Lövbrand, 2006). Kenya is a state party to all relevant international environmental conventions, mostly with translations of these conventions into applicable national policies, thus enacting international law at the national level and rendering international law de jure punishable (Wamukoya & Ludeki, 2003).

The emergence of community conservation

Given difficulties experienced and changes in international conservation discourse, recognition grew that successful environmental management might necessitate embracing these environments' social and ecological complexity. Recognising this complexity, in turn, requires an institutional design that involves flexibility and adaptability (Nagendra & Ostrom, 2012) and hence a move away from state-centric to polycentric governance models (Bushley, 2014).

From the early 1990s, an increasingly transnational scientific and normative input led to the production of the new community conservation counter-narrative and to its wide adoption in global conservation discourse and policies (O'Neill, 1996), which can be understood as one approach within the broader spectrum of polycentric natural resource governance set-ups (Nagendra & Ostrom, 2012). This new narrative was embedded in and supported a shift of thinking within the field of scientific ecology, which embraces systems-thinking and developed and promotes the concept of biodiversity. In this concept, wildlife, the traditional focus of conservation models and policies, is no longer considered a closed-off system. Consequently, in line with systems-thinking, conservation efforts cannot solely focus on protecting wildlife but must include migratory systems and entire ecosystems. An ecosystem 'is a dynamic complex of plant, animal (including human), and microorganism communities interacting with their physical environment (including soil, water, climate, and atmosphere) as a functional unit' (World Resources Institute et al., 2007, p. 3). Unlike previous 'wilderness' concepts that inspired early conservation efforts, the biodiversity concept unifies ideas and concepts emanating from both the biophysical and social sciences. Both generally recognise four levels of biodiversity, namely genes, species, ecosystems and, finally, societies and their practices (Cormier-Salem & Bassett, 2007). The introduction of the ecosystems approach led to an essential shift in the conceptualisation of nature and thus ideas about its appropriate management. Henceforth, humans were no longer exclusively considered as harmful to nature but an integral and often necessary part of it. According to Compagnon (2000), evicting humans from protected areas might even be damaging to these in the long term, as there are rarely any milieus rich in biodiversity without some form of human activity. At the same time, the idea that nature and wilderness are not necessarily 'natural' but 'constructed', which 'often require great artifice' in their creation (Sills, 1975, p. 24) gained further popularity. Cronon (1996) defines wilderness as 'entirely a cultural invention' (p. 8), far from being a 'natural' biophysically defined unit. Acclaimed environmental historian William Cronon in 'The Trouble with Wilderness: Or, Getting Back to the Wrong Nature' (1996), also suggests that 'the time has come to rethink wilderness' (p. 7).

While environmental management policies and practices had initially been founded on a static vision of what nature was supposed to be, a 'wilderness', which needed to be protected against human interference, historian Raymond Williams (1973) stipulates that 'the idea of nature contains, though often unnoticed, an extraordinary amount of human history' (p. 68). National parks as a vehicle for environmental conservation, according to Neumann (1998), hence 'are paradoxical because the culturally constructed aesthetic ideal of the natural landscape can never be "preserved" because the dynamism of ecological processes defies preservation' (p. 28) and emphasises that 'nature functions as an active agent, while simultaneously being socially constructed' (p. 29). Neil Smith (2010), in his work on the 'first' and 'second' nature, in the same vein, comes to the conclusion that 'nature is nothing if it is not social' (p. 47). According to Calas (1998), Kenya's nature, like any other, is the product of a particular understanding, a specific representation, conceptualisation and *history* of nature. While recognising the 'natural', the ecological basis of nature, it is thus 'simultaneously real, collective, and discursive … and needs to be deconstructed accordingly' (Escobar, 1999, p. 2).

Community conservation approaches gained momentum related to the acknowledgement of the historicity of human influence on natural systems and an opening up to imagining a harmonious interaction between different segments of ecosystems. Furthermore, social critiques of exclusionist practices in the name of conservation grew in the late 1980s. Arguing from a human rights point of view, the Brundtland Report, stated that 'it is both futile and an insult to the poor to tell them they must remain in poverty to protect the environment' (ReVelle & ReVelle, 1992, p. 52). In the same vein, Adams and Hulme (2001) conclude that 'conservation will either contribute to solving the problems of the poor who live day to day with wild animals, or those animals will disappear' (p. 13). Community conservation was hence drawn upon to foster new political openings through which rights to land and resources could be articulated (Dressler, Büscher, Schoon, Brockington et al., 2010).

Adams and Hulme (2001) describe these community conservation principles as 'those principles and practices that argue that conservation goals should be pursued by strategies that emphasize the role of local residents in decision-making about natural resources' (p. 13). Hulme and Murphree (2001a) add a political as well as an economic aspect beyond the involvement question and define community conservation as 'ideas, policies, practices and behaviours that seek to give those who live in rural environments greater involvement in managing the natural resources (soil, water, species, habitats, landscapes, or biodiversity) that exist in the area in which they reside (be that permanently or temporarily) and/or greater access to benefits derived from those resources' (p. 4). These definitions allude to three fundamental elements of community conservation: inclusion as such, inclusion in benefits, and inclusion in decision-making. The first highlights that the involvement of local communities in and around protected areas in managing conservation resources is paramount. This change of optic is relevant in two regards: first, because it recognises the importance of including local communities in conservation efforts, and second, because it translates an awareness that flora and fauna worthy of protection can often not exclusively be found within protected areas but also outside of their borders. In Kenya, up to 80% of wildlife live outside of protected areas during the humid season, making support of local communities, the sometimes reluctant but pivotal conservation actors, indispensable (World Resources Institute et al., 2007). The second core idea of the community conservation approach is that conservation and livelihoods are interconnected, and that conservation goals and local economic development objectives must be aligned. The rationale behind aligning conservation and livelihood objectives is that conservation should be economically sustainable for local communities and constitute an alternative source of income and subsistence to discourage potentially harmful activities such as charcoal burning or poaching, alongside certain forms of agriculture and ranching. The third element goes even further and emphasises inclusion in decision-making about managing the natural resources in a given area beyond the benefits. Many community conservation initiatives hence proposed a combination of three distinctive elements: direct income generation for those employed in wildlife management; provision of social services and infrastructure, such as clinics, schools and roads; and sometimes also political empowerment through institutional development and strengthening of local land tenure (Barrow & Murphree, 2001; Compagnon, 2000).

Considering the failure of previous approaches to environmental conservation, and since Kenya was a state party to all essential environmental international agreements, and because of the strong influence of global conservation NGOs, the guiding principles of community conservation were institutionalised within all significant ministries involved in natural resource management in Kenya in the first half of the 1990s (Okidi et al., 2008). Through ecosystem thinking and the inclusion of community conservation principles, forests in and by themselves became part of the 'imaginary landscape' of conservation theory and practice, which had previously been neglected mainly due to conservation policies' and practices' focus on wildlife. While many primary forests were de facto protected because of their inclusion in national parks, this predominantly was the case where forests were related to the habitats of the 'big five', the five large mammals on which first hunting and then photo tourism concentrated, namely elephants, rhinoceroses, lions, leopards, and buffalos. Community conservation approaches to forestry, globally and in Africa specifically, have gained momentum since the early 1990s (Agrawal, Chhatre, & Hardin, 2008; Chomba, Nathan, Minang, & Sinclair, 2015).

Community inclusion in forestry and forest governance specifically is commonly labelled as 'community forestry' (CF) or 'community-based forest management' (CBFM) and sometimes sustainable forest management (SFM). While there are various definitions and labels for related approaches (Glasmeier & Farrigan, 2005), most of these definitions include parts of three characteristics. First, some degree of forest management responsibility and authority is vested in local communities in CF; second, CF aims at the provision of social and economic benefits to local communities; and third, community inclusion is to lead to ecologically sustainable forest use and forest health restoration (Charnley & Poe, 2007). While the CF and CBFM labels are commonly used to describe and analyse community involvement in various types of forests, including private forest land, land held as common property, or forests on indigenous' people's land, most initiatives and research focus on CBFM in state forests located on government-owned lands, which comprise more than 80% of the world's forests (Charnley & Poe, 2007). Chomba et al. (2015) argue that the paradigm shift towards CBFM can be associated with three separate but related developments. First, with a recognition that traditional environmental practices of managing natural resources can contribute positively to biodiversity conservation, ecosystem resilience and improved rural livelihoods; second, that top-down forest management has not been able to address deforestation successfully; and third, the exclusion of local communities from forest management conflicts with their human rights. Community-based forest management hence addresses some of the underlying issues with previous state-centred forest management, including overexploitation of forests through industrial logging, insufficient enforcement of forest management laws due to lacking resources and resulting disengagement from forest management responsibilities and persistent rural poverty, among others, which contributed to the global recognition that CF might potentially engender more sustainable forest management (Charnley & Poe, 2007). As community conservation in general, CF is part of the broader critique of top-down approaches to development and an appreciation of bottom-up approaches (Chambers, 1993). Citing Agrawal and Ribot (1999) and Agrawal and Gibson (1999), Chomba et al. (2015) furthermore argue that power is supposedly transferred in three empirically tangible categories through CBFM: first, the power to define natural resource-use regulations; second, the power to implement these regulations; and third, the power to arbitrate disputes. Overall, CF can be understood as part of the wider shift towards community-based natural resource management (CBNRM) and conservation (Charnley & Poe, 2007), which is based on sustainable development thinking (Bongers & Tennigkeit, 2010).

Recognising alternative sources of ecological knowledge

One of CBFM's key objectives is to foster sustainable environmental development through the devolution of power in forest management (Blaikie, 2006; Kellert, Mehta, Ebbin, & Lichtenfeld, 2000), which involves a deliberate appreciation and incorporation of indigenous and/or traditional ecological knowledge (TEK) and ideas about land and resource management (Brown, 2003). With the rise of community conservation thinking, both the schism between different sets of knowledge and different modes of knowledge production, as well as the role of indigenous or TEK, also called 'local knowledge' (Geertz, 1983), received growing consideration in scientific literature starting from the 1980s (Bassett & Crummey, 2003; Berkes, Colding, & Folke, 2000; Weisser et al., 2011). Such knowledge, commonly understood as having been 'established over centuries of habitation and [to] often [be] unique to a particular community or ethnic group' (Hulme, 2009, p. 81), specifically gained popularity through the rise of climate change adaptation thinking and the investigation of drivers of resilience, understood as 'capacity to recover after disturbance, absorb stress, internalize it, and transcend it' (Berkes et al., 2000, p. 1252), and the recognition that such knowledge can meaningfully contribute to biodiversity conservation and sustainable natural resource use (Berkes et al., 2000; Gadgil, Berkes, & Folke, 1993; Gadgil & Rao, 1994).

While both TEK and scientific knowledge are based on an accumulation of observations and are often highly interlinked and co-evolving, it is apposite to oppose both since, in the words of acclaimed anthropologist Claude Levi-Strauss, referring to what he calls '*la pensée sauvage*' (the savage way of thinking), 'these two ways of knowing are two parallel modes of acquiring knowledge about the universe, ... one is supremely concrete, the other supremely abstract' (Berkes et al., 2000, p. 1251). Critiques also emerged in line with a growing scientific interest in TEK. First, the term 'tradition' has been contested in the social sciences due to various controversial underlying assumptions. One element of contention is that the lexical field from which the TEK term emanated is emotionally charged. Typically, the terms 'tradition' or 'traditional' are used by actors in a position of social dominance to differentiate themselves from the 'other', supposedly less 'developed' actors (Finnegan, 1991; Mallon, 2010). Another difficulty arises from the fact that the term 'tradition' often evokes 'a constant way of life unified and defined by the certainty of a particular continuity [which is] then identified as tradition' (Kratz, 1993, p. 32). By alluding to the fact that beliefs and rules are passed on over generations, and hence to some degree of continuity, the image of TEK as being a static composition of somewhat linear knowledge pieces is created. Despite the contested definition of what constitutes 'tradition', the usage of the TEK label became popular in the 1990s, notably through the International Conservation Union (IUCN) working group of that same name, representing a 'knowledge-practice-belief complex' defined as 'cumulative body of knowledge, practice, and belief, evolving by adaptive processes and handed down through generations by cultural transmission, about the relationship of living beings (including humans) with one another and with their environment' (Berkes et al., 2000, pp. 1251–2). Despite the broad appreciation of TEK, some authors argue that local knowledge has been challenged by transformations brought about by climate change, hence rendering TEK 'unreliable' (Morse, 2008). In that context, various authors propose differentiating between different local knowledge types. Mackenzie (2003), for instance, distinguishes between 'local knowledge', in line with TEK conceptualisations, and 'modern traditional knowledge', which claims to be traditional but is framed in the discourse of modernity. The ICRAF (2014) Policy Guidelines, Local Knowledge edition, differentiates between four types of knowledge: 'local knowledge', which is the knowledge of a defined group of people that is defined as a dynamic mixture of traditional knowledge and knowledge acquired from external sources; 'locally derived knowledge', which is part of local knowledge and based on local interpretation of locally made observations, which involves experimentation and confrontation with contemporary learning; 'indigenous knowledge', which is deeply embedded in and inseparable from cultural values; and 'traditional knowledge', which designates the part of local knowledge that is passed down from one generation to another. Hohenthal and Minoia (2018) further highlight that in a context of a plurality of socially constructed and power-laden representations of natural resources, there can be variations in ecological knowledge defined by differences in status and social recognition of their value, which they refer to as 'asymmetric ecological knowledges' (p. 1).

Terms and concepts related to 'natural heritage' or 'local heritage' are often part of TEK discussions. Cormier-Salem and Bassett (2007) specify that the 'patrimonialization' (p. 2) of nature defined as the construction of nature as heritage or patrimony, and its transmission from generation to generation, is a tool commonly used in sustainable natural resource management. The authors trace the origin of the idea of patrimony to civil law and Western religions, derived from the Latin word *patrimonium*, but widen the definition to include 'the objects and places valued in the memory of a nation, and even of humanity that are preserved and transmitted to successive generations' (p. 3). Although the notion of heritage is derived from 'Western systems of thought', they claim, it resonates with various concepts in the Global South, extending to a natural object being inherited from ancestors, transmitted to descendants who self-identify as joint stewards of that natural object. Despite being rooted in a representation of common ancestry, heritage designations are subject to change and transformation and thus a 'complex process that entails negotiations, recompositions and institutional reconfigurations ... that invariably change the meaning and substance of the patrimonial object' (p. 7). Specifically, the authors differentiate between exogenous and endogenous claims. They argue that exogenous claims typically emerge at the international scale and predominantly focus on environmental and conservation issues related to local heritage preservation. They mention, for example the CITES red list, the biosphere reserves of the United Nations Educational, Scientific and Cultural Organization (UNESCO)'s Man and the Biosphere Programme, and the World Natural and Cultural Heritage sites, which are often inspired by the presumed rarity of the object in question. On the other hand, endogenous claims typically emerge at the local scale. They tend to accentuate local communities' supposed 'ancestral rights' and social-cultural values to secure their social, cultural, and actual survival. Westra (2008), however, argues that the distinction is imperfect since cultural integrity is profoundly related to ecological integrity; and that both claims are not mutually exclusive. The idea that the environment is an essential component of indigenous cultures, specifically, is taken up broadly in international environmental law. It is, for instance, enshrined in the 1987 Brundtland Report, in Principle 22 of the Rio Declaration on the Environment and Development, in Chapter 26 of Agenda 21, in ILO Convention No. 169 or the United Nations Declaration on the Rights of Indigenous Peoples (Morse, 2008).

Despite this presumed inclusion not only of a right to a clean environment but of specific local knowledge concerning that environment, Cormier-Salem and Bassett's (2007) opposition between exogenous and endogenous processes helps to deconstruct why environmental policy and practice 'blueprints' based on 'local heritage preservation thinking' continued being the norm in supposedly 'participatory' land and resource-management policies promoted by government and non-government actors. This continuation in the promotion of top-down approaches typically manifests in the discrepancy between ideas and approaches promoted by foreign experts and Western-trained elites and their internationally accepted discourses and conservation priorities on the one hand, and the complex realities and barriers to sustainable practices on the ground on the other hand. It is hence pertinent to consider the tension between the 'environmentalism of the state' and the 'environmentalism of the peasant' (Rahmato, 2003, p. 205); or, in this case, the 'environmentalism of the state', the 'environmentalism of the Western-trained non-state actor' and the 'environmentalism of the forest dweller'. The last can furthermore be described as the result of an interaction between communities' and individual community members' identities, their rational interests and their personal preferences (Fuchs, Peters, & Neufeldt, 2019); and often include various facets of expressions of employing 'the weapons of the weak' (Scott, 1985, title), which are used to protest the imposition of coercive resource and land management measures through 'everyday forms of resistance' (Scott, 1985, title). Given the recognition that a diversity of actors and forest users is likely to result in diverging visions of how resources should be managed (Ojha, Ford, Keenan, Race, et al., 2016), and hence given social differentiation and positionality among community members, it might thus be more appropriate to speak of the 'environmentalisms of the forest dwellers' in the plural.

Who has the power? Variations in community-based polycentric governance models

Community conservation initiatives, altogether, are implemented under different names and labels, including community-based natural resource management (CBNRM), integrated conservation development projects (ICDPs), protected area buffer zones (PABZ), and buffering strategies, among many others. These are commonly called CF, CBFM, SFM, or participatory forest management (PFM) in forest management. Depending on the degree of communities' participation, various authors propose different typologies of community conservation initiatives (see Table 2).

The lightest form of community involvement is sought through minimalist park or protected area outreach (PAO) initiatives that provide communities living adjacent to national parks limited access to benefits accrued from these parks. Environmental easement strategies implemented on Private Land, which compensate private landowners for allowing a third party to manage their land to pursue conservation goals, are part of these 'conventional' approaches. At the opposite end of the spectrum are CBNRM initiatives that devolve tenure and responsibility for managing critical resources to autonomous local institutions. Many alternatives exist between these two poles (Barrow & Murphree, 2001; Compagnon, 2000; Murphree, 2000). Similarly, looking at community inclusion and participation in forest management in Africa specifically, Alden Wily and Mbaya (2001) differentiate between benefit-sharing and power-sharing CBFM paradigms, which represent the two endpoints along a continuum of participatory approaches. Core to the former is local communities' access to forests and the benefits generated from these forests through forest products and related jobs, as well as investment in local community development initiatives. Mogaka, Simons, Turpie, Emerton, and Karanja (2001) emphasise that these approaches are based on the premise that the benefits from conservation must outweigh its opportunity cost and hence be greater than the benefits from degradation. Alden Wily and Mbaya (2001) indicate that community involvement is typically limited to implementing forest regulations devised by state authorities in the benefit-sharing paradigm. The authors argue that these approaches aim to engender cooperation in and acceptance of state-dominated forest management schemes. Benefit sharing can take various forms as well, including mixed incentive schemes, PES, resource allocation to CBFM organisations, and the allocation of farming plots in forest plantations (Okumu & Muchapondwa, 2017a, 2017b). In the power-sharing approaches, on the other end of the continuum, decision-making power is devolved to communities to encourage sustainable forest use and management, considering their vested interests in forest resources. Hence, Barrow, Clarke, Grundy, Jones, and Tessema (2002) conclude that the benefit-sharing paradigm focuses on the shorter term, while the power-sharing approach relocates communities' interests in a longer time frame. The authors further argue that both the possibility of promoting specific approaches along this continuum and the community's will and interest to engage in SFM depends on forest land ownership and, related to that, forest tenure, alongside user rights. Adopting a power-sharing approach hence involves changes in state-people relations, for example, by devolving tenure administration and regulation, devolving land dispute resolution mechanisms, ensuring that land markets protect smallholders, peasants, and the rights of non-citizens, by strengthening laws that aim at land utilisation and prevent hoarding of non-utilised land, etc. (Barrow et al., 2002).

Table 2 Different approaches to participatory conservation and key characteristics.

	Protected area outreach	Collaborative management	Community-based conservation
Objective	Conservation of ecosystems, biodiversity, and species.	Conservation with some rural livelihood benefits.	Sustainable rural livelihoods.
Ownership/ tenure status	State-owned land and natural resources (e.g., national parks, forests and game reserves).	State-owned land with mechanisms for collaborative management of certain resources with the community. Complex tenure and ownership arrangements.	Local resource users own land and resources either de jure or de facto. State may have control of last resort.

Management characteristics	State makes all decisions about resource management.	Agreement between state and user groups about managing some resources that remain state owned. Nature of management arrangements critical.	Conservation as an element of land use. Emphasis on developing the rural economy.
Roles assigned to local communities	Passive providers of information.	Consultative, functional.	Interactive, self-mobilisation or empowerment.
Phases of conservation policies in Africa (Murphree, 2000)	Conservation *for* (or against) the people.	Conservation *with* the people.	Conservation *through* the people.
CBFM paradigms (Alden Wily & Mbaya, 2001)	Benefit-sharing paradigm (potentially).	Benefit-sharing paradigm (likely).	Power-sharing paradigm, including benefit sharing.

Sources: Adapted from Alden Wily & Mbaya, 2001, p. 2; Barrow & Murphree, 2001, p. 28; Compagnon, 2000, p. 15; Murphree, 2000, pp. 42–43.

Based on conservation models promoted in the early 2000s, Vaccaro et al. (2013) distinguish three phases of conservation, namely 'fortress conservation', 'co-management' and 'neoliberal conservation'. Building on that distinction, benefit-sharing approaches might more appropriately be defined as 'neoliberal' approaches, while the power-sharing approaches fall more neatly into the 'co-management' phase, which both continue to qualify as polycentric governance models.

In Kenya, conservation authorities predominantly employed PAO community conservation approaches, which was also the most dominant approach in the wider East African region. Based on the hypothesis that the support of people surrounding a protected area will enhance the conservation of biodiversity, PAO initiatives seek to improve the biological integrity of protected areas by educating local communities to create buffer zones around protected areas. Communities are commonly involved in two ways. The first is 'participation through information', which entails establishing education centres inside protected areas, managed mainly by KWS, or supporting sensitisation in schools. The second is 'participation through benefit sharing', mainly by sharing parts of the benefits made through protected areas with communities while the state retains legal land ownership. Overall, PAO typically prioritises conservation objectives more than development goals (Kangwana, 2001).

Similarly, benefit-sharing approaches were dominant in PFM in eastern and southern Africa, with little evidence of power-sharing approaches (Alden Wily & Mbaya, 2001). This assessment is in line with observations that confer that in natural resource-management set-ups, the most considerable discrepancy between state-enforced, conventional science-based approaches to management and traditional resource-management systems is likely to be found in forest management.

How much community is in community conservation – and which community?

A simple underlying assumption of community conservation approaches is that the values of a community with strong historical ties with a given landscape are likely to lead to the successful and sustainable development of the natural resources in their area. Community-based management is promoted as the most appropriate form of natural resource management (Gibson & Koontz, 1998). Yet, related to the variety of 'environmentalisms', various authors caution that concepts such as 'local' and 'community' are not self-evident and 'often conceal more than they reveal about natural resource access, control and management' (Bassett, Blanc-Pamard, & Boutrais, 2007, p. 105). They also caution against taking for granted the definition of who the 'local community' supposedly is and of what their interests are on the one hand and about the roles this community plays in natural resource management on the other hand.

A primary challenge in community conservation relates to defining who 'community' is. According to Barrow and Murphree (2001), the community is 'one of the most vague and elusive concepts in social science and continues to defy precise definitions' (p. 24), while Agrawal and Gibson (1999) stipulate that a definitive conceptualisation of what constitutes a community does simply not exist. Initially, the term draws on the German sociologist and philosopher Ferdinand Tönnies' (1887) differentiation of *Gemeinschaft* and *Gesellschaft*, community and society. Agrawal and Gibson (1999) argue that 'community' is commonly represented in three main ways in the community conservation literature: a spatial unit, a homogenous social structure, and shared norms. Today, the term community is often ideologically and morally connoted, bearing a hidden pro-poor ideology (Compagnon, 2000), according to which a community's presumed homogeneity implies a set of shared values, which leads to optimal social outcomes (Gibson & Koontz, 1998). This is problematic in several regards, notably because it implies that communities are taken as a monolith and as homogenous by default, that their values are considered homogenous, and that this supposed homogeneity of values is the central yet exogenously considered variable that explains successful community-based management. Some authors argue that such approaches overlook the ability of communities to manage their values by creating homogeneity, typically by forming supportive institutions, considering that values are not static but change across individuals, time and space (Gibson & Koontz, 1998). This definitory challenge can be problematic in community conservation initiatives, for instance, in cases where the legitimacy of the 'local community' involved is questioned or deemed socially inappropriate. This can, for example, be the case when a 'functional' community, typically derived from administrative units inherited by the colonial state and thus not necessarily representative of the local social organisation, is chosen to represent 'the community'. The selection of a 'community' can be ineffective and inappropriate, either because administrative units are too large for an effective community initiative or hardly representative of a given area (Compagnon, 2000). If the spatial unit is too small, and the definition of the 'community' solely focuses on sedentarised locals, seasonal residents or resource users might be excluded (McLain, 2001), or members of non-traditionally forest-dwelling communities, for instance (Agrawal & Gibson, 1999). Charnley and Poe (2007) argue that community, in CF initiatives, is most commonly place-based and geographically delineated. Yet, such place-based definitions overlook community dynamics in which the central elements of equity and justice are embedded (Ojha et al., 2016). Other challenges arise when 'community' is defined in ethnic terms, and the word 'community' can easily be 'ethnicised' (Gibson & Koontz, 1998), specifically in environments where 'community' is defined along ethnic lines. Ethnically based 'community' ascriptions became common in the context of the creation of 'Native Reserves' (also referred to as 'ethnic reserves') under colonial rule, addressed in detail further below, and remained a critical 'vehicle' of social organisation and mobilisation in Kenya, including in 'community' development contexts.

Furthermore, who is designated as 'community' often depends on the interests of local power brokers (Compagnon, 2000). In such cases, the search for 'homogenous' communities can become 'misdirected and politicised', particularly in the context of externally funded development projects, and subject to political patronage and favouritism (Bayart, 1989; Klopp & Sang, 2011; Wrong, 2009). Theoretically, the *'terroir'* approach that grew popular in French academic geography in the 1960s has been at the forefront of the conceptualisation and definition of socio-natural spaces in which local communities and their identities are linked to specific spatial entities, to certain places. In line with community conservation initiatives that link people to a particular community to a given place, following the assumption that environmental stewardship is more likely to develop in an area in which people have strong historical ties, the 'terroir' approach has also been used to 'construct locality' exogenously. Anglophone ecologists later approached the question through a 'landscape' lens from the 1990s, defining the latter as 'creations at the intersection of social history and biological/climatological process' (Guyer & Richards, 1996, p. 4) and hence emphasise historical and spatial dimensions of biodiversity (Bernard, 2014). In the 1990s, the *terroir* approach then became a fundamental basis for bottom-up rural development undertakings, which was less based on the scale than on a conception of locally relevant rural spatiality for the promotion of activities between the national and the household level, particularly in Francophone West Africa influence (Bassett et al., 2007). However, by attempting to define structural-functional spaces within which the resource-management role of the 'local community' is supposed to be enhanced, the very concretisation of a social construction of space interacts with existing, sometimes deeply politicised intra-community conflicts over the control of resources, and about the very meaning of the socio-natural heritage. Hulme and Murphree (2001a) concede that while 'consensus', 'partnership' and non-conflictual 'participation' are highlighted in the community conservation narrative, local competition and conflict can de facto be generated and reinforced by community conservation initiatives. They point out that those who hold power at the local level are likely to use their power to capture additional income resources and solidify their position in society. Citing an example from Cameroon, they argue that community conservation has allowed local elites to capture resources by ethnically distinguishing between 'indigenous' and 'strangers'. Others emphasise that 'community' includes complex sets of actors whose characteristics, including wealth, gender, age, and ethnicity, contribute to differences in access to resources and power, which they use to pursue various interests (Chomba et al., 2015; Leach, Mearns, & Scoones, 1999). Hence, existing power hierarchies must be considered, and attention needs to be given to how powerful actors use them to marginalise further less powerful segments of the wider community (Agrawal & Gibson, 1999; Leach et al., 1999; Peluso, Turner, & Fortmann, 1994). Intra-community stakes, stakeholders, and power relations also contribute to differences in stakeholder interests, particularly in communities that are highly heterogeneous (Barrow et al., 2002). On a related note, Bassett et al. (2007) specify that 'a terroir is more accurately described as a mosaic of lineage lands in which rights to resources vary among social groups (indigenous vs immigrant, men vs women, early vs late comers)' (p. 122) and that, consequently, 'the new spaces of conservation and development become arenas of conflict between juniors and seniors, as well as between indigenous groups and immigrants, resulting in political instability that impedes rather than promotes conservation and development' (p. 106). Cormier-Salem and Bassett (2007) also caution of 'naive and populist conceptions' of what and who constitute local communities since 'there is no one definition of the "local" since it is always a socio-spatial arena in which identity and resource control are tightly intertwined in determining who is local or who isn't' (p. 14).

Hence, these community dynamics do not only have to be considered theoretically, but consideration of variations in identities, interests, and preferences among and between communities needs to be translated into the actual institutional design of CBNRM ventures (Fuchs, Peters, & Neufeldt, 2019) to avoid social capture and a reinforcement of societal inequalities (Nagendra & Ostrom, 2012) and to be successful and make an impact (Fuchs, Orero, Namoi, & Neufeldt, 2019). Yet, most initiatives have no adequate mechanisms to deal with elite capture of power, despite attempts to insist on democratic processes within the groups with which such projects work (Martin, 2005), which effectively prevents the development of value-based institutions and the development of the values in the first place.

Insufficiency of local knowledge can also be an issue, for instance, when communities and their knowledge are idealised in an undifferentiated manner. This can be a particular problem in systems that systematically neglect, devalue and even repress local knowledge for long periods and potentially render it inadequate (Constantin, 1994). It can also be co-opted whenever a 'politically correct' term for some population segments is needed, independently of who is meant and why. This issue is particularly pertinent when various institutions at various levels, including local user groups, community associations, civil society institutions, and community-centred government ministries and representatives, are tasked to represent 'community' (Chomba et al., 2015). Local inequalities can be reproduced or accentuated by defining who and what constitutes 'community' in a way that is not considered legitimate by various stakeholders, and community conservation can ultimately become counter-productive.

Participatory conservation and land rights: Conceptual and practical challenges

Since natural resource use and management primarily concern questions of access and use of resources, one can argue that the natural resource-management question is fundamentally a land question. In that vein, the interaction between conservation and land tenure and/ or ownership has remained a core issue of contention in the broader conservation debate, generally and specifically in the context of participatory approaches.

As discussed, 'traditional' exclusionist approaches to natural resource management were primarily based on and perpetuated through a discourse that combined the neo-Malthusian 'carrying capacity' argument with Hardin's (1968) 'Tragedy of the Commons' argument. While CBNRM approaches, overall, critique these 'traditional' arguments, and while many authors agree that 'land ownership rights are possibly the single most important determinant of stakeholder identity and power' (Barrow et al., 2002, p. 10), different authors propose different approaches to the land ownership question.

On the one hand, there seems to be considerable congruence between some actors' interests in promoting participatory approaches alongside reforms that would eventually lead to land privatisation. The parallel promotion of these two approaches is typically based on the assumption that the privatisation of property rights will incentivise various users to manage their resources well (Gibson, Lehoucq, & Williams, 2002). It reveals a tendency to define communal management and private land rights as going hand in hand. In Kenya, a popular way in which land privatisation and community-based environmental conservation were pursued from the 2000s in areas that traditionally fell under communal tenure was to promote the establishment of community conservancies, which unified conservation and livelihood objectives (King, Lalampaa, Craig, & Harrison, 2015; World Resources Institute et al., 2007; Zeppel, 2007). Interestingly, many of these were superimposed on previous group ranch schemes. The promotion of group ranches had been an early attempt to align community development with the privatisation of Trust/Community Land, which had previously somewhat eluded direct state control; without directly calling it 'community conservation' at the time. Group ranching systems were gradually introduced to Kenya's Maasailand after Independence in 1963, in line with overall policies targeting a transformation of Maasai land-use systems within the pastoral economy. These reforms divided former communal lands and put them under a regime of individual or collective private ownership. Collectively owned ranching systems were formally known as 'group ranches' or 'group ranching systems'. Single titles for each ranch were conferred to a collective of landowners represented by an elected committee. The collectively owned land was held as *freehold* property, while livestock remained individual property (Beinart & Hughes, 2007; Collett, 1987; Hughes, 2006; Southgate & Hulme, 2000; Woodhouse, Bernstein, & Hulme, 2000). The 1968 Land (Group Representatives) Act (Cap. 287) and the 1968 Land Adjudication Act (Cap. 284) were introduced as legal frameworks for group titling that was based on semi-traditional clan boundaries (Lovatt-Smith, 2008). The first group ranches in Kenya were established in Kajiado District in 1968 under the World Bank-funded Kenya Livestock Development Project (KLDP). Even though little attention seemed to have been paid to the existing traditional herd management system and the need for mobility during droughts (Southgate & Hulme, 2000), the group ranch system was widely rolled out in pastoral areas, particularly in the Maasai lands. However, a clearly positive and sustainable relationship between private property regimes and sustainable land management remained weakly documented, particularly in communities that rely on mobility-based livelihoods, including pastoralists or hunter-gatherers.

Bassett, Koli Bi, and Ouattara's (2003) case study about fire control measures in Northern Côte d'Ivoire, for instance, illustrated that land privatisation was introduced and represented as a solution to environmental stress without a prior assessment that would have justified relating the environmental change experienced in the area to the land rights system in any way. The authors hence inferred that land privatisation was a pre-existing interest of those promoting environmental conservation in the area, in line with Fujimura's (1992) 'boundary object' idea and the idea of Weisser et al. (2011) and of Bollig, Doevenspeck, and Müller-Mahn (2013) that actors 'climatically' re-brand existing activities to allow the maintainance of pre-existing priorities.

On the other hand, other authors argue that power-sharing in land and resource control does not necessarily involve a conversion of Public or Community Land ownership to individual private property holdings. Conversely, numerous authors advocate for maintaining and guaranteeing community tenure over commons (for instance Ostrom, 1998; Ostrom & Gardner, 1993; Patel, Robinson, & Ng'ang'a, 2018; Serrano Alvarez, 2014); some of them cite the negative implication that land privatisation had on these commons, for instance, the 'failure' of the Maasai group ranch schemes (Markakis, 1999) and, interestingly, particularly on the Maasai Mau community forest reserve due to its proximity to a group ranch (ENSDA, UNEP, KFWG, & KWS, 2005; Kahora, 2015; UNEP, ENSDA, KFWG, KWS, & RSRS, 2006). While insisting on the importance of land and guaranteed land access, power-sharing can include devolution of resource user rights. Specifically, resource users and communities holding power to decide who can access and use resources, and to exclude and sanction, do indeed have power over their resources (Barrow et al., 2002), independently of the legal status of the land and the resources. Pacheco, Mejía, Cano, and Jong (2016) analysed the influence of tenure rights in stimulating sustainable smallholder forestry and found that having legal tenure did not automatically lead to the adoption and implementation of SFM principles, for instance, when tenure rights were disputed and extraction poorly monitored. Similarly, Gibson et al. (2002) found that efforts to link resource outcomes to specific property rights regimes were challenged by a substantial difference between de jure and de facto rights. They further showed that, while forests with better-enforced rules seemed to be in better biophysical condition, this was outperformed by one communal forest in which the community had set up and enforced sustainable forest use rules. The authors concluded that de facto institutions and their enforcement (alongside other factors) were, rather than de jure property rights, a sufficient predictor for conservation outcomes.

While guaranteed land-use rights, whether through formalised ownership or not, seem crucial to successful community engagement, PAO approaches and the creation of buffer zones with limited benefit sharing were the most commonly pursued strategies for greater involvement of communities in environmental management in the wider eastern African region. These approaches predominantly focused on education and sensitisation, as well as limited benefit sharing, but not on a guarantee of user rights or transfer of formal tenure and/or ownership (Woodhouse, 1997). In a context of PFM being predominantly pursued in state-owned forests and forest plantations, and typically limited to implementing forest regulations devised and set up by centralised government ministries in response to rational resource management, production and exploitation priorities (Chomba et al., 2015), and which often generated vital revenue for the state, the vested interests in guarding control continuously challenged the devolution of both resource use and ownership rights. The pursuit of benefit-sharing approaches was paralleled by privatising land and conversion to individual or group property through the conservancy outfit. Those who had contributed to the set-up of formalised user rights, including in the conservancies that had not previously been group ranches and whose constituents hence did not hold formal land tenure, continued lobbying for privatisation of the land (King et al., 2015); displaying a dynamic that lent little attention to the set-up of guaranteed user rights outside of formalised private property regimes.

Some authors argued that, by de-emphasising the role of land tenure for environmental conservation, PAO was attractive for a variety of actors, including governments, that are typically interested in relieving pressure from identitary movements fuelled by alleged land injustices without making concessions in terms of land ownership. Some of these critics, including Woodhouse et al. (2000) hence argued that community conservation was 'attractive to [the] minimal government stance of international aid agencies' (p. 13) in a neoliberal logic of 'not state but market, and if not market then "civil society" or "community"' (p. 13). Kangwana (2001) added that centralised governments typically like PAO programmes because they do not directly challenge the nature of relationships between the people and the Government while allowing them to respond to new conditionalities imposed by international donors. At the same time, de-emphasising land ownership and tenure allowed maintenance of the political function of land allocation and distribution for 'patronage' purposes that were comprehensively theorised in terms of political favouritism by Bayart (1989), Klopp and Sang (2011), and Wrong (2009).

The continually shaping national environmental agenda, legislation, and governance

Considering the legal and regulatory background against which environmental management is defined and implemented, both land and natural resource use and management in Kenya were regulated by the 2010 Constitution (Republic of Kenya, 2010b) by the time of the research in 2011–2013. The Constitution's entire Chapter 5 concerns the environment and land. Article 42 states explicitly that 'every person has the right to a clean and healthy environment, which includes the right ... to have the environment protected for the benefit of present and future generations through legislative and other measures', which could be pursued in court (Republic of Kenya, 2010b).

Beyond the Constitution, several laws related to the environment, as well as forests, wildlife, and water, were particularly relevant for analysing the dynamics of non-protection of the Mau Forest. First, environmental management, overall, fell under The Environmental Management and Co-ordination Act (EMCA) No. 8 of 1999 (Republic of Kenya, 1999), signed in December 1999 and enacted in January 2000. The EMCA led to an 'institutionalisation of the sustainable development concept in the legal framework in Kenya through a framework environmental legislation' (Wamukoya & Ludeki, 2003, p. vi) and was hence celebrated as a 'milestone in promoting sustainable environmental management'.[2] The EMCA also provided for the creation of the National Environmental Management Authority (Nema), which was tasked with general supervision and coordination of all matters relating to the environment and which was also the Government's principal instrument to implement all policies relating to the environment (Heinrich Böll Foundation, 2006; Okidi et al., 2008). Nema's role further was to coordinate and harmonise environmental management activities undertaken by the various lead agencies. These state institutions included several vertically structured government bodies that largely resisted horizontal integration and often also policy coordination. Overall, as of 2007, all protected areas were subordinated to the Ministry of Environment and Natural Resources, which was jointly responsible for environmental management outside of officially protected areas with the Ministry of Forestry and Wildlife, which was incorporated into the Ministry of Environment and Natural Resources in 2013, and the Ministry of Tourism. In the same spirit of coordina-

---

2   NEMA, 'About NEMA', www.nema.go.ke/index.php?option=com_conte nt&task=view&id=28&Itemid=37 (no publication date, accessed 10 October 2009).

tion and harmonisation, the compatibility of all environmental policies with the EMCA must be confirmed by Nema before their final adoption (Okidi et al., 2008). Despite only having been contained in Article 87, which was a mere declaration of policy, and hence not enforceable as such, the EMCA also enshrined the idea that the state should 'work to achieve and maintain tree cover of at least ten per cent of the land area in Kenya' (Okidi, 2008). This guideline was commonly cited in discussions about the state's environmental engagement, in line with its Vision 2030 (Ogweno, Opanga, & Obara, 2009).

The regulations for the management of forests specifically changed drastically with the enactment of the Forests Act (Republic of Kenya, 2005), which was implemented in 2007 and revised in 2016, henceforth called the Forests Conservation and Management Act (Republic of Kenya, 2016b). Before the enactment of the 2005 Forests Act, forest management was mainly regulated by two Acts: the Forests Act, commonly referred to as Cap. 385 (Republic of Kenya, 1982), and the Timber Act, typically referred to as Cap. 386 (Republic of Kenya, 1970b). Cap. 385 had been widely criticised for conferring vast discretionary power to the Minister for Environment and National Resources and the Forest Department, tasked with the everyday management of the gazetted forests. Among the Minister's competencies were the power to declare any unalienated land to be a forest area, to declare the boundaries of forests, and to alter the boundaries. The Minister furthermore held power to reverse the 'forest reserve' status of any given forest as long as a 28-day notice was observed and presented to the public via a Kenya Gazette notice. The Minister also held the power of issuing licences for the use of forest products. Under the 2005 Forests Act, any changes to forest boundaries and changes in forest status needed to be approved by Parliament. Furthermore, after much of the practical deforestation during Moi's Presidency was blamed on 'post box sawmillers' that were not actually in existence, the Government also tightened regulations for licensing sawmills. It addressed reforestation in Section 43 (1), which prescribes that, to curb previous 'hit and run' behaviours, 'immediate compulsory revegetation' needed to be undertaken by the harvesting sawmiller (Klopp & Sang, 2011; Standing & Gachanja, 2014).

The 2005 Forests Act also explicitly addressed challenges communities living adjacent to the country's forests faced. The most crucial change to forest management was introduced by including local communities through PFM, commonly referred to as CBFM. In line with community conservation approaches in wildlife conservation, local communities henceforth were to be included in the management of their environment and in benefits drawn from that environment. To achieve community participation and benefit sharing, the Forest Act stipulated the creation of specific local user groups. The Act allows these CFAs to be created at the forest station level. They are to partake in the conservation and protection of the forest, as well as in the mobilisation of the community to improve their livelihoods and in the education of the youth on non-forest-based livelihood strategies. According to Section 46 (1) of The Forests Act, 'a member of a forest community may, together with other members or persons resident in the same area, register a community forest association under the Societies Act'. Section 46 (2) further states that 'an association registered under subsection 1 may apply to the director for permission to participate in the conservation and management of a state forest or local authority forest in accordance with the provisions of this Act'. According to the KFS & KFWG (2009) 'Manual on Forming and Registering Community Forest Associations (CFAs)', a CFA is 'a group of persons who are registered as an association under the Societies Act (Cap. 108) and who are resident in an area close to the specified forest' (p. 6). It further states that 'for communities to be engaged in forest management they should be organized into CFAs' (p. 7) and hence that the Forests Act 'recognizes CFAs as the only legal entity through which communities enter into a management agreement with the Director of KFS' (p. 7). According to Section 47 (1), the functions of CFAs include (a) the protection, conservation, and management of the forest in question; (b), the formulation and implementation of forest programmes in line with traditional forest user rights in accordance with sustainable use criteria; (c), the protection of sacred groves and protected trees; collaboration with the KFS to enforce the Forest Act and so forth. Most importantly, in line with the collaborative management approach to community conservation, a CFA was to participate in the elaboration of a joint forest management plan for the zone covered by the respective forest station with which it was registered, and to sign a joint management agreement together with the local KFS staff, which was to ensure participation, benefit, and power-sharing of local communities [3/059], as specified in Section 47 (1) (e). Another important provision of the 2005 Forests Act in terms of community participation was the re-introduction of the 'shamba' system under the name of 'plantation establishment and livelihood improvement scheme' (PELIS), through which registered CFA members could acquire small plots for cultivation within forest plantations, as stipulated in Section 47 (2). The *shamba* system is a 'Taungya' system popularised in Burma/Myanmar in which short-term food crops are cultivated within forest plantations with woody perennials species (Chomba et al., 2015).[3] The *shamba* system was first introduced to Kenya by the colonial government, regulated through the 1968 Forest Act (Ludeki, Wamukoya, & Walubengo, 2006), and discontinued in the

---

[3]   While Taungya is said to have been developed from the Burmese context, this practice is also said to be similar to 'Chena', which was being practised in Kenya (see von Hellermann, 2007).

late 1980s (Chomba et al., 2015; Standing & Gachanja, 2014). Under the *shamba* system, foresters used to allocate *shambas* in the forest plantations to individual farmers who could cultivate the land in exchange for taking care of the tree seedlings until the seedlings grew to a specific size. The idea, as elsewhere where similar Taungya systems are implemented, is that the allocation of *shambas* in the plantations helps to keep these plantations intact because they allowed combining forest production and livelihood requirements. Despite important arguments in favour of such *shamba* systems, the system was abolished in the 1980s, supposedly because of contributing to deforestation (Chomba et al., 2015; Standing & Gachanja, 2014). The PELIS system foresaw community mechanisms that were supposed to prevent the destruction of seedlings and thus guarantee the survival of plantation trees by registering only CFA members, by name, under the supervision of the CFA chairman and under threat of deregistration of the CFA in case of digression. Through PELIS, conservation and livelihood concerns were to be addressed conjointly [3/062].

The 2005 Forests Act furthermore provided for forest management to be passed on from the state Forest Department to a newly created KFS, a semi-autonomous parastatal and paramilitary institution. The KFS was established with the enactment of the Forests Act in 2007. After that, it took charge of developing, conserving, and managing the country's gazetted forest reserves. Specific functions comprised in its mandate included the preparation and implementation of management plans for public forests, the issuance of licences for the use of forests and forest resources, the management of water catchment areas to ensure the provision of environmental services, the promotion of forestry education, and training, as well as tourism. Beyond that, after the territorial reorganisation and devolution of powers to subsidiary levels of government brought about by the 2010 Constitution, the KFS' mandate involved support for county governments in forestry development in both community and private forests. Concerning the PFM provisions included in the Act, the KFS website mentioned that part of its role was to establish and implement benefit-sharing arrangements,[4] In line with Section 47 (1) of the Forests Act, the KFS website proposed that the implementation of the plans involved community participation under the CFA vehicle, whose functions were to '[f]ormulate and implement forest programmes consistent with the traditional forest user rights of the community', and to 'assist the Service in enforcing the provisions of the Act'. Forest user rights that could be conferred included the collection of medicinal herbs; harvesting of honey; harvesting of timber or fuelwood; grass harvesting and grazing; collection of forest produce for

4   KFS, 'About KFS', www.kenyaforestservice.org/index.php/about-kfs/core-functions (no publication date, accessed 10 October 2018).

community-based industries; ecotourism and recreational activities; scientific and education activities; plantation establishment through non-resident cultivation; contracts to assist in carrying out specified silvicultural operations; and development of community wood and non-wood forest-based industries.[5]

Gazetted forests, the forest areas under official state protection outside of national parks, were also subjected to EMCA framework regulation and hence placed under Nema's supervision. These forests were placed under the Ministry of Forestry, which was incorporated into the Ministry of the Environment and Natural Resources in 2013 (Republic of Kenya, 2016b).

Other relevant legislation included the 2002 Water Act (Republic of Kenya, 2002), which translated international standards related to holistic water management and integrated water catchment area management into national law. The 2002 Water Act provides for the creation of water resource user groups in the form of the Water Resource Users Associations (WRUAs), equivalent to the CFAs, whose mandate was to establish CBNRM in water management. Another important law was the 2013 Wildlife Conservation and Management Act (Republic of Kenya, 2013). Before that, wildlife management fell under The Wildlife (Conservation and Management) Act from 1985 (Republic of Kenya, 1985), commonly referred to as Cap. 376. This had been the most critical piece of legislation related to wildlife and environmental conservation until the introduction of PFM through the 2005 Forests Act. Concretely, national parks remained the keystone institution of environmental conservation in Kenya. In 1989, the KWS, a semi-autonomous parastatal, was created to manage, secure, and conserve all national parks, including the wildlife, plains, forests, rivers, and lakes within them. It replaced the former Wildlife Conservation and Management Department (WMCD) (Connan, 2007). Until the enactment of the 2010 Constitution brought about a territorial reorganisation of the country, National Reserves were managed by the county council of the respective administrative unit in which they were located. The geographical limits of these elected assemblies were generally in line with the then district borders. Beyond the Water and Wildlife Acts, the Kenyan government also adopted the Climate Change Act in 2016 as in the Kenya Gazette Supplement No. 68 (Republic of Kenya, 2016a). As listed in Article 3 (1), the Act's objective was to guide the 'development, management, implementation and regulation of mechanisms to enhance climate change resilience and low carbon development for sustainable

---

[5]   KFS, 'Participatory Forest Management Plan Implementation', www.kenyaforestservice.org/index.php/2016-04-25-20-16-21/2016-05-27-19-26-24/2016-05-27-22-32-12 (no publication date, accessed 10 October 2018)

development of Kenya' and hence guide climate change mitigation and adaptation policy and practice.

Despite significant changes in regulations about natural resource use and management, empirical evidence suggests that the conservation practice continued lagging behind the ambitious plans formulated, notably through various new environmental management Acts. According to Bongers and Tennigkeit (2010), it is a common problem in East Africa that conventions and action plans for adequate environmental protection are signed and officially enacted but hardly ever put into practice.

Conservation priorities and actors in the Mau Forest

The conceptualisation and planning of the 'Save the Mau' initiative and its concretisation on the ground were rooted in global dynamics in environmental management thinking and practice. At the same time, its implementation depended strongly on the institutions tasked with the initiative's coordination and management while strongly influenced by the structures and institutions traditionally responsible for environmental and forest management.

External influence on environmental policy and practice

In Kenya, as in many post-colonial countries, international donors play an essential role in funding transnational and international conservation priorities and thus in shaping and implementing environmental policies. Historically, these international donors, including multilateral and bilateral aid agencies, were the most decisive actors within the system of environmental policy actors in the country (Hicks, Parks, Roberts, & Tierney, 2008). With the homogenisation and standardisation of international conservation discourses and narratives through the spread of international environmental agreements, and thus international environmental law, their importance increased further. A second major driver of the uniformisation of the country's conservation agenda was brought about by the standardisation of international aid through the establishment of the Kenya Joint Assistance Strategy (KJAS) 2007–2012. It resulted from an effort to streamline and coordinate foreign aid, signed by the Kenyan Government and seventeen development partners in 2007. The strategy led to a clearer distribution of roles among donors. It lent more discursive and financial power to the bilateral and international institutions in charge of the environmental aid docket (Asuna, 2014).

Overall, the 'international community' in Kenya was predominantly represented by Western countries. The United States had historically been Kenya's largest and most crucial bilateral aid donor, followed by the United Kingdom, Japan, Germany, France, Denmark, and Sweden. Beyond these, the World Bank's International Development Association (IDA), the European Commission and the International Monetary Fund (IMF) were central multilateral aid donors. Altogether, these ten donors contributed a vast majority of overall aid volumes (Brown, 2001, 2009). Among these, several groups of donors were predominant influencers on Kenyan environmental policies and practices, including the World Bank, the GEF controlled by UNEP and the EU, as well as bilateral aid agencies, namely the United States Agency for International Development (USAID), the French Development Agency (AFD), German International Cooperation (GIZ), the Japan International Cooperation Agency (JICA), and several others. Tertiary donors were large international NGOs, such as the World Conservation Union (commonly known under the acronym of its previous name IUCN), the World Wide Fund for Nature (WWF), and the International Fund for Animal Welfare (IFAW) (Heinrich Böll Foundation, 2006). Funding benefited various levels and actors within the field of environmental conservation. Significant amounts were first directed at the Government in the form of budgetary aid, which was then redistributed and used. The KWS was one of the preferred direct recipients of external environmental aid. The third recipients were NGOs of varying sizes and importance, including various famous African conservation organisations such as Nature Kenya (formerly known as East Africa Natural History Society), the East African Wildlife Society (EAWLS), and Professor Wangari Maathai's Green Belt Movement (GBM), mainly by granting specific conservation projects. As environmental aid donors used large sums of money, the influence of these donors on individual projects and policy outcomes at a more significant level was important (Heinrich Böll Foundation, 2006).

International environmental aid increased steadily since the early 1980s, accounting for approximately USD $4 billion in the 1980s and the 1990s combined: $1.15 billion in the 1980s, representing 13.6% of total aid to Kenya during that period, and 2.82 billion in the 1990s, representing 11.6% of total aid. During that time, the top environmental aid donors included the IDA, donating $402 million, the German cooperation agencies contributing $306 million, and the Swedish Development Agency (SIDA) with $249 million (Hicks et al., 2008). Hicks et al., in their 2008 study, projected international environmental aid to have grown further in the first decade of the 2000s. The rapid increase in environmental aid in the 1990s was considered to be an expression of the fact that environmental conservation projects had become aligned with international concepts and concerns during that time, notably the streamlining of sustainable development as a guiding principle for development projects. The alignment of conservation objectives with livelihood concerns through community conservation projects furthermore allowed conservation actors to tap into funding sources earmarked for human development, which, in turn, not only increased budgets for conservation activities considerably but also the donors' control over related policies (Hulme & Murphree, 2001a). After the democratic transition of 2002, the relationship between Kenya and various development partners visibly improved, which led to a steep increase in the volume of development aid. Since then, bilateral official development assistance (ODA) rose from $276 million in 2001 to $777 million in 2006 and $952 million in 2008 (Brown, 2001, 2009; Jones, Nyamongo, & Thomson, 2008).

The EU's interests dominated the environmental management docket [1/022], despite the prominence of the USA in coordinating and leading activities of external actors in the forest and wildlife sectors from 2007 to 2012. Apart from the USA, the environmental management docket also included the African Development Bank, bilateral aid agencies of Denmark, Finland, France, Japan, Netherlands, and Sweden, as well as the European Commission, the United Nations, and the World Bank (KJAS 2007–2012). The KJAS was not renewed after 2012, and other aid effectiveness arrangements were pursued through the Government's Second Medium Term Plan towards achieving the Government's Vision 2030, covering 2013 to 2017 (Asuna, 2014).

Considering the influence of international donors on the 'Save the Mau' campaign specifically, the clout that the Mau crisis had gained among prominent local, national, and international environmental actors in Kenya and beyond was further enhanced when the Mau crisis was highlighted at the December 2009 Copenhagen World Summit on Climate Change (Kagwanja, 2010). Many NGOs seized the moment and proposed conservation activities and projects in and for the Mau Forest. After the Water Towers Conservation Fund was gazetted in July 2010, various development partners agreed to support the rehabilitation of the Mau Forest (Republic of Kenya, 2010a). The Task Force initially proposed a budget of $81 million, which was later adapted to $100 million (GoK, 2009d). Prime collaborations for specific projects were set up. These include an EU-funded bamboo-promotion project (Euro 2.3 million, then valued at $3 million), USAID's ProMara programme ($7 million), the Community-Based Integrated Forest Resource Conservation and Management in the Maasai Mau (COMIFORM) project funded by the Spanish Government through UNEP (Euro 1 million – $1.3 million) and the French AFD (Euro 2 million – $2.6 million; with additional support to generate Euro 10 million – $13 million – through carbon credits).[6]

---

6   These major grants and collaborations were complemented by various smaller-scale engagements of national and international NGOs as well as

Institutional provisions for cross-sectoral and holistic management

Legally, management of the Mau Forest fell primarily under the 2005 Forest Act by the time of the research. The Act placed the entire forest cycle management under the KFS. Beyond the regular management structures, the ICS, in line with a central recommendation of the Task Force Report (GoK, 2009e), was created immediately after the adoption of the Report (Republic of Kenya, 2009a). The ICS was placed under the Office of the Prime Minister. This institutional arrangement was to ensure smooth coordination and supervision of activities devised by the Task Force, including local land and forest rehabilitation activities (GoK, 2009d, 2009e, 2010c). The Secretariat's initial term was limited to two years but was later extended for two more years until July 2013 [1/006, 1/022]. According to the ICS/KWTA forestry specialist, the Secretariat was to achieve what had not been achieved previously: coordination among different actors in general, and specifically among various ministries and parastatals. Instead of taking a sectoral approach to managing the Mau Forest, looking at aspects such as wildlife conservation, timber production, and water quality and supply individually, the ICS was to foster an integrated and holistic approach. The cross-sectoral approach was also translated into the internal structure of the Secretariat, in which technical experts of different sectors were brought together in five committees, namely restoration, planning, security, resource mobilisation, and publicity [1/007].

Initially, the Government announced the intention to create a Mau Forests Complex Authority, a separate semi-autonomous body. This authority was to be responsible for the implementation of a holistic approach to the Mau Forest's management that involves special protection of water catchment areas and biodiversity hotspots, which was to supersede the prevailing forestry-based perspective and philosophy that had mainly focused on commercial wood and timber production (GoK, 2009e). The ICS was to lead the way to the creation of this institution, scheduled to take over the coordination for the Mau Forest restoration at the end of the ICS' first term. With time, the plan of setting up a separate Mau Authority was abandoned, and a broader Kenya water towers authority was created. This organ was to be responsible for the rehabilitation of the Mau Forest, alongside Kenya's four other central

---

government agencies, for instance, five organisations that established the Save the Mau Trust Fund – the Kenya Wildlife Service, East African Breweries Ltd, Equity Bank, Nation Media Group, and the Green Belt Movement – to which they committed KES 50 million ($500,000). The Ministry of Forestry and Wildlife, together with the ICS, also established a Committee on Rehabilitation and Livelihoods, through which the African Wildlife Foundation, Malaika Ecotourism, Coral Cay Conservation UK, the Save the Mau Trust Fund, and the Kenyan 'Ministry of State for Defense [sic.]' took responsibility for the rehabilitation of specific forest areas (GoK, 2009e, 2010a, 2010d).

and thirteen smaller water towers.[7] It was created as a state agency called the Kenya Water Towers Agency (KWTA) in 2012. Since it was to succeed the ICS, it only became operational in July 2013, after the expiry of the ICS' second term. Legal Notice No. 27 supplements the State Corporations Act (Cap. 446) to the Kenya Gazette of 2012, gazetted the KWTA, and provides details about its mandate (Republic of Kenya, 2012b). According to Article 5 of the Legal Notice, the KWTA has seven functions. The most important functions are: (a) to 'coordinate and oversee the protection, rehabilitation, conservation, and sustainable management of water towers'; (b) to 'coordinate and oversee the recovery and restoration of forest lands, wetlands and biodiversity hot spots'; (c) to 'promote the implementation of sustainable livelihood programmes in the water towers in accordance with natural resource conservation', among others, through (d) resource mobilisation from various public and private actors. Apart from that, it also proposes definitions for crucial concepts, such as 'water tower', 'watershed', 'biodiversity hot spot', 'carbon reservoir', and 'forest land', to capture its mandate and reach as clearly as possible. The change in approach from more mitigation-based to more adaptation- and livelihood-centred approaches is translated into these objectives.

While the ICS was supposed to coordinate the Mau Forest Rehabilitation Programme, individual activities were to be implemented by various actors largely independently, including in the Eastern Mau. Structurally, de facto day-to-day management of the Mau Forest, as of all other forests, continued being assumed by the KFS. In line with PFM provisions included in the 2005 Forest Act, this state-centred forest management was sometimes complemented by CFAs, alongside various ad hoc NGO-type actors and activities.

Conservation aid in the Eastern Mau Forest

Considering existing land, water, forest, and environmental laws, and in line with the Task Force Report recommendations, the Government took a multi-layered approach to recover the Mau. Overall, both implicit root causes were addressed: supposed poverty-related forest destruction by the forest dwellers was addressed through projects and programmes to transform local livelihoods, and institutional failure

---

[7]   The complete list of all officially recognised water towers through the 2012 KTWA order comprises: Aberdare Range; Cherangani Hills; Chyulu Hills; Huri Hills; Kirisia Hills; Loita Hills; Marmanet Forest; Matthews Range; Mau Forest Complex; Mount Elgon; Mount Kenya; Mount Kipipiri; Mount Kulal; Mount Marsabit; Mount Njiru; Ndotos; Nyambene Hills; and Shimba Hills (Republic of Kenya, 2012b, Paragraph 5(2)).

by pursuing institutional reform, on the other hand. This approach was influenced and complemented by activities led by external actors. The Mau restoration initiative, overall, was embedded in the country's broader environmental policy framework, including both colonial legacy and terminology as well as approaches emanating from international environmental regimes.

The Mau Forest Rehabilitation Programme's spatial-temporal plan focused on the Eastern Mau in Phases I and IV (see Map 2). In Phase I, the land was to be recovered with immediate effect that had been excised in 2001 but was unparcelled and largely unoccupied. This included 530 ha within Likia Extension, 2,950 ha in Mariashoni, and 1,050 ha in an area the Government called 'LR 25148', all within the wider Eastern Mau Forest. In Phase IV, approximately half of the land that was to be recovered overall was in the Eastern Mau. It included all the additional land that had been excised in 2001 but was not part of Phase I. These ca. 30,000 ha of land were classified as critical water catchments. Yet, because settlements had been formalised and title deeds issued to some residents, more consideration was needed than in Phase I (GoK, 2009c). Beyond that initial plan, numerous additional activities were carried out in the area to 'Save the Mau' by state and non-state actors. Environmental and conservation NGOs first arrived in Mariashoni with the Mau Task Force popularising the crisis in the making in 2009. The Mariashoni residents had previously predominantly interacted with civil society actors concerned with land and human rights.

The different activities pursued in the context of the 'Save the Mau' initiative in Mariashoni centred around three priority activities: tree planting, poverty eradication and livelihood development, and local institution building.

Meeting deforestation with reforestation

In line with the Government's overall strategy, forest destruction in Mau Forest, in the first place, was to be addressed by forest re-establishment and forest restoration. In the Eastern Mau, forest rehabilitation was conceptualised as a linear reversal process in which forest reduction was to be countered by forest increase through tree planting. Different tree-planting drives had been undertaken in the wider Eastern Mau by 2013. First, in 2009, then-Prime Minister Raila Odinga initiated the planting of thousands of trees together with several ministries, including the Lands Ministry and Nema. In 2010, many other actors engaged in tree-planting activities, including government actors, such as the National Youth Service (NYS) and the Kenyan Army, as well as different universities, including Nairobi, Egerton, and Kabarak [5/233]. The British High Commission planted trees in Mariashoni, and a group of 'Misses', including Miss Kenya and Miss Ethiopia, planted trees in Sonki Kabiet Forest, close to Kiptunga Forest [1/008].[8]

Most seedlings planted in the area were sourced from the Mariashoni tree nursery, which was set up and belonged to the KFS. In line with KFS interests, most tree seedlings raised and managed at the nursery were exotic, including cypress, pine, and blue gum seedlings. A nursery attendant explained that a group of people he called 'the Nakuru saw-millers' sponsored a new nursery section through the Timber Manu-facturers Association (TMA) in May 2012. They exclusively sponsored exotic tree seedlings to support plantation reforestation. The TMA had previously undertaken tree-planting drives in the Kiptunga area in which community members were involved and paid. The 'Green Zones Development' Project also gave money to KFS for the tree nursery, which mainly helped to pay for the sixteen casual workers who sup-ported the four KFS staff employed to run the nursery [3/066]. One of the KFS officers in Mariashoni explained that the Green Zones project helped them set up and develop the indigenous tree seedling section of the nursery. Most tree seeds had been purchased from the Kenya Forestry Research Institute (KEFRI) [5/158], while the tree nursery workers also collected seeds in the forest and raised seedlings autono-mously [3/066]. Even though there was a small section for indigenous tree seedlings, the KFS did not promote planting indigenous trees per se and mainly encouraged residents to grow exotic trees for economic purposes [4/090].

Fighting poverty by transforming local livelihoods

Beyond the promotion of active reforestation, most restoration activities supported by external actors targeted biodiversity conser-vation from a livelihood-centred perspective in the Mariashoni area. Between the onset of the Mau restoration initiatives in 2009 and late 2013, when we concluded our fieldwork, four major projects or programmes were implemented by external actors in Mariashoni, namely the World Bank-funded Kenya Agricultural Productivity and Agro-Business Project (KAPAP), the USAID-funded ProMara programme, the Forest Conservation and Livelihood Improvement Project (FCLIP) funded by the Community Development Trust Fund (CDTF), and a cross-cutting project funded by the Italian NGO Mani-Tese and implemented by Necofa. These initiatives were different regarding actors, targets and philosophies but similar in the prov-enance of funds, the targeted sectors, and the activities promoted (see Table 3 for a brief overview).

8   See also: Njoroge, K., 'PM's drive to plant 20,000 trees in Mau', *The Standard*, 22 April 2010.

The Kenya Agricultural Productivity and Agro-Business Project

The implementation of KAPAP started in Mariashoni, and the neighbouring areas of Sururu and Nessuit, in 2011. The Project was a multi-million-dollar World Bank-funded project implemented through the then Provincial Administration, and monitored at the county level [1/023]. It was the largest agricultural project in the country at the time [1/025]. After a first project phase called KAPP, which piloted the overall approach and tested the underlying assumptions and models of the project, the KAPAP project scaled up and out to the five components of the project, namely 1) farmer empowerment and extension, 2) policy, 3) research, 4) coordination, and 5) extension to twenty regions in the country. Overall, the objective of the project was to develop agri-enterprises in six agricultural value chains: dairy, fish, rabbit, and poultry farming, as well as cassava farming and beekeeping. While the District Environmental Officers (DEOs) identified relevant areas of operation within a county, the District Agricultural Officers (DAOs)[9] of a given county jointly prepared a 'community integrated plan', which prioritised enterprise development in the priority value chains supported by the overall project according to what they deemed most relevant for their respective districts. These priority activities were also roughly in line with the agro-ecological zones in the areas. A 'regional service unit' of each region later sat together and defined action plans for each location in line with the district recommendations but subject to the availability of KAPAP support [1/023].

Due to changes in the project's focus between the first and second phases, and the World Bank's interest in funding projects focusing on indigenous people, Mariashoni became one of the targeted areas in 2011. It was chosen because it was considered suitable for business development in the honey value chain. Specifically, the project intended to increase the productivity of local beekeepers by introducing and popularising modern beehives. These hives are typically more productive and secure since they can be kept close to people's homes and are less exposed to wild animals [1/023].

To ensure broad participation of the residents in an area, each location in which the project was implemented was subdivided into four 'blocks', called 'common working groups' (CWGs). In the wider Mariashoni area, eight CWGs were formed. Each of these was then encouraged to elect a 'unit of operation' consisting of a chairperson, a secretary, a treasurer, and four assistants. These groups were then encouraged to register with social services and have a group constitution providing for

---

9   Despite Kenya having undergone a territorial reorganisation with the 2010 Constitution that effectively abolished the districts, phasing out offices, plans, and staff at that level had not been achieved by the time of the research.

the mode of designation of leaders, fixing a minimum threshold of 30% of women in leadership positions, setting the overall objectives, and defining the scope of activities of the respective group. Residents of the area were then trained in activities related to the selected value chain, ostensibly modern beekeeping in Mariashoni, at the CWG level. All eight CWGs were further aggregated in a joint 'common interest group' (CIG) through which marketing of the produce was to be facilitated. The project addressed different objectives by attempting to ignite interest for individual engagement through highly decentralised technical training 'on the ground', by organising individual farmers in groups to benefit from group effects (at CWG level), and to market produce through a superimposed interest group (at CIG level) and thus achieve farmer empowerment [1/023].

'Service providers' were chosen as the primary delivery mechanism. These external service providers were contracted and responsible for implementing specific activities at the farm level. At the beginning of the project, three service providers were identified through a tender for each value chain in each county. The service providers then worked with targets and benchmarks and were paid in four performance-based steps. Initially, 20% of the total budget was released to the service provider for community mobilisation and organisation. Once the communities were mobilised, a further 20% was released after the service providers proved that they registered at least 500 farmers per district and that those farmers reached specific production targets related to yield, harvest, and income generated. In the context of the beekeeping group, for instance, at this step, the service provider had to prove that an additional KES 1.5 million ($15,000) was generated through sales of previously harvested but neglected honey and that 20% of farmers harvested 'clean' honey. The third step was reached, and 30% of the budget was given out once an additional income of KES 4.125 million ($41,250) was generated, half of the harvested honey was sold, and at least 10% of farmers had improved hives. The final step was reached when the farmers trained had a cumulative additional income of KES 30 million ($300,000), and 80% of the harvested honey was sold. The money was released from accounts held by the farmers themselves, with individual farmers being signatories to the group account that was to pay the service provider based on income estimates provided by the same farmers. Their data were triangulated with data collected by local agricultural extension staff whose indications made during the development of the 'community integrated plan' served as the baseline against which progress was measured.

In Nakuru County, under which Mariashoni fell administratively, the service provider selected for the development of the beekeeping value chain was a company named Agritek Solutions Africa. Agritek was given KES 1 million ($10,000) to develop the entire value chain in the four divisions targeted within the County. While the initial plan was that service providers would establish functioning value chains within one year, these plans were changed, and service providers were expected to accompany the farmers for three to five years, depending on the value chain in question. Ultimately, in the context of the bee-keeping enterprise promotion, increased production and improved quality of the honey were to satisfy both the local and export markets. In the case of the honey value chain, the project foresaw benefiting from the United States' African Growth and Opportunity Act (AGOA), which provided a window of opportunity for duty-free honey exports to the USA[10] that had not been seized before KAPAP, due to lacking quantities and quality at the national level. Besides training opportunities, local farmers also obtained small loans from KAPAP, which required farmers to prove that they were engaged and would continue investing in sustainable production. The KAPAP project was implemented alongside the National Agricultural and Livestock Extension Programme (NALEP) at government level. At the policy level, the results obtained fed into the Kenya Agricultural Production and Sustainable Land Management Project (KAPSLM) [1/023].

By 2013, KAPAP activities in Mariashoni had remained limited to the first community mobilisation component, besides some technical training. Considering these delays, the KAPAP monitoring and evaluation (M&E) officer provided details about some of the complexities of the project. First, after obtaining clear results from their research component, the project set out to avoid giving out materials and other handouts to community members for free. This was based on the idea that 'free things are not good' [1/023] and that using one's own means would create 'ownership' and responsibility, and ultimately the sustainability of the engagement. Another challenge was that there was no appropriate collaboration and coordination between different programmes and projects at the local administration level nor on the ground in the different localities where activities were implemented. Since other projects operated with different approaches, the project's more asset-based approach became less likely to succeed. The M&E officer also suggested that the performance-based payment of their service providers was flawed because beehives given out for free by another project in Mariashoni, for instance, by the CDTF, were integrated into the assessment of the service provider's performance. She, however, called the fulfilment of KAPAP objectives through CDTF-funded activities 'mutual benefits' because 'it does not interfere with us reaching our objectives' [1/023].

10   See e.g., African Growth and Opportunity Act, http://trade.gov/agoa (n.d. accessed 19 December 2016).

Forest Conservation and Livelihood Improvement Project

The CDTF-funded FCLIP was launched in February 2012 and was intended to run for a duration of three years with a budget of KES 31 million ($310,000), of which KES 3 million ($30,000) were counted as an indirect community contribution.[11] The CDTF itself was financed by the European Union. The FCLIP supported conservation in Mariashoni, Kiptunga, Molo, Baraget, and Ol Posimoru areas and was the first CDTF project in Eastern Mau. The project worked at the intersection of conservation and livelihood improvement through the CDTF-funded Mau East Forest Conservancy (MEFoCo). One of the project's objectives was to set up tree nurseries in five targeted forest stations, including in Mariashoni. While the CDTF tree nursery was to complement the KFS nurseries in Mariashoni and Molo, the project intended to set up new nurseries in Baraget, Kiptunga, and Ol Posimoru. Overall, the CDTF promoted four different but interrelated activities: tree nursery establishment, modern beekeeping, rehabilitation of riverbanks in the forest, and fruit tree farming [3/059, 3/065]. The CDTF funding was supposed to support FCLIP activities to rehabilitate the forest through riverbank protection, prevention of soil erosion, rehabilitation of water sources, and improving community livelihoods through 'nature-based' initiatives. By December 2012, the project had mainly been successful in planting indigenous tree seedlings along riverbanks within the gazetted forest areas in Ol Posimoru, Baraget, Molo, Eburu, Sororo, and Mariashoni/Kiptunga [1/036]. Since the project was still young in 2012–2013, there was little evidence of further project activities or outcomes.

ProMara programme

The USAID funded the ProMara programme for two years, from 2010 to 2012. The project aimed to restore the upper sections of the Mara River, especially the Mara River catchment located in Kiptunga Forest, approximately 9 km from Mariashoni Centre. The overall objective of the two-year project was integrated management of the Mara catchment. This integrated management was addressed in four components. First, the project sought to address land tenure issues and worked towards ensuring the enactment and respect for property and land rights. Second, it aimed to implement a comprehensive natural resource-management framework. This framework was to address issues of community participation in the regulation of access and use of water, land, and forest resources. The third component tackled public information and education, intending to provide awareness and information to relevant stakeholders. Fourth, the project focused on livelihoods and finding

---

[11] The project was given KES 28 million ($280,000) according to the MEFoCo project manager [1/036].

the right frameworks for sustainable livelihoods of forest dwellers to enable sustainable conservation. It also addressed cross-cutting issues of gender, youth, and conflict resolution [1/014]. In terms of restoration of ecosystem services, the project's main objective was to reduce soil erosion and hence siltation into the Mara River, stabilise the river water flow, and increase infiltration [1/029]. Concerning the project's approach, the conflict specialist said 'our approach is people-centred because we know in the ecosystem, we have people. And we focus on the livelihood of people, we focus on the challenges that the people are going through, we focus on the needs of the people and the concerns of the people' [1/014]. As such, the project planners, for instance, ensured that the project would not only collaborate with members of one ethnic group in a given area, and the formation of cross-ethnic organisations, such as CFAs, was supported.

ProMara also organised conflict-resolution meetings in which representatives of different groups that were ostensibly in conflict were brought together – for instance, those that claimed to be indigenous Ogiek and those that claimed a broader 'Dorobo' identity, among whom there had been animosity in many parts of the forest – and attempted to foster dialogue [1/014]. The project further worked with schools within the public information and education component to make children 'ambassadors of change' [1/020] in their private lives. In that vein, they selected thirty-five schools in four divisions in the Eastern Mau, among which was Mariashoni Primary School in which they facilitated the establishment of environmental clubs. ProMara also supported the implementation of activities encouraged by the curriculum, such as tree planting and environmental awareness creation through songs and plays. The outreach centre furthermore acted as a resource centre, providing free internet access and a library with literature about different aspects related to conservation, agricultural good practices etc. [1/020]. The Wildlife club at Mariashoni Primary School was registered in February 2012. The school had been called by ProMara and informed it had been selected to join the conservation of Mau Forest. The headteacher was invited to a meeting in Kericho, alongside the headteachers of twenty-nine other schools and some KFS representatives. ProMara then selected several teachers who were asked to meet again and develop a curriculum to guide pupils on conservation matters, and later a teachers' guide on how to teach the pupils. Both were launched in February 2012. Through the environmental clubs, which all headteachers were encouraged to form and register as 'Wildlife Clubs of Kenya' (WCK), matters of management and conservation of soil, water, wild animals, and forests were addressed as sustainable agricultural practices. A crucial lesson was that 'communities need to be integrated into conservation' [3/063]. Participation in the club was voluntary in Mariashoni.

In the legal awareness and literacy work related to component, one on land and the other addressing the legal basis for holistic natural resource management, ProMara collaborated with the NGO Kituo Cha Sheria, also called 'The Centre for Legal Empowerment'. The organisation was created in 1973 to provide legal aid on land, labour, and housing to ordinary citizens who might not have the means to consult regular lawyers. A team of their lawyers held legal awareness education meetings in which community members in the Mau Forest were taught about their rights and responsibilities regarding land, water and forest use, and management. The education programme was implemented over six months, from October 2011 to April 2012, in Mariashoni, Kiptunga, Olenguruone, and Baraget. The primary approach of the centre was to teach community members about the new 2010 Constitution, about which most participants knew very little. They also focused on women's and youth rights and held separate meetings with these focus groups. One of the lawyers reported that they encountered lots of opposition from the village elders to whom women's rights, especially to land, were alien and who typically held onto their land tightly, leading to conditions in which succession and inheritance issues are rampant. She added that they were not allowed to take up any land cases in the Mau Forest [1/028].

When asked about the background of the programme, the conflict specialist provided details about the rationale behind USAID's interest in the Mau:

> It's around KES 500 million [$5 million] ... As we said earlier, the programme is USAID-funded. The money for the program comes from 'climate change' and 'biodiversity' ... USAID is divided into various components [and] climate change and biodiversity [are at the core of] USAID's interests in Kenya, ... issues of NRM [natural resource management], particularly issues around property rights and issues around resource governance because those are key issues for any economic growth, and also for mitigation around conflict-related issues. So, if we are sure that communities are sure about their property rights, then you're sure about them living in a peaceful way. And, at the same time, them addressing their poverty issues. And at the same time, about resource management, having a sustainable framework to use the resource that you have in a way that is sustainable and in a way that ensures your future. So, USAID is the biggest donor – the donor and the client. [1/014]

Associates for Rural Development (ARD), later called Tetra Tech-ARD, a private American contracting firm, was implementing the ProMara programme. While the project objectives had been developed for a proposed ten-year project, they had only obtained funding for a two-year project, from September 2010 to September 2012 [1/018]. Since the available time was significantly reduced, project activities were concentrated around the upper Mara catchment, including Mariashoni and Kiptunga Forest; Keringet in Kuresoi, where the source of Nyangores River is located; Baraget, where the source of Amalo River is; as well as Ol Posimoru and Olenguruone [1/004]. After the lapse of the two-year contract, project employees expected to get a five-year build-up, but they did not and had to cut short most of the initiatives that had been started by the project [1/017].

Ten community mobilisers received training as trainers (ToT) with the mandate to train other community members. They were selected by ProMara after being secretly nominated by community members during a community meeting. Three women and seven men were chosen. One of them explained that ProMara operated in four zones in the Eastern Mau, namely Kiptunga, Baraget, Olenguruone, and Ol Posimoru. After being trained in June and July 2011, the ten community mobilisers had a work plan spanning the period August 2011 to June 2012, in which five modules were to be taught to community members: group formation, group dynamics, leadership, entrepreneurship, and conflict management. However, the training schedule got delayed, and no training was held from December to March after ProMara cut the 'lunch' money [3/057].

Necofa project

Necofa was the fourth external actor implementing a forest restoration and conservation-related project in Mariashoni during our data collection. The network was established at the international level in 1998. It resulted from an international workshop on ecology and farming, funded by an organisation that later became part of the German GIZ. The idea behind the network was that gaps in communication and information sharing about ecological farming practices between different communities and societies that are often part of traditional ecological knowledge systems should be overcome. The aim of the network was thus to popularise 'traditional' and 'modern' ecological farming practices and work with communities to understand the contribution these practices can make to wider society. The organisation's overall objective was to empower local communities towards sustainable livelihoods, comprising aspects of food security, sustainable environments, social dignity, and access to education. Necofa Kenya was created in 2002 and registered as a community-based NGO whose membership is composed of local communities and schools. The network's engagement in Mariashoni was part of a strategic plan developed for the Molo River basin.

This plan was developed in response to research undertaken by two university students, who had studied the complexities of local livelihoods, including challenges faced and aspirations formulated by community members living in the basin. During activities in Molo (the upper basin), Mogotio (the middle basin), and Marigat (the lower basin), the Molo River Resource Users Association was formed, which encompassed the areas in question. Forest conservation and conservation of the land in forest-adjacent areas were defined as priority activities. Since Necofa was too small to implement and manage a project in the entire Molo River basin, the organisation chose to provide targeted support for specific activities of the Koibatek CFA, the Eldu irrigation scheme in Baringo, and the Molo River Resource Users Association. Activities in Mariashoni were later added to the project, mainly due to the country coordinator's personal attachment to the area. The Necofa country coordinator explained that he spent his childhood between Mariashoni and Elburgon when the Kikuyu community he belonged to and the forest-dwelling Ogiek were living in harmony. Later, he started witnessing what he terms 'wanton destruction' of the forest in the area 'through the political system' [both 1/027]. He then started including Mariashoni in his project, targeting biodiversity conservation of the upper catchment of the Molo River. After witnessing the drastic changes that the area had undergone when first setting out on project activities in Mariashoni in 2010, he decided that Necofa should take time to understand the complex dynamics that contributed to the changing environment in the area. He particularly worried about population changes, through the in-migration of members of other communities and changes within the local Ogiek community, and the interaction of 'in-migrant'[12] and 'host' communities, as well as local and national politics. In 2010, Necofa first came to the area in the context of a meeting organised by the Slow Food Movement held at Mariashoni Primary School. After the meeting, a needs and capacity assessment about food security, biodiversity conservation, and natural resource management was carried out, finishing in June 2011. At the same time, Necofa was indirectly working to be accepted by the community through their continuous presence and the manifestation of genuine interest, according to the country coordinator. Based on the insights generated, a two-year project was launched in May 2012.

The project centred on three main activities: inclusive tree planting that gives communities pride through active involvement instead of mere spectatorship; support of modern beekeeping through targeted training and exchange visits; and support of environmental clubs in schools to sensitise and mobilise the youth to understand the bio-

---

12 The expression of 'in-migrants' is derived from the fact that the Ogiek referred to non-Ogiek as 'foreigners' in English and '*wageni*' (guests) in Swahili. That term designates persons who have settled in the forest since the mid-1990s and mainly belong to the broader Kalenjin community, including Kipsigis, Tugen, and Nandi – and sometimes also Kamba and Kisii. Due to the somewhat derogatory connotation of the term, it is used in quotes.

diversity within which they often live obliviously. Since many of the activities were cross-cutting with other activities supported in Mariashoni, and because the country coordinator expressed the belief that uncoordinated external influence confuses local community members, he attempted to liaise with ProMara and KAPAP during project planning and when launching the project. While ProMara accepted his invitation, collaboration with the other external actors on the ground in Mariashoni had not materialised by 2013 [1/027]. In the end, Necofa chose to join all the ongoing beekeeping activities in Mariashoni and work with the participants to reach their objectives [3/068]. A project manager was employed to work on beekeeping on the ground. As part of the project activities, eight beekeeping groups were formed in the area. Each group was provided twenty-five beehives, eight modern hives of the Longstroth type, twelve modern Kenya Top Bar Hives (KTBH), and five improved log hives with an installed queen excluder for a stronger colony and higher productivity. These were given to the groups in October 2012. So-called 'catcher boxes' used to facilitate the trapping of bees were to be supplied to the groups by February 2013. Before giving out the beehives, the project brought external trainers, including the Agritek trainer who worked for KAPAP in the area, to train the group members on modern beekeeping. The four groups then identified eight locations in the wider Mariashoni area where the beehives were set up: one in the home of the Necofa field officer, close to Mariashoni Centre, and one each in the nearby Kapcholola Primary School, in Kapsinindet Primary School and in Mariashoni Secondary School. The four remaining ones were established in the outskirts of Mariashoni, mainly settled by non-Ogiek, namely in Kikingi Tatu close to Chai Moto, Ndoswa, Oinoptich, and Lawina Secondary School [1/038].[13] In June 2012, Necofa and KAPAP together also provided a honey production unit with a refinery located at the Necofa offices close to the 'Chief's place' (i.e. his office in Mariashoni Centre, in which honey could be extracted from the modern beehive elements and refined. Necofa then attempted to mobilise the community to bring their previously harvested honey for refinement, but there was close to no response because honey levels were low due to the cold and rainy weather in 2012. The field officer explained that they timed their activities in a way that would allow the refinery to be fully functional by the traditional November to January honey harvesting period [3/068]. He insisted that they had also offered the farmers a good

---

[13] Several areas in the wider Mariashoni Location are commonly understood as 'Ogiek strongholds', including Mariashoni Centre, as well as Tertit, Kapcholola, Kaprop, and Kiptunga, while other areas are understood as 'in-migrant-strongholds', including Ndoswa, Rombei, Oinoptich, and Lawina (Fuchs, 2014). These are related to what qre later described as 'upper' and 'lower' Mariashini (see Map 4 in Chapter 2).

price – KES 120 ($1.2) per kg – while the Baraka Agricultural College, located in Molo, that commonly purchased raw honey from small-scale producers in the area, only paid KES 100 ($1) [3/082]. The project further tried to have the bees moved into the modern beehives by December and for the honey to be ready by September or October the following year. Honey production supposedly was slower and took around eight months in the highlands, while it was much faster in warmer places such as Bogoria or Nakuru [3/068]. The overall idea of the project was to produce high-quality honey and operate through the Mariashoni Community Development self-help group (MaCoDev SHG),[14] an umbrella group for all the beekeeper groups. The KAPAP M&E officer referred to the same as the CIG that was to act as a cooperative for local beekeepers [1/023]. Necofa had assisted the formation of MaCoDev and the SHG grew with the support of the two local Necofa employees [3/082]. Ultimately, the idea was that MaCoDev could be empowered to process and package locally produced honey, get approval from the Kenya Bureau of Standards (KEBS) and sell local Mariashoni honey at competitive prices of around KES 250 ($2.5) per 500g. Before exporting their honey, one of the objectives of KAPAP, the intention was first to build a strong brand locally. However, one of the Necofa field officers also said that only two groups used these hives eight months after the project's inception and almost five months after giving out the beehives. Interestingly, those who used the hives were the groups in Lawina and Oinoptich, the non-Ogiek groups [3/082].

Furthermore, Mariashoni Primary School was included in Necofa's '1000 gardens' project that aimed to establish gardens in 1,000 schools after successfully conducting various sessions of the Slow Food Movement training at their school [3/063]. During that project, Necofa also launched botanical gardens in four schools in the wider Mariashoni area, namely in Mariashoni, Kaprop, Ndoswa, and Oinoptich Primary Schools, in which native plant species were planted so that the children learn about and experience the characteristics and significance of plant species that used to be crucial to the local communities [1/038]. The project further targeted additional farm diversification by promoting pyrethrum planting on-farm, and Merino sheep keeping for wool [3/068]. The MaCoDev chairman later confirmed that Necofa had secured a further round of funding for one or two years after the lapse of the first cycle in 2014 and that MaCoDev would build a cultural centre close to Mariashoni Quarry [3/087].

Overall, the four programmes directly targeted livelihood activities, most importantly beekeeping (see Table 3). Beekeeping is a traditional income-generating activity among members of the Ogiek community.

---

14   MaCoDev is not to be confused with MEFoCo, the Mau East Forest Conservation Group, also called Forest Conservation Committee or the 'Forum'.

Supporting the local community in professionalising and modernising their honey production aligns with an appreciation of local ecological knowledge and objectives related to the sustainable use of the forest and its resources. The concentration on beekeeping and honey production satisfied conservation objectives since bees primarily depend on flowers from indigenous trees and bushes for honey production. ProMara and Necofa also included active tree-planting activities into their portfolios and promoted fruit tree planting. Business skill development with the intention to support autonomous marketing and the sale of produce was an integral part of these strategies. This approach was based on the assumption that wealth creation, beyond mere poverty reduction, would reduce the forest dwellers' pressure on the forest [1/021]. The two organisations also worked with environmental clubs in primary schools to sensitise forest dwellers on forest conservation, food security, and food diversity from a young age. These clubs were furthermore used as platforms for environmental sensitisation through which information on relevant legal, political, administrative, and financial issues was shared. Most established, in terms of information provision, was ProMara's Mau Outreach Centre in Olenguruone. Information sharing through community training carried out through training of trainers (ToT) was another popular innovation in the area. ProMara had an additional conflict management component intended to help local community members resolve their conflicts. The CDTF project supported forest management and conservation through capacity building of local and regional institutions, particularly in creating and professionalising a CFA in Mariashoni [3/059, 3/065].

Due to the Baraka Agricultural College's long existence and proximity to the Eastern Mau Forest, the institution was involved in several activities to transform local practices and systems in Mariashoni. The Catholic Diocese of Nakuru created the institution in 1974 to support rural development by training small-scale farmers in sustainable agriculture. The College was set up when most white settlers had left the surrounding highlands. At that time, the five big farms that used to exist between Molo and Nakuru were subdivided into small plots and sold to individual smallholder farmers. Most of those who purchased the fields or were employed to work on the small fields for the new owners had previously worked with the white settlers, so they knew about farming. According to Baraka's deputy principal, they knew well about wheat, sheep, and dairy farming on a large scale but had limited experience in small-scale agriculture. It became Baraka's mission to train the small-scale farmers on how to be independent by farming sustainably. At the time of research, the college concentrated on matters of agroforestry, environmental management, and energy conservation. Their college ground still had space to accommodate groups for short-term training courses, and a functioning honey processing station, where

Table 3 Overview of main conservation aid actors and their activities in Mariashoni (as of late 2013).

Actor	Donor	Timeline	Target	Target sector	Activities	Approach	Philosophy
KAPAP	World Bank & GoK	2011–(2016)	Ogiek community	Livelihoods	Beekeeping (training)	Farmer field schools (FFS)	Non-provision
FCLIP	CDTF (EU)	2012–(2015)	Eastern Mau Forest	Livelihoods and conservation	Beekeeping (supplies); forest management and conservation	n/a	Provision
ProMara	USAID	2010–2012	Mara River Basin	Livelihoods (and conservation)	Beekeeping; fruit trees; environmental clubs; conflict management, and peacebuilding	Training of trainers (ToT)	Provision
Necofa	ManiTese (Italian NGO)	2010–(2015)	Molo River Basin	Livelihoods (and conservation)	Beekeeping; fruit trees; environmental clubs	n/a	Initially non-provision

Source: Author compilation based on interviews with relevant stakeholders. Note: In this context, provision refers to whether an external actor pays community members for engagement in proposed project activities. Some actors call this 'facilitation', while community members broadly refer to such payments as 'sitting allowance'.

high-quality honey, the 'Pure Baraka Highland Honey', was produced. The deputy principal explained that the college sourced the raw honey from small-scale beekeepers in the area. Since the Baraka College was known for its expertise and experience in beekeeping matters, some of the external actors operating in Mariashoni came to them for advice. ProMara, for instance, consulted with Baraka for both learning and teaching support on the one hand, and material supplies, including bee-hives, and protective gear, on the other. The deputy principal said he personally engaged in two types of training with ProMara. Between April and November 2011, he conducted beekeeping training sessions in the field in Eastern Mau. Later, a group of farmers working with ProMara came to the college to learn about group dynamics. In August 2011, preparations for a formal memorandum of understanding (MoU) between ProMara and Baraka were underway, but ProMara went quiet, and their collaboration subsided silently. Lastly, he also started collaborating with Necofa since both were part of the same Participatory and Ecological Land Use Management (PELUM) network, a Swedish-funded initiative. This network centred on sustainable and ecological agriculture, and members met bi-weekly to learn and exchange about good agricultural practices [1/024].[15]

Altogether, evidence of project activities, especially project outcomes, was sparse on the ground by 2013. While KAPAP service providers carried out training sessions in modern beekeeping, and ProMara held meetings in Nakuru, Mariashoni, and other towns outside the forest, very few actual outcomes were visible, and even fewer impacts. Two visible results were installing several modern beekeeping units close to Mariashoni Primary School and in Kapcholola, and the set-up of the honey production unit at the Necofa office in Mariashoni Centre, funded by various projects.

Local institutional adaptation towards participatory forest management

In parallel, the conservation aid actors supported an adaptation of forest management structures towards PFM through community inclusion in both environmental management and in benefits generated from these environments.

Public Forest Land placed under government management had significantly reduced in Mariashoni Location with the creation of the settlement scheme in 1997. Even though the designation of the settlement scheme was unlawful and a court case to challenge the legality

---

[15] By the time of the interview, Necofa had not yet officially launched their project in Mariashoni but were already planning this in consultation with the Baraka College. It is likely that Baraka's deputy principal would have approved their approach.

of the settlement scheme had been pending since 1997 (addressed in more detail in the following chapters) the forester of Mariashoni Forest Station described the settlement scheme as de facto existing. Based on the somewhat unclear de jure definition of existing forest land in Mariashoni, he explained that there was only about 1,000 ha of forest land in Mariashoni Location under his mandate because 6,000 ha of the overall 7,000 ha were settled [3/062]. Since most of the remaining forest land was located in the Kiptunga area in the eastern part of Mariashoni Location, which officially fell under a separate forest station, the Mariashoni residents were encouraged to form their CFA under the Kiptunga rather than the Mariashoni Forest Station. Hence, several Mariashoni residents organised as Kiptunga CFA because 'the forest in Mariashoni is too small' [3/059]. The CFA acted as an umbrella organisation for several community-based organisations (CBOs), which, in turn, were composed of several user groups (see Figure 3). By 2013, thirty-two so-called user groups were part of the Mariashoni CBO federated under the Mariashoni/Kiptunga CFA [3/059].

The CFA played several different roles. First, it was fundamental for conserving and protecting the forest; second, it was responsible for working jointly with the community members to improve their livelihoods; and third, it was to educate the youth not to depend on the forest. Regarding activities, the CFA had its own tree nursery to contribute to forest conservation and rehabilitation by reforesting degraded forest areas. In terms of improving local livelihoods, the CFA supported modern beekeeping to make Mariashoni 'an industrial area for bee production and export of honey' [3/059]. To address all three roles described, the CFAs were supposed to elaborate joint forest management plans for the forest area under their respective forest stations in collaboration with the local KFS representatives. Through the community's inclusion in the joint management plan development, which was to address matters such as modes and location of attributing harvesting rights for mature trees, the definition of livestock grazing areas, firewood collection areas, as well as the designation of places in which to hang apiaries and designate secret sites for traditional rites, both participation and benefit of local communities were to be ensured [3/059]. In the eight years following the adoption of the 2005 Forest Act and the six years after its enactment, the KFS and the CFA had not come together in Mariashoni, and no joint management plan had been set up. According to the MEFoCo division representative, this shortfall was mainly conditioned by lacking funds, which he considered necessary to pay for external expertise required to complete the task. Furthermore, the CFA initially expected to get technical advice from the KFS. Later, they expected ProMara to prepare the management plan for the Kiptunga CFA. Still, since both did not materialise, he said they either needed funds for external expertise, citing a figure of KES 4 million ($40,000)

Forest Conservation Commitee/ 'Forum'

CFA

CBO

User group

District

Forest Station

Location

Village

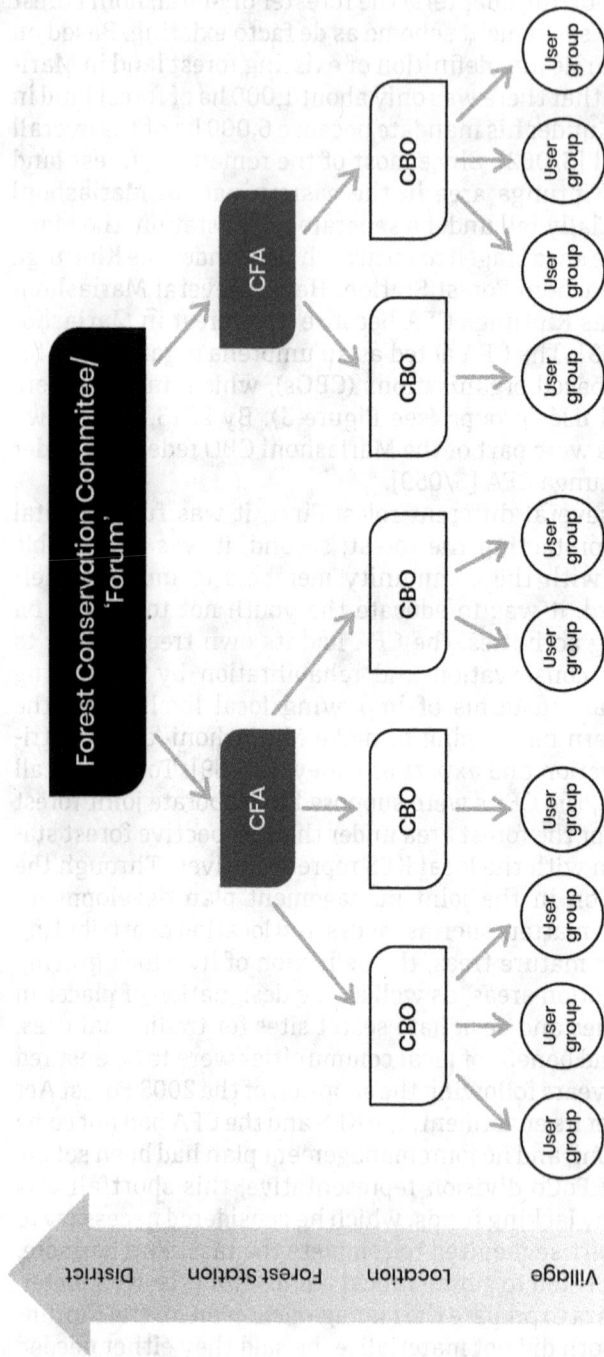

Figure 3 Organisation and mechanisms of local environmental governance institutions in the Eastern Mau Forest.

Source: Author illustration based on explanations obtained in interview [3/06].

or time and the opportunity to learn how to develop a management plan by themselves [3/059, 3/065]. The Necofa country coordinator supported this point and argued that training and adequate management of the CFA were fundamental to enable the CFA to be a vital partner in negotiations with other institutions, notably the KFS [1/027].

Apart from the creation and formal mandate of CFAs in forest management, as noted above, the formerly abolished *shamba* system was to be re-introduced under the name of PELIS to foster community participation and benefit sharing. Under the previous *shamba* system, individual farmers had been given user rights for crop production in forest plantations in exchange for taking care of the tree seedlings. Similarly, under PELIS, individual farmers were entitled to apply for cultivation plots for small-scale agricultural production within new forest plantations until the trees acquired a certain height. Like the previous *shamba* system, plantation and cultivation were to go hand in hand as the individual community member who cultivated a given plot of land was also responsible for the health of the previously planted tree seedlings. What changed, though, is that only registered members of the CFA qualified to apply [3/062]. Furthermore, CFA members were required to establish a CFA-run and managed tree nursery to help in the establishment of forest plantations that were assigned for PELIS [2/266]. Another particularity of PELIS was that the individual members of the CFA and their chairperson guaranteed the survival of tree seedlings jointly and that the CFA faced deregistration in case of destruction or reduction of tree seedlings. This responsibility clause was considered a significant improvement by numerous actors (including environmentalists, human rights activists and organisations, the Government, and the forestry department) compared to the previous sanction-free *shamba* system that, some argue, incited people to prevent seedlings from growing to allow them to continue cultivating the productive forest land [3/062]. Despite CFA members' hopes, PELIS had not been introduced in the forest plantations managed by the Mariashoni or Kiptunga Forest Stations by 2012–2013 [3/069].

The Kiptunga CFA was also part of the Mau East Forest Conservation Group (MEFoCo), created in 2009, and also called the Forest Conservation Committee or the 'Forum', a CBO acting as an umbrella organisation for all CFAs in the Eastern Mau region (see Figure 3). According to the MEFoCo division representative, twelve CFAs were registered in the wider Eastern Mau stretching from Kuresoi to Naivasha. The mandate of MEFoCo included holding meetings with representatives of relevant parastatals such as the KFS, the KWS, Nema, and KAPAP or ministries to discuss forest issues. The representative of the Kiptunga CFA to MEFoCo further explained that his role was mainly to take community concerns to the KFS and to represent community interests, as well as to mediate between the community and KFS and thus represent

KFS positions in the community. Describing himself as 'the eye of KFS at the grassroots level' [3/059], the division representative also reported to the KFS about matters related to illegal logging and transporting of trees, as well as charcoal production and transport. The Forum also provided the possibility to address the KFS Directors' Board on behalf of the CFAs regarding urgent matters. The EU-funded CDTF had supported both MEFoCo and the Kiptunga CFA since 2012. According to the division representative, the CDTF directly supported sustainable management authorities on the ground by engaging in the capacity building of CFAs through MEFoCo [3/059, 3/065].

Apart from attempting to feature the CFAs together with government representatives under the Forest Committee umbrella, a small NGO called the National Association of CFAs (NACOFA) tried to provide a platform for exchange and mutual learning among CFAs. By late 2012, there were around 350 CFAs in Kenya, 215 of which were registered with NACOFA. The organisation's mandate was to assist CFAs with capacity building, complying with the law, and fundraising through the Government and externally, for instance, by sensitising groups about international funding streams related to carbon markets, REDD, and REDD+. The Association also offered agency development to enable them to negotiate joint management plans with the KFS representation at their respective forest station level. A NACOFA programme assistant described their work as challenging. He said that, while the Ministry for Wildlife and Forestry was supportive of the CFAs overall, the KFS, in many instances, boycotted the CFAs and attempted to shut down their initiatives. Beyond focusing on the inclusion aspect of PFM, NACOFA also supported the development of a joint management plan template that focused on benefit sharing, in line with constitutional provisions. NACOFA's work was challenged by limited government support, while the county governments pushed for a concurring template that considered community inclusion into management by providing them user rights but neglected the central provision on benefit sharing. NACOFA entirely depended on international donors such as the NGO, Act!, SIDA, and USAID [1/034].

Outcomes and impact of conservation aid

While most projects had not been concluded by 2013, the local community and knowledgeable observers shared various opinions about their actual and potential impact.

Has deforestation been linearly reversed through reforestation?

One of the core axes of the 'Save the Mau' initiative was tree planting, and tree planting was a central element of both the forest restoration discourse and practice. In practice, the tree-planting drives implemented in the Eastern Mau all faced the same problem. A Timsales employee responsible for plantation management and re-establishment said, 'they are all trying to do something, plant 10 ha, but then they just leave the seedlings there. They plant indigenous trees following Wangari Maathai's ideas, but plant in the wrong places and at the wrong time, and most don't attend to the seedlings', and added that 'they are all dead by now ... also Raila's cedars [in Kiptunga Forest] are dead ... all of them destroyed by livestock' [both 5/233]. He referred to common problems in forest rehabilitation undertakings: forest planta-tion establishment required special skills, including knowledge about locally appropriate species, the right timing and proper management. He added that this knowledge must be embedded within a more compre-hensive institutional set-up that allows for implementing the required management. Since tree-planting drives attracted much limelight, attention was often given to the planting as such, while the sensi-bility and sustainability of these undertakings remained secondary. Crucially, forest plantation establishment specialists that could guar-antee that trees planted are appropriate and adequately managed were not included in these tree-planting drives. Overall, the tree-planting drives often contributed very little to actual reforestation [5/233]. Ulti-mately, all tree-planting sites visited in the Eastern Mau throughout the field research period were deserted, and the seedlings in every site had dried up.[16]

Has the promotion of improved income-generating activities transformed livelihoods?

The likelihood of succeeding in transforming practices towards more sustainable livelihoods was influenced by various factors. The first factor is related to the engagement mechanism external actors pursued with the community in Mariashoni. All activities were implemented through community groups, in some instances 'organic' groups, in others newly created groups. All projects proposed workshops and training sessions on group dynamics and leadership to build and foster a certain level of trust among group members to develop an alternative 'community'. Apart from genuine and somewhat idealistic motiva-tions for such training, these alternative communities were primarily

---

[16]   A team of journalists who visited the site in early 2017 described the same scene: 'Less than 10 metres from the wetland is a seven-year-old plaque dated 15 January 2010, commemorating the day when then-Prime Minister Raila Odinga and the late Prof Wangari Maathai led a host of government bureau-crats, politicians and environmentalists on a tree-planting ceremony in the area as part of the efforts to restore the complex's ecosystem. Sadly, however, just like the ill-fated vegetation surrounding the wetland, all the trees planted on that occasion have been destroyed' (Obi, L., 'Efforts to restore main water tower achieving little', *Daily Nation*, 28 February 2017).

created to pursue economic development, specifically to facilitate the aggregation of efforts and produce. Furthermore, KAPAP, ProMara and Necofa actively pursued production for export through these groups. ProMara specifically formed activity-based CBOs, such as beekeeping groups and livestock cultivators' groups, to allow using these CBOs as economic vehicles. Each CBO had its clear financial objectives, further federated at a higher level through the CFA [1/029]. While aggregation of produce remained insufficient in most areas, and while the CIGs that KAPAP had promoted remained 'somewhat like welfare groups' [1/023], no-one seemed to question the rationale behind the promotion of agricultural production for export. Another popular motivation for external actors to form and operate on the ground through groups was related to the interest in promoting institutional micro-loaning and micro-funding through microfinance and commercial banks [1/023], trusts and NGOs, as well as government funds, for instance, specific funding schemes for women, youth, and sports.

In terms of modes of engagement, community members' so-called facilitation was important. Specifically, the project diverged between those that provided cash and/or in-kind support and those that did not. The provision of 'transport' or 'lunch' money and other materials required in the implementation of specific projects was an issue of considerable contention. While some claimed that project participants must be 'compensated' for the time they dedicated to participating in projects [1/018], others opined that provision of cash and/or kind could also lead to 'negative encouragement' as people do not 'own' processes they engage in [1/024, 3/057]. According to the Baraka College's deputy principal, ProMara had the wrong approach by inviting random farmers to meetings and providing them with 'lunch' or 'transport' money, thus attracting opportunists who were not really interested in the matter and who did not 'own' the process [1/024]. Indeed, after ProMara cut the 'lunch' money, attendance in meetings dropped considerably. Several ProMara trainers addressed the matter with the ProMara supervisors, arguing that paying 'lunch' money spoiled the residents' motivation because they supposedly only sat in meetings passively and waited to receive money instead of actively engaging in the training. ProMara apparently defended the programme's stand that 'lunch' money needed to be paid [3/057]. In the same vein, it was believed that people did not attend Necofa meetings because they only provided participants with KES 200 ($2) in transport money [3/057]. Furthermore, there were rumours among community members that some of the project implementers had misappropriated the funds that were intended as 'lunch' money, particularly within ProMara [5/245]. Residents did not trust ProMara because 'they make people sign the sheet for handouts but never fill the slot for the amount ... and then they are given KES 200 ($2) to KES 300 ($3)' [5/228]. While interpreting authoritatively that this allegation was true might be difficult, it was witnessed during fieldwork that participants of a ProMara workshop were asked to sign sheets to confirm the receipt of 'lunch' funds, but that no amounts were indicated, hence leaving it at the discretion of ProMara staff to fill the empty space for the amount. The project manager of MEFoCo also criticised that CFA members only mobilised when an external actor called and paid for it and that most members would only come after the CFA leadership told them they would be getting something. She explained that they had initially planned not to give any money to CFA members for their engagement in tree-planting activities, but that people had just left their meetings, which forced them to adapt. Ultimately, they decided to give each individual KES 250 ($2.5) in Kiptunga and KES 200 ($2) in Mariashoni per workday. They explained that 'there is a cultural need in Kenya that you need a 'direct' impact' [1/036], referring to the fact that people want to be given something for their pocket to guarantee their interest.

At a meta-level, despite consultative rhetoric, the activities implemented through these projects were decided upon and planned outside of Mariashoni and reflected top-down project design and decision-making processes. As voiced by a few observers both from Mariashoni and from outside the area, the involvement of external actors in forest and environmental conservation and the implementation of top-down measures in Mariashoni lead to a diminishing emphasis on truly community-driven conservation activities [e.g., 1/024, 3/072] and hence to a shrinking of the democratic space that had been acquired in natural resource management, at least on paper. The Kiptunga CFA and MEFoCo division representative said it was a significant problem in the Eastern Mau that NGOs came with their budgeted projects and were not flexible in adapting to the community's interests. In that vein, he said: 'these days, conservation is in fashion ... but what about the living standard of the people? They cannot only depend on trees' [3/065]. Many other residents voiced concerns about some of the actors' motives and opted to engage in some form of 'NGO shopping', a practice in which community members came, listened and left with the 'sitting allowance' without truly getting involved and without investing time and resources in the proposed activities.

Inclusivity and de facto inclusion were other contentious issues in the Mau Forest restoration projects. The KAPAP M&E officer agreed that their project, for instance, was not necessarily inclusive since it specifically targeted members of the Ogiek community and promoted an activity – beekeeping – that formed part of the indigenous practices of the host Ogiek community, but not necessarily of other community members living in the areas [1/023]. Some *wageni* reported feeling excluded from conservation activities promoted by external agencies. One resident explained that the few 'connected' Ogiek called 'their own' to form groups and participate in proposed activities when external actors ask to mobilise community groups for project activities and that they 'closed off' access for others [5/229]. This statement furthermore alludes to the importance of power struggles within the resident community, not only between different ethnic communities but equally within them. One NGO staff member also explained that only a handful of critical actors held all 'community' positions requested by the NGOs, leading to the same persons assuming the roles of 'community mobilisers' for ProMara, 'field officers' for Necofa and 'activity coordinators' for KAPAP. In his assessment, this small group of relatively well-educated and somewhat well-off individuals and families that were able to establish good relationships with the world outside of Mariashoni, including project and programme leaders and even donors, formed a kind of layer between the community and the external actors. Every programme that came to the area was either brought by them or had to pass through them to take root. He further explained that the same people typically held leadership positions in all projects and forums but did not necessarily actively participate in these groups. This included a resident who served in a government position outside the area, a local parastatal employee and his son, and a central representative of the local authority and his wife. One of them was said to be a busy man who mainly resided elsewhere but monopolised many functions and effectively contributed to the lack of activity of some groups because he did not engage actively. The same man supposedly appointed himself as chairman of the Kiptunga CFA. He registered the same CFA, thus effectively blocking others from doing the same, yet he did not call for meetings or guide people in relevant activities. Others supposedly held leadership positions in all forums, including the CFA and MaCoDev, and were actively and positively participating and contributing to meetings outside of Mariashoni, but did not call meetings with the local community members and effectively intimidated and domineered other members. The representative of the local administration was said to be 'always out of Mariashoni attending to his personal business' [1/027]. Due to their frequent absences, the men were often not personally involved with activities but remained dominant due to their wives' involvement [1/027]. This situation arguably led to inequity in exposure and acquisition of relative wealth, benefiting a few individuals and families while others were further marginalised. The NGO staff member called this community self-organisation a 'primary hurdle' to the successful and sustainable engagement of external actors in Mariashoni [1/027]. Considering that situation, other members of the Ogiek community expressed concerns that projects were 'owned' by selected individuals and emphasised their perceived exclusion and alienation from potentially interesting activities and programmes [5/200, 5/245].

In terms of content, all externally supported programmes and projects attempted to tackle the destruction of the Mau Forest in Mariashoni by targeting the local population's income-generating activities. In that vein, all projects implemented in the area focused on improving and modernising people's beekeeping techniques and skills. As for most forest-dwelling communities, beekeeping was one of the traditional Ogiek livelihood activities. While beekeeping continued being practised in the area, it had not previously been exploited commercially in Mariashoni. Apart from being in line with the local community's traditions and relevant to existing local ecological knowledge systems, some also argued that 'beekeeping is a magic in itself' [1/024] since bees need a sound environment and mainly indigenous trees to produce good honey. This supposedly encourages people not to cut indigenous trees because they were directly related to their source of income. Basing their programmes on the same rationale, all external actors set up their programmes to contribute to 'Saving the Mau' by promoting socially and economically sound practices which were environmentally friendly at the same time. Care for their pocket thereby was to foster environmental care among those who participated in the initiatives in question. Several residents who engaged in honey production confirmed that it could indeed have been a worthwhile endeavour. An old Ogiek man, for instance, explained that he still had around five hundred beehives in the Mariashoni area. Since one *debe*, a twenty-litre bucket that weighs around 18kgs,[17] can earn up to KES 5,000 ($50), he said he could easily make KES 100,000 ($1,000) in a year without harming the environment in any way [5/108]. One of the young Ogiek men who displayed clear interest and engagement in traditional beekeeping said that he had approximately 200 beehives in the indigenous forest and that he produced more honey than anyone else in the area; supposedly more than two hundred *debes* per year. He said one bucket could be sold for approximately KES 10,000 ($100) [5/123]. Another young Ogiek man explained that he had twenty-three beehives, harvested four big *debes* and sold them at KES 8,400 ($84) each. He added that depending on the season, a *debe* could earn up to KES 12,000 ($120) [5/148]. Many other residents reported only having between five and ten beehives left and harvesting between a half and three *debes* of honey [5/173, 5/176, 5/186]. Those who indicated harvesting little honey mainly kept it for household consumption. Specifically, honey was saved and given to children when they were sick. Some also sold their honey locally, to neighbours, in small quantities, and often for KES 100–200 ($1–2) per litre [5/184, 5/194, 5/225, 5/226, 5/234, 5/237, 5/241]. Most residents continued using traditional beehives, made from

---

[17] One debe of honey is standardised to weigh 18kg according to the Kenya Gazette (Republic of Kenya, 2009b).

hollow indigenous tree logs hung in indigenous trees. The Mariashoni residents cited different indigenous trees that they used to make these beehives, including *Kesiengit* (English/Latin names not available) and *Torokwet* (East African cedar), as well as *Pondet* (*Engleromyces goetzei*). The beehives were then hung in different indigenous trees, including *Silibwet* (*Dombeya goetzenii*), *Sabtet* (Podo), *Masaita* (*Olea capensis* sub-species, East African Olive), *Pondet* (*Engleromyces goetzei*), *Tepesweit* (*Croton macrostachyus*), and *Torokwet* (East African cedar) [5/144, 5/169, 5/174, 5/179, 5/187, 5/189].[18] Only very few residents spoke of owning and using modern beehives. One young educated Ogiek man was one of these few individuals, and he explained having bought two KTBHs after visiting Keringet and seeing them there [5/257]. Another young Ogiek man explained that he had a few modern beehives in the neighbouring Nessuit area [5/210], while a middle-aged Kipsigis man explained that his family had some in Keringet [5/213]. An old Kipsigis man from Kikingi Tatu close to Chai Moto said he owned and manu-factured modern beehives [5/202]. Other community members also reported obtaining modern beehives for their community groups from external actors [5/116, 5/117, 5/173, 5/194].

While promoting improved beekeeping practices was mindful of the complexities at play and holistic in its nature, the Baraka College's deputy principal cautioned against putting all eggs in one basket. He also emphasised that people needed alternatives as much as he believed in the 'magic' of beekeeping. He said that changing weather conditions and the erratic climate overall, as well as prolonged cold spells, delayed honey production in the area. Forest dwellers need something to occupy them in the meantime and should develop integrated farming systems that are sustainable in case one of them fails, he added [1/024]. One of the Necofa field officers confirmed that, despite the organisation's efforts to mobilise local honey producers to bring honey to the com-munity refinery, only very few did. He attributed the hesitance among community members to the fact that it had rained so much throughout 2012 that the overall honey production was low [3/068]. A communi-ty member added that modern beehives promoted by the projects were flat on the top and that the bees fled the 'toc toc toc' of the rain, and that proper structures in which to keep these beehives were required [5/207]. Furthermore, in the context of reducing nectar-providing indigenous tree and bush populations and widespread use of chemi-cal fertilisers on farms that potentially endangered wild grasses and plants, and even the bees themselves, focusing on beekeeping alone might not be intrinsically sustainable.

---

[18] An overview of common tree uses in the Eastern Mau can be found on p. 8 of the OPAT (Muchemi and Ehrensperger, 2011). Appendix 1 provides an over-view of tree uses inventoried during the research.

The Baraka College's deputy principal further emphasised that the biggest challenge for any training, school, project, and programme implemented on the ground was transforming attitudes. He said that most trainings had an impact on skills but not attitudes, which was why they failed. At the same time, he conceded that changes in attitude were difficult to engender due to various interconnected reasons. The first reason was that 'we have culture sitting on us' [1/024]. Individual farmers carry much history due to who they are and how they have lived, with women doing most of the work on the farms, men providing the resources, and children being mainly in schools and not available for farm work, he added, and changing the way people work and work together is difficult. The second challenge was that small-scale agriculture does not pay as well as formal jobs, mainly because profits are liable to challenges with what he termed 'production factors', including unpredictable climate and rainfall. The third challenge he mentioned was that rural community members are often reluctant to take risks, be innovative and change traditional ways of doing things. Hence, while considering indigenous and historical knowledge was important, rural populations' reluctance to try new things could hinder the required change in attitude, so KAPAP's approach was hence interesting, he said. He acknowledged their 'farmer-field-school' approach, championed by the FAO, where farmers are trained on specific topics in their own 'open grass schools'. According to him, they did right to have continuous exchange and learning since the community groups formed came together weekly for well-structured lessons facilitated by a teacher accompanying the farmers through a complete cycle from preparation to harvesting on a demonstration farm. Individual farmers were then encouraged to apply their knowledge on their own farms. After completing one cycle, in the case of beekeeping, a graduation ceremony was held for the participating farmers after the first harvest of honey. After graduation, the project also proposed follow-up activities [1/024].

The cited examples reveal the overriding problem that NGOs and their activities in the Eastern Mau were not vetted through an official body, governmental or non-governmental, or strategically deployed and monitored. Furthermore, their activities were often overlapping and sometimes contradictory, a common problem in situations where considerable external attention is paid to a specific area [1/025]. Some called the confusion created by the external actors or 'service providers' a 'big challenge'. Different NGOs came with different stories and approaches, 'do this, do that; spray this, spray that' [1/024] while targeting the same people. The training facility staff explained that, after being exposed to several different NGOs with different approaches, activities and ideas, some rural community members decided not to go to any NGO meetings anymore because, in the end, if anything did not go according to 'plan', they were the ones suffering from their losses alone. He added that the exposure to different external agents with varying agendas led to 'NGO fatigue' in Mariashoni and ultimately to dissatisfaction and lack of involvement of local community members in any of the proposed activities [1/024]. The duplication of activities with different objectives and approaches often led to contradictory teachings and a confusion of the targeted individuals and groups. One observer spoke of the creation of redundant and potentially harmful parallel systems. ProMara, he said, created a separate system that included forest associations, coordinating committees, and local and international companies that duplicated national structures and effectively confused both the the residents and the existing system and structures [1/005]. This 'NGO fatigue', according to another observer, was facilitated by and rooted in the fact that most NGOs did not want to collaborate and wanted to outshine one another. Even his institution, an agricultural training college located at the edges of the Mau Forest that had witnessed agricultural and environmental practices, changes, and challenges in the area for decades, fell prey to the same problem. While NGOs consulted them for their technical knowledge, most organisations came with fixed work plans that were not flexible enough for the college staff to bring in their own thoughts and expertise and merely used them as service providers [1/024].

In the absence of external regulation, another observer blamed elite capture among the communities in the Eastern Mau for the failure to engage in solid community self-organisation. He regretted the situation because only a strongly organised CBO could partner with external actors, including NGOs and government agencies. A strong CBO would also be able to call partners to a round table and could lead activities implemented by external partners in their home area. He added that 'the community should not be spectators' [1/027]. Ironically, this problem was also apparent in the CFA representative's argument. According to him, the Mau Forest could be an industrial zone of honey production, and every farm and household could grow fruits. Both could be exported, and living standards could increase significantly. However, he displayed the very attitudinal issue raised by claiming that Mariashoni had not reached that stage yet because the success 'depends on who brings projects to the community; and it depends on the donors if it will work', and added that the situation in the Eastern Mau could be significantly better 'if the NGOs in the area were fulfilling their promises' [both 3/065]. He, however, also said it might be best if the local community registered their own NGO and applied for project funds directly, an approach he pursued successfully through the CFA. He added that the Ogiek Welfare Council (OWC) served as a yardstick for what can be achieved and for the potential sources of conflict since 'money can unite people but can also disperse people' [3/065]. As explained, Necofa attempted to avoid making similar mistakes by integrating pre-existing project activities and structures. In some instances, they did so successfully; in others, less so. This coordination was, however, solely driven by the interest and strong will of Necofa's coordinator rather than as a requirement posed by any regulatory body.

Has the promotion of participatory forest management led to the sharing of benefits or power?

Looking at local institutional changes, many Mariashoni community members criticised the CFA despite acknowledging the attempt to include members of the forest-dwelling community further in managing and benefits from the forest. The MEFoCo division representative, who somewhat was the 'face of the CFA', criticised that the CFA had been created after hearing on the radio that each forest station should have one. They then submitted their application to the KFS and were accredited, but they critically lacked funds to live up to their mandate. He contextualised the CFA's difficulties by invoking that while it had access to technical advice from the KFS, the creation and introduction of CFAs represented a significant change for the KFS, particularly for foresters at the forest station level. Since the Mariashoni forester was hesitant to work with the CFA, it was difficult for the CFA to have a stand. Ultimately, CFAs depend on the KFS, and they could not claim their right to be heard and included in cases in which the local KFS representatives did not allow them to. In Mariashoni, the 2005 Forest Act was 'in the books, but its implementation is very difficult' [3/065].

Another NGO staff member mentioned that capacity building of alternative forest management organisations, especially the CFAs, was a major concern and should feature more prominently in the NGOs' programmes in the Mau rehabilitation. He added that the KFS was not keen on the 2005 Forest Act and the idea of joint management with the CFAs, and said that while PFM was a good idea, 'it will not have any content' [1/031] until community members are able to defend their stand. The director of another influential NGO emphasised the same dilemma and stated that the CFAs had become weaker than they initially were in 2007. He added that the KFS was trying to frustrate and wear them out by giving them neither funds, attention, nor space. He said that the KFS was attempting to undermine the CFAs' reputation and importance. He added that the KFS was successful because after a 'keen and enthusiastic start' of the CFAs in 2007, 'reality hit them' [both 1/033], and their efforts largely remained unacknowledged and unappreciated, which led to reducing membership numbers. He concluded that few CFAs had proved to do a good job, including the ones in Koibatek and Lembus, both outside the Mau area [1/033]. Another expert agreed with that analysis and said that the CFAs had remained social organisations and 'agents of destruction' rather than rehabilitation agents. He added that all over the country, community members were frustrated with the CFAs because of the KFS' hesitance to share power with them [1/040]. The NACOFA programme assistant said that representatives from many CFAs called them and attempted to get the association's support, especially when dealing with local KFS representatives, particularly the foresters of the forest stations to which the representatives were attached, but that it was not easy to empower them [1/034]. Another NACOFA employee opined that the KFS was trying to keep the community out of benefit sharing at all cost, to the extent that even the remaining 'big three' timber companies in the country, Timsales, Raiply, and Comply, cut and carried everything from the root to the branch when harvesting forest plantations.[19] According to her, this 'total harvesting' proceeding was to ensure that communities would not enter the forest, would not use any residues, and would not remain there. She also added that the big companies replanted immediately after cutting the trees to lock the community out and to prevent the implementation of PELIS [1/034]. In Kiptunga Forest, in the wider Mariashoni area, Timsales carried out the same 'total harvest' approach [5/233]. Overall, in Mariashoni, there was no change in forest management structures and practices, and the CFA was not effectively included in devising forest management plans, which many described as the result of the forester's attempt to block such changes [e.g., 5/200].

Among community members, the assessments and analysis of the importance and performance of the CFA were less conceptual or contextualised and more matter-of-factual. One outspoken and engaged young man recounted that the CFA was not working as it was intended. He said that the CFA that was initially in place was no longer in existence and was not the one that registered as Kiptunga CFA after more than half of the initial one hundred members deserted the group. He said that they had initially paid KES 300 ($3) per person to register as members and that Necofa gave additional money to the CFA but that the CFA leaders 'defrauded' them [5/148]. Another vital critique raised against CFAs in general and about the Kiptunga CFA specifically was that 'now it is external ideas, not the elders, who guide the CFA' [5/148] and hence community engagement and contributions to forest management. One resident said that this external influence led to the CFA essentially being a 'joint outfit for the exploitation of the forest' [3/070], a sentiment echoed by another resident who said that the CFA officials collaborated with the KFS, and insisted that all they were interested in was money [5/200]. The TMA chairman suggested the same when insisting that the

19 The term 'timber companies' is used to refer to these three major commercial players in the timber and wood producing industry, while the term 'small and medium scale sawmillers' or simply 'sawmillers' is used to refer to all the other, smaller, players in the industry.

'CFAs are not empowered because they also want to become sawmillers' [2/048]. Some experts and community members alike lamented that the very idea that the CFA was to ensure that community members partake in benefit sharing introduced a fundamental change in mindsets away from the conservation of the forest and towards commodification and monetarisation of forest resources. Taking a pragmatic stand, the TMA chairperson, on the other hand, criticised government and NGO involvement in general, and USAID's ProMara initiative specifically, saying that these failed to acknowledge that forest matters were intrinsically related to the demand for timber. He suggested that forest conservation could not be successful if it were not based on a joint strategy with the private sector. It should include organisations like the TMA because they represent and know the interests, shortcomings, and opportunities related to all relevant market forces [2/048].

Whether the CFA leaders actually 'ate' money that had been collected through the CFA 'vehicle' and whether they indeed aspired to be future sawmillers was perhaps less important than the manifestation of potentially harmful social dynamics, which was somewhat engendered by the involvement of external actors. Many problems were related to the fact that the leaders of most externally supported organisations tended to be the same few people and that most community representatives collaborating with external actors were effectively the same persons, which led to confusion, suspicion, and rumours. It also contributed to the alienation of those who might potentially have been interested in natural resource-management matters but who did not feel 'belonging'. The involvement of external actors seems to have led to community perceptions that externally designed agendas were pursued with the help of some individual community members who were suspected of benefiting from their involvement with the external actors on a personal level. Whether the organisation, activity, or idea promoted appealed to other community members often lost relative importance and thus became somewhat secondary. These complex social issues are discussed in depth further below.

Considering institutional changes generally and provisions concerning participatory forest management specifically, despite bold changes in the conceptualisation of forest management structures, meaningful implementation in Mariashoni remained short of expectations.

The politics of conservation aid and the crisis in the Eastern Mau Forest

Implementing the 'Save the Mau' initiative in Mariashoni manifested the different tendencies in and pathways of priority setting in line with the state's 'initial dilemma' between commercial forest protection and sustainable forest conservation (Bryant & Bailey, 1997). Historically, Kenya's environmental policies had been largely shaped by European ideas and ideals, and were initially imposed by the colonial administration. After Independence in 1963, the post-colonial government largely maintained the same policies, adopting almost identical discourses with vastly similar effects on the environment and society (Klopp & Sang, 2011; Standing & Gachanja, 2014). The management of the Mau Forest, before the 'Save the Mau' initiative implemented since the late 2000s, bore witness to that heritage. Even though forest reservation in Kenya began as early as 1911 (Bassett & Crummey, 2003), and even though a majority of the Mau Forest was gazetted in 1932 (GoK, 2009e), forests all over the East African region were preserved for commercial production of wood and timber by imposing enclosures and were not considered in ecological terms (Bongers & Tennigkeit, 2010; Standing & Gachanja, 2014). Forest reservation consequently had little effect on the actual preservation and conservation of the Mau Forest and even less on its ecological integrity (GoK, 2009e; Mugo et al., 2010; Njeru, 2012; Standing & Gachanja, 2014; UNEP, 2008).

Looking at the activities implemented on the ground in Mariashoni to 'Save the Mau', the involvement and dominance of external actors in environmental affairs (Brown, 2001, 2009; Fairhead, Leach, & Scoones, 2012; Hicks et al., 2008; Hulme & Murphree, 2001a) was clearly reflected. The engendered transnational streamlining of approaches, terminologies, and activities (Bongers & Tennigkeit, 2010; Johnson, 1976; Mackey, 2008; Meyer et al., 1997; O'Neill, 1996) was also evident in the similarity of the individual programmes implemented. Activities were implemented along three principal axes: reforestation, livelihood enhancement, and local institutional transformation.

The minimal success of the big mediatised tree-planting drives illustrated graphically how important are the consideration of the *context* in planning and management, the context-specificity of tree species used, and management arrangements set up for such initiatives to have an actual environmental impact in line with (Coe, Sinclair, & Barrios, 2014; Smith-Dumont, Bonhomme, Pagella, & Sinclair, 2017). It also emphasises the importance of tree *growing* beyond tree planting (Duguma, Minang, Aynekulu, Carsan, et al., 2020).

The extraordinary focus on the promotion of improved beekeeping practices in the context of targeting biodiversity conservation from a livelihoods-centred approach revealed that while 'traditional ecological knowledge' or 'local knowledge' of the local community, as well as 'context-specificity', were considered, as supported by various authors (Brown, 2003; Coe et al., 2014; Smith-Dumont et al., 2017), they were approached mainly through region-specific 'community conservation blueprints' in which 'locality' and 'context-specificity' were constructed exogenously. These were exclusively defined and implemented by stakeholders who were external to the Eastern Mau without engaging in a proper participatory and consultative process in which local community members could express themselves and set their own priorities and agendas, and largely prevented the development of a sense of agency and ownership among community members (Fuchs, Peters, & Neufeldt, 2019; Maathai, 2010; Martin, 2005), but were rather in line with what Cormier-Salem and Bassett (2007) call 'exogenous claims' to natural heritage, as criticised in other instances (Adams & Hulme, 2001; Cormier-Salem & Bassett, 2007; Dressler et al., 2010; Siebert & Belsky, 2014; Weisser et al., 2011). The focus on beekeeping also displayed that the place-based community definition was too narrow and solely focused on members of the sedentarised local Ogiek community, either explicitly or implicitly, as observed in other instances by McLain (2001), Agrawal and Gibson (1999), Charnley and Poe (2007), and Ojha et al. (2016).

The fact that all projects almost exclusively promoted beekeeping furthermore stands in awkward opposition to the popularity of climate change literature and climate change adaptation approaches that promote the farm and income diversification as fundamental strategies to increase households' adaptive capacity given changing climatic conditions (Akinnagbe & Irohibe, 2015; Hassan & Nhemachena, 2008; Howden, Soussana, Tubiello, Chhetri, Dunlop, & Meinke, 2007; Noriega, Dawson, Vernooy, Köhler-Rollefson, & Halewood, 2017). The external definition of regionally relevant, context-specific practices and the neglect of broader climate change adaptation approaches illustrate the fundamental and momentous problem of there being no officially mandated organisation to channel, align, and vet external actors' offers. While the Necofa project team visibly attempted to integrate various project activities to generate synergies and co-benefits on the ground, presumably also in an attempt to reduce the risks of 'NGO fatigue' among community members in case different actors proposed different activities, and the relatively smooth integration of various projects was exclusively due to the Necofa country coordination's personal interest, this integration was not in any way required by any regulatory state institution. There were, hence, no centralised attempts to create vertical or horizontal linkages within and among different governance levels in the Eastern Mau. Vertical linkages among different projects and actors at the local level might have been critical due to resource areas belonging to larger integrated landscapes being divided by governance boundaries, in line with observations made by Nagendra and Ostrom (2012) and Fuchs et al. (2018).

The fact that project implementers planned to give community members 'per diems' for participating in the activities they offered, a practice problematised, for instance, in Peters (2010), D. Smith (2003), Vian (2009), and Vian, Miller, Themba, and Bukuluki (2013), was interesting in several regards. First, it displayed to what extent the project implementers understood that community members had an underlying expectation of receiving a 'sitting allowance'. At the same time, it also illustrated that activities implemented by external actors were designed to be 'exogenous' to local community members since these projects were implemented from the onset 'against' a local community that was represented as 'hostile' to what the projects had to offer and whose interest in preserving their environment supposedly needed to be guaranteed by involving them in a wage-labour relationship. These approaches are critiqued in Martin (2005) and Maathai (2010), highlighting the fundamental conceptual difficulties with PES schemes, despite their popularity.

Both the setting of priority activities and the casualness with which 'per diems' were planned revealed that the project's very design was exclusionist since it exclusively proposed practices that were in line with the externally attributed 'identity' of one specific group of forest dwellers, the Ogiek. This was problematic in many ways, for instance, because it defined the Ogiek as a largely monolithic group of people whose internal divisions and varying interests and preferences were supposedly overridden by their historical identity as 'guardians of the forest', in line with common 'community' ascriptions as addressed for instance in Gibson and Koontz (1998). Tailoring the project activities towards only one of the forest-dwelling communities contained an underlying connotation that they were primarily held responsible for forest destruction; and that they were the only ones considered responsible, but perhaps also able, to rehabilitate the forest. Other forest-dwelling communities were left out 'by design' and during implementation, which led to them not being able to partake meaningfully. While local Ogiek elites and 'power brokers' arguably also deliberately contributed to centring existing project offers around themselves and those within the local Ogiek community that were 'loyal' to them – revealing considerable elite capture in both descriptive and substantive representation, which further solidified their position in society, as found in various other studies including Agrawal and Gibson (1999), Leach et al. (1999), Peluso et al. (1994), Compagnon (2000), Hulme and Murphree (2001a), Poteete and Ribot (2011), and Chomba et al. (2015) – it also displayed that the projects had no mechanism for dealing with social differentiation and power imbalances among the local community, in line with observations made by Martin (2005). As a result, community inclusion and the very notion of 'community' in the Eastern Mau became 'ethnicised' and became equivalent to being Ogiek, in line with similar results in Gibson and Koontz (1998).

Beyond that, the specific nature of promoting modern beekeeping and honey production for export was also problematic. While producing and selling agricultural produce to international markets can be beneficial, such undertakings involve numerous risks that are often ignored or downplayed by those engaged in their promotion. One major risk factor is the value chain actors' vulnerability to changing policy environments that might see a window of opportunity for accessing foreign markets duty-free changed without warning, either by changing the standards and enhancing requirements or by closing the window altogether. Another risk is that production for export might increase and outweigh production for subsistence, with farmers engaged in the former registering significant profits and thus being able to acquire more land. At the same time, the latter might lose their land for the benefit of a crop being cultivated that is not locally consumed. The combination of potentially changing policy environments with the cultivation of locally irrelevant crops can lead to an essential under-supply of local markets that, at the same time, can also not act as a safety net and absorb additional production in case of problems with the export business (Achterbosch, van Berkum, & Meijerink, 2014). In the context of promoting export business development, the projects also promoted the uptake of various microfinance products. While access to working capital and hence credit are essential for business expansion, research on microfinance institutions over the past few decades provides important lessons in terms of the financial and particularly social and psychological burdens that engagement in microfinance schemes can engender in rural communities whenever proper training and financial literacy were not sufficiently considered (J. Anderson & Ahmed, 2016; Collins, Morduch, & Rutherford, 2009). The external actors on the ground in Mariashoni did not seem to be aware of or particularly interested in addressing the potential risks of their engagement in these terms.

Sustainable management of natural resources was further sought by building and strengthening the capacity of the local CFA. Strengthening institutions that are intended to involve the 'community voice' in joint environmental management planning with state institutions is in line with more progressive streams within the power-sharing paradigm on PFM and the overall community conservation spectrum (Blaikie, 2006; Kellert et al., 2000). According to one expert, the EU's engagement in local institution building at least translated some degree of interest in power-sharing approaches to PFM and interest in investing further in long-term sustainable resource-management structures and mechanisms and not only in shorter-term livelihood programmes [1/022]. However, the limited support for CFAs through government offices, and the KFS' active denial of support for any kind of power-sharing arrangements that were, on paper, provided for by the 2005 Forests Act, including the establishment of a joint management agreement, or even the establishment of PELIS, which falls under the benefit-sharing paradigm, prevented the CFA or any other community vehicle to define, implement, and arbitrate resource-use rights, and hence prevented meaningful power-sharing, in line with Agrawal and Ribot (1999), Agrawal and Gibson (1999), and Chomba et al. (2015). Indeed, the only role the CFA seemed to play was to be 'the eye of the KFS on the ground' and to witness the observance of the 'fences-and-fines' regulations for the forest reserve and report any suspicious incidents to the KFS, which is in line with both an instrumentalisation of the CFA, which allowed the state to outsource forest patrolling to community agents in line with observations made by Chomba et al. (2015), and a de facto increase of state control over both forest reserves and communities by co-opting the CFA into enforcing coercive forest regulations, as argued in Charnley and Poe, 2007. It further illustrated the resistance of the traditional resource managing ministries and institutions, as well as the wider traditional resource-management system, to change and embrace polycentrality in forest governance, in line with Charnley and Poe (2007); Chomba et al. (2015); and Dressler et al. (2010). Beyond that, it seemed that co-opting CFA officials into 'thinking' forest production at once increased the acceptance of forest commodification approaches among influential community members since the CFA officials were arguably exclusively drawn from the local Ogiek elite and contributed to the CFA vehicle being used exclusively in a benefit-sharing optic, while it could have been a powerful and legally backed tool for requesting powers over the forests to be shared. The existing CFA hence failed in two fundamental aspects that, according to Gibson and Koontz (1998), render community conservation successful: the CFA members failed to develop shared values regarding the Mau Forest and a vision for how the forest should be managed on the one hand, and the CFA, as an institution, did also not translate any supposed values into rules that the members would follow and that could have defended these values the other hand. Since the 'form' of the CFA was preconceived, there was no institutional development based on any shared values, any 'content', in the first place; and the CFA vehicle remained essentially meaningless.

The very existence of a CFA furthermore displayed another interesting dynamic: while the 2002 Water Act provided for the creation of WRUAs, whose internal organisation and tasks in terms of contributing to watershed management are mainly parallel to the ones of CFAs in forest management, there was no WRUA in Mariashoni – displaying the fact that the Mau Forest crisis was predominantly framed as a forestry problem, and not as a water management problem, and this contributed to national and international actors mainly focusing on forestry-related activities and support.

Considering the core contributions made by external actors to 'Saving the Mau', several meta-level observations can be made. First, the focus on supporting supposedly sustainable livelihood activities translated an alignment of the 'Save the Mau' initiative to current evolutions in priorities and framings, both in terms of the Government's problem identification and the definition of solutions, within the aid industry. The promotion of livelihood activities hence potentially manifested an underlying understanding of the Mau destruction as a function of poverty, a popular framing of environmental crises in terms of the Poverty-Environment Nexus in general (Martin, 2005; Nunan, 2015) and the destruction of Mau Forest particularly (GoK, 2009e). As discussed, the support for sustainable livelihoods was furthermore aligned to the shift witnessed in 'thinking' environmental conservation with the adoption of more holistic ecosystem approaches, which appreciate human beings as central actors in 'natural' environments (Compagnon, 2000; Cronon, 1996; World Resources Institute et al., 2007). Most actively promoted activities were based on the assumption that further environmental conservation measures would only bear fruit once the livelihood question was addressed, in line with Adams & Hulme (2001). This assumption further included the idea that the forest could only be recovered if people found alternatives to a life in which their livelihoods primarily depend on forest resource extraction and destruction, in line with, for example, Barrow and Murphree (2001) and Compagnon (2000). Beyond that, external support for the establishment and sustenance of sustainable livelihoods also targeted the provision of incentives for the local communities to support conservation in line with the moral argument made by the sustainable development thinkers according to which it was not justifiable for environmental conservation to disadvantage local community members (World Commission on Environment and Development, 1987). The approaches taken in the Eastern Mau were also in line with promoters of benefit-sharing approaches to participatory natural resource management, who argue that incentives need to be set in a way to allow for the benefits of environmental conservation outweighing the benefits of environmental destruction (Mogaka et al., 2001).

Beyond the alignment of activities on the ground with transnational evolutions in terms of appreciating community's rights and potentially positive impact on natural resources on the one hand, and in detecting and fighting against the presumed contribution of the Poverty-Environment Nexus to the Mau crisis, on the other hand, the activities implemented on the ground also demonstrated that actors in the field were able to seize the opportunities presented by the 'season of climate change' [1/026] on the world agenda to obtain funding for presumed climate change mitigation and adaptation activities, and, in line with Weisser et al.'s (2011, 2013) argument, it also illustrated the 'plasticity' of the climate change debate to accommodate various preconceived 'development' activities under a new 'Save the Mau' frame. The efforts made by the Prime Minister's office, under whose responsibility the coordination of the Mau restoration initiatives had initially been placed, to brand the Mau crisis in terms of 'climate change', 'sustainable development', and 'biodiversity preservation' (GoK, 2009d, 2009e, 2010c) can be understood along the same lines. The former Prime Minister's engagement illustrated at least two dynamics. On the one hand, it manifested the internalisation and familiarisation of current international environmental discourses and priorities. On the other hand, it showed the extent to which environmental crises at present were 'boundary objects' (Fujimura, 1992, p. 168), characterised by a 'deliberate and useful vagueness' (Guyer & Richards, 1996, p. 7), which allowed various actors to appropriate the situation and have it serve existing agendas (Timura, 2001). In that vein, previously introduced and proposed environmental conservation measures were 'climatically reframed' and hence 'legitimised by making reference to climate change' (Weisser et al., 2011). One critical expert claimed that the Mau restoration narrative was a welcome justification for the Kenyan government to reclaim Public Land. Since the 'world agenda focuses on climate change' [1/026] and environmental protection, environmental rhetoric and presumed conservation objectives were foregrounded to mask the Government's underlying goal to reclaim these lands. He added that because reclaiming land from those to whom it had initially been illegally allocated was risky for the state, the Government let the conservation aid NGOs struggle and solve the problem [1/026].

Another expert remarked that the plasticity of the Mau crisis encouraged opportunistic behaviours in NGOs and that many of them used the destruction of the Mau to make money without effectively doing anything [1/040]. This 'seizing of the moment' behaviour was, for instance, evident in the fact that all NGO activities in the Eastern Mau Forest concentrated on land and human rights issues before the Task Force visited the area. In contrast, NGO engagement exclusively focused on conservation and livelihood concerns after their visit.[20] The importance of framing these activities in internationally 'fashionable' terms also manifested in the fact that the funding source of ProMara, the most visible internationally funded initiative in the Mau Complex, shifted from the 'economic growth and conflict' docket within USAID to the 'climate change and biodiversity' docket without undergoing any programmatic changes [1/018]. One KWTA expert called the climate change labelling of efforts undertaken in the Mau, including by the KWTA, at least 'partly opportunistic' [1/010]. He said that addressing the Mau Forest rehabilitation and the management of the country's water towers in terms of 'climate change' allowed them to tap into different funding sources. In the context of REDD and REDD+ projects that compensate countries of the Global South for avoiding deforestation during agricultural expansion through 'green finance' mecha-

---

[20] Observation on the transformation of NGO engagement in Mariashoni, 13 April 2012.

nisms or carbon trade markets, they were able to apply for funding for forest recovery projects. He said they also tapped into resources for private-public partnerships through which private sector companies 'green' their businesses. Since Kenya, at present, did not have a legal framework for involving industries in the 'greening' business, institutions such as the ICS and the KWTA were able to accommodate activities that might typically fall under the 'corporate social responsibility' dockets of the companies in question. He further opined that these 'green labels' should, in principle, be based on Kenya's National Appropriate Mitigation Action plan (NAMA), which looked at emissions of different sectors of the country's economy and attempted to strategise how these emissions could be reduced. REDD money and other 'greening' money could be used in a relevant way to support the National Appropriate Mitigation Action plan. He, however, added that Kenya had no relevant environmental policies that legislated and monitored energy over-use or inefficiency. Since these major climate change contributors were not well regulated, it remained difficult to tap into global resources on the one hand and make an impact on the other [1/007].

The Government's opportunism and lack of clear strategy were also evident in the fact that it accepted any available funding, even if it meant taking World Bank money for the economic empowerment of the Ogiek in the Eastern Mau, while at the same time accepting donor funds supporting a 'fences and fines approach' to forest restoration that were to support evictions of local dwellers from the forest. The absence of coordination was also evident in the billion-dollar KAPAP project, whose employees confirmed that they did not have any official relations with the ICS in Nakuru County, under whose mandate the coordination of Mau restoration initiatives fell, despite being hosted at the Provincial Administration office in Nakuru town [1/023].

The importance of international agendas was translated into the kinds of projects that attracted funding and the timing when activities stopped, or funding stopped. According to ProMara's Chief of Party, the good personal relationship between the former US ambassador and the former Prime Minister, who had previously joined hands in tree-planting drives in the Eastern Mau, facilitated the engagement of the US government in the Mau restoration effort in the first place [1/018]. At the same time, another ProMara staff member expressed the belief that USAID did not extend the programme after the initial two years because it did not want to be perceived as siding with the former Prime Minister before the 2013 elections (when he stood for the Presidency) [1/031]. The failure of the project to obtain another round of funding after its lapse in 2012 might, given the political changes brought about by these elections and the accompanying narrowing interest in conservation in general and in 'Saving the Mau' in particular, thus also be understood in political terms ahead of the 2013 elections. ProMara's

Chief of Party highlighted the importance of external actors since 'the Government has a conservation-focused approach' [1/018] only, and neither addressed the relevant underlying causes and issues of forest destruction nor released the funds required to tackle the crisis. USAID consequently opted to support a regional climate project, targeting policy and legal issues rather than action on the ground [1/031].

Overall, it is evident that, despite a long history of conservation and environmental policies, there was no integrated environmental agenda and no underlying holistic approach to the conservation of the Eastern Mau, in line with approaches to other forests in the country outside of national parks. It seemed that specific, limited interests and actions established existing conservation policies, often defended and justified by a suitable discourse and rhetoric elaborated *a posteriori* that was aligned with what was 'fashionable'. Furthermore, external actors remained crucial for conceptualising, funding, and implementing initiatives to 'Save the Mau', displaying to what degree the protection of vital national resources was outsourced. Furthermore, in promoting a specific version of what PFM was supposed to look like, by defining 'desirable' activities, alongside 'desirable' project beneficiaries and hence somewhat 'desirable' identities, and in providing space for local elites to capture resources, knowledge, and exposure, conservation aid contributed to a de facto reduction of democratic spaces in natural resource management, which had at least been acquired on paper through the 2005 Forest Act, and thus led to a diminishing emphasis on truly community-driven conservation activities, as documented for similar situations in Martin (2005). Dressler et al. (2010) found that disempowerment of local communities through the design and delivery of alleged CBNRM projects was particularly common due to protectionism resurging in the context of 'green political visions' related to the fight against climate change, which was certainly true for the 'Save the Mau' initiative specifically, and the Kenyan government's general approach to securing the 'water towers', for instance by extending the label 'water tower' to more and more wetlands, which came with 'nationalising' these territories and placing them permanently under the control of the central Government[21] after the 2010 decentralisation had been implemented in natural resource governance.

---

[21]   Apollo, S., 'Agency to gazette 70 more water towers in race to save forests', *Daily Nation*, 13 March 2018.

2

Institutional Failure or Setting Priorities? The Continuation in Exploitation-focused Forest Management

The scramble for the Mau Forest began with the colonial government's need for fuelwood, especially for their newly built railway, by the end of the 19th century [1/021]. After forest reservation had begun as early as 1911 in some parts of the country (Bassett & Crummey, 2003), most of the Mau Forest was gazetted in 1932 (GoK, 2009e), which allowed the colonial government to define the forest as an exploitable commodity. The Eastern Mau Forest, specifically, was gazetted in 1941 (Republic of Kenya, 2016b). The primary purpose of creating this forest reserve was to produce timber and wood, two of the most critical resources needed during the construction and expansion of the new colonial economy, and the sprawling railway line particularly [1/021]. After Independence, the Government's approach to forest management continued relying on forestry-based perspectives that had concentrated on commercial wood and timber production since colonial times (GoK, 2009e).

The central paradox of the politicised environment: The state's roles as both developer and protector

The features of the politicised environment of forest governance in Kenya were discussed in detail in the previous chapter. Additional features introduced here focus specifically on commercial forest exploitation as an important sector of the national and local economy, its principal actors, and its ties to the Government.

Structural focus on forest production and development rather than protection

The state is the most influential actor in defining environmental and land-use management priorities, practices, and policies in Kenya, as in most countries. Yet, the state's role in terms of shaping the environment is fundamentally influenced by a 'central paradox', 'an inherent, continuing potential for conflict between the state's roles as developer and as protector and steward of the natural environment on which its existence ultimately depends' (Walker, 1989, p. 32). This paradox is often particularly evident in forest management policies since forests are primarily framed as a renewable source of forest products, including wood, timber, and non-timber forest products (NTFPs), also called non-wood forest products (NWFPs), despite encompassing primary natural and secondary plantation forests, and despite the recognition that forests play various other roles. In terms of forest products, forests are the source of timber products, including fire-wood, office paper, newspaper, paper for books, toilet paper, construction timber, plywood, and wood for furniture, as well as NTFPs including rope and roofing materials, fruits and nuts, and other edible plant parts, floral greens, fibre, dye, oils, resins, plant-derived medicines, etc. (Charnley & Poe, 2007; FAO, 2012). Tellingly, only 11.2% of the world's total forested area was designated for conservation in the early 2000s, with an African average of 16.4% (FAO, 2006), while more than half of the world's original forest area had been converted to other uses (Diamond, 2005).

While 96% of Kenya's forests officially fell under a status that implies forest conservation (FAO, 2010), active forest management, in Kenya, as elsewhere, is traditionally aimed at securing timber and wood supply (Mugo, Nyandiga, & Gachanja, 2010; Thenya, Wandago, Nahama, & Gachanja, 2008). By 2013, forest production fell primarily under the 2005 Forest Act that replaced the controversial Forests Act, more commonly referred to as Cap. 385, and the Timber Act (Cap. 386). In line with the 2005 Forest Act, the KFS managed forests and entire forest management cycles. Despite important changes, the Act endorses scientific forestry and silviculture and is primarily concerned with the rational management of a commodified resource and hence 'a political-economic system for resource control' (Peluso, 1992, p. 237). Silviculture has traditionally involved high levels of social and spatial control, favoured national interests over all others, prioritised industrial raw materials like pulp or timber over other forest uses (Klooster, 2009), and has typically struggled to include community-based forest management (CBFM) principles.

Much of the tension in environmental and land-use management can hence be explored against the background of the inherent potential for conflict between the pursuit of economic interests, which often entails a commodification of the environment and natural resources for the sake of development on the one hand, and sustainable environmental conservation priorities on the other hand. As evident in consecutive forest policies and especially practices, forest management in Kenya prioritised achieving objectives of the state's role as the developer rather than as steward of the environment.

Attempts to end deforestation by imposing restrictions on forest access

The Government's practical approach to regulating forest extraction included introducing a logging ban in the late 1990s. At the time, the country experienced significant problems conserving its forests and keeping its timber and wood supply constant. These difficulties had become apparent during President Moi's era and escalated towards the late 1980s and 1990s (GoK, 2009e). According to the Mariashoni KFS forester, the forest mismanagement experienced at that time mainly occurred in three forms. First, forest plantations that were easily accessible, for which harvesting costs were thus relatively low, were often harvested too early, before the trees reached maturity. Second, the harvested areas were poorly or not at all replanted. Third, plantations that were more difficult to access were not harvested at all: consequently, there were remnants of over-mature forests that should have been harvested since not harvesting those trees meant losing them to their slow decomposition. He added that the digression from the initial plan went to the extent that the country's forests were slowly dying while politicians and foresters were pointing fingers at each other for the destruction of the forest [3/062].

Academics mainly blamed corrupt management structures and practices involving various government officers from the Forest Department at the top to the district officers at the local level for forest depletion and underproduction of wood and timber, which peaked in the 1990s (Mugo et al., 2010; Njeru, 2012; Standing & Gachanja, 2014).

Considering the problems experienced with widespread depletion and destruction of the country's forests, a countrywide logging ban was introduced in 1999 (Republic of Kenya, 2009b).[1] The logging ban, presumed to be an instrument employed by the Government to protect the country's ailing forests, put a moratorium on logging activities. However, it only applied to small and medium-sized sawmills since the flawed registration process for these sawmills was considered to have played an essential role in the forest destruction experienced.[2] While the logging ban restricted logging activities of most sawmills, a few timber companies continued being allowed to harvest forest plantations. Specifically, the ban excluded the country's four biggest timber companies, namely Timsales, Raiply, Comply, and (the intermittently

---

[1]   See also: Gitonga, M., 'Logging ban blocks Sh40 billion from the economy', *Daily Nation*, 22 May 2010.

[2]   The terms 'small and medium scale sawmillers', 'sawmillers', and 'sawmills' is used to refer to all the smaller companies operating in the timber and wood industry apart from the 'big three' commercial and politically connected timber companies.

defunct) Pan African Paper Mills (Standing & Gachanja, 2014).[3] These four companies had also been given extensive concessions to about approximately half of the country's forest plantations, especially in the Mau Forest (Standing & Gachanja, 2014). Beyond that, the ban had an interesting legal status since it was solely based on a three-month moratorium on logging activities in 1999. After these three months, the moratorium was 'put on a shelf' [2/048] and never officially revoked until October 2011 [1/008],[4] despite the enactment of the 2005 Forest Act and its implementation in 2007.

The lifting of the ban was brought about by an appeal from the KFS, who petitioned the Government, supported by the influential Kenya Forestry Society [1/012]. The Society argued that the ban led to wasted revenue because trees in overgrown forests were falling and rotting. This was particularly relevant in exotic tree plantations with trees older than forty to fifty years. Spokespersons of the KFS argued that the logging ban in public forests had locked up KES 40 billion (USD $400 million) in revenues, notably because of the remaining local timber industry's inability to harvest approximately 38,000 ha of over-mature exotic tree plantations valued at KES 36 billion ($360 million). They added that another 18,000 ha of trees aged between ten and twenty-two years were due for thinning, valued at KES 3.5 billion ($35 million).[5] The KFS further argued that a lift would empower the KFS financially and help them afforest and reforest the country. After the KFS petitioned Parliament, and after Parliament approved it, the Cabinet confirmed the countrywide lift alongside a re-introduction of a concession management framework (Republic of Kenya, 2016b), which re-introduced a competitive tender system for forest user rights allocation, specifically logging or felling rights for timber companies. Henceforth all registered sawmills, including small and medium-scale sawmillers, could submit bids for logging rights in tendered forest sections again. Part of the request submitted by the KFS was a systematic reforestation plan in which sawmillers would be responsible for replanting the sections previously harvested under the supervision of the KFS [1/008]. The request further included a provision that positioned the Board of the KFS as a decision-maker in an apparent attempt to curb the widespread corruption witnessed before the ban's introduction. Then, the power of

[3]   See also: Wairimu, I., 'Timsales takes Nema to court over tree felling ban', *The Star*, 29 October 2011; 'Dire shortage of timber forcing merchants to import commodity', *Coast Week*, 19 November 2010.
[4]   According to the Dean of the School of Environmental Studies at Kenyatta University, the logging ban was a mere political declaration, whose legal implication was unclear. Since it was a purely political declaration, it required a political declaration to revoke it [1/012].
[5]   Gitonga, M., 'Logging ban blocks Sh40 billion from the economy', *Daily Nation*, 22 May 2010.

allocating tenders was in the hands of District Forest Officers (DFOs), and thus the direct representatives of the President at the district level [3/077]. The forest management units, the Forest Department at the national level and the DFOs at the district level used to work together with the President. In the Mau Forest, for instance, logging rights were allocated to the big timber companies to clear the land for settlement schemes devised by the President [1/008]. Mariashoni was one such settlement scheme.

Before the lifting of the ban, the Timber Manufacturers Association (TMA), the association representing the interests of sawmillers, had protested their exclusion from the timber business and appealed to the Government numerous times in vain [1/008]. The former chairman of the association, in office from 2009 to 2014, said that the TMA was utterly paralysed during the logging ban. After the lift of the ban in late 2011, sawmillers started gaining in importance again, and with them, the TMA, which, in 2012, associated approximately six hundred saw-millers all over the country [2/048]. Despite widespread criticism of the ban, various actors protested its lift because of its association with the introduction of the Concession Management Framework [1/030].

Historical and technological legacies of commercial forest production in the Mau Forest

The Molo DFO, who was the primary person in charge of the manage-ment of the Eastern Mau Forest, retraced the beginnings of the Mau Forest's commercial use to 1902, when the colonial administration's interest in timber production led to the establishment of plantations containing fast-growing exotic tree species. This followed the publica-tion of the first Crown Lands Ordinance. In the early stages of colonial forestry, eucalyptus species were planted on sloping areas within the Mau. Later, cypress (particularly *Cypressus lusitanica*) and pine (*Pinus patchula*) became the first and second most commonly planted trees in Mau Forest, followed by eucalyptus species [2/047]. According to Mari-ashoni's famous Ogiek leader, the progressive clearing of the Eastern Mau started in 1918. The first sawmill in the area was taken into oper-ation in 1932 when most of the Mau Forest was gazetted. From 1941, when the eastern part of the Mau Forest was gazetted specifically (Republic of Kenya, 2016b), large-scale legal exploitation of the forest in the area began [3/055]. Big and small sawmillers commercially extracted resources in all gazetted forest plantations until 1999, when the informal logging ban was introduced. While plantation forests were mainly established at the edges of the indigenous forests in Njoro, Nessuit, and Molo, on the outer edges of the Eastern Mau Forest, the FAN Director argued that the Government supposedly only started cutting the indigenous forest and started replanting the deforested areas with exotic trees after Independence, around 1964/65 [1/033].

Changes in forest management structures and institutions over time

While being subjected to colonial forest production and exploitation from the turn of the century, the organisation and management of the Mariashoni area through the Mariashoni Forest Station specifically began in 1959, according to its forester. In 1959, British national W. McDonald was appointed as the first forester of Mariashoni Forest Station to sustainably manage the local forest's commercial exploitation [3/069].

Forest management was initially under the responsibility of the colonial and post-colonial Forest Departments and was only handed over to the newly created KFS in 2007. Considering that the Forest Department had been mainly held responsible for the mismanagement and illegal allocation of forest land to influential individuals under the previous government, the new government prioritised the creation of the KFS to improve forest management after the democratic transition in 2002. According to the Molo DFO, the tasks and responsibilities of the forest guards on the ground remained constant since modern forestry's inception during colonial times, despite institutional changes [2/047]. The KFS forester stationed at Mariashoni Forest Station explained that the KFS assumed responsibility for managing the country's forests in 2007, including both indigenous forests and exotic tree plantations, if the land in question was officially gazetted as forest land and thus placed under government stewardship.

The tasks and realm of forest management institutions

The primary tasks of the KFS in Mariashoni were the same as everywhere in the country and primarily related to the planning and management of forest harvest cycles, including planting, pruning and thinning, advertisement of mature trees, vetting of licensed bidders, sale to the highest bidder, issuance of permits, monitoring harvest and transport, replanting forest plantations, etc. [3/062]. The KFS was furthermore responsible for policing the forest areas, ensuring that obligations in forest rehabilitation and conservation were followed, and addressing illegal forest activities. These responsibilities were delegated to the foresters assigned to each forest station, both for policing and for conserving the area under their jurisdiction. While the KFS was responsible for both indigenous and secondary exotic forests, the KFS' main task was to ensure continuous forest production, mainly for timber and wood supply. Hence, the KFS was only responsible for planting trees in forest plantations and was even 'not supposed to'

[3/069] plant trees in settlement areas, according to the Mariashoni forester. In indigenous forest parts, the KFS patrols only had to ensure that people did not encroach [3/062]. At the same time, some 'enrichment planting' with dominant indigenous trees was also done in areas where the primary forest remained, alongside replanting of exotic trees in the forest plantation areas [3/069]. This clear focus on the 'developer' and 'provider' role, as opposed to the 'steward' or 'guardian' role (Bryant & Bailey, 1997), might also explain why indigenous trees were progressively removed and replaced with more 'useful' exotic trees. Forest management and policies had thus mainly been concerned with managing an extractable, exploitable, and divisible resource and much less with holistic conservation of vital ecosystems and habitats, in line with the implementation of a 'fences and fines approach' through forest gazettement, which was an expression of forest commodification for sustainable forest production rather than biodiversity conservation [3/055, 3/059].

To manage forest cycles in all gazetted forests, the Government established a 25-year Kenya Forest Master Plan in 1991 (Chomba et al., 2015). Mariashoni's forester explained that this 'felling plan' included information about the extent of land under forest plantation and earmarked the same number of hectares for harvest at defined times, depending on the maturation cycles of the respective tree species. Once harvesting came, the KFS placed advertisements in the country's major newspapers inviting tenders for these specific forest portions within a particular time window. As previously addressed, this tender system was re-introduced after the logging ban was lifted in 2011 [1/008, 1/030]. He gave the example that if a plantation of 20 ha of cypress was established, and it was fixed that the maturation period of cypress was twenty-eight years, then permits would be given out for these same 20 ha of mature cypresses after twenty-eight years. He added that only licensed sawmillers could enter bids and that only prequalified sawmillers could get these licences. To be licensed, a company's machinery needed to be inspected, and the sawmillers needed to prove they could harvest and saw without producing waste. Only when they passed the inspection did the local authorities license them. The forester said several sawmillers in the Eastern Mau area were licensed to submit tenders. Ultimately, he said, the highest bidder would get the portion on sale. The sawmill then had to pay the agreed price for the material and apply for the relevant transport permits. The KFS transport permit forms provided extensive information about the type of trees that could be loaded and transported. In cases in which sawmillers bought advertised trees, KFS officers then were at the scene during loading to confirm the trees loaded were the trees sold [3/062].

Allocation of permits for legal forest use was part of a forester's job. There were three different categories of permits. The first was a firewood permit 'for women', meaning for household consumption. This permit cost KES 100 ($1) per month and allowed women to collect dry and fallen wood as firewood within the forest plantations in the range of one headload per day. In Mariashoni, these permits were only required if one was interested in getting firewood from the remaining 1,000 ha of forest land under the Mariashoni Forest Station's jurisdiction, but since there were trees within the settlements, and women could collect firewood from there, only very few permits were sought. The second type of permit was for those who collect firewood for sale. For instance, this type of permit was required for the men who transported firewood on their bicycles, whom we often met on our way to and from Mariashoni. One could collect two headloads per day, which required the second type of permit that costs KES 200 ($2) per month. Again, this permit was only necessary if one wanted to collect that firewood from within the forest plantations, a practice that was even encouraged since it was believed that the collection of fallen and dry branches for firewood reduced the risk of forest fires. The third type of permit was required for those engaging in the timber and wood business. These permits were mandatory to transport tree logs, regardless of whether those who transported the logs had a right to cut them. The trees were sold in a separate process, and the wood prices were calculated according to the value and species of the trees in question [3/062]. However, the prices of the transport permits for tree logs depended on the tonnage of the vehicle used. Vehicles with a capacity of two to four tons had to pay KES 1,000 ($10), those with a capacity of five to seven tons had to pay KES 1,500 ($15), and those above seven tons had to pay KES 2,000 ($20). After a permit was obtained, the sawmillers could transport as many logs as they wanted for two working days. These were restricted to working hours from 6 am to 6 pm [3/069]. The forester further said that transport permits had to be obtained by anyone ferrying trees, even by residents who wanted to take the trees they harvested on their farms to town. Since he was responsible for licensing the transport of forest commodities, it was also his responsibility to apprehend those who were found transporting firewood or logs without a permit and those caught cutting trees without a permit.

Due to the de facto establishment of the Mariashoni settlement scheme, only around 1,000 ha of the initial 7,000 ha of forest land, or 'forest blocks', that used to fall under the jurisdiction of Mariashoni Forest Station, had remained. These were parts of blocks eight and ten, according to the Forest Master Plan. These were also the only areas that armed KFS forest guards patrolled. It was also only within that area that the KFS controlled logging activities and arrested persons found cutting trees illegally. While the thirteen forest guards seconded to Mariashoni Forest Station mainly patrolled the remaining forest blocks, the forester said that they were also supposed to protect the remaining trees within the settlement scheme because people were not supposed to cut the trees on that land either and added that cutting indigenous trees was 'very illegal' [3/062], even on Private Land, unless environmental impact assessments were carried out. The Molo DFO compared cutting indigenous trees to the poaching of wild animals [2/047]. He furthermore explained that he had two ways of punishing those found engaging in small-scale timber and wood businesses illegally; either take them to the police or 'sentence' them to 'community service' by working in the KFS tree nursery. He added that he preferred a 'personal approach and try(ing) to understand the intentions for cutting' [3/062], so he hardly ever took anyone to the authorities.

With the implementation of the 'Save the Mau' initiative, the tasks of the KFS in the Mau Forest were slightly adapted because the KFS was part of the joint enforcement unit and hence responsible for the implementation of rehabilitation measures as designated by the ICS, including for evictions of forest dwellers and the conversion of former settlement areas to forest land. The ICS furthermore ordered that all exploitation in the areas that used to hold primary forest should be stopped to rehabilitate the Mau. Consequently, a moratorium was put in place for all areas where settlements had been established on forest land to allow the Government to define the forest boundaries [2/047]. However, from 2011 to 2013, commercial forestry in the Eastern Mau continued day in and day out by both big timber companies and small sawmills. Hence, it was unclear whether this moratorium was ever effectively enforced.[6]

Continuation of commercial forest production in the Eastern Mau

In the Eastern Mau, forest management continued to fall under the KFS' responsibility, despite the grossly reduced unambiguous forest land area within Mariashoni Location. While a change in land use was prompted by a de facto change in the legal status in much of the Eastern Mau Forest after the establishment of various settlement schemes in the 1990s, the remaining forest land in the Eastern Mau was still managed to support commercial forest production and exploitation.

Despite the 'Save the Mau' initiative, and to the surprise of many observers, state-sanctioned and thus not illegal forest exploitation

---

6   Depending on how the provision was interpreted, continuous logging in the Mau Forest might be explained by the fact that commercial forest harvesting continued being allowed in areas that could not be defined as having been forest that was illegally transformed into settlement schemes, appealing to the fact that forest plantations had existed before the controversial land excisions and settlement establishments between the late 1990s and the early 2000s.

continued day in and day out in the wider Mau Forest, including in the Eastern Mau Forest, both in official state forests and on 'private' farms after the launch of the 'Save the Mau' initiative.

Unrestricted forest exploitation for politically connected timber companies

Despite the imposition of a logging ban in 1999, deforestation continued unabatedly. Experts considered the logging ban ineffective because it excluded the country's four biggest timber and wood-producing companies, namely Timsales, Raiply, Comply, and Pan African Paper Mills. Since there was no halt to commercial forest exploitation, the logging ban was not really enforced [3/062]. 'In a real sense, it was a partial ban' [2/047] to allow the big companies to exploit the rest of the forest resources. At the same time, the logging ban led to a cessation of previous forest management practices, including replanting trees [3/062].

While Raiply and Comply operated primarily in the western parts of the Mau Forest and at a smaller scale in the western parts of the Eastern Mau close to Baraget [5/233], Timsales operated at a significant scale in the Kiptunga Forest in the Mariashoni area. Timsales' main factory was in Elburgon, the transit town at the edge of the Eastern Mau and approximately 10 km from Mariashoni Centre. It employed large numbers of residents of the area.[7] A Timsales worker named the fact that the company employed around six thousand persons as one of the major reasons why the logging ban was not extended to the company. Timsales' capacity was important since the sawmill ran on a 24-hour system, with a morning shift from 7 am to 4 pm, an afternoon shift from 4 pm to 10 pm and a night shift from 10 pm to 7 am. Following national policy, lorries could transport logs out of the forest from 6 am to 6 pm. The Timsales worker further explained that each lorry operating in the area typically made three daily round trips, driving into the forest, loading trees, and taking them to the timber mill in Elburgon. He added that Timsales lorries, altogether, made up to thirty daily trips from Kiptunga Forest to the mill. In February 2013, and right ahead of the 2013 general election, six ten-ton trucks transported logs three times daily. Logs were cut and prepared for transport by men operating power saws. In February 2013, ten power saws were used daily in the forest plantations in Kiptunga [all 5/233]. When attempting to assess the level of tree extraction through Timsales in Kiptunga Forest by

[7]   According to the 'corporate profile' on the Timsales website, which seems to have been written in the early 2000s, the company 'has a workforce of 1,500 and supports approximately 6,000 family members' (Timsales Ltd website, 'Corporate Profile', https://timsales.webflow.io/about (n.d. accessed 27 September 2013).

simply observing the number, type, and load of lorries that passed Mariashoni on their way to Elburgon, between two and eight daily trips, and an average of five trips by Timsales transits, each consisting of a truck with a trailer, were counted each day during an observation period of five days 26–30 March 2012. During that period, Timsales transported an estimated one thousand six hundred cypress or pine tree logs of five-metre length to Elburgon through Mariashoni. According to official records, Timsales only harvested pine and cypress trees from matured plantations within the Mau Forest and transformed them into plywood. Since Timsales produced soft boards, hardboards, doors, school chairs, blockboards, plywood and furniture, it officially did not use indigenous trees but cypress (*Pinus radiator* and *Pinus patchula*) and blue gum (eucalyptus) species. To service the high demand for its products, Timsales operated industrial wood dryers at the Elburgon factory [5/233]. Timsales was the only plywood supplier in the country, producing both chipboards and hardboards. Access restrictions would mean producing less than market requirements, resulting in plywood being imported [3/062]. According to the TMA chairman, both the Kenyan and the export markets were dominated by Timsales, Comply, and Raiply. He said that there were rumours that these companies combined made up to KES 20 million ($200,000) in a single day. He also said that they held over-mature plantations valued at more than KES 50 billion ($500 million) by the time of the interview in 2012 [2/048]. Mariashoni's forester confirmed that the big companies in general, particularly Timsales in the Eastern Mau, got tenders for bigger portions to be harvested because they were more competitive than smaller ones [3/062].

The Timsales worker explained how the company operated in the Kiptunga Forest. In his position as supervisor of reforestation exercises, his job was to clear tree stumps after tree harvesting by burning them, and to plant new trees. Depending on the rains, the replanting cycle was three to six months long. He said the Government started obliging all sawmills, including Timsales in the Eastern Mau, to replant trees in 2002. At that time, Timsales had cleared around 50 ha of forest within two weeks while fully operating more than forty lorries. The 2005 Forest Act then obliged the companies to whom forest tenders were awarded on Government/Public Land and in gazetted state forests to replant the land after harvest. After replanting, the new plantation was to be reverted to KFS management. The worker observed that Timsales had been depleting the forest at a significant rate despite paying lip service to forest restoration. He first said that replanting concentrated on areas easily observable from the road to maintain the impression that reforestation was done, and the forests were not harmed. He further indicated that during times of uncertainty, such as before the 2013 elections, Timsales increased trips to the forest because 'no-one knows how things will be during and after the elections' [5/233].

Another little-known but very harmful side-effect of the timber business was the lack of waste management. Since Timsales specialised in producing plywood, which uses even the smallest wood particles, there was no waste from the logs. However, highly toxic wastewater was produced while manufacturing plywood boards. According to the Timsales worker, the chemicals required for plywood production were released into the river during heavy rains, making it impossible to trace the chemicals back to the factory. During dry seasons, he explained, the company transported the toxic brew away from Elburgon town and released it elsewhere [5/233]. On multiple occasions, we observed foaming, dirty, and strongly smelling water in Elburgon's streams and rivers that transport water to downstream areas in various regions.

The environmental effect of Timsales' continuous presence in the Eastern Mau was considerable. Many locals stated that the forest line had receded steadily since the early 1990s. The results of the declaration of the settlement scheme in 1997 are discussed in more detail later, particularly the allocation of logging rights to Timsales in line with the allocation of individual plots and the quasi-total removal of trees from the settlement area during the early 1990s. The Timsales employee said that deforestation rose steeply in recent years, and while Mariashoni Centre used to be in the middle of dense forest, 'now you have to enter 30 km further to find forest' [5/233]. He cited another primary reason for deforestation in the area that, at best, puts the intricate nature of the international timber business in a nutshell and, at worst, illustrates the duplicity of international organisations: in 2008, Timsales was awarded a significant contract by the United Nations to supply wood for the construction of houses in a UN-run refugee camp in South Sudan, thereby deforesting the Mau Forest in the UN's name just one year before UNEP championed the 'Save the Mau' campaign [5/233].

Adapting to restrictions: Sawmillers' momentous strategic reorientation

While the big players in the timber industry were commonly referred to as 'timber companies', smaller-scale companies were typically called 'sawmillers'. According to Sang (2003), approximately 150 sawmills were located along the Eastern Mau Forest in the early 2000s and 200 'illegal tractor-mounted saw-benches all over the forest'.

The owner of one of these companies spoke in detail about the sawmillers' involvement in deforesting the Eastern Mau. He explained that he had taken over the business from his father in 2010, who had bought it in 1996. By then, he said, the Mau Forest was still 'intact' – and that massive deforestation was only witnessed in the Eastern Mau after 1996. The company owner further explained that he used different tree species for different purposes. He said he mainly used exotic tree species, namely cypress, pine, and blue gum (eucalyptus). Cypress and pine poles were cut when they were two to three years old and had a diameter of five to ten centimetres, and were typically used for the roof trusses of private houses. Older and bigger cypresses were sawn into boards or planks, and the remainder cut up as firewood. The man further explained that his company specialised in producing wooden doors manufactured from these planks. He added that all sawmills had to prove they operated on zero waste, and he sold his sawdust to the Menengai Oil Refineries Ltd as a firelighter component. He further used young eucalyptus poles as the foundation for the private mud-plastered houses that were common in the area, and he sold older eucalyptus poles for electricity posts. Apart from exotic trees, he used an indigenous tree known as East African Rosewood (*Hagenia abyssinica*), for furniture. He obtained most of his poles from private farms in the Kaprop area in Mariashoni [2/053].

The TMA chairman explained that the sawmillers found themselves excluded from their previous businesses 'overnight' after the introduction of the logging ban in 1999. Previously, sawmillers had benefited from direct allocations, a 'felling plan' for sawmillers, which rendered their businesses reliable and 'comfortable'. The sudden change brought about by the logging ban, announced on one day and put into effect the next, entailed devastating personal consequences for the sawmillers. He said several sawmillers died after suffering from stress-related strokes due to their inability to repay loans and mortgages and pay for machinery taken on loan. Consequently, people's properties were auctioned, and many sawmillers were economically and psychologically ruined [2/048]. The KFS Senior Deputy Director was stated to have calculated that the logging ban led to the closure of 300 sawmills with loss of 50,000 direct jobs and an estimated 300,000 indirect ones.[8] According to one sawmiller, the sawmillers had little choice but to diversify to deal with the suddenly imposed restrictions. He said most sawmillers chose between two different adaptation strategies [2/053].

The sawmiller's primary adaptation strategy was to turn away from harvesting full and mature trees for timber production and instead concentrated on using and collecting shorter and younger trees and tree segments. The small timber manufacturers thus became the 'cleaners' who were let into the forest plantations that the big companies had previously harvested. One used to send his lorries to recover leftovers from the plantations in Kiptunga Forest that Timsales had harvested. In legal terms, instead of getting permits for transporting full trees, his company would henceforth get permits for transporting firewood [2/053].

---

[8]   Gitonga, M., 'Logging ban blocks Sh40 billion from the economy', *Daily Nation*, 22 May 2010.

The second, more detrimental adaptation and diversification strategy that sawmillers started pursuing after the introduction of the logging ban involved a concentration on privately owned forests and trees. The logging ban's mandate extended to state-held forest possessions alone and excluded small companies from obtaining concessions and logging permits for these. However, it did not contain any provisions for Private Land. The sawmillers thus started targeting private landowners' trees. In practice, many legal hurdles persisted, particularly in Eastern Mau, where private individuals had been given allotment letters, but no title deeds, and legal ownership of the land hence remained unclear, another dynamic of non-protection discussed in detail in the following chapter. In Mariashoni, this lack of legal clarity was ignored, sawmillers directly negotiated deals with those who occupied a given piece of land, and trees were transported without attracting any further regulations. In the few years in which the logging ban was active, mature and immature trees spotted by sawmillers were sold, harvested, and removed from the forest on private farms at a large scale and, depending on the bargaining power of the resident concerned, often for minimal financial compensation. According to a resident of Elburgon town who used to operate a sawmill with her husband, there were local contact persons in Mariashoni who brokered deals between sawmillers and locals who were willing to sell their trees [5/255]. The woman added that a few young local Ogiek men bought trees from people's private farms and sold them to sawmillers in Elburgon, effectively working as brokers [5/117]. A resident Ogiek man said the Ogiek youths mostly gathered together trees bought from different private farms in Mariashoni Centre. They only sold them once they were sufficient to serve a given order and could be loaded [4/091]. The sawmiller confirmed that, up to the time of the interview, he was working with brokers from Elburgon who had contact with brokers in Mariashoni to seal deals [2/053]. The Timsales worker said that most sawmills up to that time were run by members of the Kikuyu community [5/233]. Another suggested that more than twenty small and medium-sized sawmills were operating semi-legally in the Mariashoni area [5/200]. Yet, a Kipsigis man who plied the Elburgon-Mariashoni road with his motorcycle taxi said, 'no Ogiek is on the winning side of that business because no-one has a trailer' [4/092]. The older men said there used to be a sawmill in Kaprop, Kaingo Sawmills, initially established by the colonial government and later handed over to one Mr Kaingo, who sold it to a local Ogiek named Kalego in 1998. However, the sawmill burned down in 1998, and since then, no other wood processing company had opened in the area or was run by an Ogiek person [4/097].

Several residents in Mariashoni, both Ogiek and *wageni*, spoke about calling to the sawmillers and selling them the trees from the land they identified as 'theirs' when they needed money [5/118, 5/168, 5/239], both within the settlement scheme and beyond. According to one resident, the sawmillers cut the trees themselves after placing an order. In other cases, residents paid local cutters to cut the trees [5/250], most likely the 'broker' youth previously discussed. By and before 2013, Mariashoni residents were often seen selling the trees on their farms to small-scale traders. Despite the legal 'coating' of their logging ventures, the sawmillers mostly seemed in a rush and often tried to conceal their activities when being observed. Many times, sawmillers were seen targeting residents for purchases who presumably had low bargaining power, such as one mentally impaired woman and one very old woman. Several residents furthermore raised concerns that improvements in the roads connecting the Mariashoni area to towns outside of the forest played an essential role in the forest destruction because *'barabara inavutia wafanya biashara wa miti'* (the road attracts tree businesspeople) [here 5/254; voiced in similar ways by numerous residents]. The small sawmillers' focus on trees from private farms often contributed to tension between neighbours because of unclear boundaries between different plots. While some claimed that boundary markers (also known as 'beacons'), which indicated the subdivisions and allocations of the land in the 'lower' sections of Mariashoni Location, were sometimes fraudulently moved to claim ownership of more trees and thus legitimacy to sell them [5/250], such conflicts played out even more vigorously in areas in the 'upper' sections of Mariashoni, where land had not been surveyed, and residents settled informally (see Map 4). Here, neighbours often did not agree on the border between the land and thus on the ownership of trees and the legitimate use of these trees [5/257].

Residents' opinions on the small sawmillers' businesses diverged as much as the prices sawmillers paid for their trees. One young Ogiek man said that the sawmillers were the worst because they targeted local farms directly, benefited from people's surprise when faced with their offer, and proceeded to carry the trees at low prices [5/148]. When discussing prices with one sawmiller, he said that one lorry's worth of logs was approximately KES 20,000 ($200) [2/053]. Confronted with the fact that some locals cited prices as low as KES 4,000 ($40) per trailer [5/207], and KES 10,000 ($100) to KES 12,000 ($120) per lorry [5/208], or KES 5,000 ($50) for a lorry of 200 pieces of cypress [5/227], the sawmiller confirmed that 'people in Mariashoni are satisfied with very little money' [2/053], particularly between December and January when access to the forest was easy due to dry and warm weather and the residents needed money to pay school fees. He also added that prices depended on the kind of trees obtained. The extremely low prices cited by some Mariashoni residents were most likely paid for very young and thin cypress poles [2/053]. Another Ogiek man opined that the small sawmills were worse than the big timber companies because they oper-

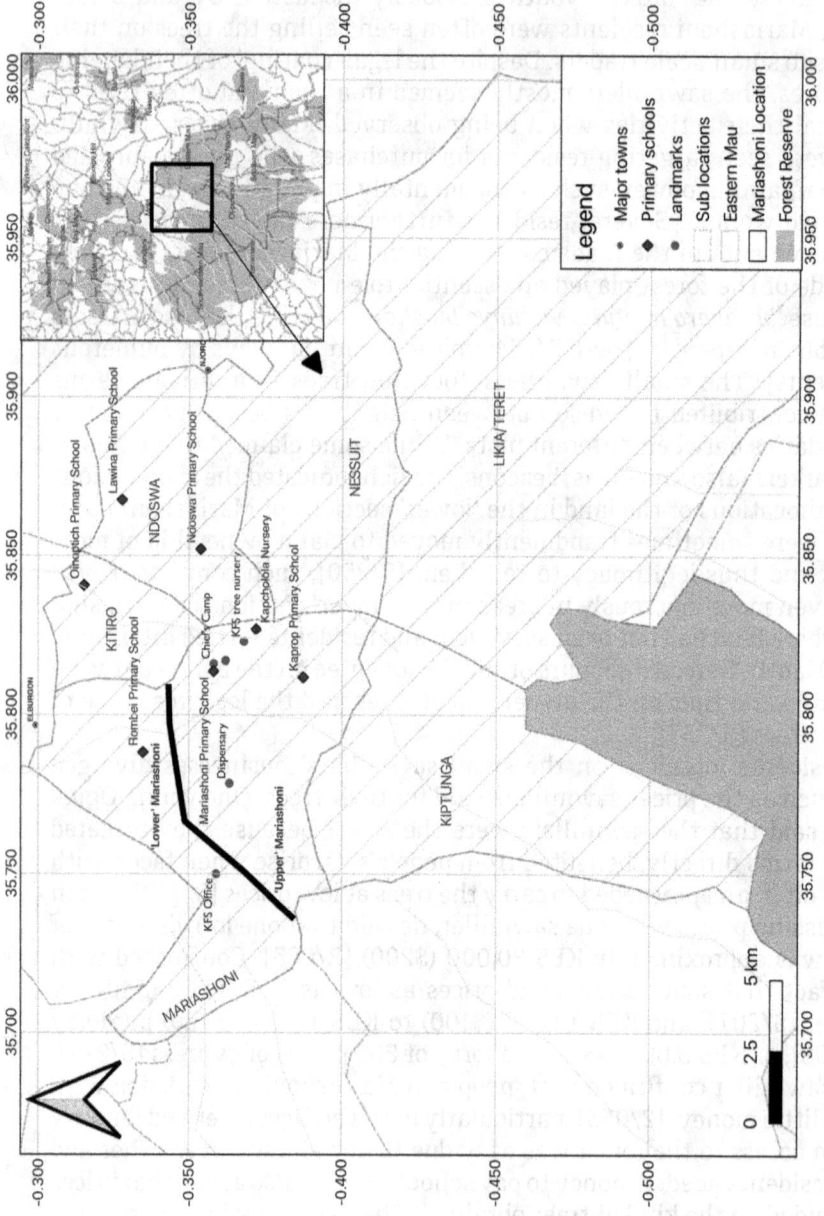

Map 4 The different settlement 'zones' in Mariashoni.

Source: Author composition using QGIS. Note: The wider Mariashoni area is separated into what residents typically refer to as 'upper' and 'lower' Mariashoni. This separation loosely follows the indicated line.

ated on one-time contracts with those whose trees they cut and did not replant any. He further said that the small sawmillers mainly operated from January to April, avoiding the area because of rains and the cold during the other months [5/200]. The sawmiller also explained that he usually cut trees in the forest and intermixed them with those from private farms, thereby deforesting private and forest land. Intermixing trees was also how he could stock indigenous trees, despite primarily using exotic trees [2/052]. An Ogiek resident confirmed that illegally adding indigenous trees to the legally purchased exotic trees was a big problem in the area [5/200].

The sawmiller further explained that his father was one of the many Kikuyu businessmen who had benefited from former President Moi's policies, especially the designation of forest areas for settlement since the privatisation of land signified that there was a change in land use from forest to agricultural land and thus often an interest in selling the trees on one's farm. He said that in the early 1990s, faced with an important supply of trees from recently allocated farmland, Kikuyus, who knew the value of timber, could fill entire lorries for only KES 200 ($2) [2/053]. In line with that assessment, many of the residents to whom the land was allocated in 1997 when the land in the presumed settlement scheme was surveyed and distributed confirmed that most of the trees on their land had been harvested by the Government with the help of the country's major timber companies [5/156, 5/236]. Not having been surveyed, land that was de facto added to the settlement scheme was not directly captured in these analyses. Some residents reported that most people who lived within the settlement scheme had sold their trees and contributed to the state-sponsored destruction of forest stands and land [5/181]. It was against this background that the logging ban was introduced in 1999.

Commercial forest production after the lift of the logging ban

The lift of the logging ban in late 2011 led to the opening of forest harvesting rights to sawmillers. This, however, also came with stricter regulations for small sawmillers who henceforth were required to obtain transport permits for trees bought from Private Lands. During the logging ban, the purchase and transport of trees from privately owned land was effectively not regulated. This loophole had allowed these sawmillers to deplete trees from privately owned or held land. After introducing new regulations and abolishing the logging ban, sawmillers started needing permits to transport the privately owned trees as well. Despite the territorial reorganisation and the substitution of the centralised land administration with a decentralised one through the 2010 Constitution, these permits generally continued being obtained from the District Forest Office, located at the District Commissioner's office. When applying for a permit, the trees in question first had to be cleared. There were two ways to obtain clearance depending on where the trees were sourced. One could pay directly at the Forest Office when planning to transport trees or firewood from government plantations. To obtain a permit for the transport of privately owned trees involved more steps. First, a letter from the owner of the land on which the trees were located was needed. In case there was no formal land ownership, the local chief could certify that a given person lived on the land in question and that the trees in question emanated from this land. A photocopy of the national identity card of the original land and tree owner had to be attached. After being cleared by the KFS Zonal Manager, transport permits could then be applied for at the DFO's office. Prices of these permits varied depending on the vehicle's size and the load type [2/053, 5/255]. The sawmiller mentioned another essential feature of the business and explained that, while a permit was required to be allowed to ferry trees, a company's license determined the type of permit for which it qualified. Getting these licences was not very expensive, according to him, but the process was tedious since the authorities made numerous visits and checked the machines to confirm that the licensed sawmills did actually exist and were not mere 'box office sawmills'. These 'box office sawmills' were a common problem before the introduction of the logging ban, and their regulation was part of the requirements when the ban was lifted. Henceforth, only correctly registered and licensed sawmills could cut trees and transport full trees. The new proceedings for giving out tenders also differed significantly from former practices. Whereas the DFO used to allocate pieces of forest plantations to individual bidders, such tenders at present had to pass through the national board of KFS and thus be approved at the highest level [3/077].

Despite having regained legal access to the forest, sawmillers continuously engaged in the illegal practice of using others' permits when entering the forest [2/053]. Many residents were aware of that practice. A Kikuyu woman, who used to engage in the business with her son, said that 'people have always found their way to do business' [2/053, 5/255]. One sawmiller noted that his company was not properly licensed, and he only held a permit for transporting firewood, so he used another company's permit when he wanted to transport full trees [2/053]. However, when transporting the logs, he said, he has to plan for bribes of KES 200 ($2) per checkpoint, independently from the existence of a permit [2/052]. His example illustrates that the persistence of widespread corruption rendered 'going the official way' neither necessary nor sufficient since even those possessing the correct permits faced unauthorised demands from the authorities' representatives.

After petitioning the Government and requesting a lift of the logging ban for many years, the TMA, alongside other organisations, disputed its lift in 2011 by taking the Government to court. They claimed it introduced unfair competition that effectively excluded small sawmillers from competing for tenders due to the requirements for obtaining harvesting rights. According to the Association's chairman, 'if the forests weren't closed, we'd have over twenty companies today that do plywood' [2/048]. He explained the plight of the associations and individual sawmillers. He said the association was founded in the early 1980s to represent the interests of Kenya's small and medium-scale sawmillers. The association was registered with the Government and, following official requirements, had a chairperson, a secretary, and a treasurer with assistants for each position. The chairperson was elected for five years, with the possibility of being re-elected once. It further had a board of directors composed of nine members representing Kenya's sawmillers. The chairman said that the organisation lost a lot of influence during the twelve years of effective exclusion from the timber business imposed by the logging ban, mainly due to their public portrayal as destroyers of the environment. Considerably reduced resources and ongoing conflict with the Government further weakened the association. Since then, the organisation was revived, with the Finnish Government assisting in the establishment of offices in Nakuru, Nairobi, and Nyeri. According to the chairman, members of the TMA employed almost two hundred thousand people directly and indirectly in the timber sector in 2012. Since the beginning of his tenure, his agenda had been '100% access to forest resources in a sustainable way' [2/048], and his most important task was to convince the members that their future was at risk in the long run if they were unable to change to more sustainable practices. He added that they needed to change the public perception of their role in the country's economic and environmental state. In the end, he succeeded in rallying a majority of sawmillers behind the idea that they needed to curb the 'cut and run' attitude and contribute to the reforestation of former forest areas and the afforestation of formerly bare lands. After a rocky start, the TMA started setting up tree nurseries and encouraged its members to replant after harvesting trees. Interestingly, the first tree nursery set up by the TMA was in Mariashoni [2/048]. The Molo DFO confirmed the TMA's investment in tree nurseries and said that the sawmillers collaborated with the KFS. Due to their experience in the matter, the latter advised the sawmillers on areas, appropriate species, and numbers of trees that should be planted. The DFO also affirmed that the sawmillers wanted to rehabilitate and replant forest areas after cutting trees – to avoid backlogs that could endanger their businesses [2/047]. One of the casual workers employed at Mariashoni's tree nursery confirmed that the TMA started contributing to the development of the nursery in mid-2011, around the time the logging ban was abolished. Unlike the KFS seedlings that were for both exotic and indigenous trees, the section sponsored and used by members of the TMA only contained exotic tree seedlings. These seedlings were exclusively planted for commercial purposes. A KFS officer posted in Mariashoni Forest Station also said that the TMA established the tree nursery because sawmillers were now forced to replant trees after harvesting, unlike before. He said this change came relatively quickly since sawmillers could no longer cut if they did not replant [5/158]. The tree nursery worker also mentioned that the sawmillers usually included local community members in their tree-planting drives and paid them. He added that, after seedlings were commissioned, the workers usually raised the seedlings themselves after collecting the relevant seeds in the forest [3/066]. To be able to fund these activities, sawmillers had been contributing money voluntarily to pay for tree nursery establishment, as well as for watchmen to protect plantations and to set up PELIS systems, the marked-up version of the previous 'shamba' system in which food crops could be cultivated in young forest plantations. The organisation's chairman thereby illustrated a pragmatic vision of the sawmillers' influence on Kenya's forests in general and the Mau Forest particularly. According to him, it was technically impossible to stop the exploitation of the forest since 'what was planted for commercial use must be used commercially' [2/048]. He thereby referred to an essential feature of the Mau Forest that highly contributed to its non-protection: with the cutting of the indigenous forest and the reforestation of forest land with exotic species, the forest became commodified since exotic trees are, by definition, cut and used as timber.

The TMA chairman added that he remained sceptical about the lift of the logging ban and said that he did not think the Government could sell trees through the tender system. He advocated for a system in which land would be directly allocated to sawmillers, who could then plant and harvest within these boundaries. He was, however, also wary of concessions, at least the concessions the Government wanted to give out in 2012, and affirmatively shared his opinion that 'Kenya is not ready for concessions' [2/048] because the country could not manage them properly. He argued that one of the most important things was to clarify the responsibilities of different actors and levels of government, specifically the inclusion of counties in natural resource management, which, according to him, also crucially lacked capacity before engaging in concession discussions. He added that, since harvesting cycles can take up to sixty years, it was fundamental that successive governments accept concessions given by previous governments [2/048].

To estimate the magnitude of the commercial forest production in Mariashoni's surroundings, the following observations were made during five days in 2012: the sawmillers transported 2.6 times more five-metre tree logs past Mariashoni Centre than Timsales and also made 4.7 times more trips (see Table 4); clearly displaying Timsales' superior extractive capacity overall.

Table 4 Timber transport through Mariashoni Centre in five days in February 2012.

Vehicle type	Timsales	Sawmiller 1	Sawmiller 2	Sawmiller 3	Sawmiller 4	Totals
Lorry	1	15	0	11	0	27
Truck	2	19	2	14	17	54
Transit (truck + trailer)	22	12	0	1	0	35
N.A.	0	0	0	0	1	1
Total trips by company	25	46	2	26	18	117
Estimated no. of logs by company	1,594	1,691	34	591	300	4,210

Source: Author data.

Overall, forest dwellers expressed different views concerning who contributed the most to the Mau Forest's active destruction. One common argument was that small sawmills supposedly had a 'hit and run' mentality [5/120, 5/202, 5/205, 5/233], while Timsales must replant [5/120, 5/148, 5/194, 5/214, 5/236, 5/256]; or that small sawmills cut everything [5/148, 5/194, 5/256], while Timsales only harvested mature trees [5/255]. Those community members tended to shift the blame on the sawmillers. Others insisted that Timsales cut large fields at once [5/218, 5/225], while small ones could not effectively deforest larger areas of land [5/191]. Another argument was that Timsales was too well connected and ran no risk of being penalised if they failed to comply with regulations because politicians owned the company and because they employed many people [5/233], so they did not have any incentive to comply and hence did not replant areas well after harvesting trees.

An unprecedented 'cutting craze' in the wake of uncertainty

Despite the continuous exploitation of forest plantations by big timber companies and the parallel exploitation of trees on private farms in the Eastern Mau, lifting the logging ban, according to many testimonies, nonetheless led to a massive increase in forest exploitation and ferrying of trees. Most observers said tree transporting increased from mid-2011 [3/070, 5/228, 5/229]. Yet, 2011 was one of the peak years in which the UN and the Kenyan government, alongside NGOs and CBOs, engaged in tree-planting drives and drumming up support to 'Save the Mau'. Numerous formal and informal conversations displayed the widespread perception that such a campaign would go hand in hand with a targeted logging ban for the Mau Forest. However, that was not the case, and the lift of the general logging ban opened a competition for tenders to harvest trees from mature forest plantations in the Mau Forest. Following an ICS directive, the only restriction on logging concerned 'all the areas that used to be forest' [2/047] within the Mau, which the Molo DFO translated into there being a moratorium on logging within the settlement schemes on forest land, but not the forest reserves, until such a time when the Government finalised and defined clear boundaries. Yet, Mariashoni's forester insisted that he was in no position to enforce the logging restriction because 'it (was) not serving anybody' and was 'just there politically, not professionally' [3/062]. At the same time, there were no particularly strict obligations attached to these tenders that would ensure that the Mau Forest was indeed 'saved'. Furthermore, the implementation of existing policies remained incomplete, and the replacement of trees, for instance, did not match the removals. Consequently, forests continued shrinking, including in the Eastern Mau [1/021].

Several persons spoke about uncertainty contributing to increased forest exploitation. One of the KFS guards stationed in Mariashoni Centre spoke about the factors that had contributed to the massive destruction of forest plantations during the 2007 elections. First, he mentioned the uncertainty over what the elections would bring in terms of official forest policies, local forest protection practices, and, perhaps most relevantly, the unrelenting willingness of local officials to take bribes in exchange for their silence on forest destruction. The second main driver of destruction he identified was the lack of actual control on the ground since most security forces, including the Kenya Police, the Administration Police, and members of the paramilitary KFS and KWS, were deployed to election-related venues. He said this reduced supervision, alongside a general concentration on election matters, also bolstered illegal tree harvesting by locals, non-locals, and KFS employees [3/077]. The Timsales worker recounted that the 2007–2008 post-election violence (PEV) had affected the company adversely, since workers burned vast numbers of logs stashed at the sawmill in Elburgon, after which the boss fired all their non-Kikuyu workers and kept the mill running despite the clashes going on outside its gates [5/233]. Similar behaviour was reportedly witnessed after the Mau Forest Task Force visited the area in 2008, carrying a wind of potential change to the status quo. Concretely, both locals and 'outsiders' interested in the forest's resources were said to fear that settlers would be evicted, logging licences revoked, the forest fenced, and access barred [5/228, 5/229, 5/255]. Consequently, forest destruction and depletion rose steeply.

In early 2013, the elections were nearing, and the incumbent President Mwai Kibaki did not run again. Then-Prime Minister and opposition presidential candidate Raila Odinga was perceived by many as interested in forest restoration due to his role in the 'Save the Mau' campaign. Consequently, many feared that the status quo of forest exploitation would change if he won the presidential election. Various sawmillers interviewed said they supported Uhuru Kenyatta's candidature 'because he is the only one who defends the interests of businesspeople and of the Kikuyu' [2/052]. They alluded to their opinion that political instability, conceptualised widely, contributed significantly to forest destruction. Hence, in anticipation of potential changes, those who could harvest the forest under the old regime made sure to increase their benefits while their privileges lasted. The Timsales worker added that the 'big boss' of the company did not hide the fact that he disliked the opposition candidate, since he feared being thrown out of the forest, and clearly instructed his workers to make sure that all the trees that the company had paid for were harvested before the elections. The NACOFA programme assistant said that the 'cutting craze' phenomenon could be observed in all forests, explaining that members of CFAs had been calling from all over the country because of excessive tree cutting witnessed in their respective areas already months before the elections were held in March 2013. He emphasised that the 2013 elections were especially crucial because of being the first elections held after the 2010 Constitution and thus the first time the new county government officials were to be elected. Since natural resource management was supposed to be devolved to the new counties, he added that uncertainty about who would be in charge overall and who would keep control of access, use and sale of the trees, led to a 'big, big problem' [1/034]. By the week before the 2013 elections, almost all local KFS employees were sent to supervise polling stations, maintaining only two guards for the supervision of the forest [3/077].

One government expert confirmed that excessive cutting during political changes was a problem [1/040]. In an attempt to anticipate forest destruction related to political uncertainty, the Government published a notice in all the national newspapers on 25 February 2013 that cutting and transporting of trees would be prohibited throughout the country from ten days before until four days after the election on 13 March 2013.[9] A former sawmiller indicated that such notices did not concern companies like Timsales since the only effect was that no transport permits could be obtained from the KFS, which the big timber companies did not need [5/255]. During the observed period, Timsales lorries continued transporting logs along the main road tangent to Mariashoni Centre, although at significantly reduced capacity.

---

9   *Daily Nation*, 25 February 2013, p. 11.

Exploitation-focused forest management and the crisis in the Eastern Mau Forest

During and after the logging ban, like all other gazetted forests containing forest plantations, the Mau Forest remained an exploitable commodity, primarily to produce timber and wood products. Hence, the management principles of the Mau Forest were in line with much of the literature that conferred that scientific forestry was mainly concerned with rational resource management (Peluso, 1992), in which economic rationales dominated (Bongers & Tennigkeit, 2010), and hence contributed to support the state's developer rather than guardian function (Bryant & Bailey, 1997). At the same time, while the CFA played a minor role in forest patrolling, participatory forest management (PFM) remained absent from the forest reserve, both in terms of benefit- and power-sharing. Management of the 'official' Mau Forest consequently remained exclusively in the hands of the KFS and the central state. This is in line with Chomba et al.'s (2015) observation that the highly centralised nature of the state was evident in forest management, which was further illustrated in the extraordinary hesitance to delegate powers to subsidiary levels, and indicated that community-based natural resource management (CBNRM) was *systemically* unable to achieve set objectives.

Beyond the Government generally prioritising its 'developer' over its 'guardian' role, another dynamic became apparent that contributed significantly to the political ecology of the Mau Forest crisis. While the Government allegedly attempted to curb forest destruction and deforestation by changing policies and regulations that supposedly were to bring about sustainable forest management, the state was not able, or willing, to prevent different actors in the industry from using various strategies to ensure continuous forest exploitation, and hence both legal and illegal extraction, production, and trade of forest products, in line with Bushley (2014), Charnley and Poe (2007), Chomba et al. (2015), and Peluso and Vandergeest (2001).

Furthermore, the Government-imposed logging ban excluded sawmillers from participating in the harvest cycles, through which state authorities managed the productivity of public forests, but not in relation to the big timber companies. The 'partial' nature of the logging ban clearly illustrated the power these timber companies held, which, in Bryant and Bailey's (1997) words, were able to exert control over others' environments by controlling access to and use of the Mau Forest, and by preventing alternative resource use and management approaches from being imposed on them. At the same time, the logging ban itself can be understood as an extension of a 'fences and fines approach' (Adams & Hulme, 2001, p. 13), which allowed the state to 'take back' power from communities and other alternative actors, and hence to reduce previously acquired democratic spaces by imposing strict controls in the name of conserving the country's ailing forests.

This alleged injustice in the system was addressed repeatedly in Parliament, for instance by Honourable Mr Sumbu on 3 April 2003. Professor Wangari Maathai, at the time Assistant Minister for Environment, Natural Resources, and Wildlife, admitted not knowing 'why the ban was discriminatory in favour of the big Indian-owned companies' (Republic of Kenya, 2003). The same issue was raised again in 2009. The Assistant Minister for Forestry and Wildlife, Mr Nanok, was questioned in Parliament as to why Timsales, Raiply, and Comply were exempted from the logging ban. In response, he explained that it was based 'on the premise that they will provide value-added products such as wood panels, fibre boards, and wood laminates that would [otherwise] have to be imported'. He added that 'the companies employ a large workforce and are involved in the replanting of the areas they clear' (Republic of Kenya, 2009b). Honourable Musa Sirma asked whether 'the Assistant Minister (could) confirm that M/s. Comply, M/s. Timsales and M/s. Raiply are one and the same thing practising monopoly in this country', to which the Assistant Minister replied that all three companies belonged to 'what is famously called the Rai Group' (Republic of Kenya, 2009b).

In May 2004, when debating the Forests Bill, Honourable Mr Sambu confessed that 'I was saddened the other day, when names of Africans were tabled here as the owners of Timsales. Those are not the owners of M/s. Timsales ... They are all Indians. Why are we being racists on our own resources?' (Republic of Kenya, 2004a). Members of Parliament had previously decried 'neo-colonial practices' in the timber industry ever since Independence. Indeed, National Assembly records from 9 July 1970 show Honourable Mr Kuguru, at the time Assistant Minister for Works, criticising the fact that Indian and European traders were given preference in the trading business and insisting that African traders were relegated to second and third-class licences, with only a handful of African traders being allowed to operate on a first-class licence. Ownership of the company and bias in access to licences and the timber business, in general, had been questioned for a long time.

While the big players' political connections were evident, the question of who factually owned and benefited from these companies' revenues continued arousing controversy. One expert said that while the 'old father' of the Rai family managed and controlled Raiply, the first-born son held Comply, and the second-born son managed Timsales.[10] Since these large companies generated tremendous amounts

10 In 2016, the Rai family furthermore purchased the previously closed Pan-African Paper Mills and further enlarged their monopoly in the Kenyan market (Andae, G., 'Billionaire Rai family buys PanPaper for Sh900m', *Business*

of revenue, interest in company shares among wealthy businesspeople was considerable as well, he added. Consequently, former President Daniel arap Moi was said to be a major shareholder of Raiply, while then-President Uhuru Kenyatta owned parts of Timsales. Since the same people controlled the largest companies in the market, the circulation of wood products was also centrally controlled, which drove up their prices in the market. He further explained that the Rai family and their businesses had been intertwined with the political elite for a long time, citing that former President Moi signed a 'development' agreement with the family in exchange for a cash loan when he needed liquidity. The agreement allegedly stipulated that the family was a 'partner of the Government to build the economy through tree-harvesting'. The nature of the contract reportedly was such that it could not be revoked because the family could claim that their position as a major employer in the region served said 'development'. Consequently, the Rai family was able to undermine all attempts to restrict and control their access to Kenya's forests [1/005, 1/008]. The Molo DFO confirmed that the logging ban was not extended to the big companies because of special agreements, predominantly because of their bargaining power as significant employers in their respective regions [2/047]. An investigative newspaper article about the same was buried [1/005, 1/008]. The Timsales worker, who also said that Uhuru Kenyatta owned 50% of Timsales' shares, insisted that it was unlikely that the company's access to the Mau Forest would ever be restricted [5/233]. Apparent alignment of personal interests of both political and economic elites clearly contributed to these actors imposing their visions and interests on other stakeholders, including government ministries and institutions, and hence to 'control their environment' (in line with Bryant & Bailey, 1997) leading to power relations expressing themselves in the destruction of the physical landscape.

Related to the same, the National Assembly records from 9 July 1970 also display long discussions among Members of Parliament who questioned why Timsales held a monopoly in exporting timber from the Mount Kenya region at that time. Honourable Mr Kuguru, the Assistant Minister for Works at the time, said: 'Timsales ... are working as a middleman; they have been given monopoly over all export timber, as it must pass through them ... and then they market the timber after which they pay our people' (Republic of Kenya, 1970a). In line with the company's apparent monopoly in exporting timber and/or timber products, one knowledgeable observer opined that the Mau Forest was mainly destroyed for the benefit of outside markets [1/021].

Beyond continuous forest exploitation by the remaining 'big three', and specifically by Timsales in the Eastern Mau, during and after the

---

Daily Africa, 29 April 2016).

logging ban, the latter also contributed to further the environmental crisis in the Eastern Mau. Furthermore, the ban's impact was diametrically opposed to what people commonly assumed since the twelve years of exclusion from state forests were enough for sawmillers to effectively deplete the trees from private farms in the area, leaving much of the settlement area land bare [2/048]. One sawmiller formulated a clear statement concerning the effects of the Government's reluctant attempt to regulate forest exploitation: '*ni sisi, tunaharibu Mau*' (we are the ones who destroy the Mau) [2/052].

Differences of opinion among community members about the relative importance of different timber industry players to the destruction of the Mau Forest was also related to social positionality, discussed further below. Some local community members worked with the sawmillers to assemble, load, and transport the trees they cut, sometimes 'legally' from their farms and sometimes illegally from the forest. These locals typically defended small sawmillers and defined them as small-scale destroyers, while Timsales was portrayed as a much worse destroyer who only benefited its stakeholders. One expert said that many residents also understood the logging ban as a neo-patrimonial practice aimed at enriching the elites of the country rather than an attempt to protect the country's forests since the big, politically connected companies continued harvesting while the sawmillers were banned [1/005].[11] Such patronage practices were comprehensively theorised in terms of political favouritism by Bayart (1989), Klopp and Sang (2011), and Wrong (2009), in which state resources are redistributed in favour of influential individuals and groups in pursuit of and as compensation for political loyalty. Thus, the environmental crisis in the Eastern Mau, like other environmental 'stories', was indeed 'a story about power' (Weiner, 2005, p. 409). Furthermore, continuous illegal forest exploitation ventures were fuelled by a lack of law enforcement in the forest and along major trade routes, which was commonly facilitated through bribes. Corruption was thus at the core of the perpetuation of forest destruction from the highest to the lowest level, from the largest to the most minor scales and quantities, in line with Adams and Hutton (2007), Bushley (2014), and Timura (2001), and an essential underlying enabler of the political ecology of the Mau Forest crisis.

Given the fact that the big timber companies were owned and operated by non-residents who rarely employed local workers, here evidently the Ogiek community, and who did not invest in local infrastructure, commercial logging continued excluding local communities in the Eastern Mau Forest, as elsewhere in the country [4/260]. Hence, the

---

11 See also: Wairimu, I., 'Timsales takes Nema to court over tree felling ban', *The Star*, 29 October 2011; 'Dire shortage of timber forcing merchants to import commodity', *Coast Week*, 19 November 2010.

only legal option for locals to benefit from the forest was to help the KFS to prune, thin, and sell the removed branches and immature trees. One Ogiek elder succinctly summarised the forest utilisation dilemma by pointing out that 'if I cut a tree, I will be arrested, if Sokoro [Timsales] cut a tree, it will be taken to town' [5/226]. Another Ogiek elder argued that the main challenge that forest restoration and conservation faced was that *'mipango ya serikali ni ya kuangusha'* (the plan/intention of the Government is to cut trees) [5/234], revealing the tension between attempts to save and restore the forest on the one hand and the continuation of the Government's approach to forest management in terms of commercial forest exploitation, in line with the 'central paradox' of its roles (Bryant & Bailey, 1997), on the other hand. He added that, due to the pursuit of commercial forestry, *'vitu zetu zimekwisha'* (our 'things' have disappeared/ended) [5/234], specifically animals and plants that used to form the cornerstone of the Ogiek socio-cultural identities and their traditional livelihoods. He voiced what most Ogiek elders said: that the Government's interests and activities were opposed to their traditional identities, interests, and preferences.

In sum, while high-profile talks about biodiversity conservation in the Mau Forest were held in Nairobi's classy hotels, and while politicians, celebrities, and companies manifested their environmental concern by feeding the media with footage from their tree-planting sessions, Timsales continued holding logging permits in the Eastern Mau, particularly in Kiptunga Forest [1/005] and engaged in massive logging day after day; ironically, right next to the Elapuyapui swamp, and hence right next to the source of the Mara River. The Mara River is the primary water source of the world-famous Maasai Mara Game Reserve, which might have been one of the main drivers for USAID's ProMara programme to attempt to restore the Mara River.

The power of the political and economic elites that benefited from the country's deforestation manifested again in the shake-up of the KFS leadership in June 2018, which was accused of 'having been complicit in illegal logging'.[12] At the same time, the very shake-up led to the nomination of Jaswant Singh Rai, the supposed head of Timsales, as the Director in charge of the Forestry Industry, and followed the re-introduction of the logging ban for state and community forests in February 2018.[13] Similar to conditions imposed in 1999, the ban halted all logging activities of small and medium-scale sawmillers, and also abolished PELIS (GoK, 2018). These changes unmistakably displayed

[12]   Munda, C., 'Kenya Forest Service chief replaced in shake-up', *Business Daily*, 13 March 2018.

[13]   Ndonga, S., 'Peter Kinyua formally appointed as KFS Chairman', *Capital News*, 7 June 2018; News Desk, 'President Uhuru Asked To Revoke Rai's Appointment To KFS', *Angaza News*, 8 June 2018.

the power of the timber-producing conglomerates in the country, and the Government's sustained interest in maintaining commercial forest production for the personal gain of the political and economic elites in place in the country.

The manifest continuation of perspectives, philosophies, and practices focusing purely on forest production – despite various reforms in the forestry sector and of the institutions tasked with forest management, particularly considering the creation of the Interim Coordinating Secretariat followed by the Kenya Water Towers Agency that supposedly were to guarantee a holistic forest management approach – entailed a particular consideration for water catchments and biodiversity hotspots (GoK, 2009e). Beyond translating a prioritisation of commercial forest production in pursuit of national interests in terms of forest uses over all others' (Klooster, 2009), commercial forest production was maintained for the personal benefit of the political and economic elite. This displayed the extent to which power relations are visible and can be 'read' in the physical environment (Bryant & Bailey, 1997; Weiner, 2005), and again, the extent to which these struggles between different interests of different actors contributed to the political ecology of the Mau Forest crisis.

3

The Political Economy of Land: Maintaining Control over Forest Land Allocation and Distribution

The Kenyan government defined recovery of Public Land as one of the main actions required to enable the rehabilitation of the ailing Mau Forest, indicating that 'illegal and ill-planned' (GoK, 2009e) land distribution had significantly contributed to the environmental crisis in the Mau. In the same vein, the five-phase spatial-temporal plan pursued by the Interim Coordinating Secretariat (ICS) in the very beginning of the 'Save the Mau' initiative in late 2009 and early 2010 focused primarily on securing forest land that had been degazetted in 2001. The over 30,000 ha of forest land that was transformed to settlement schemes in the Eastern Mau in the 1990s (see Table 1 in the Introduction) fell into that category. As illustrated by the fact that Chapter 5 of the 2010 Constitution is concerned with 'Land and Environment', and in line with the overall assumptions of political ecology, land and regulations about land are of primary importance for environmental crises.

The politicised environment: Seeing the land below the forest and the trees

Since the livelihoods of about 80% of Kenyans require direct access to land (Development Partnership Forum, 2010), while only about one-fifth of the land receives enough rainfall for extensive and productive agriculture (Lusigi, 1981), and hence qualifies as fertile (Ville, 1998), presumed inequalities in land tenure continually have been one of the most important sources of social and political conflict in Kenya.

Injustice in distribution and access to land at the basis of the modern Kenyan state

Injustice in distribution and access to land can be described as one of the founding *momentums* of the modern Kenyan state (Anderson, 2005; Calas, 1998; Connan, 2005; Woodhouse, Bernstein, & Hulme, 2000). Injustices in land distribution were established as a historical fact, from the colonial period to the present. Historically, since the beginning of the colonisation of the Kenyan territory, much of the most productive land was alienated by colonialists. Ever since the institutionalisation of the White Highlands, these European settlers established vast properties, either for cattle rearing or for the cultivation of crops. By 1922, about 10,000 Europeans had settled in the territory, holding a virtual monopoly over the best lands (Cheeseman, 2006). On three million hectares of fertile lands, they established only four thousand farms and estates, figures providing interesting insights into the average size of the respective properties. In opposition, African farmers who resided on the lands attributed to colonialists became squatters, mostly tolerated in exchange for a concession tax to the new owners (de Lame, 2006). Those who did not accept working as agricultural proletariat were displaced to ethnic reserves or forced to squat the lands the colonialists had obtained forcefully. Henceforth, land and representation in Parliament, and African demands for both, became central to Kenyan pre-Independence politics. Related concerns about common access rights to land and natural resources greatly fostered social conflict among the different non-European communities, mainly based on claims of ancestral occupation and customary rights to land and resources. The Mau Mau uprising that lasted from 1952 until 1956 and strongly contributed to Kenya's Independence in 1963 is considered a prime example of convergence of experienced land injustice, identitary claims and the overall struggle for freedom from colonial domination (Anderson, 2006; Berman & Lonsdale, 1992a, 1992b; Branch, 2011; Odhiambo & Lonsdale, 2003).

More people were displaced with the creation of national parks from the mid-1940s, a process that Neumann (1998) describes as 'one component of the broader process of colonial appropriation of land and natural resources ... and the symbolic legitimation of that process' (pp. 34–5). After their designation, state control was established over the new national parks. At the same time, the areas were cleared of communities that had occupied these lands. National parks became zones for the exclusive use of paying colonialists and tourists. Such dispossession became a recurrent feature of many conservation enterprises, as did violent resistance to these depriving measures. Eviction of landless peasants or squatters from Government/Public Land, including gazetted forests such as Mt Elgon, Mt Kenya, and the Mau Forests, were some of the most crucial features of this dispossession, alongside denial of access to land for peasants following legal privatisations, loss of land by peasants due to politically instigated ethnic conflicts, and neglect of peasants during land redistributions by the state to compensate cases of evictions. Altogether, Africans were deprived of roughly half the country's fertile lands during the colonial period, notably in the Kikuyu, Nandi, and Maasai zones (Médard, 2008b).

Even though conflicts about land distribution practices were at the heart of the 1952 Mau Mau rebellion and the fights for Independence, inequalities in land distribution barely changed after 1963. The failure of the post-Independence state to enact sensible land redistribution policies further aggravated land insecurities since only 20–25% of the former White Highlands were redistributed to African farmers (Calas, 1998). Due to the specificities of the procedures conditioning loan attribution, farmers from Central Kenya, predominantly members of the Kikuyu community, benefited over-proportionally from land sales. In sum, most land was redistributed to big landowners, or multinational firms, some of them African-held. Some academics argue that this land distribution policy was driven by a state priority to create a modern agricultural elite capable of countering the movement of landless farmers (Calas, 1998; Connan, 2007). This redistribution of lands led to further displacements of farmers who had previously used and settled on these lands. Some argue that contemporary social conflicts in Kenya were rooted in this initial division between the land haves and the have-nots, which shaped the formation of the country's social classes. According to Calas, *'le dualisme foncier constitue sans aucun doute une des caractéristiques durables et essentielles du Kenya contemporain'* (the dualism in land (attribution) constitutes without any doubt one of the durable and essential characteristics of contemporary Kenya) (1998, p. 35). These social inequalities engendered considerable tension, particularly in rural settings, which regularly contributed to violent conflicts (Homewood, Coast, & Thompson, 2004; Neumann, 1998).

Indeed, land grievances were central to most of the violent and controversial conflicts witnessed in the country. Conflict over land was also one of the leading underlying causes of violence the country experienced before and after the 2007/08 elections, as well as during the 1992 and 1997 elections (Human Rights Watch, 2008; International Crisis Group, 2008; Médard, 2008a; Republic of Kenya, 2008b; de Smedt, 2009). The Report of the Commission of Inquiry into the Post-Election Violence (CIPEV) (Republic of Kenya, 2008b), popularly known as the 'Waki Report', investigating the post-election crisis, ascribes the importance of land to

> a feeling among certain ethnic groups of historical marginalization, arising from perceived inequities concerning the allocation of land and other national resources as well as access to public goods and services. This feeling has been tapped by politicians to articulate grievances about historical injustices which resonate with certain sections of the public. This has created an underlying climate of tension and hate, and the potential for violence, waiting to be ignited and to explode. (p. 23)

The Report furthermore states:

> Constitutionally, individuals may own land in any place in Kenya and in law, no part of the country belongs to an ethnic group. Nevertheless, this phenomenon is de facto a characteristic of many areas,

particularly as many of the newly created districts since the nineteen nineties have been ethno-specific, leading to the creation of ethnically homogenous effective 'native reserves'. This in turn has created the notion of 'insiders', who are native to a place and 'outsiders' who have migrated there, a notion that has been tapped by aspiring politicians. (p. 31)

Médard (2008b) illustrates how such discourses were used, notably about land, by asserting that

autochthonous claims have been used for political gains. Autochthony as political discourse, legitimates the recourse to violence to settle land grievances ... The political position of defending autochthony enables a leader to hide his real motives while acting as the champion of a collective cause such as land. (p. 382)

While land grievances often had legitimate and justifiable bases, the quote also illustrates that land was an emotive issue and that land conflicts often masked deeper grievances related to perceived political domination or inequity. As in many similar post-colonial contexts,

(m)ost of these conflicts are expressed in the form of an opposition between autochthonous populations and strangers. Citizenship is conceived in ethnic and territorial terms, and an individual's enjoyment of civil rights depends on his appartenance to an ethnic group or locality. (Mbembe, 2000, p. 46)

The connection between land claims, belonging to a particular group and service provision was further fuelled by the fact that land allocation and management were intertwined with corruption and impunity, two of the other significant risks identified for contemporary Kenya (Republic of Kenya, 2008b).

The 2007/08 post-election violence crisis brought the profoundly political nature of land conflicts back to the fore. It served as a potent reminder that the existing complicated and insecure land tenure system rendered use and ownership of lands and, therefore, most ordinary citizens highly vulnerable. Land reform prominently figured among the fundamental issues to be solved according to Agenda Four of the National Accord and Reconciliation Act that was adopted in March 2008 (Republic of Kenya, 2008a) following the National Agreement of 28 February 2008 (Brown, 2013). While comprehensive land reforms were engaged from the mid-2000s, critical challenges remained.

Land, the kingmaker: The politics behind land conflicts

Until the adoption of the new Land Policy in 2009 (Republic of Kenya, 2009c), 'processes of intervention and change in land tenure have repeatedly allowed elites to manoeuvre to their own advantage' (Homewood et al., 2004, p. 602) by dispossessing some individuals and communities of their land, and by redistributing it to others. Benefiting from the chaotic legal situation and its room for manoeuvre, notably the provisions of the 1882 Indian Transfer of Property Act (ITPA) that was revised to the Government Lands Act (Cap. 280) in 1948, the President 'kept a complete and absolute control of allocations of lands'.[1] These Acts also allowed the President to extend these powers to the Commissioner of Lands. Successive commissioners used their power and granted land directly to favourable beneficiaries through allotment letters while ignoring legal requirements requiring that commercial plots be allocated through public auctions. According to a 2009 Africa Centre for Open Governance study, 'this facilitated the illegal and irregular allocation of public land, in total disregard of the public interest, leading to the pervasive corrupt practice popularly termed as "land-grabbing"' (2009, p. 2).

Successive presidents and their governments redistributed natural resources, mainly land, in search of and as compensation for political loyalty; a practice commonly referred to as political favouritism, patronage or *clientélisme* (Bayart, 1989; Klopp & Sang, 2011; Wrong, 2009). The land was primarily allocated to reward individuals deemed 'politically correct', which led to an irreversible politicisation of the land allocation process, as prominently documented in the Ndung'u Report.[2] According to the Report, all Kenyan presidents have employed such practices since Independence. The country's first President, Jomo Kenyatta, redistributed the former White Highlands mainly to loyal Kikuyu. In contrast, President Moi rewarded Kalenjin and Maasai for their political fidelity by awarding them parts of forest reserves. Considering forest depletion especially, the Moi era was further characterised by plundering forests and forest land by appointing political cronies to head the Forest Department (Mugo, Nyandiga, & Gachanja, 2010; Njeru, 2012; Standing & Gachanja, 2014).

These practices intensified after the restoration of multiparty democracy in late 1991 and the organisation of elections in 1992, as the latter presented the need to attract and reward political loyalty in a context of growing competition for state resources and an overall reduction of available resources that could be distributed (Klopp & Sang, 2011). At that time, President Moi, who had to accept defeat and abolish Article 2A of the Constitution that had instituted a de facto single-party state since 1964 after months of largely peaceful mass mobilisation in the country and internationally, had to face his opponents at the polls

[1]   Bowry, P., 'Do land title deeds mean anything?', *The Standard*, 5 August 2009.
[2]   The correct citation is: Republic of Kenya, Report of the Commission of Inquiry into the Illegal/ Irregular Allocation of Public Land (The Ndung'u Report), Nairobi: Government Printer, 2004.

for the first time since his ascension to power in 1978 (Branch, 2011; Hornsby, 2013; Hornsby & Throup, 1998). Alongside considerable flaws in the implementation of the elections, which did not satisfy international standards on free and fair elections, the incumbent government engaged in various strategies to ensure it would win the 1992 elections. Ensuring popular support was essential since, according to the electoral laws, a presidential candidate had to obtain at least 50% of votes in at least five of the then-eight provinces to be elected. The allocation of land to politically loyal individuals, predominantly members of the President's Tugen community and members of other Kalenjin subgroups whose leaders pledged allegiance to President Moi, thus mainly served to create so-called voting blocs in strategically important areas (Lonsdale, 1992, 1994; Lynch, 2011). Other members of the ruling Kenya African National Union (KANU) party also had to compete for their positions in the concurrently held parliamentary elections, again rendering land vulnerable to political usage. Land in the Mau Forest was either directly allocated to specific individuals by representatives of the local administration, which the President appointed down to the lowest level (the Assistant Chiefs) or conceded to political representatives, often Members of Parliament (MPs), who were to distribute the land to potentially loyal voters. The redistribution of land was facilitated by the fact that all important political positions at the time were held by members of the wider Kalenjin group, including the Presidency, the Ministry of Lands, and the post of the Provincial Commissioner in the then-Rift Valley Province [e.g., 1/002]. The primary purpose of the Ndung'u Report, commissioned by President Kibaki and released in December 2004, was to name and shame the persons who benefited from illegal land acquisitions throughout the country (Connan, 2005). Illustrating that land was used as a prime political resource, most incidents of manipulation of land attribution and distribution occurred during the 1992, 1997, and 2002 electoral periods (Klopp, 2012; Lafargue & Katumanga, 2008).

Understanding the legal basis of land insecurity and conflicts

Land ownership and use have been controversial throughout colonial and post-colonial Kenyan history. Some of this controversy was caused by an unclear land law situation, in which a multiplicity of legal sources co-existed and in which oral sources, for instance, competed with written ones. The legal situation around land tenure had mainly remained unaltered since the colonial period and hence ambiguous for almost 50 years after Independence, until the enactment of the 2009 National Land Policy (Republic of Kenya, 2009c).

During the colonial period, various legal instruments were used to allow for colonial appropriation of land and other natural resources, which contributed to a contradictory legal set-up. In 1902, the first Crown Lands Ordinance was published. Having declared all lands and natural resources in Kenya property of the Crown, the redistribution and sale of the resources began. Derived from the British Common Law, a double-jurisdictional regime was introduced, providing separate spaces for the natives and the colonialists. Thus, twenty-four Native Reserves (or ethnic reserves) were created for the members of native Kenyan communities recognised by the Crown. These and the lands reserved for European settlers, the so-called White Highlands, were institutionalised between 1926 and 1933. The White Highlands were allocated to white colonialists, initially under a leasehold regime. This regime provided for Crown Lands to be leased for variable durations in exchange for rent to the relevant administration while legally remaining state property (Connan, 2005). Each ethnic reserve, on the other hand, was reserved for the exclusive use of a given African community, administered by local authorities, while remaining legally the property of the state. As indicated, there were no formal property rights for native Africans under colonial rule (Compagnon, 2000). Socially, these changes in legislation had far-reaching consequences because the introduction of customary jurisdiction, in the case of these ethnic reserves, replaced existing 'ascribed' forms of relatedness with more rigid ethnic or tribal definitions of community membership (Barrow, Gichohi, & Infield, 2001). Ethnic membership thus became a precondition for the right to access land under customary or communal land tenure, and the land became a resource defined in ethnicised territorial terms. Ancestry in land tenure, a central theme of past and present imaginary and actual land conflicts, is a colonial artefact rather than an absolute reality as it is essentially the colonial administration that confined citizens to a region of origin.

The continuing jurisdictional dualism was derived from two different laws, inspired by the British Common Law. First, the 1882 ITPA regulated the Crown Lands that later became Government Land, which was put under the direct control of the central administration. This Act legalised the eviction of Africans for the benefit of colonialists leasing the then-White Highlands. The 1948 Government Lands Act (with its subsequent revisions), the inheritor of the ITPA, was not revoked and thus continued to allow land alienation on simple presidential orders until the enactment of the 2009 National Land Policy. 'In the interest of the Nation', the President was entitled to attribute title deeds or leases for free or a fee to whomsoever he wanted. The second written source of land rights was the 1963 Registered Land Act (RLA), which provided for transferring formerly communal lands to private *freehold* ownership. These communal lands were mostly the ethnic reserves, classified as communal Trust Lands after Independence (Connan, 2005). The RLA was inspired by the colonial Swynnerton plan of 1954 that sought to address land scarcity after the eruption of the Mau Mau revolt in 1952, which had crystallised around land claims (Odhiambo & Lonsdale, 2003).

After Independence, many rangelands in Kenya, like most other East African rangelands (Homewood et al., 2004), underwent a gradual but widespread shift from the communal tenure of common property resources to widely privatised tenure. These post-Independence land reforms led to the creation of ranches allocated to individuals or collective private owners. Until then, most rural areas had remained under customary management and tenure regimes specific to each ethnic group that had not always been fixed in writing. To achieve these privatisations, the sometimes very different and often oral sources of communal tenure had to be legally registered by the Commissioner of Lands, which involved demarcation, surveying, 'beaconing' (marking) and registration. The duality, overlay, and sometimes contradiction of oral and written legal sources have caused significant confusion, notably in the form of superimposing ownership claims for the same parcels of land (Anderson, 2005; Calas, 1998; Connan, 2005). Beyond that, corrupt government agents' denial of access to land was also the norm (Collett, 1987). Land registration procedures, and conversion of communal lands to Private Land holdings, started right after Independence in 1963. After Independence, the former White Highlands continued being regulated by the Government Lands Act (1948) and could thus only be leased. It was, however, possible to purchase these former Crown Lands from the post-Independence government and have them placed under the RLA regime. One of the core intentions of the enactment of the RLA was to convert the more than twenty land acts into one universal and comprehensive system of land legislation. Since this initial uniformisation failed in 1963, the land reforms that were engendered only after the 2002 democratic transition and the election of Mwai Kibaki to office then had to consider and harmonise more than fifty land acts.[3] The enactment of the 2009 National Land Policy and the 2010 Constitution ended some significant issues related to previous land regulations that had contributed to land conflicts.

Due to considerable national and international pressure, former President Moi established the Commission of Inquiry into Land Law Systems, commonly referred to as the Njonjo Commission after its chairperson and then-Attorney General Charles Mugane Njonjo, in 1999. The acclaimed 2002 Njonjo Report proposed an initial framework for a new land policy ahead of the 2002 general elections that eventually led to the democratic transition. The Njonjo Report would later become known as one of the first key events in Kenya's land reforms (Manji, 2014). Acknowledging that land conflicts were central to the

---

3   Aluanga, L., '"Government" land reclassified as public', *The Standard*, 15 August 2010.

country's social, economic, and political issues, the Kibaki administration officially engaged encompassing land reforms. The appointment
of the Commission of Inquiry into the Illegal/Irregular Allocation of
Public Land, commonly known as the 'Ndung'u Commission' after its
chairperson Paul Ndung'u, in 2003, represented a critical step towards
uncovering connections between inadequate land law systems, land
distribution – and corruption. Apart from naming and shaming both
those who allocated and those who received land irregularly, the Report
also proposed a catalogue of recommendations, notably about how to
revert illegally allocated land to its intended use. Concerning forests
specifically, the Report recommended that 'all excisions of forest land
that were made contrary to the provisions of the Forests Act and the
Government Lands Act [1948 and its revisions] should be cancelled' and
that 'all titles which were acquired consent upon the illegal excisions
and allocations of forest land should be revoked. The forest lands affected should be repossessed and restored to their original purpose'. Due to
the commitment of former Lands Minister James Orengo, the Ndung'u
Report became vital in informing the 2005 Draft Constitution as well
as the 2009 National Land Policy (Africa Centre for Open Governance,
2009), and certainly influenced the 2009 Mau Task Force Report and
the subsequent rehabilitation programme. During the so-called Bomas
process (after its location), the consultative process on constitutional
reform under the chairmanship of Professor Yash Pal Ghai, the land was
also singled out as one of the most critical issues to be addressed, hence
framing and defining land distribution as a constitutional matter.[4]
After the post-election violence crisis, further attention was drawn to
the necessity of solving land conflicts. In that vein, land reform prominently figured in Agenda Four of the 2008 National Dialogue and Reconciliation Act. Comprehensive land reforms were herein termed as
'vital before the 2012 elections' (Brown, 2013), a point taken up by the
Waki Report (Republic of Kenya, 2008b).

The formulation process of the National Land Policy began in 2004.
The first draft was completed and adopted through a National Sympo-
sium in April 2007. Despite significant opposition to the policy, led by
then-Deputy Prime Minister Uhuru Kenyatta and then-Minister for
Agriculture William Ruto,[5] the Cabinet approved the draft National
Land Policy on 25 June 2009. On 3 December 2009, Parliament approved
the Sessional Paper No. 3 of 2009 on the National Land Policy formulated by the Ministry of Lands in August 2009. This policy was 'to guide
the country towards efficient, sustainable and equitable use of land

---

[4]   Odhiambo, F., 'The new Constitution and land legislation', *The Standard*, 25
August 2010.
[5]   Star reporter, 'Land policy debate rages on as some MPs plot bill's defeat',
The Star, 3 December 2009, p. 2.

for prosperity and posterity' (Republic of Kenya, 2009c) by addressing critical issues such as land administration, access to land, land use
planning, productive management of land resources, restitution of historical injustices, environmental degradation, conflicts, elimination of
gender discrimination, and many more. It also recognised the need for
security of tenure for all Kenyans (Kenya Land Alliance, 2010; Klopp &
Lumumba, 2016; Manji, 2014).

The adoption of the new Constitution on 4 August 2010 further supported the land reform process. Fundamentally, Article 40 (1) defines
the principles governing land policy by providing that 'Land in Kenya
shall be held, used and managed in a manner that is equitable, efficient, productive and sustainable' (Republic of Kenya, 2010b). The
new Constitution elicited great hopes from the beginning due to its
assumed potential to 'facilitate economic development and promote
national cohesion' since the land reforms stipulated were 'key to
sustainable peace, security and socio-economic development of the
country'.[6] It also laid a strong foundation for the implementation of
the 2009 National Land Policy with several articles being relevant
for access to and tenure of land, including Chapter Four, Article 40 on
the protection of the right to property under the Bill of Rights; Articles 60–68 in Chapter Five – 'Land and Environment'; Article 174 in
Chapter Eleven – 'Devolved Government'; Articles 248–54 in Chapter
Fifteen – 'Commission and Independent Offices' about the National
Land Commission (NLC); the Fourth Schedule that lists the functions
of national and county governments; the Fifth Schedule that lists the
time frame within which new land laws or changes had to be enacted;
and the Sixth Schedule about the transitional status of existing laws
until new laws would be passed, specifically about the transitional status of freehold land and land held under leases greater than 99
years by non-citizens (Kenya Land Alliance, 2010). The 'Land and
Environment' Chapter Five, specifically, embedded the 2009 National
Land Policy (Manji, 2014).

The Constitution provided for some fundamental changes, keeping
in mind that legal provisions remained inherently complex and
subject to interpretation since the actual practices of implementing legal provisions determined their true relevance and meaning.
The initial provisions concerning land stipulated that existing laws
should be harmonised into one comprehensive land law. Furthermore,
to enhance transparency and accountability in land administration,
service delivery roles were to be moved from the Ministry of Lands
to the autonomous National Land Commission (Art. 67). New clas-

---

[6] According to the Institution of Surveyors of Kenya (ISK), quoted in
Mwanzia, M., 'Experts: New laws to aid land reform', *The Standard,* 19 August
2010.

sifications of land also were to be enacted: Government, Trust, and Private Lands were to become Public, Community, and Private Lands. Concerning the Community Lands, the 2010 Constitution confirmed that the communities themselves were owners of the land, not the county councils that had previously administered them for the communities. The articles concerning the devolution of powers to the county councils stated that the rights of communities to manage their affairs should be protected, which might be interpreted as relating to access and decision-making. Community Lands, registered or not, especially land held by hunter-gatherer communities, were also subject to enhanced protection. These lands were to be protected from deliberate alienation for alleged public or private interests. Furthermore, the acquisition of land by the Government became illegal without 'prompt payment in full and/or just compensation' (Article 40 (3) (b) (i)).[7] This provision, however, did not apply to those who were found to have acquired their land illegally, whose lands could henceforth be reclaimed without compensation. At the same time, the Government retained the right to repossess and alienate Private, Community, and Public Land if compensation was paid to the owner, and only in line with the Constitution and in accordance with new land laws that were to be enacted by Parliament. Other crucial measures foreseen by the Constitution included minimum and maximum landholding acreage, intended to enhance economic productivity and prevent land from lying idle, as well as fixing land tax and premiums on immovable property (Kenya Land Alliance, 2010; Klopp & Lumumba, 2016). Important provisions for the legal protection of the rights of wives, widows, and orphans were also considered [1/263]. Concerning the rights of non-citizens, the 2010 Constitution also provided important changes. Crucially, it denied foreigner's rights to freehold ownership of land, and limited leasehold rights to 99 years. Consequently, all previous freeholds and leaseholds held by non-citizens were to be reduced to leaseholds with a maximum duration of 99 years, starting from the date of effect of the new Constitution. The Constitution was, however, silent about potential possibilities of renewing leaseholds (Kenya Land Alliance, 2010).

Despite many changes in land rights, the making of the land law was criticised by numerous observers and experts. Manji (2014), for instance, says that the review process before and after passing the law was 'marked by haste', leading to a 'confused, contradictory, and rushed legislation' (p. 122) that 'threaten[s] further to undermine the rule of

---

[7]   According to a lawyer of the Kenya Land Alliance, 'full and fair' 'means the full market value of the land and additional consideration for the disturbance caused. I guess fair also brings in the aspect of timeliness of the compensation' [1/263].

law and to perpetuate Kenya's long-running land problems' (p. 125). Klopp and Lumumba (2016) also highlight the *systemic* insufficiency of the process, and detail various situations in which the persons in power had attempted to frustrate and delay the enactment or implementation of crucial land legislation. Furthermore, there were numerous inherent challenges. One of them concerned the fact that, despite historical land injustices being addressed as such in the Constitution, there was no obligation for the tate to do more than investigate and recommend action. The NLC carried out these investigations and recommendations. Article 171 of the National Land Policy committed to developing a legal and institutional framework for the restitution of illegally seized land, but it remained unclear which kinds of land would be concerned. In the case of land being alienated to national Parks or forest reserves, the Constitution expressed a clear preference for them to remain subject to the Public Land regime and, therefore, national property. At the same time, it allowed communities to claim ownership of ancestral land and lands traditionally occupied by hunter-gatherers, which applied to many of Kenya's national parks and Forest reserves (Kenya Land Alliance, 2010). Competing ownership claims were also likely in areas where big landowners produced cereals or tea or held private conservancies on 'ancestral land' that was alienated by the British colonial regime.[8] Conversely, community rights, potential conflicts between communities, the risk of ethnicisation of such 'ancestral lands' and the very 'community' notion remained contentious. This was further emphasised by the provision that communities could register their 'ancestral land' as private property. In that context, experts warned that 'there is reasonable concern that it could reinforce the idea that certain ethnicities "belong" in a certain area, creating a risk of ethnic chauvinism and even the forced displacement of so-called outsiders in ethnically diverse areas'.[9] Not all of these matters were addressed in the final draft of the highly controversial Community Land Bill, adopted in August 2016 as the Community Land Act.[10]

Land and forests specifically were related in a problematic way. Beyond looking at land policies, policies and processes related to *forest land registration*, and hence technicalities, were fundamental for the political use and misallocation of forest land, according to the Dean of the School of Environmental Studies at Kenyatta University [1/012]. To understand these processes, it was necessary to compare the suc-

---

[8] An interesting example of East Africa Tanning and Extract Company (EATEC)/Lonrho vs Nandi squatters is detailed in Klopp (2002).

[9] Brown, S. 'Two cheers for Kenya's new constitution', *Deutsche Welle*, 9 August 2010, www.die-gdi.de/en/the-current-column/article/two-cheers-for-kenyas-new-constitution-1 (accessed 19 August 2010).

[10] Wily, L.A., 'The Community Land Act: Now it's up to communities', *The Star*, 17 September 2016.

cessive Forest Acts, including the 1960s Act (Cap. 385), the 2005 Forest Act, he said, and the 2016 Forest Conservation and Management Act. He argued that the structures and distribution of powers in the degazettement of forests, which allowed for the conversion of Public Forest Land to Private Land, were at the root of the depletion of the Mau Forest. Cap. 385 placed most relevant powers in the hands of the Minister for Forestry, at times subordinated to the Ministry of Environment and Natural Resources, and notably attributed him the sole authority of gazetting and degazetting forests. This process, the Dean explained, was inherited from the British Colonial Administration. He said that the provision was not bad as such but conceded that it was misused for political purposes. He further insisted that misuse of the provision was unheard of under colonial and early post-Independence rule and only started in the late 1980s. He added that misuse of the prerogative increased after 1992 when multi-party democracy was re-introduced, and politicians supposedly began to worry about forming political majorities again. According to Cap. 385, conversion of Public Forest Land to Private Land was not complicated and needed to follow a simple order: First, a piece of forest had to be officially degazetted by publishing a notice in the Kenya Gazette that a specific piece of forest land, at the time forest land fell under Public Land status per definition, was no longer forest land. The boundaries of the forest piece whose use was to be changed also had to be drawn without necessarily having to provide significant justification. Only after official degazettement could the land be allocated to someone and registered in their name [1/012].

The Dean also confirmed that the Government retained the right to harvest the trees, even after allocating the land to private beneficiaries after forest land was degazetted. Due to the simplicity of forest degazettement, a lot of forest land was allocated to politically connected big players, including in the 2001 excision of the Eastern Mau, as revealed by the Ndung'u Report (Republic of Kenya, 2004b). However, despite the legal process being simple, the parts of the Eastern Mau Forest in which the Mariashoni settlement scheme was established were not degazetted before its declaration and the allocation of plots to individual beneficiaries.[11] When the land was finally degazetted in 2001, and the forest land officially excised, land allocation within the settlement scheme had long been completed. The Dean argued that political actors continuously capitalised on the weak registration and policy regulations and intentionally kept them weak during the Moi era. The 2005 Forest Act introduced important changes in forest regis-

---

[11]   According to the Dean, this was the case in many areas since President Moi commonly gave out land without previously informing the Minister and thus without instructing the Minister to degazette the relevant land [1/012].

tration and deregistration processes, which had been fundamental for forest land misallocation. Forests could no longer simply be degazetted at the discretion of the Minister for Forestry but needed to follow a more comprehensive procedure. Degazetting forest land henceforth required prior discussion in Parliament and conduct of an environmental impact assessment [1/012].

Changing forest land use and occupation in the Mau Forest

Against the general background of changing regulations of Public Land, and specifically, Public Forest Land, and the effects and implications of changes in legal provisions concerning the use and ownership of this land, tenure and occupancy of the Eastern Mau Forest changed considerably throughout history. Both changes from pre-colonial to colonial regimes and changes within the post-colonial period were relevant to the 'Mau crisis'.

Historical changes in socio-spatial organisation and livelihoods

The Eastern Mau Forest is said to have always been the 'national habitat' of the Ogiek (Towett, 2004).[12] The Ogiek are considered forest-based hunters and gatherers who had traditionally lived in different forest areas in western Kenya and northern Tanzania. Most of the remaining Ogiek were found within the Mau Forest Complex and the Mt Elgon Forest areas (Muchemi & Ehrensperger, 2011). They were arguably the largest remaining hunter-gatherer group in Kenya (Ohenjo, 2003). The chairman of the Ogiek Welfare Council and the Ogiek Council of Elders claimed that 'the true face of the Ogiek is in Eastern Mau, mainly in the Mariashoni area' [3/055].

The wider Kalenjin community has received little academic attention despite its prominence in Kenya's history and current political affairs. The few available studies mainly focus on specific Kalenjin sub-groups (Lynch, 2011). In that vein, several localised micro-studies on the Ogiek have been undertaken since the beginning of the 20th century. As noted in the Introduction, most outstanding are the works of Hobley (1903), Huntingford since the 1920s (1929; 1931; 1942; 1951, 1955), and since the 1970s Blackburn (1970, 1974, 1986), Kratz (1980, 1993, 1996, 1999) and van Zwanenberg (1976). Apart from in Blackburn's studies, the Kalenjin-speaking Ogiek of the Mau Forest, like most other hunt-

---

[12] While most early anthropological and a few current studies spell Ogiek with a 'k' instead of the 'g', hence Okiek, I consistently spell Ogiek with the at-present more common 'g'. Furthermore, even though the official singular of 'Ogiek' is 'Ogiot', the term Ogiek is used here to refer to members of the community in singular and plural, as is commonly done.

er-gatherer groups, have not figured in any major linguistic or historical studies (Distefano, 1990). Furthermore, little has been written about the recent transformations of contemporary Ogiek societies beyond these classical anthropological studies. One exception, while not academic per se, is the very notable 'The Ogiek Peoples Ancestral Territories Atlas' (OPAT) – jointly produced by ERMIS Africa, the Eastern and Southern Africa Partnership Programme (ESAPP) and the Centre for Development and Environment (CDE) from the University of Bern, Switzerland – that was first published in Kenya in A3 format in 2011 (Muchemi & Ehrensperger, 2011). The results of their participatory mapping exercise, combining advanced spatial technologies such as aerial photography, the Global Positioning System (GPS) survey, and geographic information system (GIS) technology, as well as an intensive process of community involvement, and ethnographic recording and inventorying of clan narratives (Muchemi, Ehrensperger, & Kiteme, 2015) were unprecedented and led to the production of in-depth maps of the different Ogiek communities' territorial and cultural heritage, their natural resources and a guide to traditional land and natural resource use and related systems of meaning.

The wider Ogiek community was composed of twelve different subgroups, or sub-tribes (Muchemi & Ehrensperger, 2011),[13] whose total population in 1970 was estimated at 50,000 (Blackburn, 1970). Three of these twelve sub-groups, the Tyepkwereg, Morisionig, and Kipchorng'woneg, were traditionally represented in the Eastern Mau. Those three sub-groups were further subdivided into twenty-one clans (Muchemi & Ehrensperger, 2011). The mother tongue of the Ogiek, also called Ogiek, is a Kalenjin language of the Southern Nilotic group (Kratz, 1999). Due to the language-based definition of the wider Kalenjin community, whose common identity was not professed until a Nandi radio presenter proposed the term in the 1940s to unite all Nandi speakers, the Ogiek are hence understood as part of that community (Lynch, 2011).

According to the Ogiek elders consulted during the elaboration of the OPAT, three Ogiek sub-groups still lived in Eastern Mau that used to occupy different areas within the forest (see Table 5).[14]

---

[13] Here, the term sub-group, rather than sub-tribe, is used, despite the latter's prominent use in the OPAT.
[14] Apart from the OPAT Atlas that provides details about the social and spatial structures of the *traditional* Ogiek society, most insights into the ethnographic, economic, and social structures in the past and present were gathered in Interview 4/097.

Table 5   Traditional territories of the Ogiek sub-groups in the Eastern Mau.

Sub-group	Approximate localisation	Specific forest blocks and areas
Tyepkwereg	Forests south-east of the Eastern Mau Forest towards Lake Nakuru and southwards.	Sururu Forest: named after the Ogiek traditional chief Sururu Tarimbo Olekiwanja.; Likia Forest: named after a cluster of clans called 'Likyo' and comprising the Gaplepul, Gaploibor, Gapshoi and Gaptiepopo clans, as well as the Kirasi family of the Gimengich clan; Logoman Forest: named after the *logomeg* plants which are common in the area; Teret (Tiritap Susweeg) Forest: named after a grassland area within the forest.
Morisionig	Northern, central and south-western areas of the Eastern Mau Forest.*	Nessuit (Nesoit): named after a sacred stone in the area. Elburgon Forest (Lembega): A traditional dancing ground. Marioshoni (Moreseei soogot) Forest: named after fresh branches which the Morisionig would place at the junctions of paths leading into the forest to inform others whether one has gone into or come out of the forest; among residents, there are alternative explanations about the origin of the name;* Keringet Forest (part): a place with numerous natural pits.
Kipchorng'woneg	Western and northern parts of the Eastern Mau Forest.	Molo Forest: named after an Ogiek elder called 'Mololo' from the Gapyemit clan; Baraget Forest: referring to the sound of trees swinging in a strong wind; Keringet Forest (part): a place with numerous natural pits.

Source: Adapted from Muchemi & Ehrensperger, 2011, p. 2. Note: *Information here is complemented based on author observations.

The Ogiek spatial organisation was traditionally strictly organised. The forest land used to be subdivided into forest tracts, main lineage territories called *konoito*. Each clan was given its own *konoito*,[15] within which clan members had land-use rights. The OPAT provides the following explanation:

> Over time, the Ogiek partitioned Mau Forest into clan territories (*gonoitweeg*). The boundaries of these territories are clearly delineated using natural markers, topography and vegetation features. The records of these boundaries are held as an intangible cultural heritage by such means as oral traditions, songs, dances, ceremonies, folklore, and riddles. The ancestral boundaries are recognised and respected by all the clan members inherited along the lineage, through intergenerational learning processes, and through the intangible cultural heritage and landscape exploration. The clan-based territories formed the basis of Ogiek occupation, ownership, utilisation, protection, conservation and governance of the forest as well as the resources therein. (Muchemi & Ehrensperger, 2011, p. 2)

As part of these land-use rights, members of the respective clan could hang their traditional log-based beehives in trees, harvest honey, and hunt animals within their clan territories. They could also harvest the white honey produced by small honeybees, often in stones under the soil [5/184, 5/234]. Blackburn (1970, 1986) argued that *konoito* lines primarily demarcated honey, but not necessarily game use, rights. According to a group of elderly Ogiek men, the hunter-gatherer lifestyle of the Ogiek also involved semi-permanent settlements that families would establish in open forest glades within their *konoito*. They added that families moved within the *konoito* to 'follow the honey', as well as the game, and thus rebuilt their leaf-houses (*gotopteleeg*) in open glades along the way. Each *konoito* was devised in a way that it spanned over different altitudes and eco-climatic zones, giving each clan access to different sets of natural resources at different times. The elderly men also said that families would migrate from around 1,500 to 3,000 metres in altitude, what the OPAT describes as 'vertical transhumance', following what they called the 'natural cycles of the land' [4/097]. Each clan territory was furthermore subdivided into family transect units, called *koret*, ranging from one to ten square miles (Blackburn, 1970), which ran parallel to the overall clan territory lines, allowing for transhumance through the different eco-climatic zones from the highlands to the lowlands (Blackburn, 1970, 1986; Muchemi & Ehrensperger, 2011). A *koret* was typically inherited by a man from his father but could also be transferred to another person, most significantly as

---

[15] Throughout the text, I use this spelling since it reflects how the Mariashoni residents pronounce it. The OPAT proposes an alternative spelling, *gonoitweeg*.

compensation for having caused the death of another. Giving a *koret* was synonymous with providing continuous access to honey and hence to life (Blackburn, 1986).

Underpinning the Ogiek transhumance was a traditional classification of eco-climatic zones from the Mau Escarpment to the Lake Nakuru plains. While earlier literature differentiated between five major zones, namely *Soyua, Sasaondet, Tirap, Sisiyuet* and *Mau* (Blackburn, 1970; Kratz, 1993), the OPAT provided an Ogiek classification system that differentiated between ten major existing climates and ecosystems, despite the existence of numerous climatic 'pockets' within the Mau Forest area. Eight of the eco-climatic zones – *Sooywo, Saapo, Tiriig, Logom, Tuimasat, Teegeg, Rogroget,* and *Gaporowo* – 'faced north' (*moipagee*), while two 'faced south' (*ingotogoon*), namely *Mooo,* and *Mosop*. The direction of the zones was based on the water divide, which defined the direction in which the numerous rivers flowed that originated around the summit of the escarpment. The Ogiek defined, delineated, and described the climate of the entire Mau Escarpment and the Lake Nakuru plains based on temperature, humidity, rainfall, and wind, as well as topographic details such as location and altitude, topographic features such as rivers, hills, valleys, and caves, alongside soil types, vegetation types and composition, quality and type of honey, and presence or absence of wild animals. Each of the eco-climatic zones was characterised by different vegetation types, wild animals, types of honeybees, as well as medicinal plants.[16] Land-use practices and spatial movement, particularly, used to follow the rhythm of seasonal changes in forest ecology. According to Muchemi and Ehrensperger (2011), the Ogiek furthermore differentiated five seasons with distinct weather patterns and natural resource dynamics.

The arrival of the colonial government, which set up forest plantations and workers' villages in the Mariashoni area in the Eastern Mau, marked a turning point in previous land management regimes and practices. While the Ogiek continued being allowed to manage and use the remaining primary forest land according to their traditional usages and customs, the colonial government restricted access and movement in the newly established forest plantations. The older men said that clans whose *konoito* was cut off by the plantations could ask to be given user rights in another clan's *konoito*. Despite this initial adaptation, the pre-conditions required for a forest-based life were altered permanently through the plantation establishment. The choice of species, referred to as 'exotic' and fast-growing species not indigenous to the area, for instance, was not conducive to the existing fauna and led to changes

---

[16] An overview of common tree uses in the Eastern Mau can be found on p. 8 of the OPAT (Muchemi and Ehrensperger, 2011). Appendix 1 provides an overview of tree uses inventoried during the research.

in the local ecosystems. The establishment of forest plantations also led to a network of roads within the wider Mau Forest, including in the Mariashoni area, which facilitated exchange between the people inside and outside the forest [4/097]. Customarily, the Ogiek mainly traded their honey for other goods, notably meat, and later potatoes and maize. Before the arrival of the Kikuyu, the Ogiek mainly entertained contact with the neighbouring Maasai communities (Blackburn, 1970; Distefano, 1990). While they were somewhat exposed to 'hard money', the absence of places to spend that money made barter trade the preferred means of exchange until the 20th century. Kratz (1993) locates the wider Ogiek community's full integration into the market and consumer economy at the beginning of the 1980s. The establishment of various settlement schemes in the 1990s brought about further fundamental changes to the socio-spatial organisation in the Eastern Mau Forest.

Winners and losers in historical land conflicts

In the 1990s, seemingly official, as well as straight-out illegal degazettement of forest land for the benefit of individual owners, accelerated considerably in the Mau Forest, including in the Eastern Mau (Republic of Kenya, 2004b). While the Ogiek were made to believe it was for their benefit (Sang, 2003), it quickly turned out that most of the land was not attributed to the Ogiek but sold or given out to politically connected persons. Misappropriation of land in the Mau Forest was addressed in the Ndung'u Report and the list of beneficiaries included in Annexes Vol. II. It illustrates that two hundred thousand non-regular land title deeds had been distributed in the previous twenty years, often leading to the expropriation and eviction of specific individuals and groups for the benefit of others (Connan, 2005).

While most of the major politically significant land beneficiaries were taken out of the publicly accessible version of the Report (Klopp & Lumumba, 2016),[17] one media expert insisted that land issues in the Mau Forest were 'typical land issues' and added that 'there is no politician who has no issues with land [and that it is why it is] difficult to tackle them' [both 1/005]. He also cited several cases in which the country's important political and/or economic elites had benefited from illegal and mostly large-scale land allocations. Most prominently, he mentioned the Nyayo Tea Zones in Kiptagich in Transmara Forest Reserve. The vast tea estate, which extended over 938 ha, was supposedly created as a 'buffer zone' between the settlements outside of the forest cutline and the actual forest. This zone officially was to prevent encroachment into the forest and thus conserve the forest [1/005].

---

[17] The analysis of the publicly available Annexes II thus does not allow for easy insights, and evidence presented in this section had to be extracted from interviews with experts.

Klopp (2012) explains that the Nyayo Tea Zones were established with the help of a World-Bank-supported project, which aimed at protecting government forests by creating 100 m-wide 'buffer zones' around the forests in which tea was planted. These tea zones were represented as 'simple but effective way' to prevent people from encroaching into the forest. The media expert further explained that President Moi used this 'buffer zone' narrative for many tea estates that were created in or along the edges of the Mau Forest, most of which were created through gazette notice only. The notice for the establishment of the Nyayo Tea Zones was gazetted on 3 March 1989, however without posting legal notice of the forest excision. The area thus remained gazetted forest and the excision was de jure illegal.[18] Since the land on which the tea zones were established was grabbed and henceforth belonged to one of the companies of what the journalist called former President Moi's 'family empire', the creation of buffer zones, and the conversion of forest to agricultural land, led to considerable monetary gains for his family, and important net forest losses for the country. The expert further cited a famous politician [1/005], whose constituency extended to parts of Eastern and South-Western Mau, as did his personal land possessions [1/002]. According to the Ndung'u Report (2004b), he obtained more than 29,000 acres of land in the Mau Forest while serving as Permanent Secretary for Internal Security during Moi's Presidency. At the time, he was a close ally of then-Deputy President William Ruto.[19]

Despite the political change, former President Mwai Kibaki, who was internationally recognised as the first democratically elected President of the country, made use of the same repertoire of practices as his predecessors. Despite climaxing during Moi's Presidency, the political use of land did not end with the formation of the NARC multiparty government after the 2002 elections. Land was used as a political resource during election periods, but equally served to garner support during other political events. One of the most important occasions was the 2005 constitutional referendum. The referendum was to mark the concluding step of the democratisation period that began with the re-introduction of multiparty elections and eventually was to lead to a replacement of the 1963 post-Independence Constitution. Former President Kibaki, elected as head of the NARC Government in 2002, led the 'Yes' Campaign for the heavily contested so-called 'Wako Draft' of the new Constitution, while the opposition within his coalition government, headed by leader Raila Odinga, at the time leader of the Liberal Democratic Party (LDP), drove the 'No' Campaign. A league of many different

[18]   Additional information about the size and the legal situation from UNEP (2008); UNEP et al. ((2005).
[19]   Many other 'big men' got land as well, specifically 'big men' of President Moi's entourage [1/002].

parties carried the 'No' Campaign and political figures, and the symbol allocated to the 'No' in the referendum, an orange, later led to the formation of the Orange Democratic Movement (ODM), the party at whose head Raila Odinga competed for the contended presidential elections in 2007 and 2013. Most political leaders and parties from the Northern Rift Valley, and thus most prominent Kalenjin politicians, supported the 'No' campaign. President Mwai Kibaki found himself in the predicament of wooing the Kalenjin who had previously settled in the Mau Forest (Kagwanja, 2010; Médard, 2008b). In breach of the initial order of the High Court about the allocation of forest land in 1997, against the recommendations of the Ndung'u Report, and contrary to a new court order issued regarding the attribution of title deeds for illegally allocated land specifically, Kibaki's Government decided to give out title deeds to forest dwellers in the Mau Forest [1/002, 1/005]. It was established, for instance, that a majority of the 12,616 title deeds issued in the Mau Forest were distributed to dwellers by President Kibaki ahead of the 2005 Referendum, disregarding a former High Court Order and therefore illegally.[20] The political objective, at that point, was understood to be related to attracting the 'Kalenjin vote' that was challenged by two different sources at the time. Most importantly, much of the debate surrounding the new Constitution included discussions about historical injustices in land allocation, one of the main issues driving the political agenda in Kenyan politics since the emergence of the Mau Mau uprising in the 1950s. Many settlers feared losing their land. The Government supposedly planned to reassure Kalenjin settlers that their land was safe by attributing them title deeds. The other major problem that the 'Yes' campaign faced in the Mau Forest stemmed from the fact that most Kalenjin leaders actively supported the 'No' campaign [1/002]. Kenya, generally, is a country deeply marked by voting patterns along ethnic lines (Branch, 2011; Hornsby & Throup, 1998; Klopp, 2001), which are often motivated by what (Lonsdale, 1992, 1994, 1996) calls 'moral ethnicity' that concretises in the form of redistribution of state resources to members of one's ethnic group, or the provision and delivery of state services in the area of origin of a respective politician. Attempting to 'buy' the Kalenjin vote with title deeds can be understood as a display of a certain sense of realism on the Government's side. In some instances, the Government had distributed so-called 'flying titles' to forest dwellers. These highly insecure 'waiting to be allocated' title deeds were mainly given to members of the Kipsigis community on land in the Likia Extension settlement scheme on the northern edges of the Eastern Mau, which had led to much tension with other settlers in the area [1/002].

---

[20] Standard Team, 'Explosive Mau forest dossier', *The Standard*, 27 July 2009.

Another study prepared by the Mau Task Force and presented by the then Prime Minister in July 2009 illustrated that various present and former MPs, power brokers, senior officials in the present and past governments, big businesses owners and the like had benefited from political favouritism and obtained land in the Mau Forest.[21] According to that study, five hundred acres were given to twenty-five influential individuals between 1996 and 2005 in eighteen settlement zones, namely Mariashoni, Likia, Korao, Ndoinet, Kapsita Molo, Kapsita, Sururu, Ngongongeri, Saino, Teret, Nessuit, Tinet Sotik, Kiptagich, Kiptagich Extension, Baraget, Likia Extension, Londiani Jourbet Kedowa and Changeya. The study revealed that eighteeen companies received land ranging from four to eight hectares each in 1998 alone in the Mariashoni settlement scheme. Beneficiaries included a former President's son, various MPs, and other persons holding political positions. At the same time, many other '[c]hiefs, district officers, district commissioners, provincial commissioners and departmental lands and forest officers benefited' as well.[22] These reports also showed that county councillors, previously in charge of administering Trust Land on behalf of a given community, vastly contributed to the misallocation of land: 'the most pronounced land grabbers in these areas were the councillors themselves ... The corruption within central government has been replicated at the local level through the activities and omissions of the county and municipal councillors' (Republic of Kenya, 2004b, p. 147).

In the Maasai Mau, the most southern forest reserve of the Mau Forest, 'big men' accessed and acquired forest land by benefiting from specific policies in that area. The status of the Maasai Mau Forest was different from that of the other forest blocks since it was a community forest exclusively populated by mostly indigenous *cedar* and *podocarpus* species (ENSDA, UNEP, KFWG, & KWS, 2005; UNEP, KFS, & KFWG, 2005; UNEP, ENSDA, KFWG, KWS, & RSRS, 2006). Due to its location on Trust/Community Land, the Narok County Council was the custodian of the forest (DRSRS & KFWG, 2006; GoK, 2009e) until the 2010 Constitution introduced the territorial reform. Since members of the Maasai community had traditionally inhabited the Maasai Mau, land use and management in the adjacent communities were influenced by group ranch policies implemented by the Government under the auspices of the World Bank in the 1970s. A media expert explained that, with the help of corrupt officials, the group ranches along the Maasai Forest

---

[21] Kimutai, V., 'Raila censures hostile Rift Valley MPs', *The Standard*, 10 August 2009; Ndegwa, A., 'Who is who in Mau Forest land allocation', *The Standard*, 30 July 2009; Tanui, K., 'Water is life, now please shut up!', *The Standard*, 31 July 2009.

[22] Agutu, M., 'Revealed: Big names given Mau Forest land', *Daily Nation*, 2 April 2009.

slowly encroached into the forest reserve. Consequently, the forest surrounding the farm became a 'cash cow', and politically connected figures acquired 'unreasonably big' [both 1/005] land. Apart from using their land for large-scale agricultural production, politically well-connected persons purchased large tracts of land in forest areas, subdivided them and sold them directly or swapped them against 'clean' pieces of land outside the forest. The turnaround between acquisition and sale was typically kept short to reduce risks associated with engaging in this illegal practice, notably dispossession [1/008].

In the Mau Forest, as in many other places, the allocation of land to selected individuals implied that other individuals and groups had to be evicted from the same. One expert explained that different supposedly 'disturbing' groups of people were expelled and dispossessed from the Mau Forest by successive regimes throughout modern Kenyan history. First, the colonial government brought in members of the Kikuyu community and sought displacement of members of the wider Kalenjin group, particularly of the Kipsigis community, since the Kalenjin were generally considered as opposed to colonial rule and the colonial government. Later, the Government displaced the Kikuyu workers and their families after the beginning of the Mau Mau uprising in the early 1950s, which, according to the expert, started in Olenguruone in the South-Western Mau. In response to the rebellion, the colonial government evicted the Kikuyu from the forest and sent them back to the Central Province, while others were transported to *Ukambani*, the homeland of the Kamba community, in what was then the Eastern Province. In the Eastern Mau, the Mau Mau rebellion also touched Mariashoni, and the Kikuyu were evicted from the forest. After Independence, the Kikuyu returned to both Olenguruone and Mariashoni areas, only to find that members of the wider Kalenjin community had taken over their lands. According to the expert, these men had, in the meantime, been recruited as Home Guards, the colonial guard composed of members of different Kenyan communities whose task was to fight the Mau Mau. After Independence in 1963, President Jomo Kenyatta displayed interest in maintaining a robust Kikuyu presence in the Mau Forest and enabled many Kikuyu households to acquire land in the Mau Forest again. The forced displacement of the Kikuyu continued under post-Independence governments, particularly during the Presidency of Moi, who sought to remove political opposition from the land, especially after the failed coup attempt of 1982 [1/002].

Further trends in forest evictions and population displacements in the Mau Forest included workers from other parts of the country being brought to the Mau Forest by the colonial administration as part of the forest production enterprise from as early as 1927. Most of the forest workers were displaced from Central Province, the area where most of the Kikuyu are said to originate from and settled them in the eastern parts of the Mau Forest, most prominently in Mariashoni. The workers were mainly employed for the day-to-day management of the forest plantations. From the 1930s, more and more Kikuyu workers were brought into the area, especially Olenguruone. Here, the Kikuyu were mostly used as farm hands in the cultivation of vast farms created on the fertile forest land. Kikuyu workers were supposedly also used to 'push back' members of the Kalenjin community who refused to collaborate with the colonial government. Before bringing in the first Kikuyu workers in 1917, the colonial government had displaced members of the Kipsigis community from the south-western sides of the Mau Forest to an area called Chepalungu, around the towns Kipsingei, Siongiroi, and Kipsuter, approximately 65 km south-west of Olenguruone. Before being displaced, the local Ogiek and the Kipsigis had intermarried, and the Kipsigis laid claims to the land. They finally returned to the South-Western Mau in 1969 and established nine villages but were evicted once more by then-Provincial Administrator Mathenge. According to the expert, around one-quarter of the inhabitants of these nine Kipsigis villages moved deeper into the forest, while the remaining three-quarters returned to Chepalungu. By then, the colonial government had established tea estates in Chepalungu, and the Kipsigis were not allowed to resettle in the area. Most of them after that returned to the slopes of the Mau Forest, particularly to the southern part of the Eastern Mau, where Kikuyus lived by then. The Government displaced the Kipsigis from the area one final time in 1974. After President Moi took office in 1979, the Kipsigis' struggle for legitimate residence in the Mau Forest reduced in intensity [1/002].

The political economy of land allocation and distribution in the Eastern Mau Forest

Mariashoni settlement scheme was de facto carved out of the Eastern Mau Forest in 1997, including the Mariashoni Trading Centre area. Within the settlement scheme, five-acre plots were allocated to individual households. There were three settlement schemes close to Mariashoni Centre, namely Mariashoni, Kapsita (Elburgon), and Ngongongeri (DRSRS & KFWG, 2006) [3/058], and ten in total in the wider Eastern Mau (see overview in Table 1). The settlement schemes started being carved out after former President Moi, through the Provincial Commissioner of the Rift Valley Province at the time, had begun giving out good and easily attainable forest land to individual contenders in an unstructured manner from as early as 1992/1993. Later, in 1997, the Government integrated these areas in which land had previously been parcelled and allocated to the newly created settlement schemes. Degazettement and hence excision of the forest land followed in 2001 [1/002].

The characteristics and proceedings of land distribution within these settlement schemes provide insights into the presumed objectives of the actors involved. The analysis of the different types of individuals and groups who obtained land areas shows that the Government pursued many objectives, presumably informed by different sets of rationalities. While narratives included here concentrate predominantly on the wider Mariashoni area and thus on the Mariashoni settlement scheme, similar realities found in neighbouring settlement schemes are addressed where appropriate.

Consolidating the support of the 'Big Men'

The Mariashoni settlement scheme was officially established with the objective to compensate the Ogiek for past land injustices by giving them land. While estimates varied, various observers agreed that members of the Ogiek community had only benefited marginally. According to local officials, less than one-quarter of the total land excised in the Eastern Mau was attributed to Ogiek beneficiaries [3/056, 3/062].

Those who did benefit were mostly the political and economic elite of the country, including members of different arms of Kenya's security forces, the local administration, and a few ordinary people [1/002]. The head of Mariashoni's local authority specified that around one-quarter of the land in the Mariashoni settlement scheme was allocated to government officials, as well as half of the land in the neighbouring Kapsita (Elburgon), and three-quarters of the land in Ngongongeri settlement schemes [3/058]. The forest dwellers who had petitioned President Moi had assumed they would be the primary beneficiaries. Yet, in the process of registering legitimate contenders, other Kalenjin from outside the forest joined their peers throughout the Eastern Mau, and the authorities could no longer differentiate between those who were initially supposed to obtain land and those who sought out new opportunities [1/002]. The Chief traced the inclusion of other community members in the beneficiary lists back to the Kenya Indigenous Forest Conservation (KIFCON) project. He said that KIFCON, funded by the UK Department of Overseas Development Agency (later the Department for International Development, DFID and, since 2020, the Foreign, Commonwealth & Development Office, FCDO), carried out a study in the early 1990s that was supposed to identify the Ogiek who lived in the Mau Forest area. However, the exercise was allegedly 'influenced', and 'bogus Ogiek' were included in the register, particularly members of the Kipsigis community and some Tugen. In the same vein, around 800 members of the Kikuyu community who had been evicted from Olenguruone in 1992 were settled in Kapsita between 1998 and 1999 [3/058]. The ballooning of contenders to the land that had been excised, alongside illegal allocations of the land to various elites, rendered the available land insufficient. The President repeatedly increased the size of forest land tracts that were then excised, deforested, commodified, and allocated. After excising more than half of the Eastern Mau, most of the bush and the indigenous forest were cleared between 1993 and 2003 [1/002].

In terms of land sizes, there was a critical difference between the land allocated to 'big men', often hundreds of acres, and land given to ordinary farmers. One Mariashoni resident said that 'there are people who got six hundred acres, three hundred acres, one hundred acres and some got nothing' and added 'obviously, there are conflicts' [5/236]. A member of the local authority mentioned that 'many people who got big plots are past or present government officials' and that, consequently, there was 'no openness to talk problems out and find solutions' [3/061]. The political and economic elites who kept their land for their own benefit, instead of subdividing it and reselling it, mainly used it for agricultural production, providing them with an important source of income. A government employee added that most of the 'big people' did not live on their land but had caretakers look after their farms. Since many of these farms were of considerable size, they were often monocropped, typically with maize or wheat. Since trees would disturb the machinery used for harvesting these fields, there were almost no trees left in these areas, and the promotion of agroforestry and planting of trees would be unlikely to yield any successes [3/062]. Farms of a considerable size used for larger-scale crop farming could be observed mostly in the 'lower' parts of Mariashoni Location, almost until the supposed 'cutline', up to which plots were surveyed, demarcated, and allocated in 1997. These farms were obviously used productively.

Various persons spoke about having benefited from land initially attributed to 'big men' in different parts of the Eastern Mau, including Mariashoni. An Ogiek man, for instance, explained that some land to be given out during the land allocation exercise was hidden and subsequently sold out by the *'wakubwa'* ('big men') [5/251]. Another young Ogiek resident also insisted *'wakubwa wanang'ang'ania mashamba'* (big men steal land) [5/172]. A Tugen resident of Chai Moto village within the wider Mariashoni area estimated that approximately three-quarters of the people who owned the surrounding *shambas* in the area were *'watu wadosi wakubwa'* (big, rich men) [5/204]. In Mariashoni, 'big men are all over the place' [5/108], said an outspoken resident. He further spoke about a senior politician who supposedly owned a 200-acre farm. The other beneficiaries he mentioned were a wealthy hotel business owner from Nakuru, a son of the former President, alongside different representatives of the provincial and local administration [5/108].

Another aspect of compensating the 'big men' manifested in land allocations to acknowledge 'service to the Nation'. To recognise their 'service', members of different branches of the country's security forces obtained land in the Mau Forest over the years. While there was no widespread allocation of land to security forces in the Mariashoni area, the practice was common enough for it to be worthy of mention. In the Maasai Mau, south of the Eastern Mau, a place called Sierra Leone made the news in 2010 because violent opposition to planned evictions erupted during Phase III of the Mau Restoration plan.[23] The area's name was derived from the fact that the land was allocated to Kenyan soldiers who had been involved in the civil war in the West African nation under an African Union (AU) mandate at the turn of the century [1/005]. The 'compensation for service to the Nation' aspect aside, the majority of the soldiers who benefited from land allocations in these areas were members of the Kalenjin community. One expert explained that different parts of the Mau Forest were allocated to specific groups of people. Land in Sururu, on the eastern edge of Eastern Mau Forest, for instance, was given to members of the General Service Unit (GSU), a special para-military force under the direct command of the President, while officers working for the Administration Police Service (AP) received land in the wider Eastern Mau area [1/002].

Opinions about the purpose of land allocations to members of the armed forces varied among Mariashoni residents. One resident explained that President Moi exposed paranoid behaviour towards members of the Kikuyu community, who, after all, had started a revolution from a forest base with the specific objective of nationalising land during the Mau Mau rebellion that eventually led to Kenya's Independence and who, at this point, had manifested a degree of alienation from President Moi's rule [1/002]. Others opined that allocating entire forest blocks to politically loyal groups and protégés targeted creation of buffer zones against the Kikuyu [1/002]. The power of these groups became apparent when the violent protest of those who had obtained land in Sierra Leone led to a permanent halt in the eviction of forest dwellers from the Mau Forest in 2010, merely a year after the publication of the report of the Special Task Force and the beginning of the actual forest reclamation exercise under the auspices of the ICS. Doubts were clear about the Government's ability to carry out the evictions in Maasai Mau since the area's residents openly challenged it and refused to vacate the land that had been allocated to them twice [1/005].

A Tugen resident of Chai Moto village explained that his neighbour was supposedly one of the persons that were compensated for 'service to the Nation'. He explained that the older man owned fifteen acres but continued laying claims on the land allocated to him, pointing out that the entire area had been given to him as grazing grounds for his animals. He said that the older man had already come six times to his homestead to threaten him into leaving, sometimes armed with a sword. He even

---

[23] Sigei, J., 'Why Mau restoration has stalled', *Daily Nation*, 4 September 2010.

sought the local authority's intervention, but no solution was found. He remained wary of the older man's claim to the land because of his presumed long-standing connection to the Government [5/199]. The older man said that he had lived in Chai Moto for more than ten years and was a Maasai hailing from Narok. He explained that his grandfather had been a Chief during colonial times and his father, a Chief after Independence. He added that the Mau Forest used to belong to the Maasai. He said the 'Dorobo' came to the area through the colonial administration to work in the forest and then started laying claims to the land. Yet, he also acclaimed that *'sisi wote ni wenyeji ya misitu'* (we are all locals to the forest), displaying the historicity of divergent claims to ancestral possession of forest land [5/196].

Creating clusters of political loyalty

The distribution of fertile forest land to members of the wider Kalenjin community during Moi's Presidency served many purposes. The IDP coordinator explained that the excision of forest land and the accompanying land redistribution to members of non-forest-dwelling communities in the Mau Forest was triggered by a group of Kalenjin elders approaching the President. They supposedly complained about poor living conditions on the south-western slopes of the Mau Forest and about being less well-off than the Kikuyu in the area despite claiming that the land was ancestral Kalenjin land, and petitioned him to improve their living conditions. In response to their request, land in various parts of the Mau, including in the Eastern Mau, was allocated to individual Kalenjin households from the early 1990s [1/002]. President Moi evidently targeted improving the economic situation of his 'kin' by giving out fertile forest lands. However, many observers said President Moi's strategic consideration was to consolidate a 'Kalenjin zone' by allocating small parcels of land to individual members of the wider Kalenjin community. These allocations allowed his government to increase the numbers of Kalenjin residing in the central Rift Valley in a short period. This ethnic mobilisation for votes had long-lasting political implications [1/005].

The Ndung'u Report revealed that land allocation to politicians was widespread in all the settlement schemes carved out in the Eastern Mau Forest in the late 1990s (Republic of Kenya, 2004b). In the Mariashoni settlement scheme, according to the testimony of a local authority representative, one-quarter of land was directly allocated to government officials under whose discretion further sale and redistribution of land fell thereafter [3/058].

Many non-Ogiek Mariashoni residents confirmed having obtained land in conjunction with specific political events. An educated young man who had studied abroad but failed to find a job and moved to Mariashoni in 2000 explained how he and his family arrived in the area. At the time, a Rift Valley MP mobilised and tried to convince young families and members of the Tugen community struggling to seek greener pastures to move into the Mau Forest. The man explained that the offer represented an opportunity because temperatures in his home place Baringo were very high, the soil was poor and laced with rocks, and water was sparse. He said he came to Mariashoni to pursue a better life, while many families resisted the temptation because they feared the changes and did not want to give up on their homeland. He was not asked to pay anything for the five-acre land allocated to his family, and no liabilities were imposed. However, they were requested to register as voters in their new home instead of returning to Baringo to vote [5/199]. Creating a voting bloc with loyal Kalenjin was thus clearly one of the main objectives of attributing land to him. The man explained that when he arrived in Chai Moto in 2000, there were only two houses in the area, and other people started moving in after that date. Chai Moto was mainly settled by members of the Kipsigis and Tugen communities. At the same time, he said that the Government primarily settled members of the Kikuyu community 'down there' in Kapsita (Molo) and confirmed that different areas in the Mariashoni area were allocated by different persons to different groups of people [5/199]. A Tugen resident who hailed from Baringo as well described a similar situation. He said the same MP had asked each local chief in the area to nominate five households that were then taken to Mariashoni. The individual households nominated by each chief were divided and settled in different parts of Mariashoni Location. Hence, when he and his family arrived in Chai Moto, they did not know anyone, despite being settled alongside other Tugen from Baringo [5/203]. Another Tugen man who benefited from a similar land allocation exercise in Chai Moto explained that residents in some areas of Baringo had entered their fifth year without obtaining any harvest, when some mysterious sickness broke out in 1997. The MP then petitioned the President in search of a solution for his ailing people. Since the President was about to 'redistribute the White Highlands for settlement schemes', as he framed it, they were lucky, and each of the nominated households obtained five acres in Mariashoni [5/204].

Other residents explained that they obtained land because of personal connections. Another vocal individual of the Tugen community who received a five-acre plot free of charge, for instance, explained that he got his land due to connections between his area MP and the local authority in Mariashoni. However, it was unclear to him if the local authority had to comply with orders from above or, on the contrary, if they could favour him when giving him land [4/264]. A Nandi resident explained that he obtained land because he had an Ogiek friend who was part of the local elite. He added that he met the head of the local authority, who invited him to stay and gave him a piece of land [5/256].

Others indicated having bought their land. An old Kipsigis woman from Kericho, whose family owned a visibly well managed farm on the completely deforested lower slopes of Mariashoni Location approximately 3.5 km from Mariashoni Centre, explained that she got land after visiting her brother, who had married a woman from Mariashoni. She said she was just visiting when a broker approached her and offered her five acres for approximately KES 200,000 ($2,000). Since her land in Kericho was small and not enough for her children, and because the land in Mariashoni was so good that 'no-one can sell a *shamba* here after having found one' [5/247], she bought five of the fifteen acres the owner had obtained. She added that the owner sold five more acres to another Kipsigis woman [whom we interviewed in 5/246] and that there are still more *shambas* being sold up to the present day. She also stated that land prices had increased, and five acres were now sold at KES 300,000 ($3,000) [5/247].

Starting from the late 1980s, in the context of voting-bloc creation for President Moi's KANU party, which led to the described allocation of land to members of the wider Kalenjin community, the forest-dwelling Kikuyu were displaced once again. A Timsales worker who, due to his duty station being in Elburgon and his work assignments being in Timsales-managed forest plantations inside the nearby Kiptunga Forest, regularly frequented Mariashoni Centre, himself a member of the Kikuyu community, explained that the former District Commissioner had members of the Kikuyu community evicted from the Eastern Mau in a highly violent fashion in 1987. He described that the police beat down the Kikuyu forest workers' maize fields, burned their houses, destroyed their *shambas* and killed or drove away their livestock. His explanation attempt was that President Moi wanted the Kikuyu out of the forest because they were too rich, cultivated their fields too successfully and had vast livestock holdings in the Eastern Mau. At the same time, he said they 'refused Moi' because 'Moi wanted [our] allegiance in poverty' [5/233]. He explained that his grandfather had worked under the colonial government in the forest and was one of the households evicted in the late 1980s. Before the eviction, the Kikuyu settlers had received notice to vacate the area, but since most people did not have anywhere else to go, they stayed put. After their eviction from Mariashoni, the Timsales worker's family and many other Kikuyu families moved to Elburgon, where his family resided up to that date [5/233]. An Ogiek resident of Kaprop spoke of the same and said that Kaprop Primary School was closed, cattle possession forbidden, and that specific on-farm forestry practices permitted through the *shamba* system were abolished, which led to a complete economic disempowerment of the Kikuyu residents. He also said that President Moi evicted people who had been perceived to sympathise with the opposition, especially the Kikuyu and Luo, to 'remove his opposition from the forest' [2/051].

A young Ogiek man explained that there used to be a village inhabited by Kikuyu forest workers opposite Kaprop Primary School. He recalled that the entire village was evicted in 1987 and that there had not been any Kikuyu residents in Mariashoni since then. The eviction of the Kikuyu and the subsequent closure of the Primary School in Kaprop interrupted the lives of non-Kikuyu in the area as well, including that of the young Ogiek man himself, because Kaprop Primary School that he was attending was closed in 1987 when he was in Standard Six [5/148].[24] The middle-aged Ogiek woman, who was a member of the Ogiek Council, on the other hand, and who, according to her name, is the daughter of a Kikuyu man and an Ogiek woman, explained that her father was one of the few Kikuyu who were not evicted because he was working with the forest service at the time [5/118].

Several areas in the Eastern Mau Forest had also benefited from the politically motivated attribution of illegal title deeds. According to various testimonies, the political objective of reassuring the Kalenjin settlers was compounded with an ongoing 'requirement' of manifest-ing some degree of 'moral ethnicity' towards the Kikuyu community as well. In that vein, numerous settlers of the Kapsita settlement scheme, where Kikuyu IDPs had been settled, got title deeds in 2005 [e.g., 1/005, 5/201]. The eastern part of the wider Kapsita, called Kapsita Elbur-gon, was one of the three settlement schemes in Eastern Mau Forest. Kapsita was the settlement on the outer northern edge of the Eastern Mau, in an area that had supposedly not physically resembled a forest for generations. The wider Kapsita also included Kapsita Molo, part of the Western Mau Forest. The media expert said that while former Presi-dent Moi proposed to give title deeds to around twelve thousand mostly Kikuyu households in Kapsita Elburgon between 1998 and 1999, which his administration had previously evicted from Chepakundi in Kuresoi in 1992, land in Kapsita Molo was initially given to the then-area MP [1/005]. He was said to have first distributed parts of the land to other political figures, including one politician elected as area MP for Molo Constituency in 1997 after serving as MP for the Nakuru North and Laikipia West,[25] before selling to individual settlers. The media expert argued that the Kikuyu households to whom land had been promised only benefited marginally. By 2010, he added, the same land had already been sold to the fourth round of people [1/005].

The distribution of title deeds led to the further arrival and set-tlement of people in the forest, many of whom had not been directly affected by the evictions, discussed in detail in the following chapter.

---

[24] Standard Six is the sixth year of Primary School in Kenya, typically repre-sented by children aged 12–13 years.
[25] Wachira, P. 'Kihika Kimani: The master political clown', *The Standard*, 6 June 2010.

One expert called them 'land masqueraders' who claimed to be affected by evictions and internal displacements and hoped to benefit from government compensation programmes [1/002]. The media expert explained that the in-migration of presumed victims of evictions had severely interfered with the forest restoration. Initially, it was unclear whether the evicted households should be compensated for losing their land. Later, the Government decided that they would not, and then that first-generation beneficiaries would not be compensated, but subsequent generations of landholders would. The confusion led many residents to believe there would be compensation after all. Since the Government struggled to explain why their policies produced more IDPs, the relocation question eventually became the scapegoat for the forest restoration process stalling altogether [1/005].

Looking at the magnitude of land allocation to smallholder farmers who hailed from areas outside of the forest, the *wageni* clearly outweighed the local Ogiek in terms of population numbers within Mariashoni Ward in 2013. Assessed in the run-up to the 2013 general elections, local estimates proposed a distribution of 2,800 *wageni* voters against 1,600 Ogiek voters [5/229]. Almost two-thirds of the approximately 4,400 registered voters within Mariashoni Ward were arguably not originally from the area. This imbalance rendered the local Ogiek vulnerable to the perception that they might potentially be overruled by them (Fuchs, 2014). These underlying fears also led to the creation and circulation of rumours that further contributed to deteriorating social relations between different groups in the area. Local Ogiek representatives said that 30,000 households were brought from KANU-friendly areas into the wider Eastern Mau in the late 1990s (Sang, 2003). One external expert confirmed the same figure and indicated that these households were distributed from Mauche at the outer edge of the Eastern Mau further afield. He added that Mauche was targeted mainly because the area had been an opposition stronghold before [1/033].

Declaration of the Mariashoni settlement scheme and the great dispossession of the Ogiek

Looking at a recently built makeshift church opposite the entrance to Mariashoni Centre, one Ogiek resident said, 'this is my land, but because I supported the court case [HCCA No. 635/97, noted below], the Chief brought other people to take my *shamba*'. He explained that his family used to own two 'lines' within his family clan's *konoito*. He added that land was allocated to him and his wife during the land allocation exercise in the 1990s but that he had found himself at the centre of a land conflict since then [5/200].

The man described what transpired in 1997, a year that marked an important transition in access and use of land for inhabitants of the

Eastern Mau Forest around Mariashoni. Since the arrival of the colonial forestry enterprise in the Mau Forest, the forest's biophysical and human landscape has been subjected to continuous change. These changes eventually climaxed when the declaration of the Mariashoni settlement scheme led to de facto changes in the land rights regime and introduced private land holding on previously government-controlled Public Forest Land. Since then, land allocation and management in Mau Forest have remained contentious, particularly in the South-Western and the Eastern Mau [1/002].

Mariashoni's famous Ogiek leader said that despite having suffered a long history of deprivation, the most traumatic and disruptive event the community had to experience was the official excision of 35,301 ha of forest land in the Eastern Mau in 2001. According to him, less than one-quarter of the land had been allocated to members of the Ogiek community at the time. Before that, since 1994/1995, the land had slowly been given to individual beneficiaries, but the number of 'outsiders'[26] moving into Eastern Mau skyrocketed after 1997, he added. In 1996, before the official excision, Ogiek activists had drummed up support for their opposition to land allocations in the area. They even brought about a vote in Parliament, in which thirty-nine Members of Parliament supported their cause. The Ogiek leader explained that the 1997 forest excision was an answer to resistance the Government had met after changing forest policies in 1987 that were intended to lead to the eviction of all forest dwellers. The Ogiek, however, resisted forest evictions and, as a reaction, the Government later attempted to pacify and silence them by allocating them individual plots, he said. 'We almost became beneficiaries of an illegal process', he added, emphasising that the Ogiek resistance to the settlement declaration only solidified after realising that 'the plan would be to settle one Ogiek alongside five non-Ogiek, mainly Kipsigis' [3/056]. With the support of the famous Kenyan human rights lawyer Gibson Kamau Kuria [3/058], a group of Ogiek activists led by said local Ogiek leader took the case to court, logged as Constitutional Suit HCCA No. 635/97, on 23 June 1997 [3/060]. On 22 October 1997, the Government responded through the then-Nakuru District Commissioner, since 2013 Nakuru Governor, that the Ogiek had been using the gazetted forest illegally, that the settlement scheme only covered plantation areas, which were the property of the Government, and did not involve indigenous forest land, and that despite the Ogiek occupation, the Mau Forest was not an Ogiek reservation and hence not Ogiek ancestral land (see also Sang, 2003). Despite this bold response, the High Court granted the plaintiffs an injunction

26 As mentioned previously, the Mariashoni Ogiek referred to members of other communities as 'foreigners' or 'outsiders' when speaking in English and as *'wageni'* (guests) when speaking in Swahili.

on 15 October 1997, which provided that further alienation and allocation of land in Eastern Mau had to cease until the case was resolved in court (Sang, 2003). Consequently, further surveying and plot allocation were halted from October 1997 (Towett, 2004); since the case had not been taken back up and was still pending in court by 2013, the order was still valid. The opposition to the carving out of the settlement schemes in the Eastern Mau became the most publicised and recognised struggle for the land of the Ogiek.

Despite the court order, land title deeds were issued on the lower slopes of the settlement schemes in the Eastern Mau, particularly in Kapsita (Elburgon), from February 1998. Attempting to disguise the illegality of these titles, the authorities supposedly backdated them to July 1997, before the injunction was obtained [3/058]. Interestingly, titles were almost exclusively given out for plots that had been allocated to 'foreigners' in the lower parts of Mariashoni Location.[27] While assessing the precise 'cutline' between the land that was demarcated and allocated by Kenya Surveyors and the remaining unallocated land was difficult during the research, some explained that some of the settlers in the lower parts of Mariashoni, from Elburgon towards the trading centre, had obtained titles [3/062]; but that the attribution of these titles[28] stopped somewhere close to Mariashoni Primary School and thus at a considerable distance from Mariashoni Centre. Consequently, people who did not obtain land formally, including a majority of local Ogiek, moved to the land that had not been surveyed, subdivided, and allocated [3/061]. Similar accounts were given by numerous local and external experts, as well as Mariashoni residents. This land remained under unclear status within the proposed settlement scheme but was de jure Forest and hence Government/Public Land. A member of the local authorities stated that despite official proceedings and court cases, most Ogiek settled on land that had traditionally been allocated to their clans (*konoito*) and that members of clans whose land had been allocated to others by the Government were given land within the traditional lands of those clans who maintained significant portions that were not officially allocated [3/061]. In the same context, one of the most candid members of the local Ogiek community emphasised that some of the regulations and restrictions associated with the *konoito* lines, mainly concerning traditional honey production, were still respected, despite the subdivision of the land [5/245].

[27] Surveying was halted close to Mariashoni Primary School. Land between that 'cutline' and Elburgon town was in majority allocated to members of other communities. People referred to this area as 'lower side' of Mariashoni.

[28] While having numerous discussions about these presumed 'titles', we were not able to establish fully, who among the settlers received actual, 'legal' titles registered with the Ministry of Lands. The Chief insisted that there were no proper land title deeds within Mariashoni settlement scheme [3/058].

Consequently, the irregular status of the land was not recognisable in the settlement of the land because almost 6,000 ha of the 7,000 ha were inhabited, independently from the land's status, leaving only 1,000 ha of the Location under considerable tree cover [3/062]. Despite the area being excised in 2001, it remained Government Land, but it was 'removed from the map as forest area' [3/062]. The 2001 excisions in the Mau, in and around Mount Kenya and several other forests, mobilised a coalition of conservation and forestry networks – including the Forest Action Network (FAN), together with the Green Belt Movement (GBM) and the Mazingira Institute[29] – and challenged the Government over the excisions in court. This case, like the 1997 Ogiek land case, was still pending by 2013. One expert explained that any progress with the case was unlikely since 'the *wageni* became part of the Ministry' [1/033].

According to an Ogiek resident, the local community in Mariasho-ni suffered a deep division after some of them moved to court in 1997, which led to a standstill in official land allocations [5/200]. Whereas many community members insisted that it was inappropriate to subdi-vide traditional Ogiek land into small parcels and to allocate five acres to each adult Ogiek registered, advocating instead for the area to be declared as an 'Ogiek Reserve' with a legal status of Trust/Community Land [e.g., 3/056], others supported the subdivision and privatisation of the land [e.g., 5/200]. Another Mariashoni resident explained that introducing private property was not the most crucial matter of conten-tion but rather the form that this private property would take. She said some manifested interest in individual ownership, while most of the Mariashoni Ogiek at the time advocated for a community title. The idea was that different Ogiek clans should be given titles for their ancestral lands (*konoito*) and then allocate land to individual households, thus maintaining the land within the community and preventing its subdi-vision and sale [3/063]. An Ogiek resident and member of the ICS Ogiek Council of Elders emphasised this argument by insisting that 'the Chief would not have been able to cut pieces of people's land and sell it to people from outside' if they had obtained a community title [5/118]. One of the most cited reasons for rejecting the subdivision of land was because such a dissection supposedly was in contravention to Ogiek customs and ways of life. Particularly, land subdivision interfered with traditional socio-spatial *konoito* land occupation and use through which the Ogiek used to be able to migrate across the various agro-ecological zones. Despite being informal, this type of land allocation came with clearly established rules and regulations concerning land and resource access and use, which arguably helped the different clans and individu-al families to live together peacefully. It also allowed them to live a life

[29]   Transnational civil society organisation, based in Kenya: https://mazinst. org (2016, accessed 5 October 2022).

in which they interfered only minimally with the ecological integrity of their environment. Apart from the fact that traditional Ogiek livelihoods were based on minimal resource use, the nature of land occupation and use, which was neither permanent nor concentrated, also gave the land and the broader ecosystem space and time to regenerate. Traditional Ogiek ways of life were largely non-intrusive and sustainable. The introduction of private property, and thus the 'commodification' of the land and the forest, was diametrically opposed to traditional Ogiek ways of spatial organisation. The restriction of available land to merely five acres per person did not only lead to the subdivision of the land, rendering it more vulnerable to being sold to individual owners, but also interrupted the community members' ability to move along clan lines to follow their primary sources of nutrition. Protests against the carving out of the settlement scheme in Eastern Mau Forest were supposedly sparked by initial requests to have at least thirty acres allocated to each person. Despite being an important alteration to traditional 'free' land use within a clan's *konoito*, the thirty acres would have allowed the Ogiek to maintain their previous livelihoods, as it would have allowed them to continue hunting and gathering. The Government's push for the new spatial organisation, which involved fencing off small parcels of land, was hence effectively understood as an attempt to alter and destroy traditional Ogiek livelihoods and to transform the community into a sedentarised, controlled, farming community (Sang, 2003; Towett, 2004).

According to the more politicised members of Mariashoni's community, the declaration of the settlement scheme formed the climax of an 'ethnocide' [the term was deliberately used in 5/200] that the Government had supposedly been committing against the Ogiek. They also said that such policies had not started with the Government of former President Moi in 1997, even though they had climaxed during his reign, but they had already existed during colonial times. These members traced the dispossession of the Ogiek from their land and historical land injustices back to colonial times. Since the turn of the century, and particularly after the 1930s, they explained, Ogiek land organisation and use were mainly altered by the massive clearing of indigenous forest, the establishment of monoculture forest plantations, and the establishment of dams and roads. The establishment of the first tree plantation in the Mariashoni area, dated 1932 by residents, went hand in hand with clearing all indigenous forests that had previously occupied the respective areas [5/236]. For plantation establishment, the Ogiek were regularly evicted from specific portions of the forest. The Mariashoni Chief confirmed that the colonial government de facto abolished the *konoito* land allocation and land-use system in the 1950s [3/058]. While it is difficult to trace the exact dates of forest evictions and changes in settlement locations and structures in the Mariashoni area, evictions were said to have been carried out in 1904 and 1911, as well as in 1987 and 1991 [5/200], while Sang (2003) mentioned the periods 1911–1914, 1918 and 1926–1927. The spatial reorganisation during colonial times was not only marked by physical changes but also by social transformations that were mainly brought about by the arrival of 'foreign', mostly Kikuyu, workers and the establishment of separate Kikuyu villages.

Overall, the Government-induced changes in the land's 'legal'[30] status in 1997 marked the climax in the eyes of those locals who held on to 'traditional' Ogiek ways of life. Alongside the active enclosure of the land and the trees and the loss of the 'traditional' Ogiek livelihoods and subsistence activities, including hunting and gathering, 1997 also marked the highpoint until then of the Government's commodification of forest land for political purposes. Some opined that the exclusion of the Ogiek from land beneficiary lists was related to their opposition to the idea of a settlement scheme with private property rights to land, as well as to their rather hostile relations with the incumbent government [3/056], as previously discussed. At that time, the Government reacted violently to protests staged in Molo and Nakuru, during which Ogiek protesters were beaten, arrested, and taken to court, but later released. Similarly a group of Ogiek on their way to protest at State House, the President's residence in Nairobi, were stopped and arrested [3/058].

Speaking about the effects that the declaration of the Mariashoni settlement scheme had on the Ogiek community, the Chief of Mariashoni Location gave insights into the circumstances of the exercise and some of the consequences. He explained that Ogiek protests against land demarcation and allocation were ongoing when Kenya Survey officers came in to establish a plan for the new settlement. Initially, they were tasked to demarcate and allocate five-acre plots and settle two hundred persons per day. Considering the pressure exerted by the protesting Ogiek and presumably 'to finish as fast as possible and 'beat' the protesters', and since their maps did not illustrate rivers, 'little attention was paid to rivers and catchment areas that just became part of the allocated land' [3/058]. The Chief conceded that only approximately half of the land within the settlement scheme was officially surveyed and allocated to individual households because the mentioned High Court Order stopped surveying and allocation from October 1997. He further indicated that only half of the surveyed land was allocated to members of the Ogiek community, while the other half was given to *wageni*. He also estimated that only around half of the Mariashoni Ogiek households were allocated land within the surveyed areas and that the settlements within the areas that were not surveyed had not officially been allocated, and the settle-

---

30 The term legal is here set in quotes because the establishment of the Mariashoni settlement scheme was de jure illegal despite government attempts to regularise the situation later.

ments had remained completely non-permanent. However, all those who obtained land only received allotment letters, and none of the persons who acquired land in Mariashoni had title deeds [3/058]. Another government employee provided a more pessimistic figure and said that 'the Ogiek only got 1% of the land, while 99% were brought in from outside and people have titles, which makes the Ogiek vulnerable to evictions as they don't have titles' [3/062].

Creating and exploiting land insecurity at the local level

Analysing the consequences of land redistribution and conflicts at the local level in Mariashoni, it became apparent that both sides were aggrieved, the ones who had acquired land and those whose land had been acquired. Among the local Ogiek, many spoke of insecurities or even the loss of land allocated to them. A young Ogiek woman recounted that her neighbour had taken a piece of her land just some days earlier and that there was nothing she could do about it [5/165]. Another young Ogiek woman explained that one day a *mgeni* ('in-migrant') came to her land with an alternative land allocation map and claimed that her land was his. She referred the case to the local authorities without resolution [5/181]. One of the outspoken Ogiek elders of the area, who indicated living on ten acres of 'Community Land without title deed', recounted a similar story in which a *mgeni* claimed ownership of the land he occupied. The man was, however, taken to court and eventually had to move out of the area [5/234]. One of the Ogiek female elders of Mariashoni said that a daughter of the Chief had just settled on her land. She reported the case to the District Commissioner (DC), but no solution was found, and the woman and her husband still occupied the land she considered hers, and for which she said she had an allotment letter [5/239]. An older Ogiek woman told a similar story of a neighbour trying to take over her land and that the case had been pending with the authorities [5/191].

A young plain-spoken Ogiek man explained that a neighbour had started asking for parts of his family's 13-acre farm in July 2012. Some elders and the authorities had intervened and resolved the case, but he said that there were many land conflicts, especially in the areas in which residents held *shambas* that had not been surveyed and allocated in 1997 [5/184]. Another young Ogiek man pointed out that his family used to accommodate another family on their land and supported that other family. One of the other family's sons later joined the National Police and returned to the area to claim their land. He added that the case was referred to the authorities but that dispute was not solved, and no-one came to the farm to understand the facts on the ground. The authorities' nonchalance, as he said, had left the young man's family wondering about their role in land conflicts in the area [5/221]. Yet another young Ogiek man said that people that he suspected to be close to the Chief had taken over his land earlier that year. A man from outside the forest just approached him with a title deed and claimed that the land was his. Since the document looked real, he could not refute his claims and decided to move and leave his crops behind. He said that most of the people laying claims on small parcels of land in the Mariashoni area came in through the members of the local authorities [5/148]. An older Ogiek man explained that in 2000, a Tugen man came to his land and told him to move because he supposedly had the title deed for the land. He addressed the authorities who merely referred him to the DO and the DC. He added that none of his attempts to get help and support had been fruitful, and he was eventually forced out of his home and had to give five acres to the man. 'There are no good things for the Ogiek from the Government' [5/147], he said. An old Ogiek woman, who said she owned approximately ten acres, half of which had trees, explained it was not only the land that was grabbed but also the trees. In her life, she often had to deal with people coming to her land and trying to cut and sell her trees. In some of these cases, she called upon the authorities who helped her defend her resources [5/160]. While these testimonies of Ogiek residents directly or indirectly blamed people from outside the forest for attempting to take over their land, they also illustrated the authorities' important role in the matter.

Other Ogiek were more direct in the criticism of local authorities and directly blamed them for illegal land allocations to *wageni*, displaying an important schism within the local Ogiek community. An older Ogiek man explained that a sitting political representative had tried grabbing his land but referred the case to the authorities, who promised to intervene. By 2013, both parties still laid separate claims to the land and the situation was not resolved. He added that his father had been evicted from the area when he was still young, illustrating the human drama that comes with such sudden evictions, leading to the loss of household goods and even livestock. He said the family then moved to a settlement in Keringet, at the heart of the Mau Forest. The land he lived on at present and whose tenure was challenged had later been given to his father and subsequently to him in 1997 [5/167]. A middle-aged Ogiek man, who lived in Kaprop close to the Primary School with his family, explained that the Chief allocated the plot he occupied to him because 'the Chief decides who can live where' but that the land had not been given to them 'properly' [5/207]. A young Ogiek woman explained that she had also obtained five acres of land from the Chief [5/208]. A middle-aged Ogiek woman living close to the Chief's place showed the house his nephew attempted to build on a piece of her land. The day preceding the research visit, the Chief had come to see her and claimed that, despite her living there, the land was his and not hers and that his nephew could use the land as he pleased. Before that, she had experienced a similar situation when a *mgeni* approached her on her farm and claimed her land. She said she had gone to complain to the DC, but nothing had changed [5/118]. Overall, the mentioned examples clearly illustrated the uncertainties faced by the Mariashoni residents. The recurrence of the same stories further showed the degree to which public service delivery in the area was personalised. The unsuccessful attempts to involve other authorities in conflict resolution additionally displayed why many residents were of the understanding that members of the local and provincial authorities knew each other and dealt with each other in one big circle of corruption, supposedly aimed at bringing politically relevant players to the forest, particularly members of the Tugen, Kipsigis, and Kisii communities.

One of the vocal Ogiek elders claimed that there was a lot of tension between the Mariashoni residents and the authorities because they brought in *wageni* and benefited from allocating land to them [5/234]. Others said the authorities had *helped* many people in the area. One resident insisted that the surveyor had come to Mariashoni in 1997 and that the Government had since forced their people in by bringing them in government cars and under police protection. He said that the Chief defied the Government and requested that four 'lines' be given to his people instead of taking over all the land in Mariashoni. The Government supposedly granted him his request, enabling him to help 'his people'. However, these people were not necessarily other Ogiek but people from outside the forest, he added [5/108]. A middle-aged Ogiek woman drew a clear parallel between members of the local authority having obtained large strips of land and the fact that they collaborated with the Government during land surveying and allocation in 1997 despite the Mariashoni Ogiek having pushed for them to reject the exercise. Some of the Mariashoni Ogiek representatives at the time were pledging for a community title, which would, in turn, have allowed them to give user rights to individual families in line with the traditional *konoito* system. The Government refused to grant them what they had requested and instead gave out land to individuals. The Chief was a personal beneficiary as well, she added. The introduction of the Private Land property regime thus became the condition and the basis for his sustained role in the allocation of forest land, 'which would not have been possible with a community deed' [5/118].

One Ogiek man opined that the land dilemma was rooted in the fact that '*hakuna umoja kati ya wenyeji*' (the locals [Ogiek] are not united) [5/172]. Similarly, another Ogiek man said that most land conflicts used to occur between *wageni* and local Ogiek, but local leaders had contributed to fuelling land conflicts among the Mariashoni Ogiek, particularly since the onset of the 'Save the Mau' campaign. He recounted that a group of local 'elite' Ogiek had attempted to dispossess him of the land that had been allocated to him, illustrating an important divide among the Mariashoni Ogiek, 'a big opposition between those who are close to the Chief and those who are not' [5/200]. One of these 'elite' Ogiek indicated owning fifty acres, a considerable amount in the area. Despite being from the 'elite', he also experienced land conflicts. He described his problems with a man from the Tugen community, who had been brought to Mariashoni by a national politician and laid claims to his land ever since. He feared the contender to the extent that he found a watchman to protect his house during nights because he did not want to spend his nights at home for fear of being killed. He added that another man had been murdered in conflict over land in the Mboroti area of Mariashoni in 2006 [5/227]. He said that, since 1997, more than fifty people had supposedly been killed in the Segut area close to Kiptunga, further south of Mariashoni, because of land conflicts. He said that members of the Tugen community expressed entitlement over forest land because they were backed by the former President's entourage and he claimed they were responsible for the murders in the area [5/108]. A member of the local authority explained that in another extreme case, competition over land between Ogiek and Kipsigis had led to the destruction of one hundred houses and eighteen deaths in the neighbouring location of Nessuit in 2006 [3/058]. In Ngongongeri settlement, a man was shot in 2016 in a quarrel over land. Following the incident, several houses were torched, and tension between members of the Ogiek and Tugen communities fighting for land tenure in the area since the mid-1990s increased.[31]

While many Ogiek residents blamed the *wageni* and the local authorities, many testimonies from *wageni* shifted part of the blame onto ordinary members of the Mariashoni Ogiek. The most common claim concerning the Ogiek's supposed contribution to the land transformation and land-use change, and to some extent to illegal land grabbing, was related to the fact that the Ogiek had refused the land allocation exercise in 1997 and were thus excluded from land ownership within the settlement scheme. Many said this had contributed to the Ogiek having had to move deeper into the forest since that land 'used to belong to the elders' [5/148]. A Mariashoni Community Forest Association (CFA) representative laid the blame for the fact that the Ogiek moved deeper into the forest onto the *wageni* coming to the area and challenging ownership of the land that the local Ogiek inhabited. Consequently, he said, the Ogiek were pushed deeper into the water catchment area because others grabbed the fertile lands between Elburgon and the area around Mariashoni Primary School as far as the 'cutline' where surveying and allocation of plots had ended in 1997 [3/059]. In that context, a Mariashoni resident from the Nandi community shared the opinion that the

---

[31] Felista, W., 'One person confirmed dead as Ngongongeri skirmishes escalate', *HiviSasa*, 14 March 2016.

Ogiek cried crocodile tears since the Ogiek presumably sold their land to people and then pretended it had been stolen to attempt to benefit twice. He stated that '*wanajiletea shida*' (they are bringing themselves problems) by 'playing a bad game' to which they were incited by 'opinion makers' [5/256]. A Kipsigis resident also explained that he had bought a four-acre piece of land from an Ogiek man that he later transformed into a farm on which he cultivated maize, peas, and potatoes all the way to the riverbank. Some months after moving to the area, another neighbour came to his land and wanted to chase him, claiming that the land belonged to his family and not to the one that had sold it to him. He was, however, successful in maintaining his land [5/185]. A Tugen resident painted a dark picture of the situation. According to his testimony, some members of the local Ogiek community had been pursuing a scheme in which they first sold the land that had been allocated to them. Once the land was sold, they would go to the land registry or the local authorities and obtain a certificate that testified that the ownership of the land had been theirs since 1997. After that, they returned to the land they had sold and claimed such a transaction had never taken place and that those who bought it from them had illegally grabbed the land. He also pointed out that the Ogiek sometimes returned to the land they had sold to cut and sell the trees they found there, while those who had bought the land had no choice but to let it happen [5/199].

A *wageni* couple, who had lived in Chai Moto for more than ten years, recounted their ordeal [5/198]. The Kipsigis woman said she was from Mau Summit, while her husband was originally from Baringo. The Government had allocated five-acre parcels to individuals in the Chai Moto area up to a place known as *Kikingi Tatu*, where the forest 'boundary' was located, according to the residents. They did not have to pay for their land, but the Government harvested most of the trees that had initially been on the land and only left the new residents with a few. Once they were settled, a group of young Ogiek men came at night and threatened them. The woman said that many Chai Moto residents had similar problems with young Ogiek coming at night, attempting to disassemble their houses and scare them away. In their case, one night, the young men even demounted their iron sheet roof while they were in the house. An even more violent one preceded this incident. Initially, when they moved to the area in 1998, they had been settled on another plot. As early as 1999, they were pushed out of that land by a group of local Ogiek claiming that the land supposedly belonged to the Chief's brother. One evening in 1999, she went out in the rain with her first-born to buy milk. Upon her return to the house, her younger children were sitting outside of the house, and the house was locked from the outside. Not understanding what the situation was all about, she broke the padlock and entered the house. After a few minutes, two young men came, one armed with a *panga* (machete) and one with a knife and told them to leave. Her husband sustained a deep cut in the ensuing conflict. After that, they decided to leave. The woman first took the children to her mother's place, who was living in *Mawe Mbili*, a little centre on the road leading to Chai Moto, closer towards Elburgon. Later, they decided to move directly into the centre of Chai Moto. The couple narrated that despite knowing the identities of those men, there was little they could do. They had tried to address their concerns to the authorities severally, without much success. The man confirmed their powerlessness considering the involvement of the local authorities and finally stated that 'God will judge them for what they did' [5/198]. A Kipsigis man, whose family had purchased five acres in Chai Moto, explained that the land in the area had been allocated to the Ogiek in big chunks, which supposedly made it easy for them to sell pieces of land to a vast number of *wageni*. His family had also gone through a situation in which a member of the local Ogiek community claimed their plot was their ancestral land. However, the Chief intervened and insisted that the land was his and its sale was thus legal [5/201].

Interestingly, Chai Moto was the only place within the wider Mariashoni area where several different people spoke openly about experiences with tribalism and tribal conflicts, particularly between the local Ogiek and members of the Tugen community [e.g., 5/197]. A Kipsigis man, who left his Bomet home and came to Mariashoni in 2000, also clarified that legally purchasing land did not necessarily guarantee that there were no conflicts. He had bought an allotment letter for the piece of land he then occupied in the quarry area right behind Mariashoni Centre, and he and the supposed owner signed an agreement at the Chief's place. However, he was later unable to obtain a title deed from the registrar's office [5/169]. A Kipsigis man who bought land in the surveyed area on the opposite side of Mariashoni Secondary School also explained that the prices for land in Mau Forest had increased significantly in the previous years. He had bought five acres in 'upper' Mariashoni for KES 50,000 ($500) in 2003, for which the value had supposedly gone up to around KES 400,000 ($4,000) by 2008. Consequently, the Ogiek who had sold him the land wanted to reclaim and resell it at a higher price [5/176]. An older Kipsigis woman in the 'lower' Mariashoni also said that land prices in that area had increased by half from KES 200,000 ($2,000) to KES 300,000 ($3,000) for a five-acre plot, rendering her tenure vulnerable [5/247]. The Kipsigis man added that the man who had claimed his land threatened to chase him, and during the mediation meeting at the Chief's place, he pretended not to know that he had sold him more than one acre. He was later beaten by the police and arrested in Mariashoni Centre in 2008 because he refused to vacate the land he had bought. He then went to the provincial authorities and attempted to sue the person who had sold him the land, but the case was discontinued without indicating the cause. Things became so bad that he temporarily relocated in 2008 since he feared for his life. He returned several months later but still did not feel safe on his land. He further stated that most of the land in the area where he lived was settled by members of the Kipsigis community and that all of them had bought land from the Ogiek, who had initially obtained land during the settlement creation in 1997. He added that all the original owners had moved deeper into the forest [5/176]. A young Kipsigis woman who lived in the same neighbourhood told us a similar story and said that another Ogiek man had tried to evict her from her land but that the one who had sold her the land came to her rescue [5/177]. Another Kipsi-gis resident who moved to the area from Baringo said that a local Ogiek attempted to grab his land as well, but he failed [5/182]. Altogether, numerous residents from Rombei and Chai Moto, which some residents called 'upande wa Tugen' (the Tugen side) [5/186] because it was mostly settled by members of the Tugen community, alongside Kipsigis from Kericho and Transmara [5/203], and some areas in Mboroti, which was predominantly settled by members of the Kipsigis community, spoke of land conflicts perpetrated by members of the local Mariashoni Ogiek. Both areas were part of the initially surveyed land for the settlement scheme in 1997.

A member of the Ogiek 'elite' confirmed that many Ogiek had sold the land that had been given to them in the 1990s quickly because they were interested in the easy money. He also related that behaviour to the fact that the very idea of private land ownership was new for the Ogiek at the time, who had been used to strict regulations and user rights related to the forest track (konoito) allocated to each clan, but not to private ownership. He stated that many of them only realised later that they could have used the land more sustainably [5/108]. An out-spoken Ogiek woman argued that land disputes in the area were mainly caused by the Ogiek, who were 'greedy for money and sell portions of their land' and came back later and tried to force the buyers out [5/188]. One very old Ogiek woman who shared her in-depth knowledge of the area also opined that most land conflicts in Mariashoni could be attrib-uted to the fact that the Ogiek had sold their land to 'outsiders' [5/189]. A well-connected Ogiek resident summarised that the Ogiek played a significant role in land grabbing and selling in the area because the wageni did not know about the land or plot numbers and could thus not simply claim ownership of the land if they had not been informed of the existence of that land in the first place. He said that the Kisii were among the most important beneficiaries of land in the area and that the local authorities were highly involved in the land business [5/178]. The Chief added that there was a police post within Ngongongeri settle-ment and a camp of the Administrative Police in Kapsita (Elburgon). At the same time, apart from the Administrative Police officers employed to protect him, there were no security officers in Mariashoni with the explicit purpose of protecting the settlers from being disturbed by the local Ogiek [3/058].

Many people observed that the Ogiek sold their productive land and moved into the forest because they supposedly were poor farmers, a narrative discussed in detail in the following chapter. In line with that observation, these people said that, instead of using their land productively, the Ogiek supposedly sold it to gain an income [e.g., 5/199].

Magnitude and popular representations of forest land misappropriation

The magnitude of forest conversion and de facto privatisation was momentous. The media expert cited various areas as particularly affected, including Baraget, Elburgon, Likia, Sururu, Mauche, Mariashoni, and Teret (in Mauche) in the Eastern Mau, as well as Saino, Kipterero, Ndoinet, Tinet, Kiptaget extension, Kapkambu, Kiptegelde, and Kipkoygor in the South-West Mau. He also mentioned Sierra Leone and Chepakundi in Maasai Mau, alongside Ol Posimoru, which initially also belonged to the Maasai Mau Forest [1/005]. While these areas were administratively separated, they were all part of one extensive ecosystem and thus profoundly intertwined. The Eastern and South-Western Mau Forest were highlands and held the sources of most of the over thirty rivers originating in the Mau Forest. The rivers then passed through areas inhabited mainly by members of the Kalenjin community, as far as the Kikuyu around Lake Nakuru, the Maasai in the Maasai Mara and so forth. Since upstream issues potentially affect the downstream areas, the land issues in the Mau Forest had repercussions way beyond the areas in question. All the mentioned areas were also part of the initial five-phase Mau Restoration plan (see Figure 2 in the Introduction and Figure 4 in the Conclusion).

Looking at the drivers of land misappropriation overall, different respondents cited different theories and experiences about the origin of the practice of fraudulent land allocation. For instance, a high-ranking member of the local authorities remarked that 'it is all the fault of the Government' [3/058]. Others somewhat echoed the idea that illegal land attribution had been driven by the Government but insisted that decisions were not always taken at the highest levels of government. They added that the 'Provincial Administration at the time was a law of its own' and 'the root of corruption' [3/060], emphasising that a power vacuum allowed the Provincial Administration to disregard government decisions [1/003]. Yet others insisted that a few MPs were behind land allocations in Mariashoni [various testimonies, e.g., 4/264, 5/199, 5/203, 5/204]. An underlying enabling factor mentioned by numerous Mariashoni residents was the innacurate idea that, since the 2010 Constitution, any Kenyan could own land anywhere in the country, with land allocated to the highest bidder in disregard of ancestral claims to land [e.g., 5/227].[32]

Speaking about the supposed motivations of those who facilitated the allocation of land to individual families and households, the media expert explained the implication that the motivation for such actions, for political figures at all levels, was often based on the assumption that land distribution not only allowed them to attract the gratitude of the persons helped but that the very act of being able to influence the distribution of fertile lands allowed them to create the image of someone likely to succeed. Land attribution was thus 'a tool to make political kings' [1/005].

Beyond serving national and subsidiary political interests, questionable land allocation practices were employed to pursue local interests in which political and economic objectives and aspirations overlapped. Unsurprisingly, the members of the local authorities supposedly played a central role in fraudulent land allocations. Land disputes arising between different residents were usually referred to the local Chief. Generally, the rule of 'first come, first serve' was applied. Independently of the particular set-up and of legal or other sources of ownership, the administration enforced the status quo; it did not have the power to evict people and to decide who was 'truly genuine'. Complaints were numerous but usually just ignored. According to the local administration, most people, who argued they had title deeds, had obtained those illegally in the first place. In addition, most of those, who claimed later on that land was allocated to them, should not have been beneficiaries since they were absent at the time of allocation. Local leaders insisted that there was too much uncertainty about land ownership in the region and did not want to act against what had established itself, the status quo. In a very few cases, elders were called upon to subdivide the land for it to be shared among two contenders. The local chief said that, since the onset of the 'Save the Mau' initiative, he had told people who had land conflicts to wait for the ICS to decide on the matter [3/058]. At the same time, he supposedly also acted as an important gatekeeper, preventing land cases from being regulated through higher instances and centrally recognised processes. Given the unequal and informally regulated access to land, several individuals and groups had filed complaints to the authorities, including the Chief and the Chief's superiors, notably the District Officer, District Commissioner, and the Provincial Commissioner, and even to the High Court of Kenya. Yet, none of their cases was taken up and resolved.

Beyond that, opinions remained divided as to whether the Chief was used as an entry point for political interests of higher-placed political figures and if he thus had to comply with orders concerning land allo-

---

[32] This fear was raised repeatedly, although freedom of settlement was already granted in the previous constitution.

cation that he received 'from above', or if, on the contrary, he was able
to give out favours and distribute the land as he saw fit. Since the Chief
supposedly was 'one of the major beneficiaries of land' [1/027] in the
Mariashoni area, both seemed plausible. In support of the latter argument, two young Ogiek brothers explained that the land they were
living on had been given to them by the Chief's brother because the
family feared negative consequences 'if the Government sees they have
big *shambas* of one hundred or two hundred acres'. They added that all
the members of the political families owned a lot of land in the Eastern
Mau and that this land was thus given out to other people, 'but not permanently' [4/093], particularly for as long as it was not clear what the
Mau rehabilitation exercise would entail for big landowners. A young
Ogiek man from the neighbouring Nessuit, who had moved to Mariashoni a few years earlier, explained that evictions from these lands were
facilitated by the fact that the rich and powerful grabbed a lot of land
and later distributed plots to residents. He added that, since the names
in the land registers were never changed, the people who occupied the
land could not resist eviction if the ones listed in the register decided to
repossess it. He also pointed out that the Mariashoni Centre was to be
established further down towards Elburgon, but it was established at
its current location because the Chief had grabbed the land in question
and sold it to third-party purchasers [5/210]. A candid young resident,
who had previously lived in many different parts of the country, added
that the Chief had supposedly sold five hundred acres to a flower farm
close to Elburgon. He also said that he ruled the area with an iron fist.
To emphasise this point, he described that he witnessed the destruction
of the Chief's camp after the 2013 Party Primaries in the area but that
an elderly man and the local AP officers advised him not to be heard
asking questions or saying what happened because 'the Chief can have
you killed'. He also recounted that unknown assailants shot his neighbour, and his brother had been incarcerated for more than ten years
by the time of the interview 'because he had a grudge with the Chief'
[5/212]. At the very least, most residents seemed to have found it difficult to access the local authorities and could thus not even ask for help.
In that vein, a resident Ogiek woman complained that the 'Chief's office
is always closed; no help, no info, no nothing!' and further explained
that 'the Chief is absent for months, sells land, takes money, disappears
for months; people can't even get their passports and IDs and register
for elections; he's just not there; and if you want an ID, you have to pay
the Chief' [5/118].

A young Kipsigis woman, who was married to a young local Ogiek
man, said that people came from outside the forest and bought or rented
land and that some even paid too much. At the same time, she said that
local authorities would make it difficult for the locals to get more land
if they required more, for instance, to increase their cultivation for food

production [5/171]. A young Ogiek man added that there was massive interest in buying land in the Mariashoni area, especially by members of the Kipsigis community from Bomet. He stated that they came with KES 300,000 ($3,000) to KES 400,000 ($4,000) and bribed the authorities, who then supposedly did not interfere if they chased the people occupying the land they were interested in [5/148].

Technically, a wide range of strategies was employed to allocate land to non-forest dwellers illegally. Most of them benefited from the fact that there was no administrative or police population register, allowing for the attribution of land to non-existing identification document (ID) numbers or existing ID numbers overwritten with other names. Manipulation of land registers was further facilitated by alternating sizes, locations, and boundaries of plots on different maps. Often, individual plots were stolen with the help of fabricated maps that altered the demarcation proposed by the surveyor before the land allocation. An Ogiek elder illustrated this with the help of two different maps in use during the time that land in his area, in Saino in South-Western Mau [2/262].[33] The Chief explained that the same had also happened in Mariashoni. He recounted that the surveyors in both Mariashoni and Ngongongeri were under pressure when attempting to finalise their demarcation and allocation in 1997. While the surveyor had presumably already settled 256 Ogiek households in the Mariashoni settlement scheme, the surveyor in Ngongongeri was under such 'pressure' that he changed the original map on which he had based the allocation of individual plots until it overlapped with the Mariashoni map. He thus effectively allocated land and gave out titles for plots within changed borders of the Ngongongeri settlement scheme that had previously been assigned to members of the Ogiek community within the original boundaries of the Mariashoni settlement scheme, who had, however, not received their allotment letters. The Chief also indicated that he had opposed the scheme and had 'stood firm', saying that he was consequently called to the provincial authorities and had to answer charges of being biased in favour of the Ogiek [3/058].

The political economy of land and the crisis in the Eastern Mau Forest

In line with political-ecological thinking, the question of access to and ownership of essential resources, here ostensibly land, strongly influences the nature and trajectory of environmental crises. This was also true in the Mau Forest. While the conversion of primary forest land to

---

[33] During our visits, the Ogiek elder who lived in Saino in South-Western Mau showed us some of the manipulated maps of the South-West Mau.

secondary forest through the establishment of mostly mono-cropped tree plantations with exotic tree stands during the colonial period considerably altered the ecological and socio-spatial realities on the ground, these changes did not lead to the massive forest degradation and destruction that became synonymous with the current Mau crisis.

In the Eastern Mau, the massive deforestation in many areas direct-ly resulted from the Government's strategy to attract, consolidate and compensate political loyalty by providing access to fertile forest land. Despite the importance of the pressure exerted on the forest by the demand for tree products, especially wood and timber, by both big and small wood processing companies, the scramble for the Mau Forest and the loss of forest land were primarily defined by the scramble for land, not for trees. Land in the Mau Forest was allocated to both 'big men' and ordinary farmers, albeit predominantly from non-forest-dwelling com-munities, and increasingly so since the re-introduction of multiparty democracy in the early 1990s. Beyond the threat that the democrati-sation represented for the incumbent, various authors also argue that President Moi developed a strong sense of persecution and paranoia after the failed coup attempt in 1982 (Branch, 2011; Hornsby, 2013; Hornsby & Throup, 1998).[34] Both aspects are covered by theories on political favouritism and patronage (Bayart, 1989; Klopp & Sang, 2011; Wrong, 2009), which focus on various aspects of the relationship between land allocation and distribution in exchange for political loyalty. These land allocation and redistribution exercises were enabled by the complex and fragmented legal situation, which allowed powerful government actors to manipulate these exercises to address a wide array of underly-ing rationalities and calculations, in line with (Anderson, 2005; Calas, 1998; Homewood et al., 2004).

Many of the 'big men' used their land for medium- to large-scale agricultural production, especially in the 'lower' parts of Mariashoni Location (see Map 4 in Chapter 2), while others, typically political con-tenders, distributed land to members of their own or other communities whose loyalty they wanted to strengthen. The latter was widespread during former President Moi's time to satisfy the wider Kalenjin com-munity's request for fertile lands while assuring a presence of these communities in various forest reserves (Lonsdale, 1992, 1994; Lynch, 2011). This spreading out of community members both created human 'buffer zones' in areas that were considered potentially hostile to the Government, and increased the proportion of these communities in various constituencies, hoping to influence election results. Ultimate-ly, the 'big men' used their power to grant and withdraw access to

---

[34] Also see Mutunga, K., 'Moment of bravado that changed Kenya', *Daily Nation*, 31 July 2012; Frankel, G., 'Scars of failed coup attempt still etched on Kenyan psyche', *The Washington Post*, 30 September 1984.

fertile land as a prime political resource. Since formal land titles were not 'legal' for land that officially retained a status of government-held forest land, land allocation remained, by definition, informal and thus easy to manipulate. Therefore, land could be withdrawn from the persons it had been given without providing them with possibilities to seek redress. The same land could be redistributed to others, following the multiple and changing rationalities of those who controlled the lands at various levels.

Furthermore, the creation and transformation of the Mariashoni settlement scheme clearly followed political objectives, which were evident in the timing of various steps in the development of the scheme. Since the early 1990s, individual households from non-forest-dwelling communities received plots of forest land in the area that would later become Mariashoni settlement scheme. The settlement scheme was declared in 1997, and thousands of 'foreigner' households were brought in just before the general elections. Then, the forest was degazetted in 2001, right ahead of the 2002 elections. It is no surprise that the most extensive forest excisions were undertaken in 2001 since the general elections of 2002 were commonly understood as the moment in Kenyan history when multiparty democracy was fully re-established. 'Free' elections were held for the first time in decades. While the democratic transition had started with the repeal of Section 2A of the Constitution in 1991 that had provided for a de facto single-party state since 1964, the 1992 and 1997 elections were far from 'free and fair'. In 2002, due to strong opposition to the incumbent government, President Moi was faced with the requirement to attract support and loyalty more than ever before (Branch, 2011; Hornsby, 2013). Consecutive displacements of the Kikuyu settlers also followed political objectives of majority creation and dissolution.

The consequences for the people who obtained land were manifold. While access to good forest land was attractive to most Kenyans, both those who could afford to engage in large-scale agricultural production and those who depended on small-scale subsistence farming, settling in the Mau Forest was neither easy for those who had 'officially' obtained access to land nor for those who had not. While the same subdivision of land and allocation of land was in contravention to the traditional socio-spatial organisation of the forest-dwelling Ogiek community, leading to opposition among the 'traditionalist' Ogiek to the land allocation exercise carried out during the establishment of the Mariashoni settlement scheme in 1997, other members of the local community accepted the allocation of individual plots. Since the official land survey and allocation was halted in late 1997, only a tiny fraction of the local Ogiek community initially obtained plots. Others remained without land allotment letters altogether. In the context of politically instigated demand for land in the area, both those who had originally received land and those who had not started experiencing that a lot of money could be made from land sales. Consequently, some members of the local Ogiek moved deeper into the un-surveyed forest areas while selling their land within the settlement scheme to members of other communities. These Private Land sales were paralleled by politically motivated land allocations, leading to a shift in the local population balance and dominance of other, traditionally non-forest-dwelling communities in terms of population numbers in the Eastern Mau, specifically in Mariashoni Location. In the context of various actors pursuing multiple motives and objectives generally dominated by political and economic rationalities, many of those who had acquired land and those whose land had been acquired by others were aggrieved. Faced with various hierarchies and rules in the illegal attribution of land that were neither fully clear nor always understandable for those affected, many people felt disempowered in confrontation with local and *wageni* land grabbers, particularly when these colluded with the local authorities.

Several points can be addressed concerning the much discussed political ecology question about the effect of land privatisation on the sustainability of land use. First, land privatisation in the Eastern Mau went along with literal forest clearing and hence had a direct negative effect on forest cover. Furthermore, the attempted change in legal status from Government to Private Land led to a de jure loss of forest land since the trees on that land officially lost the 'forest' label. Third, with a de facto conversion of the legal status of the land came a conversion of rights and duties regarding the trees on the land. While trees on public and gazetted forest land officially belonged to the state and could legally not be cut without KFS approval, trees on private farms, de jure, belonged to the owners of the land, who hence could do with them as they pleased. The subdivision of the land within the four 'lines' that had presumably been granted to the Chief effectively resembled land privatisation practices witnessed elsewhere in the context of group ranch schemes and the sustainability concerns associated with them. Consequently, how those who had obtained land in the Eastern Mau effectively used it was crucial to the contribution of the political economy of land to the environmental crisis in the Eastern Mau. This land use was determined by various factors, which are addressed in detail further below.

While the Government emphasised the importance of recovering Public Land in the Mau Forest that had been given out to individual beneficiaries or companies in an 'irregular or ill-planned manner' (GoK, 2009e) to rehabilitate the forest cover, the illegally privatised land in Mariashoni settlement scheme was not restored to the state, as foreseen in Phase IV of the spatial-temporal plan (GoK, 2009e) after the land recovery plan was discontinued in 2010 [e.g., 1/040]. While new illegal conversion of forest land to private settlements was de jure close to impossible after the enactment of various land acts in line with the 2009 National Land Policy (Kenya Land Alliance, 2010; Klopp & Lumumba, 2016; Manji, 2014), what would happen to the lands excised in the Mau Forest, including in the Eastern Mau, in 2001 remained unclear.

Theoretically, while political ecology approaches emphasise the importance of land for environmental crises, environmental governance literature seemed to largely neglect the role that the land 'below' the natural resources plays. While land tenure was recognised as a central element in terms of whether community inclusion in natural resource management falls under benefit- or power-sharing paradigms, most of the literature dealing with the central state's resistance to devolving forest governance competencies to both subsidiary levels of state governance, as well as to communities, for instance, continued relating this hesitance to the state's interest in maintaining control over the exploitation of forests and hence the revenue generated from extractive forest production practices (Charnley & Poe, 2007; Chomba et al., 2015; Peluso & Vandergeest, 2001), rather than relating it to unwillingness to relinquish control of the land and to the possibility of using it for political purposes. In contrast, the Mau Forest crisis displayed clearly that it was not only the trees but, at least to equal degrees, the land to which powerful actors wanted to guarantee access that contributed to their deliberate involvement in sabotaging the 'Save the Mau' initiative.

4

The Politics of Belonging and Exclusion in Response to Changes in the Eastern Mau: The Complex Definition of Legitimate Land and Resource Use

Since settlement on and use of land adjudicated as national parks and forest reserves was legally prohibited in Kenya, residents of government forest reserves were *legally* considered as squatters of Government/Public Land, who neither had ownership nor legal tenure of the lands they occupied. This situation remained de jure unchanged in the Eastern Mau Forest, despite de facto land subdivision and allocation in the various settlement schemes. The livelihoods of all forest dwellers, both Ogiek and others, were thus highly insecure. In the Mau Forest, the social-cultural dimension of the environmental crisis was characterised by experiences of subjugation and marginalisation of the Ogiek especially, as in many instances in which minorities occupy lands of high economic value, but also by a deep generational divide and a reinvention of what it means to be Ogiek.

The politicised environment: The role of the community in environmental management

By the 1990s, community conservation had become the new orthodoxy for thinking and practising environmental management and governance (Adams & Hulme, 2001). Due to the multiplicity of approaches to participatory conservation, typically because the state, society, and economy significantly shape the implementation and application of communities' participation (Bixler, Dell'Angelo, Mfune, & Roba, 2015), various aspects of these approaches faced important practical and theoretical critiques. Beyond aspects related to defining who 'the community' is and the question surrounding the sustainability of land privatisation, which were comprehensively addressed previously, these focus on the various roles the 'community' can play in environmental management crises and, importantly, on communitities' practices of inclusion and exclusion.

Sidelining traditional environmental protectors

'Natural' suitability of communities to manage the natural resources surrounding them is the basic premise upon which community conservation initiatives, including community forestry (CF), are based. The belief that communities are 'traditional environmental protectors' is informed both by a human rights perspective and a practical ecological-integrity perspective. There is ample empirical evidence for the validity of this premise both in 'natural' settings where communities manage their lands and resources and in externally supported community-based natural resource-management (CBNRM) initiatives. Some of the relevant works in the anthropological field include studies about various forms of ecologically sound forest management practices based on the use and appreciation of the resident communities' ecological knowledge, including sustainable management of forests by engaging in swidden agriculture for crop production (Dove, 1985), burning to increase desired plant and animal species in line with local livelihood requirements (Vale, 2002), enriching the soil to create forest patches (Fairhead & Leach, 1994a, 1994b, 1996), as well as about the correlation of forest distribution and indigenous populations (Chapin, Matson, & Mooney, 2002), or about areas of high biodiversity overlapping with the existence of traditional communities' control over resource management (Maffi, 2005).

In that context, manifestations of environmentally detrimental behaviours, including violent opposition against protected areas or certain protected species, defy simplistic interpretation, particularly against the background of a general paradigm shift towards community conservation, an appreciation of traditional ecological knowledge, and given ample empirical evidence that suggests that environmental and socio-cultural relationships between people and natural resources are often sustainable.

Despite the popularity of community conservation concepts since the late 1990s, environmental degradation and destruction continued to be attributed to poverty-driven ignorance and demographic pressure in popular discourses. This 'Poverty-Environment Nexus' is derived from two related and very influential concepts in analysing and discussing environmental degradation. First, it links neo-Malthusian overpopulation arguments with poverty and, in turn, with environmental degradation (Nunan, 2015). In the same vein, the Poverty-Environment Nexus entails the idea that 'many parts of the world are in a vicious downward spiral' (World Commission on Environment and Development, 1987, p. 27) in which poverty leads to resource over-use that leads to environmental degradation, which, in turn, leads to deepened poverty (Nunan, 2015). The second related concept is that of Hardin's Tragedy of the Commons, which predicts that 'freedom in the commons brings ruin to

all' (Hardin, 1968, p. 1244) and hence specifically links overexploitation of resources to these resources being held in common, as 'common-pool resources' (Ostrom, 1998; Ostrom & Gardner, 1993). While the
concept initially emanated from the Brundtland Report, which is also
credited with being the cornerstone of the sustainable development
paradigm, other influential reports, such as the World Bank Development reports, took to the concept as well (Martin, 2005; Nunan, 2015).
The importance of the concept can also be attributed to the fact that
the Brundtland Report is understood as 'perhaps the most significant
international environment and development report of the twentieth
century' (Nunan, 2015, p. 1). The insistence and 'fear' of this presumed
'downward spiral' between people's supposed poverty and the environment has certainly also contributed to the fact that the most commonly
pursued community conservation approaches to environmental crises
targeted benefit sharing, and hence economic or livelihoods development, specifically to those crises that involved common-pool resources.

Numerous academics propose more complex explanation patterns
for community contributions to environmental destruction, invoking
social and political dimensions. Ville (1998), for example, attributes
opposition to protected areas to a sentiment of marginalisation. He
analysed instances of organised sabotage against protected areas and
endangered wildlife species and inferred that these acts were fuelled
by disenchanted locals who had been excluded from these areas and
hence found themselves deprived of their existential resources, which
consequently expressed the perception that *'les animaux soient devenus
plus importants que les hommes dans ce pays'* (animals have become
more important than humans in this country) (pp. 239–40). In a context
of high demographic pressure on relatively few fertile lands, both the
designation of protected areas for wildlife conservation or forest plantations, as well as the distribution of vast strips of land to politically
loyal individuals or groups, led to the confinement and displacement
of ordinary citizens throughout Kenya's history. Lusigi (1981) claims
that opposition to protected areas and critical species stems from a historical trauma of dispossession from ancestral lands and customary
rights to resources, which started with the ivory trade that gave way
to the slave trade and later to colonisation. Colonisation came with its
own set of experiences of disempowerment, including relocation from
traditional homelands, confinement into 'tribal' reserves sometimes
far from people's original homes, and repressive game laws prohibit-
ing hunting without permits; effectively coercing ordinary locals to
'trespass' boundaries and thus into 'wildlife criminality'. Specifically,
the social dimension of poaching has been broadly addressed in academic literature (Lusigi, 1981; Neumann, 1998; Steinhart, 2006). As
discussed, the tendency to *think* of hunting in terms of poaching was
introduced to the Kenyan colony by the influential Society for the

Preservation of the Fauna of the Empire (SPFE), a conservation lobby created in 1903, whose core objective was to control of the 'indiscriminate slaughter of the wildlife' (Lusigi, 1981, p. 88). Various academics investigated the intents and motivations for that interest in controlling African hunting. Neumann (1998), for instance, postulates that much of the debate was rooted in a pursuit of social distinction, including the demonstration of scientific superiority. Whereas white 'sport' hunting was represented as going hand in hand with nature conservation, African hunting was represented as being antithetical to conservation. Consequently, the control of African hunting can be understood as an expression of European dominance, with hunting being part of upper-class habitus and identification, in contrast to the representation of the African. The dominant narratives surrounding the hunting ban furthermore reinforced stereotypes of racial inferiority, which allowed the questioning of the Africans' ability to conduct their own affairs. Neumann (1998) summarises the dominant way of thinking: 'the native has not yet reached the stage of civilization at which he is capable of appreciating properly the gifts of nature such as fine game population and valuable timber forests – and of conserving them' (p. 108) and concludes that many instances of environmental destruction in response to coercive conservation initiatives have 'deep historical roots in European colonialism and European ideals of the scenic African landscape' (p. 3). Similarly, more recent works address the paradox that in the context of the implementation of 'development' or 'conservation' initiatives, people are disempowered and displaced. While discursively framing these people as 'surplus', the members of these 'unimagined communities' (Nixon, 2010, p. 62) effectively become 'developmental refugees' (p. 62); or, in the same vein, 'conservation refugees'.

According to these academics, traumatic dispossession and denigration experiences, written into the collective memories of the respective communities, contribute to solidifying negative attitudes towards the environment, including wildlife and forests, and to their conservation. Continuous hunting, apart from remaining intrinsically related to local diets, food security and livelihoods, could hence be understood as a symbolic struggle against the state's discursive power. By targeting large mammals, such as elephants and rhinos, these communities were sure to attract the attention of the state since their actions threatened tourism and hence income. Neumann (1998) argues that the concept of 'moral economy', coined by historian Edward P. Thompson (1971), can be invoked to explain the motivations and intentions, as well as struggles over norms, values, and expectations related to the livelihoods of subordinated people. In the case of protected areas, it is hence unlikely that adjacent communities accept to suffer from restrictive park policies without being included in benefits generated by these policies since these endanger their subsistence instead of safeguarding it. Being exposed to moral deception, a rather hostile population is unlikely to sympathise with the park system and similar conservation efforts. Historian Steven Feierman (1990) emphasises the same by arguing that violations of the 'subsistence guarantee' through the imposition of protected areas were the primary motivation behind the subsequent resistance to colonial schemes (Neumann, 1998). In that vein, Brown (2003) argues that, historically, political unrest has often occurred when subordinated communities revolted against being made victims of political games in the name of conservation, and emphasises that ecological issues were important triggers for local and nationalist uprisings against colonial regimes in Kenya, as well as in Zimbabwe and South Africa. At the same time, the militarisation of conservation through the employment of armed guards to defend the 'hard edges' of the national parks has historically overlapped with state repression, particularly of liberation movements (Neumann, 1998).

When natural heritage-making, by imposing protected areas, is furthermore entangled with struggles over land, further tension and conflict are likely. In the African context, heritage claims are often used to mediate territorial and identity claims (Cormier-Salem & Bassett, 2007). In 'From Conflict to Peacebuilding: The Role of Natural Resources and the Environment' (UNEP, 2009), the authors warn that 'if access to the direct use of scarce land, forest, water or wildlife resources leads to marginalization or exclusion of certain groups, they become easy targets for political manipulation' (p. 1). In Kenya, such manipulation has often adopted 'ethnic' undertones. Use and abuse of land issues to solidify, reinforce, and sometimes even create ethnic identities through discourses highlighting narratives related to a 'common history' and 'common struggles' to mobilise and eventually cause mayhem are widespread. 'Tradition', here, is used by those in power as an ideological tool to create 'a false consciousness' (Kratz, 1993, p. 34). In such instances, popular notions of collective identities are instrumentalised and stylised as 'ethnic conflict' for strategic purposes (Martin, 2005; Timura, 2001). Connan (2005) also emphasises this aspect by pointing out that *'l'essentiel des manifestations conflictuelles des identités ethniques se cristallise autour du problème de l'accès à la terre'* (the essence of conflictual manifestations of ethnic identities manifest in relation to issues of access to land) (p. 13). He confers a 'triple dimension' to these conflicts, invoking the complex interactions of demographic pressure on limited agricultural land, the historical multiplicity of legal sources regulating land access and ownership, and political usage of land in a neo-patrimonial logic of solidifying political loyalty. Ethnic identities are prominently invoked when different ethnic groups occupy or use the same area or when different types of resource users converge in the same area, notably pastoralists and agriculturalists. This was particularly true during Moi's Presidency when ethnic militias were created in the context of conflicts over land and to form ethnically homogeneous districts (Calas, 1998; Klopp, 2001; Médard, 2008b). Concretely, political and social frustrations related to presumed injustices in land and resource use and management materialised in many instances in attacks against great landowners and the destruction of protected areas, forest reserves, or single key species, either in drastic attacks or through covert action and 'everyday' forms of resistance (Homewood, Coast, & Thompson, 2004; Rahmato, 2003; Scott, 1985). The Kenyan Mau Mau was certainly one of the most famous of these movements, both in Kenya and beyond, that amalgamated stout criticism of experienced land injustices, widespread indignation with the colonial state and system, and a strong sense of identity. Violent attacks against big landowners were part of their strategy (Anderson, 2006; Berman & Lonsdale, 1992a; Branch, 2011; Odhiambo & Lonsdale, 2003). Historian David Throup (1987) furthermore demonstrates that the introduction of coercive anti-erosion policies contributed significantly to rural unrest related to the Mau Mau insurrection. While Hauge and Ellingsen (1998) found that land degradation renders a country prone to conflict, and Stalley (2003) confirmed that land degradation contributed to interstate conflict, some academics note that there rarely are causal pathways between environmental degradation or scarcity and violent conflict. Hauge and Ellingsen (1998), for instance, argue that structural scarcity in terms of unequal access to resources is mainly a consequence of politics and that it is hence the politics of distribution of access to natural resources, and land specifically, that determine the emergence of conflict in a situation of environmental crisis. Martin (2005) also argues that various actors 'socially construct resource use competition' (p. 329) under the influence of a range of local variables, which determine the outcomes that result from a resource-use conflict. Typically, environmental resource competition, particularly in a setting of environmental scarcity, is 'an indirect cause of conflict by amplifying/triggering traditional causes of conflict [that are often] associated with institutional failure' (Martin, 2005, p. 330). Environmental change is hence mediated by various social, cultural, and economic factors, which can lead to competition for resources being 'mapped onto existing perceptions of inequality, resulting in a hardening of group identities and providing a catalyst for hostility towards out-groups' (Martin, 2005, p. 333). While some authors emphasise the relation between environmental conflict and 'scarcity and poverty', which arguably leads to an 'ingenuity gap' preventing institutions from engaging in constructive reform (Homer-Dixon, 1994; 1995; 1999), Martin (2005) argues that any situation in which competition over the use of resources occurs can be constructed in ways that either encourage cooperative solutions or unproductive forms of conflict. He hence critiques the much discussed work of Thomas Homer-Dixon and his so-called

Toronto group and other even simpler models, and complements these simplistic and deterministic assumptions about a supposed Environment-Conflict Nexus, as well as the Environment-Poverty Nexus, by invoking agency. Timura (2001), in the same vein, argues that several factors related to tensions that pre-exist in a given society contribute to whether competition over natural resources manifests in open conflict, including the economic and political power of involved groups, ineffective land titling bureaucracies, bureaucratic redundancy and corruption, conflicting valuations of land, land tenure law and a number of global-level phenomena including economic liberalisation programmes and political decentralisation. While Martin (2005) insists that 'in the most constructive scenario, material scarcity actually brings different groups closer together, encouraging cooperation and building forms of social capital that may then be drawn upon to deal with other, perhaps more difficult, problems' (p. 330), he also adds that 'where unproductive intergroup conflicts occur, they tend to manifest themselves as conflicts over ethnicity, class and other existing social fault-lines' (p. 333).

Martin's (2005) case study about the interaction of refugee and host communities in Bonga Refugee Camp in Ethiopia in a context of environmental stress provides important and highly relevant insights into the complex interaction of various mentioned factors. The most obvious environmental impact of the installation of the refugee camp in 1993 was deforestation in the area surrounding the camp. Tensions between the refugee and host communities were witnessed that were presumably linked to these environmental changes. However, Martin (2005) argues that the specific framing of the situation influenced social relations between the groups much more than the actual physical magnitude of deforestation. He adds that the most critical contributing factors included the fact that the United Nations High Commissioner for Refugees (UNHCR) had allegedly promised to facilitate infrastructure development, which did not materialise, and hence contributed to a representation of the situation that placed the host community as victims and the refugees as privileged. The deforestation experienced then attracted the attention of conservationists. After being made aware of the ecological importance of the surrounding forests, members of the host communities contributed to framing the concern over biodiversity conservation as a threat to their traditional livelihoods. The ensuing climate of hostility among the communities, based on an underlying ethnic-historical tension, led to a complete absence of cooperation between resource users. At the same time, the surrounding area had 'become a de facto open access resource' (p. 337).

While much of the mentioned literature addressed resistance to rather exclusionist conservation set-ups, Bixler et al. (2015) illustrate that conservation initiatives and institutions, which were to be built through community participation, also created resistance and adverse conservation outcomes. Their findings from Kenya's Biliqo-Bulesa conservancy in Isiolo County include that the conservancy was set up with the supposed intention to create an arena for local actors' interaction with the state and was represented by local authorities as a 'positive transition' of shifting from transhumant pastoralism to a sedentary livelihood and production system, in which communities drive the agenda. The establishment of the conservancy was further understood to allow for the creation of shared decision-making spaces in which power and responsibilities over natural resources would be shared between the state and communities. However, the authors found that the establishment and implementation of the conservancy had disrupted traditional social networks, which had previously provided a social safety net and upon which social cohesion in the area had been based; and that the new rules replaced customary rules and formed new forms of stratification and power relations, which eventually contributed to increased vulnerability and conflict in the area. The authors further found that decision-making in the conservancy was driven by people with pro-conservationist mindsets while lacking in-depth local knowledge of the socio-ecological system, which further illustrated that unequal power relations did not only contribute to differing decision-making powers between state and community actors but also between members of the community itself. The authors conclude that participation was 'functional' to comply with goals and objectives imposed from the outside, but fostered tyranny rather than democratic ideas by allowing powerful actors to constrain other local actors' interests and decision-making opportunities. In turn, the community conservancy model contributed to dividing rather than uniting the community and experienced critical opposition.

Similarly, Chomba et al. (2015) investigated the empowerment of communities through the CBFM vehicle in central-northern Kenya in terms of defining regulations concerning forest resources, implementing these regulations and adjudicating conflict. Overall, they found that outcomes fell short of expectations in their case study for two main reasons. First, existing institutional power structures continued limiting the de facto transfer of powers to the Community Forest Association (CFA) since state agencies, including the Kenya Forest Service (KFS), retained the powers to define regulations concerning the access to and use of the forest, as well as the distribution of revenue generated from the forest, despite having outsourced some of the enforcement of these rules to CFA guards. Second, the CFA reflected power structures within the local community and prevented members of locally marginalised groups from meaningfully partaking, which reinforced existing social and economic inequalities, including competition for environmental goods and services. Specifically, elite capture was found in the control of elective or appointed positions in the CFA lead-

ership (descriptive representation) and in the formulation and definition of activities and interests (substantive representation). Green
(2016) argues that CBNRM produces new power systems, which alters
the patterns of losers and winners in natural resource governance. She
adds that those in dominant positions often attempt to appropriate
the new structures of power to enhance control over natural resources
and potential benefits, hence reconfiguring power to serve their interests. Dressler, Büscher, Schoon, Brockington, et al. (2010) conducted a
comparative CBNRM assessment with case studies from various countries in both the Global North and the Global South. They found that
the design and delivery of CBNRM often disempowered rather than
empowered communities, particularly in a context of a resurge of protectionism related to 'green political visions' related to climate change
debates since the turn of the millennium. Opposition to the community conservation vehicle can be related to the question of which community is included, whose local knowledge is considered, and whether
this inclusion is more than rhetorical. Alden Wily and Mbaya (2001)
also hypothesise that non-recognition of customary tenure regimes by
the state law might contribute to other forms of community participation or locally based forest management not being taken up as a viable
option by communities.

Building on Rahmato (2003), it might be necessary to consider not
only one single 'environmentalism of the community' but various
'environmentalisms of diverse segments of the community' depending on the context. Differences in 'environmentalisms' are particularly
likely along various intersections, namely age and gender, or as a result
of tension between indigenous or ancestral occupants of an area on the
one hand and those who arrived later, the 'in-migrants', on the other
hand. As discussed, these 'environmentalisms', while rooted in locality and identity, are not static, and 'knowledge regimes of farmers are
as likely to be shaped by interests, power relations and institutional
considerations as those of government agents' (Munro, 2003, p. 203).
The interconnectedness of locality, identity, tradition and heritage
with interests and power relations in many instances also contributes
to what Hobsbawm and Ranger (1983) appositely call the 'invention
of tradition', which further complicates the legitimacy claims that
are often the outcome of such inventions. In the same vein, Carneiro
da Cunha and de Almeda (2000) argue that some indigenous groups
adopted Western projections of them being 'ecologically noble savages',
a term coined by Redford (1990), dedicated to environmental conservation, and hence 'invented tradition', with the primary objective of
attracting donor funds.

Overall, conflicting attitudes among local community members
towards protected areas, often judged in moral terms by external
observers, can be understood as the result of a complex combination

and interaction of symbolic and substantial struggles, identities, interests, and needs. In the circumstances where local groups understand or represent themselves as marginalised by the Government, top-down approaches to environmental and other land-use and land-management policies can reinforce marginalisation and domination. Since these policies are so crucial to the social reproduction of groups that depend on their outcomes and their mere survival, what might seem like inconsiderate approaches to protecting essential natural resources to some might equal more far-reaching fears of extermination for others.

Reading the landscape: The difficulty of assessing the outcomes of inclusive conservation approaches

Considering the translation of new approaches to environmental conservation and management in the physical environment, relatively little is known about the 'big picture', about the overall relation between community conservation and real improvements in biodiversity conservation that can be attributed to these conservation models and programmes (Kangwana, 2001). Considering forest management specifically, economic rationales have continued to dominate regulations and practices in forest use and management in the wider East African region, far from national and international holistic conservation approaches and priorities (Bongers & Tennigkeit, 2010), with a minimal shift towards more community inclusion. The World Bank-supported tea zones established in the late 1980s and the early 1990s as 'simple but effective' buffer zones between people and the forest, including in the Mau Forest (Klopp, 2012), clearly displayed the continuous emphasis on the creation of enclosures. The logging ban imposed on state forest reserves between 1999 and 2011 can also be understood as an instrument related to the 'fences and fines' repertoire (Klooster, 2009). The limited implementation of truly inclusive conservation approaches renders assessing their outcomes difficult.

Considering the effectiveness of CBFM programmes specifically, there is empirical evidence for their potential as viable approaches to forest conservation and community development and for comprehensive gaps. Participatory forest management (PFM), in Kenya, manifested predominantly in communities' self-organisation in CFAs (Okumu & Muchapondwa, 2017a). Given the importance of shared values and institution building based on these values, it is important to consider that communities' willingness to self-organise and develop or join institutions depends on various contextual factors. Looking at specific determinants of participation across twenty-two CFAs in the Mau Forest at the household level, Okumu and Muchapondwa (2017a) found that household size, household heads' post-primary education and ownership of private woodlots positively influenced participation. In contrast, household heads' off-farm employment and non-residential status negatively influenced participation. However, considering the success of the CFAs, defined as a manifestation of collective action, those with more 'natives' were more successful. At the same time, higher education of the CFA chairpersons was correlated with lower collective action success, possibly because of a link between education and elite capture. Beyond that, the CFAs formed through the support of NGOs or other external actors were less successful than those formed organically. Concerning community members' participation in CFAs, Musyoki, Mugwe, and Mutundu (2016) found that the motivation to join was highest among those who strongly depended on forests for their livelihoods. Conversely, Ojha, Ford, Keenan, Race, et al. (2016) found radical opposition to the idea of CBFM among community members in Nepal because some ethnic groups were excluded from the governance system and benefit sharing specifically, and the CBFM vehicle was hence considered only to benefit forest-adjacent communities.

Seeking to analyse conservation outcomes further, the exclusion, inclusion, and representation question remains fundamental. While the legislative frameworks that often maintain prerogatives for both max-imisation of commercial forest exploitation through centralised actors and a recognition of community and minority claims are partly responsi-ble for this, Chomba et al. (2015) found that powerful actors deliberately use a multitude of strategies to prevent comprehensive empowerment of local communities – and hence its assessment. Citing Poteete and Ribot (2011), they argue that local elites, namely large-scale farmers and con-servancy owners, invoked economic and symbolic forms of power to control the CFA alongside other local development initiatives. Okumu and Muchapondwa (2017a) came to similar conclusions and found that rent-seeking behaviour among KFS foresters led them to collude with loggers and CFA officials to benefit from deforestation and hence to elite capture, undermining both collective action and sustainable forest man-agement (SFM). Chomba et al. (2015) further showed that the forest management agreement that the CFA had entered with the KFS empha-sised benefit sharing in extractive forest activities and foreclosed a more comprehensive valuation of forest benefits, including ecosystem services, which reinforced the commodifying approach to forests that the state had exposed since colonial times. The authors hence conclude that '[i]nstead of a transfer of power in favor of the marginalized groups, the management agreement ended up not only serving, but actually reinforcing the power of larger farmers and conservancy owners' (p. 8), which resulted in 'processes of local empowerment through CBFM [being] usually neither effective nor well achieved in practice' (p. 9).

These results are similar to findings from other parts of the world. Charnley and Poe (2007), for instance, compared CF initiatives in four cases from the Americas, namely Canada, the United States, Mexico, and Bolivia, and found that in each of these cases, real community involvement and empowerment had been hampered by structural continuity, which manifested in limited devolution of forest management authority from states to communities. A study of several colonial and post-colonial states in Asia revealed that, despite the partial inclusion of customary forest management practices and institutions, state bureaucracies had remained in control of forest management (Peluso & Vandergeest, 2001). Bushley (2014) confirms the same for CF in Nepal, indicating that power struggles between community members and government representatives at the local level prevented the communities from enjoying their rights, autonomy, and benefits; and that corruption at various levels perpetuated illegal timber harvesting and trade. In the same vein, Chomba et al. (2015) argue that the limited success of many community conservation initiatives, in the Kenyan context specifically, clearly reflects the highly centralised nature of the state and its hesitance to delegate power to subsidiary levels in matters of land and natural resource management and hence manifests that the CBNRM approaches were, to a large degree, systemically unable to attain the set objectives. Bushley (2014) describes the dominance of state-centric forest governance structures, despite the inclusion of polycentric elements, as a function of the dominance of international NGO- and donor-driven conservation agendas.

These findings appositely reflect the differentiation made and difference found between benefit-sharing and power-sharing approaches to CBFM (Alden Wily & Mbaya, 2001). They hence strongly suggest that most CBFM initiatives actively implemented in many parts of the world fell within the former and thus, to some degree, responded to the 'Poverty-Environment Nexus'. Considering the limited empowerment achieved through CBFM, some criticise CF as yet another mechanism to increase state control over forests and their communities and to co-opt communities into the enforcement of coercive forest regulations or restoration of degraded forests that they did not destroy in the first place (Charnley & Poe, 2007).

Inclusion and exclusion in the struggle for environmental justice

The Ogiek, supposedly the 'traditional' inhabitants of the Eastern Mau, experienced marginalisation and subjugation throughout the country's history. This 'othering' was actively encouraged by successive governments and perpetuated by members of various ethnic communities. Since the 1990s, a group of community leaders had been actively bringing the community's living conditions into the limelight, received considerable support from various organisations and institutions, and finally achieved important legal recognition.

Experiences of subjugation and recognition: From passive to active 'othering'

Despite officially being counted as part of the wider Kalenjin community, the Ogiek's association with it has repeatedly been contested by members of other Kalenjin groups and academics alike (Lynch, 2011). Since colonial times, members of the Ogiek community were commonly referred to as 'Dorobo', a derogatory term derived from the Maasai term '*Il Torobbo*', designating people without cattle, who were thus understood as being poor (Blackburn, 1974). The prominence of the Dorobo designation illustrates that the image of the Ogiek was mainly conceived from the outside through a process of differentiation. According to Kratz (1993), the Ogiek were constructed antithetically as the 'others' following a contrasting to the self-representation of their neighbouring communities. This othering is further supported by the fact that members of other ethnic groups could 'become Dorobo' when relative poverty forced them to adapt their lifestyles and take up livelihoods based on hunting and gathering (Berntsen, 1976). Due to their lifestyle of hunting and gathering, the Ogiek have been represented as backward people 'at the end of the evolutionary scale' or even 'social outcasts' (both Distefano, 1990, p. 43). Those and other connotations associated with the term Dorobo led the 'true' Ogiek to refute that name as it is considered to be cruel, and insist on the term 'Ogiek' which is said to literally mean 'caretaker of all animals and plants' (Sang, 2003; Towett, 2004).

State actors actively pursued the 'othering' of the Ogiek since colonial times. Confronted with the 'Dorobo question' on how the 'fiscally barren' forest-dwelling communities should be conceptualised and governed (Cavanagh, 2017), a Committee on the Dorobo Question was formed in the 1920s. Based on the Committee's recommendations, the colonial administration decided to assimilate the Ogiek and recommended their relocation to the Native Reserves of bigger tribes, insisting that they 'should become members of and [be] absorbed into the tribes with which they have most affinity' (Sang, 2003, p. 118). While the colonial government arguably used 'civilising violence' to 'transform *anthropos* into *humanitas*' (Cavanagh, 2017), the Ogiek leaders labelled the missions to assimilate, dispossess and relocate the Ogiek or frustrate them by imposing veterinary controls as well as hunting and grazing bans, as attempts 'to exterminate, assimilate and impoverish them through constant evictions and disruptions of their traditional lifestyle' (Towett, 2004, Chapter 1). Sang (2003) lists various moments and periods in history during which, he argues, the Ogiek were evicted from their ancestral lands, including 1911–1914, 1918, 1926–1927, followed by a cease-fire agreement between the colonial government, the settlers, and the Ogiek in 1932. After testifying before the Carter Land

Commission in 1932, which led to the recommendation to relocate and absorb the Ogiek community into bigger ethnic groups, various eviction attempts ensued. Further sedentarisation and fluctuating adoption of small-scale farming since the 1940s and increasing economic diversification in the 1950s followed (Kratz, 1993). At the time of the research, it was not as easy to differentiate the Ogiek lifestyle as it used to be from that of other communities. Nonetheless, other communities have continued distinguishing the Ogiek based on their traditional economic activities associated with life in the forest, a characteristic that also remained crucial to the Ogiek self-representation (Kratz, 1993). Distefano (1990) also argues that while having been in close contact with their neighbours, the Ogiek have generally remained 'culturally and economically distinct ... while still changing and developing internally' (p. 53). Sang (2003) estimates that about 10% of the Ogiek in the Eastern Mau still lived traditional hunter-gatherer lives, while the others combined selected practices related to that livelihood with small-scale farming and livestock rearing. At the same time, all Ogiek land continued to be controlled by the Land, Forest and Wildlife Acts (Ohenjo, 2003). Historically, agricultural expansion, the introduction of non-indigenous tree species,[1] large-scale logging and the settlement of in-migrants contributed to the loss of the ancestral Ogiek land in the Eastern Mau. As land use and access were crucial to their hunter-gatherer lifestyle, these changes became a key feature of their economic and political marginalisation, negatively impacting Ogiek housing, health, and food security (Rolnik, 2010).

The social and economic marginalisation of the Ogiek was facilitated by the fact that they continuously held a minority status in the national set-up. Due to their dispersion in different areas and their statistical inclusion into the wider Kalenjin and sometimes Maasai categories, there were no apparent records of the evolution of their population numbers. Until the census that was carried out in 2009, there were no available statistics on hunter-gatherers in general since the Government continued pursuing a non-recognition policy. For instance, the Dorobo category listed in 1989 included other groups apart from the Ogiek, while the 1999 census was released without reference to ethnic affiliations. Estimates on the total Ogiek population range from 20,000 to 37,000 (Ohenjo, 2003), while one source proposes a figure of 78,691 for Nakuru County alone.[2] Unofficial OWC records number about 6,000 members of the Ogiek community in the Eastern Mau Forest alone (Sang, 2003). After their population census results were cancelled in the 2009 count,

[1]   These non-indigenous tree species are commonly referred to as 'exotic' in Kenya.
[2]   Number cited as representing the figures indicated in the 2009 census (Cottrel-Ghai et al. 2013).

the Mau Forest Restoration Initiative proposed to compose an alternative Ogiek register. A timely publication of the report was hindered by various factors, especially differences among the members of the Government-initiated Ogiek Council of Elders that had been tasked with the supervision of the project on who should be included in the register and who should not. According to the 'Report of the Prime Minister's Task Force on the Conservation of the Mau Forest Complex', the wider Mariashoni area was settled by approximately 12,000 persons in 2009 (GoK, 2009e). Others spoke of up to 20,000 persons that had settled in the area since the declaration of the settlement scheme, which marked a significant increase from the supposed 1,600 residents before that. While the Task Force Report identified 1,500 Ogiek families within the Mariashoni settlement scheme (GoK, 2009e), unofficial sources indicated that the Ogiek register comprised around 9,000 adult Ogiek, 3,000 of which lived in the Mau Forest [1/006, 1/040], while another estimated that the Ogiek by lineage could be as few as 5,000 [mentioned in 2/051]. The Ogiek leader spoke of 10,000 adults, of which 1,500 supposedly lived in the wider Elburgon area, including Mariashoni [3/056]. Another knowledgeable observer opined that only around 3,000–4,000 of the adult residents in Mariashoni were Ogiek [5/108]. The composition of the Ogiek register and the results had not been made publicly available by 2013.

As a response to this history of 'othering', sections of the Ogiek community actively pursued recognition and inclusion by self-defining as an indigenous minority (Towett, 2004). This self-definition played a crucial role in the socio-cultural dynamics influencing the 'Mau crisis'. Since the label became central to the Ogiek fight for recognition, it is important to highlight that, of the two terms, neither indigenous nor minority have globally recognised definitions (Nassali, 2011), and various definitions for both persist in the human rights literature. In 2005, following similar evolutions at the international scale, the African Commission stipulated four criteria for defining indigenous peoples: first, there is a spatial dimension in terms of occupation and use of a specific territory; second, there is the voluntary perpetuation of cultural distinctiveness such as language, religion, spiritual values, modes of production, laws and institutions; third, there is self-identification as well as recognition by other groups as a collectivity; and fourth, there is an experience of subjugation, marginalisation, dispossession, exclusion, and discrimination (Nassali, 2011). Unlike in societies in which a foreign minority eventually became dominant, indigeneity, in African contexts, focuses less on the question of 'who came first' but centres around exclusion, negative appraisal of alternative cultures and ways of life, as well as threats to the very survival of specific groups. Three aspects in the definition of indigenous peoples can, therefore, be extrapolated that would allow proposing a relevant definition for African contexts: first, the existence of a distinct culture intrinsically linked with a specific territory; second, self-identification as being part of that distinct culture; and third, (perceived) negative projection of that culture with regards to mainstream (developmental) paradigms (Nassali, 2011). The term 'minority' also contains the idea of self-identification as belonging to a particular group and the fact of having stayed within a given territory for a long time. According to Alfredsson (2005), the most crucial criterion, however, is numeric in that the concerned group must constitute less than half of a given population to be in a non-dominant position within that population.

In Kenya, in line with suggestions made by Henrard (2001), the Minority Rights Group International defines minorities as numerically inferior to the rest of the population within a country; in a non-dominant position; residing in the state, being either nationals or a group with close, long-standing ties to the state; possessing ethnic, religious, or linguistic characteristics that differ from those of the rest of the population, and showing, if only implicitly, a sense of solidarity directed towards preserving their distinctive collective identity (Cottrel-Ghai, Ghai, Oei, & Wanyoike, 2013). Three groups of minorities are most commonly recognised: ethnic, religious and linguistic minorities. In Kenya, indigenous peoples can be defined as the fourth category of minorities (Makoloo, 2005). Evidently, individual labels within this proposed classification are not mutually exclusive, and a given group can fall into several categories. Furthermore, the boundaries between indigenous and minority rights are not clearly defined either. The main difference between minority rights and indigenous peoples' rights is that the first are individual rights, whereas the latter are collective rights (Nassali, 2011). It is also important to note that indigenous groups can be minorities, but not all minorities are indigenous; at the same time, the minority title does not automatically convey marginalisation.

In Kenya, the origin of the definition of minority groups as 'separate entities' dates to the European colonial powers' land management policies. As prime land was forcefully acquired for agricultural production, those who formerly occupied the land were forced into economic, social, and eventually cultural marginalisation if they were not able or willing to 'adapt'. Previous socially defined spatial structures often disappeared or lost validity due to the introduction of private property dimensions into land tenure. The colonial imposition of new land-use and ownership regimes led to circumstances in which a few communities were compelled to identify as minorities or indigenous people, often to defend their land rights (Ohenjo, 2003, 2011). The minority status in Kenya is thereby not necessarily conveyed by numbers but by socio-economic marginalisation.[3] The marginalisation of certain

3   It is pertinent to ascertain here that minorities are not born but made according to prevailing circumstances and that belonging to a minority is not

groups in politics, the economy, and the civil service remained a prominent feature of post-Independence Kenya. Minority rights were far off the agenda, as in most African countries at the time, because minority rights were represented as fostering negative ethnicity and tribal division, ultimately endangering national unity. Like most African states, Kenya manifested a desire to de-culturalise and assimilate minorities into dominant cultures. At the same time, indigenous cultures were commonly represented as primitive and calls for their presumed need to become 'civilised' were common (Nassali, 2011).

Before the establishment of the Centre for Minority Rights Development in 2000, there was no evidence of any federated group lobbying the Kenyan government on minority rights at the national level (Ohenjo, 2011). Minority rights, however, had received considerable attention on the international and continental scale. Whereas neither the UN Charter, nor the African Charter on Human and People's Rights (ACHPR), nor the African Union Charter explicitly refer to minorities, the idea that minorities require special protection is not new. The now-defunct UN Sub-Commission on the Prevention of Discrimination of Minorities was created as early as 1947 and later, in 1982, established a Working Group on Indigenous Populations. Furthermore, the Permanent Forum on Indigenous Issues under the Economic and Social Council (ECOSOC) was inaugurated in 2000, and a special Rapporteur was nominated. Several international agreements relevant to minority rights protection were adopted within those forums. The most crucial document is the 1992 UN Declaration on the Rights of Persons belonging to Ethnic, Religious and Linguistic Minorities. Others are the International Labour Organization (ILO) Convention No. 169 of 1989 or the UN Declaration on the Rights of Indigenous Peoples in 2007. At the continental scale, similar advances were made in 2001 with the adoption of the Resolution for the Rights of Indigenous Groups by the African Commission. Kenya is a state party to several of these international and continental agreements (Ohenjo, 2011). Yet, difficulties in their enforcement, as well as in monitoring compliance by state parties, have bestowed only moderate successes upon those treaties (Nassali, 2011).

In the absence of specific consideration and legislation, representation of the interests of minority groups is often unrealistic. In many instances, lobby groups petition states to enforce special legislation to guarantee the full participation of members of minority communities as citizens of the democratic state, notably with the objective of engendering a sense of national belonging and security among the members of these groups (Cottrel-Ghai et al., 2013). Since the democratic regime change in Kenya in 2002, minorities had been accorded gradual recognition on the national scale, starting with the inclusion of minority

static but constantly redefined and re-negotiated (Nassali, 2011).

representatives in the constitutional review process in the same year. The 2010 Constitution explicitly recognised and protected the rights of minorities for the first time in Kenyan history. In the Constitution, hunter-gatherers are defined as marginalised because of their livelihood system, without having to prove actual discrimination (Cottrel-Ghai et al., 2013). Regarding political participation, Article 56 (a) of the Constitution stipulates that the State shall ensure that minorities and marginalised groups 'participate and are represented in governance and other spheres of life' (Republic of Kenya, 2010b). The constitutional review process was also crucial since minority representatives decided to present their claims together as indigenous peoples' voice instead of pursuing their interests as separate groups (Makoloo, 2005).

As required by law, minority representatives also took part in the elaboration process of the 2009 National Land Policy. Addressing historical land injustices and community rights to land and striving to protect minority rights, the Land Policy also clearly notes that

> minority communities ... have lost access to land and land-based resources ... that is key to their livelihood ... these groups ... deserve [sic.] special protection from the State with regards to their land rights and ability to manage their natural resources in a sustainable manner [and they] have not been represented adequately in governmental decision making at all levels. (Republic of Kenya, 2009c)

The Policy also singles out colonial assimilation policies and capitalism as primary drivers of the marginalisation of minorities. Further provisions for the participation of minorities in local decision-making processes were also included in the 2005 Forest Act and the 2002 Water Act.

The Ogiek also fought for inclusion in active decision-making, from which they had been largely excluded because they did not hold any significant political offices. The first time an Ogiek held any government office was in the late 1970s, when a few individual Ogiek were nominated as Assistant Chiefs among the Kipchornwonek and Kaplelach subgroups (Kratz, 1999). Concerning elective positions, there were only two Ogiek councillors in Nakuru County during the legislative period of 2008–2013, despite their presence in fifty-two county wards distributed over six constituencies (Cottrel-Ghai et al., 2013). At the same time, no Ogiek had ever held any high elective position in the country. Considering their continuous marginalisation and the inability to bring about substantial change through elections, some Ogiek then took to other means of political participation in the last two decades, primarily by seeking legal redress in the courts. A group of Ogiek had been fighting marginalisation and eviction from their land by taking the Government to court since the 1990s. After that, the courts were used by the same Ogiek to pursue their inclusion in public and political affairs in the run-up to the 2013 elections. Based on the precedent set by the Kenyan

High Court in 2008, which decided that the Ilchamus hunter-gatherer group, a culturally distinct minority group, had a right to influence the formulation and implementation of public policy and to be represented by people belonging to the same socio-cultural and economic groups as themselves, and, consequently, should be represented by a nominated Ilchamus Member of Parliament, the Ogiek petitioned the courts in the run-up to the 2013 elections. The High Court, in July 2012, then compelled the Independent Electoral and Boundaries Commission (IEBC) to consider the rights of minority and marginalised groups and to adjust the ward boundaries to bring the Ogiek together, hence providing that the Ogiek should be able to have one of their own represent them politically (Cottrel-Ghai et al., 2013). This was a critical albeit partial victory after the IEBC had previously announced it would not create tribal zones in the North Rift by giving specific wards to specific communities,[4] a decision nullified by the courts. Despite that decision, the ward boundaries were not adapted before the 2013 elections, and the Ogiek did not form a majority in any electoral ward, including in Mariashoni. In the aftermath of the 2013 elections and faced with the fact that neither in Mariashoni nor anywhere else was a 'real Ogiek'[5] elected or nominated to the national or any county assembly, members of the community filed petition No. 177/2013, pointing out that the state had failed to assure the representation of members of the Ogiek community as provided for by Article 56 of the Constitution. The case was first mentioned on 3 May 2013.[6] The following day, the IEBC published an updated list indicating that they had made changes to the four persons representing special interests to be nominated to the Nakuru County Assembly. After the initial list contained three representatives of the disabled and one of the youths, the IEBC corrected its list and included a representative of the 'marginalised' in the person of an Ogiek activist from Nessuit in the Eastern Mau (IEBC Dispute Resolution Committee, 2013a, 2013b). Despite this critical decision obtained by the IEBC, petition No. 177/2013 was not resolved. Ogiek leaders tried to rally members of other indigenous minorities behind their case to present a joint case.[7] The joining of forces presumably represented an essential change in strategy. It manifested that the decentralisation and devo-

---

4   Too, T., 'IEBC refuses to create tribal zones', *The Standard*, 27 January 2012.
5   Agnes Jerotich Salimu, MCA for Mariashoni Ward since 2013, celebrated as 'the first elected woman leader from the marginalised Ogiek community' whose 'election was also a clear victory for the minority community which has fought for its existence for a long time', was highly controversial (Obiria, M., 'MCA Jerotich Salimu strives to change the lives of the Ogiek', *Daily Nation*, 10 September 2014).
6   SMS text message from the famous Ogiek leader on 29 April 2013.
7   SMS text message from the famous Ogiek leader on 3 May 2013.

lution of powers introduced by the 2010 Constitution were used as a welcome vehicle to insist on minority interests.

Recognition of the Ogiek as sole legitimate inhabitants of the Mau Forest

In conjunction with the community conservation orthodoxy and PFM specifically, partly based on a re-valorisation of traditional ecological knowledge and in line with previous advances in recognising indigenous minority rights, the Government ostensibly found itself compelled to reconsider the fate of the Ogiek community in the Mau rehabilitation exercise.

The 2009 Mau Task Force Report engendered considerable discussions about the situation of the Ogiek community. Consequently, the Government embarked on several different approaches to defining the rights of those recognised as Ogiek. Initially, it was announced that, in line with the recommendations of the Task Force Report, no-one would be allowed to remain within the forest (GoK, 2009e). It was also in this spirit that the first evictions of forest dwellers, particularly in South-Western Mau, were carried out. After considerable backlash from sections of the Government and various human rights groups, it was then announced that the Ogiek would continue to have a right to stay within the forest (Human Rights Council, 2010). Matters discussed controversially included whether third-party purchasers of land within the settlement schemes should be compensated and whether evictees should be resettled by the Government or be left to look after themselves (Republic of Kenya, 2012a).[8] The resettlement question furthermore engulfed the difficulty of defining whether evictees were 'illegal settlers' or whether they should be defined as IDPs, and if they were defined as the latter, who was a 'genuine IDP' through forest evictions, and who was not [1/002, 1/005, 1/018]. The recognition of the Ogiek as legitimate inhabitants of the forest and hence their right to remain within the areas adjacent to the forest did not necessarily imply that the Government was not aware that lifestyles among the forest dwellers had changed [1/022]. This recognition can be understood as falling under payment for environmental/ecosystem services (PES) or environmental easement approaches, depending on the applicable land regime, which allows people to remain in environmentally critical areas but prescribes land-use and management practices that support environmental conservation and forest rehabilitation. In early 2011, the Government indicated wanting to move all those households identified as Ogiek from critical upstream areas within water catchment areas to less sensitive downstream areas under ICS supervision

8   Opiyo, D., 'Mau Ultimatum', *Daily Nation*, 31 July 2009; IRIN, 'Mau evictees still waiting three years on', *IRIN news*, 28 September 2011.

[1/006]. By early 2012, these plans had changed because 'donors shy away from an Ogiek resettlement downstream' [1/022] against the background of general resistance to the eviction and resettlement question because 'the Mau has been destroyed in the name of the Ogiek being resettled' [1/006].

The question about the future of the settlement scheme was intrinsically a question of how to deal with the different groups of people who had settled in the area and, more fundamentally, about how to deal with the 'Ogiek question' – first a question of who was defined as Ogiek and secondly of the rights attributed to those recognised as Ogiek. The fluidity of identity questions, together with the formal recognition of the Ogiek as the legitimate indigenous community in the Mau Forest by the initial Task Force Report, led to the necessity of defining who would be recognised as Ogiek and who would not. Due to previously discussed amalgamations in the national censuses and the Ogiek being subsumed into various other groups, official census results were de facto useless for the 'Ogiek question'. To solve it, the ICS funded an Ogiek census. One government expert said that the ICS had spent considerable time working on defining what the criteria of an Ogiek identity would be and on screening 'potential' Ogiek before composing the register. This screening was undertaken by a newly formed 'Ogiek Council of Elders', composed of what the ICS/KWTA (Kenya Water Towers Agency) forestry specialist described as 'genuine Ogiek' who established a questionnaire with the help of which 'genuine' Ogiek were to be distinguished from 'imposters' [1/006]. The Ogiek Council, whose main objective was establishing the Ogiek register, was set up on 1 April 2010, and the registration process concluded on 3 September 2010 (GoK, 2010a, 2010d). The exercise, overall, was informed by the OPAT, the Ogiek Peoples Ancestral Territorial Atlas, published by ERMIS Africa in 2011 [1/006]. While the primary purpose of the atlas had been to develop a map displaying the different resources in the Mau Forest, including the sources of the rivers, it contributed to understanding historical land management practices and the socio-spatial organisation of the different Ogiek clans across the ancestral lands (*konoito*) [1/006]. As indicated, the precise number of adult Ogiek living in and out of Mau Forest remained disputed. The Government expert further said that the register composition took longer than expected because the Ogiek tried to 'pump their numbers' [1/040] to include others who might eventually benefit from compensations or relocations. An ICS/KWTA official said that the register would not have any direct implication because no direct outputs were linked to the establishment of the register and that it was not clear whether the register would be used for possible evictions or resettlements. However, he conceded that the register would serve as 'the basis for the definition of who is Ogiek and who is not' [1/042] if anything came up.

At the continental scale, a judgement of the African Court on Human and Peoples' Rights on 26 May 2017 was celebrated by human rights defenders as a 'historic judgement' that 'sets major precedent' because the 'Court has recognised that the Ogiek – and therefore many other indigenous peoples in Africa – have a leading role to play as guardians of local ecosystems, and in conserving and protecting land and natural resources, including the Mau Forest'.[9] The judgement concluded an eight-year-long legal battle. It confirmed that the Kenyan government violated seven articles of the African Charter concerning the Ogiek land rights, including their rights to life, property, natural resources, development, religion, and culture. The Court had been in operation since 2006, and the ruling was the first on indigenous peoples' rights and the largest ever case brought before that Court. This ruling was also in line with the recognition of ancestral land rights through the 2010 Constitution and the 2016 Community Land Act, which had been expected to compel the Kenyan government to grant minority rights.

Beyond the question of the importance attributed to indigenous minorities in general, and the Ogiek in the Mau Forest crisis particularly, problematic tension among and within the various communities and between their members persisted. A matter of particular concern was the schism between claims about environmental friendliness on the one hand while the same community members adopt and adapt to what some describe as 'perverse modernisation' (Kahora, 2015) on the other hand.

The role of the community in forest degradation and the non-protection of the Eastern Mau

As addressed in various instances, the indigenous Ogiek in Mariashoni defined their identity sometimes in line with others' identities and sometimes apart. Some Ogiek leaders insisted that, historically, many of the public policies implemented in the Mariashoni area had targeted the extinction and annihilation of the Ogiek, in line with general 'othering' (Lynch, 2011; Said, 1978) policies implemented since colonial times. For instance, the widely recognised Ogiek leader invoked that the idea of assembling the Ogiek and settling them in the Mariashoni settlement scheme simply targeted their extinction. He explained that, by settling

[9]   Lucy Claridge, Minority Rights Group International (MRG)'s Legal Director, in Minority Rights Group International, 'Huge victory for Kenya's Ogiek as African Court sets major precedent for indigenous peoples' land rights', http://minorityrights.org/2017/05/26/huge-victory-kenyas-ogiek-african-court-sets-major-precedent-indigenous-peoples-land-rights (accessed 26 May 2017).

them, the Government implemented the recommendations of the Carter Land Commission from 1934, which suggested that 'whenever possible the Ogiek (Dorobo) should become members of and absorbed into the tribe in which they have closest or most affinity' (Towett, 2004, Chapter 5). He further claimed that their settlement disrupted their lifestyle, along with agricultural expansion, the installation of commercial forest plantations with exotic trees, large-scale logging, and the in-migration of members of other communities [3/055]. Independently from the validity of these claims, the 'persecution complex' that was evident in his spoken and written words profoundly influenced the Ogiek imagination of self and others in Mariashoni, as well as social relations among different communities in the area.

Being Dorobo unites beyond ethnicity

Looking at the popular representation and labels given to different communities, it was interesting to observe that (as noted) most Ogiek in Mariashoni referred to members of other communities as *wageni* (guests) when speaking in Swahili and 'foreigners' or 'newcomers' when speaking in English.[10] A young woman, one of the few local Ogiek who pursued a university education,[11] differentiated between three different groups of *wageni*. First, those who had lived in the Eastern Mau for a long time, 'with her own ancestors already', and whose lives had been highly integrated with those of the Ogiek community members. Second, those who had intermarried or adapted to and adopted the lifestyle of the Ogiek in more recent years. Lastly, those who had come 'out of nowhere' since the early 1990s, who did not integrate and who behaved contrary to what used to be understood as the quintessential Ogiek lifestyle. It was those *wageni*, she said, who were generally disliked by the local Ogiek [5/206]. In a similar vein, a young Kipsigis resident observed that 'there is a difference between "*wadorobo za asili*" [members of other ethnic communities who have been there for long] and other "*wadorobo*" [*members of other ethnic communities who arrived only recently]*' [5/201],[12] and hence a difference between the long-term forest dwellers, independently from whether they were part of the Ogiek community, and the other forest dwellers. This differentiation between the ones who originated from outside the forest but had intermarried and/or adapted to the Ogiek lifestyle and those who came from outside the forest with their families and kept their own ways of

[10] Observation made on various occasions throughout the field research.
[11] One of the most candid members of the local Ogiek community explained that, in 2013, there were only six university graduates from the entire Mariashoni region, two of which are PhD holders from the same family, and three further university graduates from another family [5/245].
[12] In Swahili, *wadorobo* is plural of *dorobo*.

doing things was effectively made by most Mariashoni residents. In line with this distinction, the relations between the local Ogiek and members of other communities largely depended on generation, time, and prevailing political circumstances.

Since colonial times, members of the Kikuyu community had lived in the Mariashoni area. The movement and resettlement of the Kikuyu in the North Rift were mainly motivated by the colonial need for labour in a region whose Kalenjin population were largely hostile to the colonial enterprise and refused collaboration [1/002]. Thus, the colonial forestry department started bringing Kikuyu workers to Mariashoni in the early 1930s, moving them into the area with the white colonial forestry officials. Some of the Ogiek elders spoke highly of the Kikuyu workers who, they said, started arriving in the area around 1937 as permanent employees of the colonial government. Since the colonial administration disrupted traditional forest life in Mariashoni, most of all through spatial reorganisation and the establishment of forest plantations amid traditional clan territories, the local Ogiek and the Kikuyu workers were settled in villages. At the time, the colonial government established different villages for the Kikuyu and the local Ogiek, but both were established on open glades within the forest. The Ogiek villages were placed in glades in the indigenous forest, where they continued being allowed to move freely. At the same time, movement was restricted in the newly established forest plantations [4/097]. According to reports given by the few remaining contemporary witnesses and their descendants and other community members, the colonial government introduced an essential division between the local Ogiek and 'foreign' workers at the time. The Ogiek men were compelled to do hard physical labour in the plantations. They had to carry individual trees on foot to the nearest sawmills on dangerous journeys along forest paths that were slippery due to the permanent moisture in the thick forest, and risk being confronted by wild animals [5/200]. Others were employed as simple forest guards, given 'modern' (i.e. European-style) clothes, and somewhat introduced into more 'modern' livelihoods [3/063]. On the other hand, the foreign workers were mainly recruited for more technical and skilled labour, such as tree cutting, plantation establishment, and management [4/097]. The settlement in villages further necessitated new types of houses because the traditional Ogiek leaf-houses (*gotopteleeg*) were not suitable for village life. The older men said that the Kikuyu taught them how to build mud houses. With the settlement of the white and Kikuyu people also came some small-scale farming. The Ogiek elders recounted that the Kikuyu taught them how to plant maize on small pieces of land for subsistence purposes. At the time, all cultivation was done within the forest plantations, using what would be known as the *'shamba'* system after 1968. Typically, people would farm their food crops, especially maize and potatoes, in the forest plan-

tations until the tree seedlings were three years of age. Each farmer
had to take care of the seedlings and ensure that the trees grew properly. The elderly men added that there were no separate *shamba*s for
food cultivation in Mariashoni apart from the ones within the forest
plantations until 1997 [4/097]. Later, people also started cultivating
pyrethrum, but this was soon given up because the previously flour-
ishing pyrethrum market had collapsed in the 1960s. In terms of social
relations, according to statements made by many of the older residents,
relations between the Kikuyu and Ogiek were mainly friendly. Many
observers said the Kikuyu adapted well to local customs and ways of
doing things. Most of them also learned the Ogiek language, while
many Ogiek learned the Kikuyu language; a 72-year-old female Ogiek
resident even joked in Kikuyu while giving us this account [5/239].

During the research, it was noted that many Ogiek understood or
spoke Kikuyu, and many areas in the forest had maintained Kikuyu
names that were sometimes slightly altered and sometimes plain
Kikuyu [4/097, 5/148, 5/188, 5/239]. While there sometimes were
minor brawls between members of different communities, the relations
between the local Ogiek and the few remaining Kikuyu were mainly
friendly. Relations with the Kikuyu who passed through Mariashoni,
mostly Timsales workers or small-scale timber business operators, were
usually friendly as well, despite some people criticising the Kikuyu for
being major perpetrators and beneficiaries of forest destruction in the
area due to their implication with big and small sawmills [3/058, 4/092,
4/096, 5/131, 5/168, 5/208, 5/225, 5/233, 5/245].

Although his experience was not representative of general relations
between the Ogiek and the Kikuyu in Mariashoni, the fate of the only
remaining Kikuyu resident in Mariashoni illustrated that historically
positive relations between communities are not always able to with-
stand divisive politicisation. He explained that despite being a Kikuyu,
his home had always been in Mariashoni. He was born in 1959 in Kaprop
to a father who was a forest worker with the then-dominant colonial
timber company, Amagamatet. He said the same company 'was later
renamed Sokoro, then Timsales' [5/236], illustrating the historical
roots of current forestry activities in Mariashoni.[13] His family lived
what he described as a peaceful life in Mariashoni until 1987, when all
Kikuyu were evicted from Mariashoni, particularly from the Kikuyu
village in Kaprop, as previously discussed. He returned to Kaprop in
1997, although he did not benefit from land attributions in the settle-

[13] According to the Timsales website, seven sawmillers formed the East
African Timber Cooperative Society Limited in 1932 and later named it
Timsales. In 1967, Timsales subsidiary Sokoro Plywood established Kenya's
first plywood factory in Elburgon (Timsales Ltd website, 'Corporate profile',
https://timsales.webflow.io/about (accessed 27 September 2013)).

ment scheme. He also said that, as a precaution, he left the area during the election period in 2002, which led to the democratisation of the country with the ascent to power of the NARC Coalition Government. He added that he never experienced any problems until 2007, when a large group of armed men surrounded his house, destroyed his fields, and took his livestock. He had been warned by an Ogiek friend and was able to escape before the attack, but he lost all his belongings that night [5/236]. Later, the middle-aged man benefited from the Government-run 'Operation Rudi Nymbani', which the Ministry of Special Programmes implemented after the 2007 post-election violence (PEV) crisis.[14] He operated his 'hotel'[15] from the same mud house built by the Government programme. Despite the Government's plans of securing the PEV's victims' livelihoods by providing them with shelter, his example also illustrated that overcoming politically induced trauma is a difficult and gradual process for all the persons involved, those who were harmed and those who harmed. While he operated his 'hotel' in Mariashoni every day and occasionally slept there as well, his family still lived in Elburgon, where he fled during the clashes. He also indicated that he did not take the attack personally but that the people perpetrating violence against 'outsiders' in the area were politically incited. He said the same people had attacked the local authority's office and the campaign trail of the future local Member of Community Assembly (MCA) in the run-up to the 2013 elections. He further said they were young men who 'supported the local candidate' [5/236].

The ProMara conflict management specialist confirmed that the Mau Forest had been one of the hotspots that experienced violence during every election, calling conflict in the Mau 'cyclic', which could 'be stirred

---

14   After the post-election violence crisis, the Government implemented the 'Operation Rudi Nyumbani' programme. The particularity of this, which in Swahili means 'return home', officially called the Restoration of Farm Infrastructure and Rural Livelihoods Project, is that the Government was to assist displaced families to re-build houses on their land. The important element here is the de facto tenure of land. Through the programme led by the Ministry of Special Programmes and Public Works, the Government planned to help approximately 260,000 families to return to their homelands by providing them shelter (Republic of Kenya, 2008c). In Nakuru County, the 'Rudi Nyumbani' project was implemented by the Norwegian Refugee Council (NRC). With support from the African Development Bank, NRC built around 3,700 rural transitional shelters between April 2011 and February 2012. Beneficiary lists were handed to them by the Ministry that compiled information provided by the DC through the DOs and chiefs without being able to address criticism related to potential bias in the compilation of the lists. A fourth phase which was to benefit 19,000 households was not funded [1/013]. A separate government programme aimed at resettling landless IDPs.

15   'Hotel', in this context, does not designate a place to sleep, but a place to eat. These are commonly small, informal restaurants/cafés.

any time because of the multiple ethnicities that exist' [1/014].[16] The violence that ensued during the primary elections in Mariashoni ahead of the 2013 elections (Fuchs, 2014) was understood by many as related to the fact that the MCA candidate who eventually won the election had supposedly promised to subdivide the land in Mariashoni. Local community members feared that further subdivision and allocation of title deeds would bring in more members of other communities, insisting that 'it is her plan to bring other tribes here' [5/216] and further marginalise the Ogiek. Land, ethnicity and the exploitation of emotionally charged moments during elections, and their amalgamation with general socio-political frustrations, were all part of the puzzle that might explain why the only remaining Kikuyu, a well-integrated and well-respected man, became a target of violence on that fateful night in 2007. Two young Ogiek men confirmed, that apart from him, none of the other Kikuyu who used to live or rent *shambas* in the area had come back until the present day [4/093]. The ProMara conflict management specialist further explained that those benefiting from government schemes such as 'Rudi Nyumbani' were often rendered more vulnerable in conflict-prone areas. He added that many understood it as being biased towards resettling members of the Kikuyu community and that members of other communities often expressed feelings of being disadvantaged, which, in turn, contributed to enhancing other conflict dynamics [1/014].

Redefining identities: Inter-generational conflict and mutual othering

Social relations between members of the Ogiek community and members of non-Ogiek Kalenjin groups differed vastly from relations with other communities. As mentioned, the Mariashoni Ogiek made a clear difference between the two groups of Kalenjin in the Mariashoni area. On the one hand, there were the ones that had been in the area for a long time and with whom the Ogiek often intermarried and integrated well, especially some Kipsigis families, which were effectively considered as 'real' forest dwellers, sometimes positively referred to as Dorobo, even by the Ogiek. On the other hand, there were the 'new in-migrants', the Kalenjin who had been brought or had bought land in Mariashoni after the declaration of the settlement scheme in the late

[16] The conflict management specialist further mentioned a number of 'conflict hotspots' in the Mau Forest, especially during election times: 'Kuresoi; Molo because of the Kikuyu/Kalenjin factor; Njoro; Mauche, Andefo; Rongai; parts of Kericho; Transmara; Dorobo; the Ogiek area; the Nandi Tinderet area; Naivasha, areas of Maella; Narok partly because of the land conflicts that exist in the place; the border area between Narok and Njoro in Ole Kutoi; and also Ol Pusimoru'.

1990s. Social relations between the Ogiek and this last group of *wageni* were generally tense, despite being their Kalenjin 'cousins' [5/206]. The politically instigated arrival of and attribution of land to thousands of Kalenjin households in the area led to fears of becoming economically and culturally insignificant; and to a rigidification of formerly more fluid identities, especially among communities defined as having a common ancestry.

Many Ogiek residents specifically spoke of bad relations with members of the area's two most dominant Kalenjin communities, the Tugen and the Kipsigis. The accusation generally was that both *wageni* communities wanted land because they were farmers traditionally, while the Kipsigis were also accused of wanting access to land to allow them to steal livestock. Cattle raids, or cattle rustling, customarily played a significant role in Kipsigis society (Omvvoyo, 2000), mainly as an initiation ritual for young men, but livestock theft that residents in the area experienced was presumably driven by economic reasons rather than cultural ones. An Ogiek resident said cattle rustling occurred in seasons, particularly before Christmas, and accused the Kipsigis from Transmara and Tinet regions in the central-southern Mau of stealing cattle from the residents, particularly from members of the Tugen community [5/209]. A few young Ogiek men confirmed that there were waves of cattle theft in the Mariashoni area twice a year. They said that groups of young Kipsigis men came armed with bows and arrows at night, locked residents into their houses and drove away their livestock and that any form of resistance could lead to being killed. They added that there was a lot of tension between the Ogiek and the Kipsigis, specifically because of these cattle raids [5/123, 5/199, 5/209]. Many residents also accused the *wageni* of cultivating food crops up to the river, claiming that the Ogiek would never do that since it reduced the water levels in the rivers. Another common accusation was that the *wageni* washed their laundry and even themselves in the river, which polluted the water and made people sick downstream, according to the common narrative [e.g., 5/148]. In the words of a member of the local authorities, the feeling of being betrayed by the Government and disadvantaged for the benefit of others had led to a kind of 'cold war' [3/061] in general between the Ogiek and all those who were not originally Ogiek, but predominantly between the Ogiek and new in-migrant members of other Kalenjin groups.

Changes brought about by the arrival of large numbers of people in the area were often blamed for changing behaviour patterns among the local Ogiek as well. Various local Ogiek argued that the supposed negative influence of this 'in-migration' came through two channels: exposure to other people's rationalities, customs, and habits through formal education on the one hand, and everyday contact and interaction on the other hand. One highly critical and plain-spoken middle-aged

Ogiek man summarised the situation eloquently: 'people don't look at the same thing when they look at the trees: they [the Ogiek] see honey, rain, food ... the "visitors" see wood, charcoal, and posts' [5/120]. Many local Ogiek made an important connection between the arrival of in-migrants in the late 1990s and a massive and evident transformation of the landscape: since the declaration of the settlement scheme and since the political elites brought 'foreigners' into the Mariashoni area, the forest had increasingly vanished. As discussed, within a few years in the late 1990s, the Mariashoni area transitioned from a dense, closed-canopy, humid forest into a mixed agricultural landscape with only a few remaining forest patches and tree formations that could best be described as agroforestry systems due to their interaction with cultivation and settlement land. The basis for the previous lifestyle of the Ogiek had hence been eradicated, including the basis for their tradable goods. Honey production had suffered particularly from changes in the landscapes with the disappearance of old indigenous trees formerly used to hang the traditional log-based beehives. Even more importantly, honey production had reduced because all kinds of flowering trees and bushes, which were crucial for the pollen and nectar required for honey production, had disappeared due to the expansion of agricultural fields and the increased use of fertiliser, pesticides, and herbicides [5/200, 5/226]. In 2013, there were almost no traditional beehives in the remaining trees in Mariashoni, and the very few still in use produced very little honey. Many of the elder Ogiek spoke in awe about the times when Mariashoni abounded in beehives. A few elderly men explained how drastic the changes in the area had been and that despite the colonial use of Mariashoni as a village for forest workers and a few sawmills, most people in the area had lived a relatively 'traditional' Ogiek life until the mid-1990s. With the declaration of the settlement scheme in 1997, the Government instructed licensed timber companies, particularly Sokoro (which later became Timsales) [5/156, 5/236], to cut most of the trees around Mariashoni, consequently rendering traditional Ogiek life impossible [4/097]. Since the declaration went hand in hand with both the political elites bringing in new residents that were not traditionally forest dwellers and the cutting of the trees on the land allocated to them, many local Ogiek amalgamated the different changes that occurred in the late 1990s and sometimes drew conclusions about presumed causalities that they were not necessarily able to sustain. A young male relative of the famous Ogiek leader attenuated the accusations against the *wageni* and said that it was indeed difficult for them to engage in active forest destruction because 'no-one can go to a place he or she is not familiar with and start cutting trees', emphasising arguments commonly made by *wageni* themselves. The latter typically emphasised that they could not enter the forest to destroy the remaining forest and that the land they bought was generally bare of trees before they purchased it [5/178].

Considering the environmental and socio-spatial changes in Mariashoni, the Ogiek did not have a chance but to turn to agriculture for their survival, according to the elder Ogiek men [4/097]. The Ogiek had traditionally lived on an animal and plant-based diet, which included mainly honey and meat, but also leafy greens, forest fruits, nuts, and berries that were gathered. As is common for most traditional hunter-gatherer groups, the Ogiek were not farming before the arrival of the colonial government. The interruption of the traditional spatial organisation of the Mau Forest land, and with it the interruption of previous modes of subsistence which required free movement and unrestricted access to all parts of the land within one's *konoito*, as well as the settlement of the white and Kikuyu people, led to the introduction of small-scale farming in the Mariashoni area. As noted above, the older men remembered that the Kikuyu workers had taught them to plant maize for subsistence within the forest plantations, taking care of the seedlings and ensuring that the trees grew properly. Despite the disruption of traditional Ogiek life from the 1930s onwards, it was not until the mid-1990s that changes in the socio-spatial and economic structure in Mariashoni started affecting what the Ogiek represent as their social and cultural heritage, including their means of subsistence and overall livelihoods. The establishment of the settlement scheme and the allocation of private plots within the scheme, alongside the Government forest plantations, significantly reduced the available or 'free' land in the Mariashoni area [3/062]. Residents also had to reduce their livestock numbers after the settlement scheme was set up since open-access land for grazing was reduced through the imposition of de facto Private Land ownership, which furthermore restricted the animals' movement [3/063]. While those Ogiek who had been settled in the colonial villages had acquired some farming skills from the Kikuyu workers and had experienced the cultivation of food crops in the forest plantations through the *shamba* system, farming on fields set aside for food cultivation was new for the Ogiek in Mariashoni until the creation of the settlement scheme. Considering gender and age relations in pursuing livelihood activities outside the household, women mainly fetched water and collected firewood, while men engaged in the more physical tasks related to life in the forest. Traditionally these tasks included the preparation, installation, and maintenance of beehives in the forest and honey harvest. Both men and women collected from trees leaves, bark, and roots, and prepared tree-based natural medicines. Many residents said that the older men were most aware of the forest and forest conservation matters and were most concerned with maintaining the forest. After shifting into a sedentarised farming lifestyle, both men and women assumed various responsibilities on the family farms. Men typically assumed more physical tasks, such as digging the soil, while women took care of most other tasks related to crop cultivation, including planting, weeding, and harvesting. It was, however, not uncommon for both men and women to work hand in hand. While some youth supported their parents on the farm, when not in school, many engaged in small businesses, including shopkeeping, motorcycle taxi riding, and other non-agricultural activities.

One Ogiek elder explained that the Ogiek, back then, were 'like a fish taken out of the water and put on a stone' [5/245]. Crop farming thus became the primary source of subsistence and income available. A young Ogiek man opined that the Mariashoni Ogiek started engaging in *maendeleo* (development) and 'developed away' from their previous hunter-gatherer lifestyle and hence became farmers and thus contributed to further changes in the environment [5/174; expressed as well in 5/178, 5/178]. Most residents were cultivating maize, potatoes, beans, and peas for subsistence and as cash crops for sale [3/061]. Apart from that, most residents kept 'kitchen gardens' in which they planted onions, *sukuma wiki* (a type of kale), cabbages and often a variety of what is commonly called 'indigenous leafy greens', including *managu* (African nightshade), *terere* (amaranth) and *thabai* (pronounced 'thafai', stinging nettle). Some residents said that it used to be too cold for the cultivation of many crops that were by then farmed in the area [5/158] and that people used to cultivate without fertilisers and pesticides, but that use of agricultural chemical inputs increased after 1997 [5/116]. Another explained that the types of seeds used in the area changed only in the mid-2000s. He said that residents started using new maize breeds only in 2002/2003 and that, by 2006, all residents had shifted to planting hybrid maize seeds exclusively [5/204].

Yet, by many accounts, the Ogiek were not necessarily good farmers. Consequently, they supposedly needed other sources of income, while other forest dwellers who traditionally engaged in crop farming, such as the Kikuyu or the Kipsigis, were able to live off their farming. One resident said that the local Ogiek were such bad farmers and used outdated farming techniques that she even brought in women from the nearby town to work on her farm [3/057]. A Tugen resident named the supposed 'bad farming' of the Ogiek as one of the most fundamental challenges for the area [5/199]. A local government employee said that the Ogiek had had to change their way of life after the declaration of the settlement scheme and the allocation of land to individual households. He regretted that 'they are still not like other communities' because most of them only had a few heads of cattle and cultivated with what he called 'very old methods' [3/062]. The supposed inability of the Ogiek to farm their lands properly was also discursively related to them being more harmful to the forest than members of other communities, evidently, members of other Kalenjin groups. In the same vein, one government expert said that the Ogiek low-input agriculture had led to massive erosion of the farmland in the area, which had furthermore led to land being abandoned regularly and new land being taken under cultivation because of unsustainable land use practices [1/006]. Such opinions were also expressed by several non-Ogiek residents who said that the Ogiek engaged in the sale of forest products because they supposedly could not farm, and some added that since most Ogiek also sold their land to *wageni*, they cut the trees on their plots as well [5/198]. A Tugen resident said that he experienced that a few individuals of the local Ogiek community approached members of other communities, who had bought land in the area which was supposedly located within the traditional *konoito* lands of their clans, and claimed that, while they accepted that the land was sold to them, the right to cut the trees on the land remained theirs [5/199]. A local teacher argued that there was a connection between these elements and said that the Ogiek depended on cutting trees illegally because they did not farm much and needed alternative sources of income [3/070]. The fact that most local farmers depended on middlemen or brokers to sell and transport their agricultural produce to outside markets rendered farmers further vulnerable. Due to the bad condition of the road, prices for farm produce were sometimes so low that farmers rather let their crops spoil in the fields than sell them at a loss [5/229, but mentioned by many residents, both *wageni* and Ogiek]. On numerous occasions during the research, ready-to-harvest crops were seen spoiling in the *shambas*. In one instance, a family reported that they had refused to sell their entire two acres of cabbages because the brokers offered them merely KES 2 ($0.02) per head, while the same cabbages were sold in Elburgon, merely 5 km from their farm, for KES 40 ($0.4) or more.[17] One resident also related the Ogiek engagement in forest destruction to the fact that hunting, a primary source of income in the past, was forbidden [3/057].

A Nandi resident retraced the historicity of environmental and social changes in the area and put them into perspective. He said the changes in Ogiek lifestyle started after people like him were settled in the area after 1997 and that things began changing rapidly, also because the *wageni* came with more knowledge, progress, and development. At the same time, he added, land distribution to the Ogiek got them interested in accessing easy money, and they started selling the land they had been given, as opposed to using it sustainably – but later started accusing the *wageni* of having stolen their land. He said that many people sold their land because they did not have money, but he also said that they were not used to looking for money with *'nguvu'* (strength/determination), meaning that they were not used to working hard, particularly in agriculture, to earn a living. Yet, he also alluded to the possibility that the Ogiek

---

17 Observed on the farm during interview [5/247].

might not have taken the land they had obtained seriously because they might have speculated to either get much more land or to be resettled or compensated altogether in case the Government went through with the forest rehabilitation plans and evicted all settlers [5/256].

As a reaction to the arrival of large numbers of *wageni*, what some Ogiek described as a government strategy targeting their annihilation, as noted above, many Ogiek entertained rather hostile relationships with these *wageni*. Such hostilities, perpetrated by members of the Ogiek against members of other communities, were sometimes tangible in everyday life and often concretised around matters related to land tenure. A few such cases were discussed previously in which local Ogiek had sold land to *wageni*, only to report an alleged land theft to the authorities, attempting to benefit from the land sale twice, sometimes while physically threatening those to whom land had been sold. Such 'schemes' were reported by several non-Ogiek Mariashoni residents, particularly in Chai Moto and other outskirts of Mariashoni Location that were mainly settled by *wageni*.

The distant and often hostile relationship between the 'host' Ogiek community and the more recent in-migrants also had important consequences on conservation initiatives to 'Save the Mau'. The conservation projects implemented in Mariashoni, which predominantly targeted livelihood adaptations and improvements through the promotion of sustainable income diversification activities, as previously discussed, often contributed to further the distance between different communities; despite inclusive rhetoric among NGOs in the area [1/014]. This exclusion happened in various ways. One aspect concerned the fact that most projects engaged residents in beekeeping, which is a traditional Ogiek activity, and thus centred on existing Ogiek traditional ecological knowledge. Another aspect was that one of the projects, the big Kenya Agricultural Productivity and Agro-Business Project (KAPAP) project implemented by the Government with the help of extensive World Bank funding, explicitly targeted the Ogiek community.[18] While the projects seemed de facto more integrated and inclusive than their funding and official activity structure might have suggested, members of non-Ogiek communities complained about feeling excluded by the Ogiek elite. One Luo resident, for instance, shared her thoughts that 'groups are just for the Ogiek, so we can't enter them easily ... they are closed to all people from outside' [5/149; voiced in similar words by 4/264, 4/265]. A Tugen resident also criticised '*sisi hapa* [us here], we are just in a dark land' [5/199] and said

---

[18] Mariashoni was only included in the second Phase of the so-called Adaptable Program Loan (APL), KAPAP, a joint project of the Government of Kenya and the World Bank, because of the World Bank's focus on marginalised minorities. KAPAP in the area therefore specifically targeted the Ogiek community [1/023].

that all external actors only focused on Mariashoni Centre and never came to the outskirts of Mariashoni Location, such as Chai Moto, where he lived. He said that this had several negative consequences. He said, for instance, that the environment could have recovered much faster if the non-Ogiek residents had been included because 'people do not refuse to plant trees, they just lack the education and opportunity' [5/199]. A second, perhaps more far-reaching consequence was that many residents, many of whom were illiterate, as he said, got 'wrong ideas' about what was happening since external actors, including the Task Force, only spoke to a particular group of people and there was no information sharing in the area [5/199]. Furthermore, the alleged fact that a small group of well-connected Ogiek was in control of 'external relations' of the Mariashoni residents contributed further to the schism between different groups of Ogiek and, even more than that, between the Ogiek and members of other communities. This 'control' of external relations was represented as 'defending their rights' and 'taking what is theirs' by those Ogiek who seemed to be part of that group. The exclusion of other community members from environmental conservation projects was often discursively related to the supposed inability of the *wageni* to take care of the forest and the environment. The 'foreigners' were often accused of being responsible for destroying the forest due to their numbers, farming, and alleged involvement in charcoal burning and the forestry business. Consequently, the necessity of excluding them from such projects was represented as 'obvious'. Many *wageni* complained about being used as scapegoats for forest destruction, while they said that most *wageni* could not even enter the forest, leave alone destroy it, since the Ogiek insisted that the forest belonged to them alone [5/198].

The Necofa country coordinator, a considerate man who partly grew up in Mariashoni and had a lot of knowledge about, and affinity with, the local Ogiek, explained that he also used to blame the in-migrants for much of the destruction of the area. However, he said that he had realised that the Nandi, Tugen, and Kipsigis in Mariashoni had invested in their land, had better farming practices, planted trees, and engaged in other forms of income generation and small-scale rehabilitation, while the Ogiek, in his opinion, had failed to improve their farming skills. Consequently, the Ogiek often rented out their land to other farmers and looked for other sources of income than farming. He also stated that 'the Ogiek are therefore a bigger risk to conservation than other communities' and added that, rather than dwelling on that problem, he attempted to support the Ogiek community in changing their attitudes and perspectives about land use and farming [1/027]. The local Necofa project manager and a local Ogiek Necofa field officer confirmed that it was difficult to encourage the Mariashoni Ogiek to engage in the modern and sustainable farming practices the project was promoting. They said modern beehives were distributed to eight groups during the project but that only two had started making use of them five months after the distribution. Interestingly, the two groups that had started using them were the beekeeping groups in Lawina and Oinoptich, the two only non-Ogiek groups included in the project. When asked about possible explanations for the non-Ogiek groups being more interested than the local Ogiek, who, by all accounts, had traditionally engaged in beekeeping and were thus highly familiar with the practice, the field officer conceded that 'the Ogiek are lazy. If you try and hurry them, they will just drop out' [3/082]. The plain-spoken leader of one of the bee groups, to which beehives had been distributed, agreed that the group had participated in activities of ProMara, KAPAP, and had been trained by Baraka College on the usage of the modern beehives but that they did not really engage. He admitted that his group was 'dead', that they were not doing anything and that the improved beehives were just standing around [5/245]. The accounting assistant at the Mau East Forest Conservancy (MEFoCo), an outspoken member of the progressive Chemusus CFA, had another explanation for the hesitancy that external actors sometimes found among members of the Ogiek when promoting new agricultural practices. Apart from the fact that she agreed that the Ogiek struggled to implement good farming practices because farming was new to them, she said: 'people are used to poverty, they do not want to improve' [1/261]. She added that despite them being idle sometimes, many Ogiek were not used to working hard and did not see the necessity of improving their livelihoods because they were already content with the little they had [1/261].

The confidence and mutuality of pointing fingers at each other for the destruction of the forest between these two groups, including the somewhat cohesive and coherent narratives, was a striking indication of how challenging and complex social relations were in Mariashoni. The candid youthful 2013 MCA candidate for the United Democratic Front (UDF) added yet another layer of complexity to the analysis of social relations in Mariashoni by insisting that '*kabila ni mbili, maskini na matajiri*' (there are two tribes, the poor and the rich) [3/080]; yet he was the candidate who was commonly represented as driving the anti-*wageni* agenda [3/081]. Negotiations of identities, boundary making between ethnicities, and related 'othering', and the definition of joint interests were continuous processes that deeply marked social relations in the area.

Beyond negotiations over identities between members of different ethnic groups, there was an apparent conflict between different groups of Ogiek as well. This schism was primarily related to how the groups were assumed to interact with the 'outsiders'. On the one hand, there were the 'elite' Ogiek, who were often accused of being responsible for and of having personally benefited from the sale of land to *wageni*, or who were at least presumed to have allowed the higher echelons of the local administration and the Government to misappropriate local land that was supposed to benefit the Ogiek, allocating instead to outsiders, and who were thus assumed to have accepted bribes in return. There was a general assumption that all those Ogiek in power had betrayed the 'real' Ogiek. Clashes between these two camps also erupted in the run-up to the 2013 general elections that saw the Jubilee Party candidate, a Nandi woman married to an influential member of the Ogiek 'elite', and thus a *mgeni*, elected as Member of County Assembly (MCA). During the clashes, a small number of her supporters were physically injured, while the Chief's camp and surrounding offices, including the Necofa office, were destroyed by a group of young armed men at night (Fuchs, 2014). One local teacher explained that false allegations and rumours contributed a lot to the tension between different groups of Ogiek and between the more 'radical' Ogiek and the *wageni*. He said that land was at the core of these tensions. One of the most common rumours during the run-up to the 2013 elections was that the Jubilee Party candidate had promised land to *wageni* and local Ogiek who support her candidacy, while another rumour was that her 'radical' opponent would expel *wageni* of the area if he was elected. Since roughly two-thirds, approximately 2,800 of the total registered voters of about 4,400 in Mariashoni were *wageni*, both rumours potentially had an important influence on the residents' voting pattern, as well as on the social relations between different groups, notably the *wageni*, the 'radical' Ogiek and the Ogiek associated with the administrative elites of the area [5/229]. The ProMara conflict specialist suggested that there was a connection between conflict, environmental conservation, and poverty in the following way: 'If you talk about conservation of Mau, you cannot talk about sustainable conservation of Mau if you don't deal with the hot question of youth poverty, and if you don't deal with the hot question of poverty in the communities [altogether]' [1/014]. He further emphasised that people should learn to

> think as a community on how they can sustainably address their challenges; on how they can come up with solutions innovatively ... We may have a beautiful new Constitution, beautiful plans for the rehabilitation of Mau Forest, peace meetings, but then you are not addressing the whole issue of youth violence; you are not sustainably addressing the conflict issue. After five years, during the election period, they use the same youths again to attack other youths. [1/014]

Fears of increased marginalisation and defining legitimate resident status

In a social situation that was already tense due to conflicts related to land, identity creation, and resources, one of the biggest challenges was that the forest dwellers in Mariashoni expressed a genuine sense of uncertainty about their fate. Some people knew about the initial plans of the Government to evict all non-Ogiek from the area, while others had heard of the possibility that the Ogiek might be resettled to an undisclosed downstream area. Altogether, government communication had been unclear, and people did not know what the future would hold for them.

As discussed, defining a forest conservation agenda for the future required deciding on the fate of the people who lived in the area. The fluidity of identity questions among and between different groups of forest dwellers, together with the formal recognition of the Ogiek as the legitimate indigenous community in the Mau Forest by the initial Task Force Report, rendered it necessary to explicitly define who was Ogiek and who was not. In that vein, the Mariashoni Ogiek were also involved in establishing the Ogiek register. To be identified as 'genuine' Ogiek, people had to answer questions and give the names of their father, grandfather, and great-grandfather, as well as their clan and sometimes the clan territory (*konoito*), held until the 1950s [3/058]. A Mariashoni resident and nominated member of the Ogiek Council said that she actively contributed to establishing lists of people who were screened for 'genuineness', since '*kila kabila ni Dorobo*' (every tribe is 'Dorobo') [5/118]. She alluded to the fact that, through the discussions about special rights for the Ogiek, the old dispute resurged between those who claimed to be 'original' Ogiek by lineage and those who claimed equal rights in the name of being long-term forest dwellers, who referred to themselves by the name of 'Dorobo'. While the final use of the register had not been determined, the fact of it being created led to a heightened awareness among residents that change might be coming their way.

Members of the communities living in the wider Mariashoni area, who were generally aware that the Government planned to attribute special rights to the Ogiek despite the Mau rehabilitation efforts, expressed differing opinions about these plans. Most of the Ogiek opined that the Ogiek should have special rights, and advanced various arguments. These included most commonly 'the Ogiek are the indigenous inhabitants of the forest'[19] [5/137; voiced in similar words in 5/189, 5/221, 5/151, 5/154, 5/190]; 'here is our area' [5/210]; 'we are the only indigenous inhabitants of the forest' [5/143]; and 'we have been here since time immemorial' [5/139; also voiced in 5/127, 5/140, 5/167, 5/191, 5/206, 5/254]. Being the indigenous inhabitants of the forest supposedly had led them to 'understand about trees and natural medicine the way the Maasai understand cows and the Luo know fish' [5/116], stating that 'the Ogiek have always taken care of Mau' [5/148;

---

[19]   Many statements are in quotes here because these were answers to a question included in the survey, and literal responses could be captured. The English translation is provided in brackets when answers were given in Swahili.

also voiced in 5/160, 5/188]. Taking care included, for instance, that 'we, the Ogiek, manage the forest and water' [5/153; also voiced in 5/150, 5/172, 5/179, 5/181, 5/186]; and that 'we take care of the trees so they do not perish' [5/141]; leading to the conclusion that 'if it weren't for [us], the forest would be destroyed' [5/123; also voiced in 5/184]. Since forest destruction was recognised as a fact by most Ogiek, some extended the argument to include matters such as that they, as the Ogiek 'know [we] have to restore because here is [our] only home, while others know where their [other] home is' [5/118]; they 'have lived here forever and do not have *shambas*' [5/208], with a strong emphasis being put on the fact that 'there is no other place we call home' [5/147; also voiced in 5/165]. Their inability to 'call another place home' was also cited as part of the reasons why the Ogiek should hold special rights in the Mau Forest, by insisting, for instance, that 'those who are indigenous to the forest know how to take care/recover the forest' [5/152; also voiced in 5/244], but equally formulated it as a request, a responsibility, for the future: 'let [us] manage the forest, so it doesn't get finished' [5/155], and also 'because [we] have to take care of their forest' [5/174]. Another line of argument highlighted that the Ogiek should remain in the forest because there should be no negative discrimination against them, because '[we] don't have title deeds' [5/217], '[we] have no power' [5/223], 'we have been very disadvantaged' [5/227], and 'we have been marginalised' [5/157], but that 'we are Kenyans' and 'we are just like those other tribes' [5/131], and the Government should thus make sure their rights were preserved. One of the matters at hand was that their rights should be preserved because 'we don't want to be bothered by other tribes' [5/168] so that 'other people cannot take the land of the Ogiek' [5/162]. Some others simply said that the Government had promised them titles, so they should get them [5/115]. A very vocal and critical Ogiek resident emphasised: 'it's a must, we have rights here' [5/200], echoed by an Ogiek elder who insisted, 'this is our reserve, and we will not go anywhere else' [5/234]. Another Ogiek elder said the Ogiek should receive special attention because 'many things have gotten lost from our home area' [5/192].

Yet, some other Ogiek conceded that they were no longer sure the Ogiek should have special rights because 'people from here are not as concerned with the forest as they used to be' [5/167] or because 'there are some Ogiek who also engage in destruction' [5/162]. On a more general note, a few Ogiek considered that 'following the law, the Government must respect all people's rights' [5/219], and also 'God created mankind so that they can live together in peace; therefore, everyone has a right to live anywhere' [5/224], but such voices remained few.

Among the non-Ogiek, opinions were more divided. Some, such as a Kisii woman married to a local Ogiek, said that the Ogiek should be allowed to remain since 'they are the indigenous inhabitants of the forest' [5/134; also in 5/148, 5/156, 5/158, 5/177, 5/180], because 'they don't have another reserve, another ancestral homeland', as mentioned by a Tugen resident [5/170], or 'they are not many, and they are being disturbed a lot', as stated by a Turkana resident [5/193], and also because 'the Ogiek do not have *shambas* and title deeds', according to a Kipsigis woman married to a local Ogiek [5/166]. A resident who hailed from the Embu community said the rights of the Ogiek should be preserved because 'the Ogiek have not developed enough so the Government must come in and support them' [5/253], 'because they have been discriminated against', as expressed by a Nandi resident [5/256], while a Kipsigis resident voiced the idea that 'they should be given a piece of land where they can stay safely so that they can take care of the forest' [5/175]. Another Kipsigis resident also said that the Ogiek should remain 'because they are taking care of the forest' [5/171; also voiced in 5/185], in line with a Kikuyu worker who said 'if any other community had lived here for as long as the Ogiek, the forest would have been finished' [5/233]. On the other hand, some doubted that the Ogiek indeed conserved the forest and should have special rights, such as a young Kipsigis resident who said 'no, because they are the ones 'eating'/selling/destroying the trees a lot' [5/183], an opinion also expressed by a young man described himself as half Ogiek and half Kipsigis who said 'no, the Ogiek community also engages in tree business' [5/222], as well as by a very candid local teacher who said 'the Ogiek are a marginalised community, but they have almost no importance because they have engaged so much in forest destruction' [5/229]. On a more general note, some said there should not be positive discrimination in favour of the Ogiek because 'the Government must protect the rights of all people' [5/169; also voiced in 5/187, 5/195, 5/198, 5/202, 5/203, 5/216, 5/228, 5/247] and 'it is the right of every person, of every community, to be seen/considered by the Government' [5/120]. One resident insisted, 'if they got special rights, it would be tribalism' [5/242]. Others advanced the argument that the Ogiek should not have any special rights because 'they got their rights from the Government a long time ago' [5/176], notably in the form of land allocations in the late 1990s. An old Maasai resident said the Ogiek should not have any special rights because 'we are all indigenous to this forest' [5/196]. Another young man, who described himself as half Luo and half Ogiek, further said that 'the land does not belong to a single community' [5/212] and a Kisii resident summarised that 'a person is a person; people are people', and all people needed a possibility to live [5/110].

Independently from opinions raised among Mariashoni residents and changing policies at the Government level about whether evictions, resettlements, or the status quo would be pursued, the absence of a clear indication of what the future would hold had numerous effects in Mariashoni. One way in which the residents' interests and expectations were influenced stemmed from the fact that there was de facto no investment in infrastructure in the area, and there was thus no solid road, no electricity, and no reliable mobile phone network [3/065], with the Mariashoni forester adding that 'there is no more development of infrastructure because people are waiting for conclusions of ICS' [3/062]. Alleged plans of a private company to install electricity in 2012 were halted, presumably to wait for the Mau restoration initiative's outcome on the undertaking [3/062]. Amid these claims, there were further rumours that the MP made sure that the newly installed electricity supply only reached as far as the neighbouring Nessuit and Kapsita locations since most voters in both areas had elected him in the 2007 general election [3/061].

Another way in which the uncertainty influenced the area negatively took the form of what could be termed unsustainable farming practices, particularly the use of heavy fertilisers and low-intensity agriculture practised in the settlement area [1/019]. These practices might have partly been related to the fact that farmers in the area, especially the ones close to Elburgon town, rented *shambas* for periods of only one year at a time from the big landowners. Engagement in sustainable farming practices that might potentially be more complicated was thus unlikely. The ProMara natural-resource management specialist confirmed that many people around Mariashoni were lease-farmers and were therefore not particularly interested in taking up good agricultural and environmental practices, including soil and water conservation measures such as windbreaks terraces or more complex agroforestry systems [1/029]. A government expert agreed that 'the anxiety is not very good for the Ogiek because they will not invest in their land' [1/040].

In terms of repercussions, increased cutting of trees was the most harmful immediate result for the forest after the Task Force's visit and increased awareness that the status quo might be changed. As addressed in relation to the behaviour of big and small sawmills, two local teachers spoke of a 'cutting craze' in the Mariashoni area where 'all actors' had been engaging because 'people were fearing consequences' of these visits. They added that indiscriminate cutting of trees had not reduced since it started after the Task Force visit, arguing that forest dwellers were still anticipating what would come next [5/228, 5/229]. One of the teachers named the fact that '*watu hawajui kama ni porini ama ni mashamba*' (because people do not know if it is a forest or farms/settlement here) as the main reason why the forest was not being recovered [5/228]. A young Ogiek man emphasised the same and insisted that 'the Government has not clearly indicated up to where people can live and from where the forest starts' [5/174]. Another Kipsigis resident said that the Government should establish a clear plan, 'a clear line that divides the forest land from settlement land, and where they do reforestation and do not let the people in' [5/175].

A Kikuyu woman from Elburgon also said that 'when people [i.e. the Government] declared that all the area was Mau [and thus officially forest land], people cut trees massively on their land because they were not sure they would keep their land' [5/255]. She emphasised that it was difficult to know what could be done about deforestation because people were uncertain where the forest begins and where their *shambas* end because 'you can cut your trees when it's your *shamba*, but if it's forest, you are not supposed to cut'. She stated that what was needed was a clear status quo [5/255]. The local CFA representative blamed much of the environmental destruction in the Mariashoni area on this 'suspension life' [3/059]. He underscored that the underlying factor for this uncertainty was related to the fact that people did not really know if their farms were located on Public Forest or Private Land and that this was because they did not have title deeds to the land they inhabited and because the court cases that started in 1997 were still pending [3/059]. A young Ogiek man further opined that the villagers did not fully engage in the restoration of the forest either because they were not sure if they would be kicked out eventually, despite those efforts. So 'people stand back and watch' [5/221]. A plain-spoken Nandi resident emphasised the same by insisting 'the unclear plans irritate people' [5/156]. An elderly Chai Moto resident added that it was even difficult to get reliable information from the villagers in the area because they feared being investigated and that speaking to the 'wrong' people could lead to evictions [4/094].

The matter of uncertainty about the future highlighted the importance of issues surrounding land tenure and ownership. Many residents and experts voiced the opinion that this uncertainty about the Government's plans and policies in terms of forest restoration was accentuated by land insecurities. One Ogiek resident, for instance, said that the absence of title deeds was the main reason why most people did not engage in any conservation practices because the people think that they could be kicked out of their *shambas* despite all their conservation efforts [5/222]. Another outspoken resident made a similar point by emphasising that '*watu wakiamua wako nyumbani kabisa bila uogo wowote watagawanya mashamba sehemu ya miti na sehemu ya kulima kwa sababu Mau hawezi rudi kama zamani hata tukitaka [kwa sababu] watu wamejua ukulima*' (if people decide that this is really their home, even without encouragement people will start dedicating a piece of their land to trees and another piece to cultivation because the Mau Forest cannot go back to how it used to be [because] people have become farmers) [5/224]. Another Ogiek man also mentioned that life was difficult due to uncertainty about the future and land insecurity, pointing out that 'life is not easy because we don't know about the Government's plans and people here have no title deeds' [5/237]. The common representation further accentuated this fear that the 2010 Constitution allowed people to 'live everywhere now' and that land was not reserved for specific groups of people; increasing fears that Kenyans who have the means could legally obtain land anywhere, including in Mariashoni, without recognition of ancestral claims to land [5/227; voiced in similar words by numerous Mariashoni Ogiek]. The fear of being dispossessed of their lands also made another Ogiek resident doubt that residents would engage in PES schemes because it would be as if they had sold their lands indirectly, and the Government might wake up one day and decide to evict them, he said [5/222]. One of the very few 'visible' Ogiek female elders made the same point by insisting that *'kulipwa ni kuuza'* (to be paid is to sell). She explained that she would not want to be paid for environmental services because it invited those who paid to come and claim they had paid and, therefore, somewhat own the land [5/239].

One local teacher shared a note of caution about the idea of resettling the Ogiek downstream, pointing out that many Ogiek found it challenging to adapt to different climatic conditions. She recounted a situation in which Ogiek from the Mariashoni area had allegedly been resettled in the Ndoinet area between 1988 and 1993, but they eventually returned to Mariashoni because of the difficulties they experienced in adapting to the new environmental conditions and climate. The resettlement had rendered them more vulnerable since they were settled on forest land and built homesteads and temporary houses on land they did not own without any land to farm, while they were allocated plots in the forest plantations under the *shamba* system [3/063]. The local CFA representative, on the other hand, suggested that the areas belonging to Elburgon, Nessuit, and Ndoswa Forest Stations in the area surrounding Mariashoni in Eastern Mau should suffice for the resettlement of all the Ogiek and forest could be re-established in the remaining area under the joint management of the KFS and the communities [3/065]. The question of resettlement of the Ogiek, yet again, echoed general dynamics and complexities related to land ownership, the form of land ownership, and land use overall.

Realistically, it seemed morally and practically difficult to expect people to adopt environmentally sound and sustainable practices when faced with such important uncertainties concerning their future. A local headteacher emphasised that the forest dwellers neither knew the way forward nor what the politicians wanted to achieve in the area, adding that it was difficult for people to get information about these plans despite the crucial role they played for everybody's future. 'People find things happening without knowing what it is about' [3/063], she said, accusing the local politicians of withholding information and disregarding the people's right to and need for information. The Necofa country coordinator summarised succinctly: 'As long as people do not know about their future, any activity is difficult' [1/027].

Being Ogiek in the twenty-first century: Challenges to indigenous identities and self-representations

By 2013, the Ogiek in Mariashoni had let go of their 'traditional' identities and had started partaking in forest commodification in various ways. Charcoal burning was one of the somewhat low-key but widespread forms of that engagement, which typically involved the destruction of indigenous tree species. Since charcoal remained the most crucial source of fuelwood among low-income town and city dwellers, with 80% of urban households depending on charcoal as a primary fuel source, while more than 90% of rural households used firewood (UNEP, 2012), charcoal production was rampant for the benefit of people residing outside of the forest. While estimating a household's charcoal consumption was difficult due to variations in household sizes, tree species used, and hence durability of the fire, one respondent set the average consumption of charcoal by his five-headed household at one-third of a *gunia* bag per week, thus around eighteen bags per year [5/233]. In the Eastern Mau, charcoal was mainly made from indigenous species whose wood was generally harder and therefore more long-lasting when burning than the softer exotic species. Species used included *Sabtet* (Podo), *Torokwet* (East African cedar), *Yemdit* (African wild olive), *Kanunga* (various Acacia subspecies) and *Masaita* (East African Olive), according to multiple testimonies from Mariashoni residents. Many residents indicated liking indigenous trees for that very reason: because they were a secure and long-lasting source of fuel.

In Mariashoni, firewood was the most important fuel source, followed by charcoal. While the Ogiek typically used firewood that they collected in the surrounding forest and more rarely that extracted by cutting down trees on their own or on forest land, most non-Ogiek members indicated using charcoal for home use. While this was in line with the dominant narrative among many members of the Ogiek community, circumstantial evidence collected during the research confirmed the trend and members of other communities more often referred to the production, use and/or sale of charcoal than the Ogiek. Superior use of charcoal by non-locals most likely stemmed from more complicated access to fresh forest resources, both on their lands that were often cleared of trees before being given out and from the nearby pieces of public forests whose use was typically represented as being reserved to members of the Ogiek community alone. Overall, while firewood was a more important source of fuel for Mariashoni residents during the dry season, the importance of charcoal increased for all forest dwellers during the rainy season [5/209]. In the Mariashoni area, trees were cut, and charcoal was burned by various groups of people who targeted different markets and used manifold strategies to go about their trade. Both residents and people residing outside of the forest were involved. Among the locals both *wageni* – who were commonly accused of destroying the forest by burning charcoal – but also many Ogiek youths engaged in charcoal production and trade. While many denied an implication of the Ogiek in any form of forest destruction, others willingly confirmed that their youthful offspring participated in the business. Some observers mentioned that there was not much of a difference between the Ogiek and other residents of the area, provided that the trade with external traders in charcoal required that residents, both Ogiek and others, burn charcoal [5/206]. A young Ogiek woman affirmed the same by confessing that '*wageni wanachoma makaa, lakini pia sisi tumejua kuchoma makaa*' (the 'outsiders' burn charcoal, but we have also started engaging in burning charcoal) [5/250].

Traces of charcoal production were visible throughout the Eastern Mau, although most of it presumably happened further afield in the forest. Some residents spoke about vast strips of forest land having been deforested because of charcoal production in the forest hinterland of Mariashoni, including Baraget and Keringet [5/108], which were typically accessed through the western edges of Mariashoni Location and the road through Chai Moto. A Luhya resident of Chai Moto said charcoal was a big business everywhere in the Eastern Mau, not only deep inside the forest [5/197]. In Mariashoni, remains of charcoal burning could be found right within the settlement scheme.[20] A local headteacher of a school located at the edges of what the locals define as the 'cutline' between the settlement scheme and the remaining forest regretted that charcoal burning was an 'everyday business' [3/070] that merely required being on good terms with the KFS soldiers. He said there was a lot of activity in the area every night, especially carrying charcoal and trees, right under the eyes of the forest guards. He also added that mostly the lower-level KFS officers engaged in corrupt practices and hid from higher-ranking officers [3/070]. The two vocal Ogiek brothers confirmed that there was a lot of charcoal production underway during the day and that there were around five hundred *gunia* bags of charcoal in an area known as Songhi in the Kiptunga Forest area that were to be transported that very evening. They further added that the bags were guarded by KFS officers [4/093]. One of the motorcycle taxi riders, who frequently plied the route between Elburgon and Mariashoni, spoke about the presumed role of the KFS in the charcoal business. Since he was moving about the roads a lot, he sometimes observed confrontations between the forest guards and persons transporting charcoal. In his opinion, the KFS was highly responsible for forest destruction because the guards, typically, did not only solicit bribes after apprehending persons found carrying charcoal and then let

---

[20] Observations made, for instance, on the land where interviews 5/187 and 5/196 were held.

them get away, but they also confiscated charcoal and ended up selling it themselves [5/218]. During the research, the perhaps most curious case of charcoal burning and trading was observed next to the main Mariashoni trading centre. In late 2012, one of the biggest and most noticeable Podo trees that used to grow on the left side of the path leading to the abandoned quarry one hundred metres below the main centre was cut and burned to charcoal right by the roadside. Two young men explained that the owner of a neighbouring plot had commissioned the removal of the tree because its shade supposedly negatively affected the potatoes he grew. They were brought to the tree that would give them ten or eleven full *gunia* bags of charcoal. Since they were called by the person who lived on the nearby plot, they had to pay him two *gunia* bags of charcoal while they planned to take the remaining bags to Elburgon, where they would sell them for KES 700 ($7) per bag. They insisted that it was usually very dangerous to burn charcoal, but since the owner of the nearby plot contracted them, they were confident that they were acting in total legality. Lastly, it turned out that the plot in question belonged to a member of the Ogiek 'elite' [3/073]. That same evening, a KFS vehicle transported two of the same charcoal *gunia* bags from Mariashoni to Elburgon without even attempting to hide them.[21]

Since much of the charcoal in the Eastern Mau supposedly came from Baraget and Keringet through the Chai Moto road, transport of the charcoal on this road was particularly common. Coming from the DO's place in Elburgon, the road to Chai Moto branched off the road to Mariashoni Centre not far from the KFS office. The road then meandered through the heavily deforested lands of the Eastern Mau to Chai Moto, the last stop on the road leading to Baraget and eventually to Keringet in the centre of the Mau Forest. During the research, groups of donkeys of varying herd sizes, with sometimes up to seventy animals, were observed being driven along the Chai Moto road into the forest in the morning and being driven back to Elburgon in the evening every single day. Typically, each donkey carried two *gunia* bags of charcoal back to Elburgon that were hauled over the animals' backs. The donkeys were accompanied by small groups of either men or women, who sometimes carried additional charcoal bags. Most regular was a small group of four or five middle-aged Kikuyu women with fifteen to twenty donkeys that were in terrible physical shape. Regardless of their physical condition, each donkey was loaded with two *gunia* bags. Along the way, donkeys often toppled over, pulled down by the weight, only to be beaten back to their feet down the hill into the city.[22] An old Ogiek resident commented on the evolution of the forest very outspokenly and explained

---

[21] Observations on illegal charcoal production in Mariashoni Centre, 14 November 2012.

[22] Observations on the charcoal trade (of Kikuyu women), 22 December 2012.

that the donkeys were taken to the charcoal production sites between Baraget and Keringet. He added that all it took was to send some money to the KFS guards' phones via M-Pesa, Kenya's mobile money transfer service, for the traders to be able to go about their business undisturbed [5/108]. During school holidays, it was not uncommon to see even the youngest members of local families help in the charcoal business. While visiting Chai Moto just before Christmas, a small group of young boys aged perhaps between ten and fourteen years jogged and played along, saying that they had purchased half-*gunias* of charcoal around the 'cutline' close to Baraget, which they were now taking back to Elburgon, a distance of ca. 8 km.[23]

Another common way of transporting charcoal from the production site to the markets was to stack the *gunia* bags on motorcycles. Since the road to Mariashoni and beyond was very unreliable, most tradable goods entered and exited the forest on the backs of motorcycles. One of the riders, who mainly worked as a taxi, explained a motorcyclist's perspective on the charcoal trade. He said that he usually undertook two or three trips carrying charcoal from the Eastern Mau to Nakuru town per day. In one trip, he could transport seven *gunia* bags. He said he mainly bought the charcoal in a small area called Kikingi Tatu, located after Chai Moto on the road to Baraget. He also broke down the business costs and profits. He said he usually bought seven *gunia* bags for KES 1,500 ($15) in total and used approximately KES 300 ($3) for fuel. His total cost was thus KES 1,800 ($18) for seven bags of charcoal. In Nakuru, he was then able to resell each bag for KES 800 ($8), providing him with a gross income of KES 5,600 ($56). For each trip, he thus made a net profit of KES 3,800 ($38). He also said that he usually did not deal with any Ogiek in the charcoal business but rather with members of the Tugen or Nandi communities who had settled around Chai Moto. He added that he sometimes also purchased charcoal in '*Maasaiini*' (Maasai land), as the areas of Ol Posimoru in the southern parts of the Eastern Mau were commonly referred to, indicating that it was easy to do business there because the police supposedly feared the Maasai [4/098]. The Timsales employee confirmed these figures by indicating that charcoal in the forest was sold for KES 250 ($2.5) to KES 300 ($3) per bag and that 'in town' it was possible to resell it for KES 800 ($8), thus giving the seller a significant profit [5/233]. The motorcycle rider further explained that officers of the Kenya Police were not as aggressive as the KFS guards. He said the regular police were '*watu wa watu*' (people's people) and that they were easily satisfied with bribes ranging from KES 200 ($2) to KES 500 ($5) by someone found transporting charcoal. He also said that he had once been arrested by KFS guards who had followed him all the way from Njoro – from where one could access and exit the

---

[23] Observations on young boys in the charcoal trade, 22 December 2012.

Eastern Mau by following the Kapcholola-Nessuit road to the Kaptembwa area in Nakuru – pushed him off his bike, impounded it, and only released him and his bike after paying a hefty bribe. He added that any vehicle was used to transport charcoal out of the forest and that he used to use a simple bicycle before he could afford a motorcycle. He also said that most charcoal, in terms of quantities, was carried by personal cars that look like taxis. He explained that the drivers usually carried three persons to make the car look like a taxi, but these cars were full of charcoal [4/098]. Many locals also said that lorries of varying sizes came in and ferried mostly indigenous trees and charcoal out of the forest at night [3/057, 3/063, 3/064, 5/210].

Beyond engagement in charcoal production and sale, local community members also contributed to producing and selling wood and timber. The sawmillers started targeting trees from privately held land for wood and timber production after the logging ban was introduced. Because the trees of most plots initially allocated to non-Ogiek settlers had been harvested even before being allocated, the sawmillers' efforts mainly concentrated on land held by the Ogiek. Given the little effort required to sell one's trees to these sawmillers who come, cut the relevant trees, and transport them off, selling trees in times of financial constraint became an easy income-generating activity for Mariashoni residents as described previously. These sawmillers often paid locals, including local Ogiek, to prospect and broker deals with other residents. The same locals also helped cut, organise, and prepare the trees for transport. A young woman spoke of the involvement of members of the Ogiek community. She said that her household benefited from the tree business since her Ogiek husband regularly got jobs as a casual tree cutter [5/166]. An old Ogiek woman also said that times had changed and that she had started selling her trees to the small sawmillers when she needed money. She said if she wanted trees to be cut, she just called upon the sawmillers, discussed a price, and the sawmillers came, cut the trees, took them and resold them in town [5/160]. Similarly, another resident insisted that young local Ogiek had become wood and timber brokers, buying trees from residents' private farms and selling them to sawmillers in and from Elburgon [5/117]. A young Ogiek man confirmed that it was widespread that sawmillers approached residents and that they quickly convinced them to sell their trees, despite being paid very poorly for their resources [5/148]. According to a former sawmiller who used to engage in the tree business in Mariashoni, a local contact person used to broker the deals between her and the locals willing to sell the trees from their farms [5/255]. Another sawmiller explained that he worked with brokers from Elburgon who got in touch with brokers in Mariashoni [2/053]. Another resident, a member of the Ogiek Council of Elders and very eloquent and outspoken in her defence of the rights of the Ogiek people, said that she cut and sold the trees on her land to these brokers, for instance, when she needed school fees. At the same time, she introduced an essential difference between the trees on the farm, primarily exotic tree species, often referred to as *'miti ya biashara'* (trees for business) on the one hand, and indigenous trees on the other hand. Only the latter qualified as 'the forest', particularly indigenous trees located behind the 'cutline' between the settlement scheme and the officially recognised forest land [5/118].

Beyond the sale of trees from private farmland to external sawmillers, many young men engaged in another form of deforestation that they called *'backshwara'*.[24] *Backshwara* involved entering the protected 'official' forest illegally at night, cutting single trees and carrying them on one's back to sawmills in town, similar to what some of their ancestors used to do as wage labourers for the colonial Forest Department. The young men who engaged in the practice carried indigenous and exotic trees. Some said indigenous trees, particularly Podo trees, were targeted the most [4/093, 5/200]. Others said that while indigenous trees were interesting because they gave them higher income, they were difficult to find and very heavy, so exotic trees were an easier alternative. In Mariashoni, the tree trunks were carried mainly on foot from the forest edge of the Kiptunga Forest to Elburgon town. The men mostly worked alone or in small groups, carrying the trunks alone or in pairs. After walking for the better part of the night to reach the town approximately 10 km away, the trees were sold to local sawmills. Indigenous trees were typically ordered by sawmills who could not obtain them legally, illustrating the interconnectedness between various types of forest destruction for forest production. Only very few young men discussed their engagement in *backshwara*. Those who did, spoke of the risks involved in the late-night business. First, one must ensure not to be caught by guards on patrol in the forest, especially when targeting the forest plantations managed by Timsales in the Kiptunga Forest. After identifying a suitable tree, the tree needed to be cut without making too much noise, which was mostly done with crude tools such as *pangas* (machetes), which increased the risk of being injured while cutting the tree. The forest was also alive with wild animals, especially cheetahs and hyenas, the young men said,[25] but since they were usually armed with *rungus* (traditional wooden clubs) and *pangas*, the animals rarely harmed them. Once the trees were cut, transporting them to Elburgon involved additional risks. One of them was meeting the authorities on duty that could either ask for bribes or

---

24 Since this is an unofficial term, its spelling is not clear. Some people we spoke to referred to the practice as *bakshwara* or *backshwara*, others say *backswarah*.
25 The brothers were the first ones to speak about *backshwara* in detail – almost a year after the onset of the fieldwork – illustrating the extent to which *backshwara* breaks a taboo in the Ogiek community.

arrest the carriers. Both outcomes of meeting with the guards negatively influenced the business, so the young men tried to avoid them as
much as possible and often preferred 'inside roads' to the official road.
These 'inside roads' were often nothing more than small paths crossing
the landscape that were neither lit nor maintained. The risk of injury
on these paths was thus even higher than when following the main
road. Furthermore, there supposedly was a difference between meeting
with a member of the Administration Police (AP) or with a KFS guard.
The former usually just took bribes, while some KFS guards took the
young men to court. However, the *backshwara* carriers said they had
an 'inside man' at the KFS and, therefore, usually knew which officer
was patrolling in which area and made sure to avoid the routes of those
who were 'strict'. They also reported having witnessed severe injuries
and even death in cases where the trees had become too heavy for their
carrier and ultimately beaten them to death [4/093].

An old Maasai resident confirmed that young men carried trees
throughout the night. He added that beyond cutting the trees themselves, the young men often purchased the already cut trees from
corrupt KFS guards [5/196]. Another young man said that it was
mostly cypress trees that were carried from Kiptunga Forest to Elburgon that earned the carriers between KES 200 ($2) and KES 600 ($6) per
tree. Small groups of youth typically organised in groups and got orders
from sawmillers in Elburgon before delivering the trees one by one at
night. The forest guards were usually aware when people intensified
the practice and intercepted them in Elburgon to pocket bribes of KES
50 ($0.50) to KES 100 ($1) from each individual carrier. Many of the carriers delivered their trees to a sawmiller whose business was located on
the outskirts of Elburgon next to a big flower farm that could be reached
via the shortest of the three direct routes from Elburgon to Mariashoni. He also said that most sawmills in Elburgon accepted *backshwara*
trees [5/257]. Others said that the prices at which trees were bought
varied and depended on the species, size, and timing. The two brothers
said that prices went down when many trees were carried. The fact that
prices for illegally carried trees reduced in case demand was saturated
was cited as one potential reason why the young men typically did not
unite beyond the small groups mentioned [4/093]. A local teacher also
spoke about the practice. Since the school was located along the main
road connecting Kiptunga Forest to Mariashoni Centre and eventually
to Elburgon, he recounted witnessing groups of two to five men carrying
trees almost every night. He described the opening of the forest through
the abolition of the logging ban as positive in that regard, citing the fact
that illegal tree carrying at night reduced afterwards because many
young men started getting casual jobs in the timber industry, mostly
in cutting and loading trees. He also pointed out that it was mainly
members of the local Ogiek youth who carried trees illegally and not

members of other communities who resided in the area and who were commonly blamed by the Ogiek for forest destruction [5/229].

According to a young Ogiek resident, 2011 marked a climax in terms of carrying trees illegally to Elburgon, indicating that 'whole families were out at night' [5/257]. Another young carrier explained that since arriving in Elburgon after the 2007/2008 PEV crisis, he had been engaging in *backshwara* regularly to make ends meet. He usually carried cypress logs four nights a week, each earning him around KES 1,000 ($10). In an area where unskilled labourers made as little as KES 150 ($1.5) for one day's farm work, for instance, being able to make KES 1,000 ($10) in a few hours visibly represented a serious temptation. He added that preventing the destruction of the forest was very difficult because people who were destroying the forest on a day-to-day basis were many more than what had been known previously [2/049]. A young Kipsigis man, who moved to Mariashoni in 2008, also explained that he carried trees at night three times a week to make ends meet [5/185]. A young Ogiek man affirmed that many young people carried trees illegally, some transporting them with lorries, others on bikes or foot. He said this illegal carrying of trees was a major issue in the area [5/148]. The two Ogiek brothers insisted that despite denying the problem in public and blaming others for forest destruction and loss, everybody knew that 'most boys' engaged in the practice [4/093]. One of the few youths from Mariashoni to receive a university education summarised the situation by pointing out that 'most people here live from forest businesses' [5/206]. The brothers also said that many parents were embarrassed and hid from others what their sons were doing, but everybody knew that Mariashoni's sons would continue to deplete the forest without any other meaningful income opportunities. They added that this kind of illegal business had been going on for the last twenty years [4/093].

Social and environmental impacts of the Ogiek youth participating in forest commodification

Residents proposed different interpretations regarding the local understandings of the Ogiek youth engaging in these practices. One Ogiek elder said that the Ogiek youth were the main driver of the destruction of the Mau Forest. He said, '*wakijana wa kisasa si ile ya zamani*' (the youth of today is not what it used to be) [5/225] and insisted that they had changed so much and refused to listen to their elders and their traditions. He regretted the 'old days' when different generations of men would sit around big fires in front of the makeshift homesteads, and the youth would listen and learn from the elders. He said, 'the youth think they have more brains than their fathers and ignore the old ways'. He added that people used not to think in terms of business, but 'everything is business now, the trees and the *shambas*' [5/225]. Similarly, the only remaining Kikuyu resident said that only the old Ogiek could be entrusted with forest management, but not to the youth, especially not without conditions, because '*vijana bila condition ni wakikuyu tu*' (the youths, without being given conditions, are just like the Kikuyu) [5/236], alluding to his opinion that Ogiek youths were just into business and/or stealing trees and ultimately interested in making money if no conditions were imposed on them on how to behave in the forest. One of the other outspoken Ogiek elders also regretted that people from outside the forest come and 'hold money under your nose', compelling their Ogiek youths to collaborate with them. He stated that '*na hawana akili*' (and they do not think) [5/234] because they participate in cutting and carrying trees at night. One female Ogiek elder confirmed the same by saying, '*watu wakati walisoma wamewachwa na asali*' (when people started going to school, they stopped with the honey) [5/239], alluding to the idea that modern education interrupted traditional Ogiek lifestyles. Another Ogiek woman also explained there was a generational divide among the Ogiek, particularly between the young and older men. She said that 'the youth do not respect the elders anymore and the elders do not teach the youth anymore' [5/227]. A young Ogiek man confirmed that there were generational conflicts in the area, pointing out that the youth and the elders 'do not understand each other' [5/257]. An older Ogiek man shared the same sentiment by insisting: '*Hakuna kazi wanafanya. Ni kulala tu. Na kuamka na kuingia misituni*' (They do not do any work. They just sleep. And then wake up and go into the forest [to sell trees]) [5/243]. The CFA representative also opined that the young idle Ogiek men held the main responsibility for forest destruction, insisting that 'it's normal that people extract illegally ... where there is a community, everybody needs something' [3/059], although he also claimed things had started to improve recently. A young Ogiek man admitted that the problem was that 'people have understood that trees equate to money; people used not to know, and there was no destruction' [5/251]. While many residents claimed that the Ogiek youths played an important role in destroying the forest, others minimised their destructive potential since 'some locals carrying three or four trees cannot finish the forest' [5/245].

Many among the older Ogiek observed changes in the behaviour of the Ogiek youth with concern. Since it was easy for the young men to make a little money by carrying trees, drop-out rates from schools were significant. While there were no official statistics about the same, many locals decried the situation, including the headteacher of Mariashoni Primary School [3/063]. The headmaster of Kaprop Primary School, located even further inside the forest than Mariashoni Primary School, spoke about the same with worry. He said drop-out rates were high, especially among boys between fourteen and sixteen. According to him, education was not valued by a majority of the adult Ogiek.

When boys reached puberty and developed an interest in other things in life, many dropped out to start burning charcoal and doing casual jobs of cutting and carrying trees for the sawmills. He emphasised that the problem was such that the few parents who took their children's education seriously made sure to enrol them in boarding schools to distance them from negative role models [3/063, 3/070, 5/200].

Many parents in the area faced the additional underlying problem of paying school fees despite free education being introduced in 2003 in both primary and secondary schools in Mariashoni. A young Ogiek man explained that parents had to pay 'informal' school fees to pay for the teachers' salaries, food, and construction and infrastructure development in the schools. Each child must pay KES 240 ($2.4) 'per desk' per term and must carry lunch to school when at the lower primary level. The fee increased after class four to KES 1,800 ($18) per term and one bag of maize per year [5/184]. Since most households had many children and limited available resources, these fees represented a significant burden for most families. A young Ogiek man termed this phenomenon a 'social problem'. He added that young girls were at present more educated than young boys because it was more likely for the latter to drop out of school and uptake some activities related to the tree business. He explained that the same dropouts hung around the Mariashoni Centre and played poker or pool during the day, waiting for the evening to come [4/090]. A local headteacher further highlighted another critical connection between lack of education and deforestation. He said the local Ogiek were easily exploited into selling their trees for too little money due to lack of education. Lacking education presumingly impeded their ability to plan long-term and prevented them from understanding that short-term cash gains from selling their trees were not sustainable [3/070]. Conversely, another young Ogiek man argued that *backshwara* had become so common because there was a lack of employment and other income-generating opportunities in the area. He said that even those who did graduate from school failed to find jobs and thus engaged in anything that might help them get some little money [5/257]. Another young man said there simply was not much work for the ever-increasing numbers of youth on the small and insecure pieces of land in the area. There were basically only two accessible occupations for the youth, and all youth engaged in either of them or both; one was to farm the *shamba*, either on one's own or as a farm help, and the other was to sell trees [5/240]. An Ogiek elder confessed that he knew the Ogiek youths were cutting and selling forest resources. He recounted that the Ogiek elders had attempted to hold meetings with their youth and that it had helped to reduce the forest destruction for a while, but that their power was limited when confronted with 'outsiders who bring money under [their] nose' [5/234]. A young Ogiek man from an influential local family said that most young people wanted to move out of the forest, go to town and forget about their traditions [4/090]. An older Ogiek man said that he feared that his children would completely forget what it meant to be Ogiek due to their exposure to school and members of other communities. He regretted that children did not even speak Ogiek anymore the way they used to [5/147]. Access to fast money, boredom during the daytime, and exposure to the 'outside' world also contributed to a significant alcoholism problem in Mariashoni. While some residents said alcoholism was mainly a problem among the older men, others noted that the younger ones were also involved.26 An Ogiek elder retraced the history of the popularisation of alcohol and said that the first bar in the area opened close to where the Mariashoni Primary School was in 1982. It sold *'busaa'*, one of the traditional fermented cereal-based alcoholic beverages similar to modern beer, for the Kikuyu forest workers. The Ogiek were 'afraid of alcohol' then, but it had since become a big problem among the Ogiek men [5/234].

The case of Kaprop Primary School was interesting since it provided another angle to the analysis of the residents' sometimes destructive behaviour towards their forest. The reconstruction of Kaprop Primary School was finalised in 2010, with funds from Timsales to support local parents who had been attempting this since 2002 [2/051]. It had been closed by the Government in the late 1980s when Kikuyu settlers were evicted from the area. The construction was one of Timsales' only visible investments in infrastructure development in Mariashoni. They offered to build the school and to maintain the road connecting Mariashoni to Elburgon after Mariashoni residents had blocked the road and protested for weeks to keep Timsales lorries out of the forest. The road in question was the road that Timsales lorries used day in and day out when ferrying trees from the forest plantation in Kiptunga Forest to their factory in Elburgon, forcing the Mariashoni residents to stand by and watch while the big politically connected timber company that hardly employed any locals deforested their home area. The Timsales worker said that the locals had threatened to cut down the trees in the Timsales plantations at the time [5/233], illustrating the fact that indiscriminate forest destruction without benefit sharing could potentially lead to more forest destruction to prevent others from accessing benefits that are represented as being illegitimate. Overall, as the protest that aimed to disturb Timsales' business activities illustrated, the local population had a lot of resentment towards Timsales for destroying their forest and not sharing the benefits. In early 2017, Mariashoni made the national news after 'fifty irate youths' set ablaze fifteen vehicles belonging to timber giant Comply Industries Limited, after a

---

26 During our fieldwork, increasingly drunk and sometimes aggressive men in Mariashoni Centre were such an inevitable reality that we usually attempted to be out of the Centre by latest 4 pm.

lorry transporting logs from Kiptunga to Elburgon ran over a motorcycle and killed two people. The violent reaction of the youth 'unearths underlying issues among the Ogiek', said the area MCA who explained that management of natural resources in the area was 'unfair', leading to grievances.[27] The protest also showed that strong emotions were involved when dealing with matters of land and natural resource use and management. One NGO staff member, in the same vein, said that they were cautious with the kind of information that was disseminated to the communities because forest matters were so emotive that 'information can spread fast and change aspects and can incite the community to adopt destructive behaviour and destroy forestry or destroy the plants of the sawmillers' [1/034]. By targeting the activities and benefits of those who destroy the forest, the Mariashoni residents illustrated that violent protest often contains a political and symbolic dimension and is not primarily an expression of poverty and ignorance.

Another rationale often voiced by those who admitted to destroying the forest in one way or another can be summarised as 'if I do not do it, someone else will'. Some of the local young men who seemingly partook in the small-scale timber business voiced related opinions by adding an 'ethnic twist' to the question of who benefited from the destruction of the forest. One young man explained that all the small sawmills that operated in the area and the senior KFS staff in the area were from 'one tribe' (Kikuyu). He said that since the Kikuyu were the ones who controlled the timber business, they attempted to keep Ogiek competitors at bay. 'That's even why they don't do the road so that the Ogiek can't transport logs easily' [4/096]. An Ogiek resident from Kaprop even named the fact that the residents were not included or reliably involved with the sawmillers and thus excluded from benefiting from the forest as one of the top three challenges facing the area [5/209]. At the same time, the bad road allowed the sawmillers to continue obtaining forest resources at very low prices. Since, via KFS, the national government received money through the allocation of transport permits for forest products, as well as business licences for all small businesses in Mariashoni Centre but 'never [did] anything for the residents' [4/096], the young men even deliberated putting up a barrier on the main road to ask for 'taxes'. One resident explained that the young men had previously put up a barrier on the road right after Mariashoni Centre in mid-2013 and charged lorries, motorcycle taxis, and private cars for using the road. The roadblock was presumably intended to compel Timsales to maintain the road, which had been in a bad state. He also stated that the roadblock was only taken down after the sawmillers agreed to contribute to maintaining the road [4/100]. Being excluded from the ben-

27 Ngure, S., 'Tragic accident unearths underlying issues among Ogieks', *Citizen Digital*, 1 March 2017.

efits of the trade in forest products while someone else benefited was understood as a moral infringement on the residents' rights, placing economic benefit and forest commodification at the centre of concern, not forest conservation.

Looking for explanations themselves, many of the elders echoed a sentiment that an Ogiek woman in Kitiro summarised succinctly: '*Ogiek wanasahau utamu wa asali sasa wakagundoa utamu wa pesa na huwezi badilisha hayo sababu ya kuokoa misitu*' (the Ogiek forget the sweetness of honey because they have already tasted the sweetness of money and you cannot change that just because you are trying to rescue the forest) [5/224]. A local government employee also confirmed '*pesa imechukua nafasi kubwa na watu*' (money has taken a toll on the people) and that the locals 'forgot their ways' because of being exposed to '*biashara ya pesa*' (money business) [3/071]. He said people even cut trees that hosted beehives, an important taboo in traditional Ogiek culture. While some said 'the Ogiek became jealous, and that's why they behave like animals now' [5/212; numerous residents voiced the same idea], many of the older Ogiek blamed formal school education for the changing values and habits of their children. Another common explanation residents gave for their children distancing themselves from their traditional cultural values was exposure to members of other communities and their norms, customs, practices, and values. Some of the local teachers related all these aspects and said that local community members, while being constantly exposed to commercial timber logging, witnessed individual members of other communities make a lot of money from burning charcoal and general forest destruction and slowly garnered interest in doing the same [3/063, 3/064]. The commercial logging had remained somewhat distanced and 'faceless', while members of other communities who worked with the sawmillers gave small-scale forest exploitation a human, and a wealthy human, face. In the words of a young Kipsigis resident, the presence of other communities made the Ogiek 'realise that them too, they could sell trees' [5/220]. Apart from formal education and exposure to other communities, witnessing, tolerating, and even participating and benefiting from everyday destruction might perhaps have had a much more critical influence since it made the local Ogiek, who used to represent themselves as custodians of the forest, accomplices in forest destruction. Those who benefited once typically wanted to benefit again. Many of the Ogiek recognised that problem when stipulating that, despite the common rhetoric that represented the Ogiek managing the forest as a panacea for forest depletion, the destruction would most likely continue if the Ogiek were left alone in the forest because, as one young Ogiek man said, 'it has been a lucrative business for a long time now' [5/172]. One local headteacher was also pessimistic in her analysis of the role of the Ogiek in forest destruction, arguing that 'everybody is after money' [3/063]. The social consequences of this involvement were visibly considerable since those who benefited effectively lost the moral high ground to criticise others for forest destruction – and thus became accomplices.

An interesting feature of this commodification was the conceptual differentiation between indigenous and exotic trees. When discussing the importance of different tree species, most Ogiek expressed the opinion that indigenous trees, generally called *'miti kienyeji'* (indigenous trees) or *'miti ya zamani'* (erstwhile trees), but also *'miti ya mungu'* (God's trees) or *'miti ya dawa'* (medicinal trees), were more important than exotic trees. Apart from having socio-cultural importance in traditional Ogiek ontologies of the world, including for purposes of worship, indigenous trees were praised for supplying medicine for humans and livestock, for providing habitat to bees and thus allowing for honey production, for retaining water in the soils and for lasting longer when burned as firewood and charcoal. On the other hand, Exotic tree species were generally described as less important. They were widely referred to as *'miti ya kisasa'* (modern trees), *'miti ya serikali'* (the Government's trees), and primarily as *'miti ya biashara'* (trees for business) and even as *'miti za wazungu'* (white people's trees). While this descriptive nomination was related to the fact that exotic forest plantations were 'alien' and not attributed with any specific traditional social-cultural meaning, it also revealed that some trees were indeed valued less than others and somewhat not even considered as 'forest'. A young Ogiek man eloquently verbalised the differentiation and different valorisation by insisting that indigenous trees were more important because *'miti huyo mingine inasaidia kampuni za mbao pekee, sio jamii'* (the other trees are only good for timber companies, not for the community) [5/219]. While many individual members of the Ogiek community recognised and valorised exotic trees, they mainly did so for their wood, firewood, and general economic qualities. It was thus not far-fetched to believe that the exotic trees did not require special treatment or protection and that such trees could be cut and sold. This commodification of exotic trees was in line as well with differentiations commonly encountered in narratives of the forest dwellers that distinguished between the *'here'*, the land they settled on, often within the settlement scheme that had been established where exotic tree plantations had previously been established, and the forest *'there'*. This distinction was sometimes alluded to subtly and sometimes spelt out very clearly, for instance, by one respondent who lived close to the 'cutline' with the indigenous forest behind Mariashoni Quarry, who explained that he was not able to say much about changes in the forest, 'because the forest is far away', and he does not know 'what is going on in the forest' [5/170]. An outspoken Kipsigis resident explained that talking about the state of the forest was not easy because 'the health of the forest depends on what you talk about' and added that '*here* is not like *there* after the cutline' [5/175]. An Ogiek resident addressed the same point by indicating that the land supposedly was subdivided into two parts: 'down there', where there are no trees, and where there was only cultivation, and 'up here', where there were trees [5/209]. The latter was aligned with the 'zones' represented in Map 4 (Chapter 2), while what is described as 'forest' is likely to refer to the remaining indigenous forest in the wider 'upper' Mariashoni.

In terms of the impact of the nightly tinber trade on the social fabric in Mariashoni, the young men's business had various vital implications. First, the money they made allowed them to find young women willing to marry them, either formally or informally. Practically, there was a strong tendency towards early marriages in the area. After previous ways of finding a spouse, which typically involved a young man's father going out and searching for a wife for his son, were somewhat overcome by modernity in Mariashoni, modes of modern-day marriages had changed. Numerous residents recounted that beyond fathers selecting potential wives for their sons, there used to be a practice that young men would 'steal' recently circumcised young women from the houses in which they were recovering in order to marry them. According to some testimonies, the young women supposedly went for circumcision once they were ready to get married. Subjecting oneself to circumcision was thus understood as a sign to the young men that a young woman was ready to be married. According to this marriage custom, as described by many, the women then waited for their future husbands to 'steal' them. Once they did, the couple was considered to be married. Many observers insisted that the 'stealing' was a custom planned between future spouses in agreement and consent. In the same vein, if a young woman was 'stolen' by another man than expected, she supposedly was free to go back home [5/212]. A young Ogiek man said that, at present, the capturing of girls after their circumcision was not as common as it used to be and that young couples now often went through a courtship phase. That notwithstanding, he confirmed that it had become widespread for young people to just get together and for young women, or rather teenage schoolgirls, to get pregnant without the couple marrying first [4/090]. One local teacher explained the details of this vicious cycle by pointing out that it started with 'there [being] so much money here' [5/229]. Because of the easy access to money in the tree business, many girls were 'lured into the life of *pikipiki*s [motorcycles], TV and generator', dropped out of school, and readily accepted to get married [5/229]. Because of early marriages, there were many young families with children. Some older Ogiek said family structures had changed drastically after the Ogiek formally settled in Mariashoni. A Nandi *mgeni*, who arrived in Mariashoni in the late 1990s, said that the local Ogiek had few children and did not have too many problems when his family came to the area. Later, the youth started drinking, dropping out of school, hanging around in Mariashoni Centre, getting girls pregnant and thus contributing to rapid change in the social structure [5/256]. Some Ogiek elders explained that Ogiek families used to have very few children, often widely spaced with up to five years between children. This was important to teach the young ones the tricks needed to survive as a hunter-gatherer [4/097]. With the sedentarisation of the Ogiek families and the vanishing of the hunter-gatherer lifestyle, families started having more children. Due to the accessibility of 'easy money', these families were started earlier, and the families, overall, were younger.

However, many of these families were challenged by the second crucial social implication: the fact that the young, 'rich' men mostly walked to Elburgon at night, spent their nights outside the matrimonial home, and only returned to Mariashoni in the morning. Some said that adultery, and particularly frequentation of prostitutes, was common. This practice often had fatal consequences. One resident spoke about a vicious cycle. The first problem was that the people in the area were illiterate and married early. Another issue was that the youth engaged in the timber business and frequented Elburgon town a lot, where they 'saw girls', contracted the human immunodeficiency virus (HIV), infected their wives and spread it to their families back in Mariashoni. Many children were equally infected, and schools were only poorly sensitised to handle the children's infections and general hygiene. A further complication emanated from the fact that many people who died from HIV/AIDS and were buried on their land, which excluded them from the public eye and prevented mutual learning. She added that there used to be a USAID AIDS program in Mariashoni, but that it was no longer operational and that not enough was done to educate the youth about the risks of HIV/AIDS [3/081]. Because of early engagements and concurrent 'libertarian' lifestyles, there were many broken families and many young single parents in Mariashoni [5/229]. A young Ogiek man said that many young women ended up in single-parent households because their boyfriends got them pregnant and took off and because it remained difficult for a man to marry a woman who already had another man's child [4/090]. A local teacher added that, in other cases, the young men's resources reduced quickly because they engaged in unsustainable businesses and spent their time playing pool and cards, which led many of their young wives to leave them. He said they often became single parents and slid into poverty [5/229].

The spread of HIV/AIDS in the area was commonly unnoticed or ignored by the public and the Government alike. However, workers of the local health facility spoke about how the disease had affected the community. One local clinic staff member said that more than half of all the adults in the area were HIV positive. While she admitted that she was not entirely sure about the actual prevalence rate, she said that the problem had only been discovered when the Government introduced mandatory HIV tests for all patients seeking medical treatment at the health clinic, independently from their condition. Practically, each patient had a card that indicated their HIV testing history and based on which the clinic staff conducted tests with the help of rapid-testing kits. Patients had to agree to be tested for HIV at least once every three months to be allowed to consult the health personnel for other matters. In her observation, most people did not know their status, or at which point they contracted the sickness. Despite the high prevalence in the area, only thirty-five individuals, three men and thirty-two women were open about their health status, and worked as unpaid volunteer community health workers to sensitise their fellow community members. These workers also used rapid-testing kits and attempted to send any positive cases they identified to the clinic for treatment [3/078]. One health worker said that their job was not easy. First, they worked for free, making it difficult for them to concentrate fully on their work. Second, people living with HIV/AIDS often refused to be singled out and hence refused to participate in programmes offered to help them. She said that she had six regular patients while another friend had five more, a mere drop in the ocean compared to the numbers of people infected in the area [5/198]. The clinic staff member confirmed that most people in the area did not take anti-retroviral medicine. Part of the problem was that most residents only found out about their condition at an advanced stage, first attempted to treat themselves with herbal medicines, and only came to her once their self-medication was no longer enough, but often too late to help them. Deaths were usually not attributed to HIV/AIDS but to other conditions, typically the prevalent cold-related respiratory infections, contributing to a generalised culture of silence [3/078]. Infections mainly came to the area through the young men engaged in the timber industry, but they were transmitted both sexually and while giving birth. Because most women still had homebirths, infection rates were high among the newborn babies and traditional midwives, who often delivered the babies without wearing gloves [3/088]. High infection rates among young women also disclosed a lot about women's bargaining power in terms of intimacy and family planning. The clinic staff member explained that most women got injections that protected them from unwanted pregnancies for three months. Most women preferred these because it was easier to hide from their husbands than other types of contraceptives. She added that most husbands were unaware that their wives used birth control. An interesting feature of her work was that she only gave injections to married women. Young women who asked for contraceptives received neither oral nor any other form of hormonal contraceptives – in line with government policy, she said – but she gave them condoms [3/078]. One *mgeni* resident further noted that the hospital was embroiled in corrupt practices. Specifically, he accused the hospital staff of selling the Government drugs allocated to the hospital that should be free for patients through a private chemist next to the hospital. His attempts at attracting attention to the situation by reporting the case to the police in Elburgon had remained unsuccessful [5/216].

The politics of belonging and exclusion and the crisis in the Eastern Mau Forest

In the Mau Forest, the interconnectedness of identities, interests, and conflicts was particularly visible in the creation and/or the revival of 'ethnic' identities, which often served political or economic interests. Identitary claims, alongside identity creation and rigidification, were evident among members of a specific group of Ogiek, mainly belonging to the 'lower' classes who positioned themselves in open opposition to the local Ogiek 'elite'. These identitary claims involved assertions about holding presumably exclusive legitimacy to ownership and user rights of the forest land and resources. While the Ogiek were officially considered a hunter-gatherer community that had traditionally lived in the Mau Forest, it was at present almost impossible to differentiate the lifestyle of most Ogiek in the Eastern Mau from that of other communities. This evolution, engendered by the exposure to other communities and their values and practices, the expansion of formal education and environmental stress, among others, posed ethical and practical problems. Since the Ogiek were defined as the only legitimate group *in* the Forest,[28] conflicts about the localisation of legitimate monopoly for defining their identity and the limits of their ethnocultural space emerged.

The existence of a collectively shared memory of Kipsigis in-migrants trying to appropriate the Ogiek identity for themselves, combined with de facto assimilation of some Kipsigis and Ogiek groups (Kratz, 1993), as well as long-standing assimilation of various groups of Maasai (Berntsen, 1976), considerably complicated the definition of criteria of 'genuine' Ogiek identity. One of the most considerable ambiguities in the identity definition related to the attempt to reconcile ancestry claims on the basis of 'traditionally harmonious coexistence of humans and nature' on the one hand, and the mere fact that many present-day Ogiek contributed considerably to the unsustainable use of the forest

---

[28] In June 2010, Prime Minister Raila Odinga stated that the only group the Government would protect in the preservation of the water tower were members of the Ogiek community, as 'the Ogieks are known inhabitants of the forest who know how to protect the environment since that is their home' (Omanga, B., 'No pay for Mau Forest invaders, Raila insists', *The Standard*, 6 May 2010).

on the other hand. Increased engagement of the Ogiek youth in active forest destruction, specifically, had led to a growing distance between the older generation of Ogiek 'traditionalists' and the Ogiek youths whose lives had little in common with their ancestors'. The youth's lifestyle further attracted important social issues to Mariashoni, including teenage pregnancies, single-parented households, and a high prevalence of HIV/AIDS. As shown, this transformation of Ogiek livelihoods was embedded in the broader self-representation of being located at the 'losing end' among the social groups present in the Eastern Mau, who presumably got rich by deforesting the Mau, while the Ogiek were forced to watch. Many of them hence 'joined in', expressing sentiments close to what Hardin (1968) calls the 'free rider' problem. Although reference was made to another context, Lynch's (2011) summary of related complexities applies to the case of the Ogiek of the Eastern Mau as well:

> [I]t is not necessarily the mere presence of market-dominant minorities that is important, but popular perception regarding their evolution, social justice, threat and opportunity, and the ways in which these narratives are shaped and channelled by political elites, institutional norms, and processes of reform. Together, these complex processes – rather than the levels of inequality per se – help to explain the origins and development of local categories of 'us' and 'other'. (pp. 51–2)

Many members of the youth themselves invoked a differentiation in time, which Kratz (1993) argues was central to the Ogiek discourse about themselves and their life in the forest: the 'then' on the one hand, which was represented as the 'Ogiek Golden Age', the time when the Ogiek were living the 'proper' hunter-gatherer life in an intact forest on the one hand, and the 'now', which was represented as the period since the Ogiek began to settle and cultivate their land, and since they adopted a more sedentarised lifestyle overall, largely in line with colonial encroachment into the Mau Forest.[29] Overall, according to numerous narratives, the Ogiek had adapted relatively well to the 'shocks' of colonial intervention, despite it leaving the socio-spatial organisation of the area completely altered. This display of 'adaptive capacity' at that time and the vast difference in how the Ogiek related to members of other communities that arrived since the early 1990s was blatant. During the early colonial stages, the overall population density in the Eastern Mau was arguably much lower, and thus allowed for adaptation by giving way and through spatial reorganisation. At the same time, relations between different communities in the Eastern Mau, during

---

[29] Kratz however also cautions against indiscriminate use of the 'two-time Western model': 'Neither colonial punctuations of Then or Now nor the national independence noted in the Now are crucial watersheds from the local Okiek viewpoint, though they also help structure historical narratives (by Okiek, by other Kenyans, by scholars, and others)' (1993, p. 41).

colonial times, mainly between the Ogiek and Kikuyu, were also less politicised and, therefore, somewhat friendlier from the onset. Less intense, less numerous and less politicised contact allowed for relatively smooth relations between the two groups at the time, which, one could argue, did not 'threaten' the Ogiek social, economic, and cultural survival in the community's perception. After Independence, relations between the different communities inhabiting the forest changed slowly. Listening carefully to the few members of the youth who spoke about their engagement in unsustainable resource use, the beginning of the 'now' might hence more appositely be placed at the beginning of the 1990s when government-driven socio-spatial changes ostensibly transformed the area; and with it the communities living in and adjacent to the Mau Forest. Many Ogiek described the arrival of large numbers of *wageni* as a government strategy targeting their annihilation. They alluded to the Government supposedly pursuing a *'colonisation de peuplement'*, a 'settler colonialism' strategy, which was widely employed by imperial power structures. Such strategies typically involve transforming a given area by bringing in settlers with 'desirable' characteristics (Wolfe, 2006). In response to the arrival of these in-migrants, many Ogiek entertained rather hostile relationships with these *wageni*, which contributed to Ogiek elites capturing opportunities offered by external actors in terms of resources, knowledge, positions etc., and to a spiral of mutual 'othering' and finger-pointing between the host and in-migrant communities.

Local identity politics, including questions of inclusion and exclusion, also involved differences in land use and land designation. The 'forest' label, legally, was reserved for the area that still fell under the forest reserve regime. However, rather than differentiating only two zones, the 'forest' and the 'settlement', most residents also differentiated between 'lower' and 'upper' Mariashoni (see Map 4 in Chapter 2), representing socio-spatial characteristics beyond legal status. Given the empirical data presented, it might be more appropriate to differentiate between three, or even four, zones: the one 'down there', where big pieces of land were fully cultivated, mainly mono-cropped with maize or wheat with minimal human settlement; a transition zone with smaller-scale plots and cultivation in what could be described as agroforestry systems along the border between what ought to be the settlement scheme and the declining forest boundary; and the actual remaining forest, containing both primary forest and exotic tree plantations. The 'forest' could be further subdivided into two different zones, one with the *'miti ya wazungu'*, the plantations, and one with the *'miti ya mungu'*, the indigenous forest. The first conversation with the famous Ogiek leader at the onset of the fieldwork already abounded with indications that the underlying differentiation between different tree types was of primary relevance to understanding local forest commodification. His welcoming remarks then were: 'It's the indigenous forest that defines our identity, not the exotic [trees]. That's why we fight the exotic ones and fight for the recovery of the indigenous ones' [3/055]. Later he explained that the forest plantations 'turned our home into private property', rendering the forest 'private assets instead of public property' [3/056]. Since the Ogiek had 'problems' with the exotic forest, as he described it, the Ogiek leader did not find it difficult to justify why he decided to cut them and benefit from this 'environmental destruction'.

While the overall impact of the Ogiek youth's engagement in deforestation might have remained minor, due to the rudimentary methods used and the persisting social stigma that prevented their assertive engagement in forest exploitation on larger scales, the 'normalisation' of the Ogiek no longer being able to represent themselves as 'guardians of the forest' was likely to have had real and far-reaching consequences. The other side of this transformation of attitudes towards increased forest commodification was ostensible in the strong support for forest enterprise development among external partners and the Kenyan government. A young Ogiek man who participated in a 'Kazi kwa Vijana' (work for the youth) programme, a governmental youth empowerment programme under the Prime Minister's office that used the Constituency Development Fund (CDF) mechanism to create income-generating activities for the youth at the time, explained that the objective of the project that had been implemented in the area was to establish small exotic tree plantations to support the involvement of the youth in commercial forestry [5/174]. A staff member of an NGO initially founded by the tea companies surrounding the Mau Forest defended their engagement in the establishment of small-scale commercial tree plantations, in their case mainly through on-farm forestry, since it supposedly targeted 'wealth creation, as opposed to poverty reduction'. According to his argument, 'people who make money forget about the Government forests' [1/021], which would ultimately lead to environmental conservation of the vital primary forest and watersheds. As demonstrated, many of the more 'traditionalist' Ogiek rejected engagement in any form of modern forestry undertaking, including PES schemes, in line with Maathai (2010) and Martin (2005). Yet, another young Ogiek man who participated in setting up 'Kazi kwa Vijana' cypress plantations in Kiptunga and Kaprop explained that the plantations had been established during a tree-planting drive in January 2010 [5/232], and sustainable commodification hence seemed to have been part of the Government's approach to 'Saving the Mau' from the onset. The commodification of the forest perhaps reached its climax when the most famous Ogiek leader became the head of a newly formed sawmillers' association called Nakuru Timber Traders and Millers Association.[30] Attempts

30 Wambugu, S., 'Timber traders form group', *The Star*, 27 August 2013; Nation

to obtain a statement on the same from the leader were unsuccessful despite regular exchange on other issues. Beyond the paradox which turned an Ogiek leader into the head of a sawmillers association, one might, however, argue that the leader's engagement was a particularly controversially employed 'weapon of the week' (Scott, 1985) since his enrichment passed exclusively through the commodification of those 'government trees' that he indicated were responsible for the Mau crisis in the first place; contributing to taking them down, and financially earning from them, could hence be equated to practising an alternative form of redistributive justice.

It remained complex to identify the underlying dynamics for the Ogiek youth's engagement in destructive behaviours related to a commodified approach. Assumptions related to the Poverty-Environment Nexus, commonly cited by various stakeholders involved in the Mau crisis and the multiple campaigns to save it, were not negligible in the Mau context. However, exerting caution in defining causes and effects in phenomena driven and defined by complex dynamics remained important, as much as differentiating between contribution and causal attribution. As previously discussed, most external actors in Mariashoni tackled biodiversity conservation from a livelihood-centred perspective. This was an apparent response to their definition of the Mau destruction as a function of poverty. However, the minimal success of these programmes also showed that, while the underlying assumption might not have been entirely wrong, it was at least incomplete. While relative material destitution might very well have contributed to changes in attitude, particularly among members of the Ogiek youth, who transitioned from a self-representation of forest protectors to being 'just like any other people', as some of them claimed, an array of other factors contributed to that change as well. Chief among these was the sedentarisation of the hunter-gatherer community through spatial restriction and confinement to land parcels of limited size, which started with the establishment of colonial forest plantations but climaxed only with the establishment of the Mariashoni settlement scheme in the 1990s. For the Ogiek, these socio-spatial changes led to the necessity to adopt small-scale farming as an income-generating or at least subsistence strategy. Since they were traditionally a non-farming community, many claimed that their agricultural skills had remained rudimentary, supposedly leading to poor yields and harvests. The poorly developed infrastructure and lack of transport to take agricultural produce to the nearby towns led to brokers offering very low prices for agricultural produce, which rendered it difficult for many Ogiek to sustain themselves on small-scale agriculture. The sedenta-

correspondent, 'Small saw-millers form own lobby', *Daily Nation*, 4 September 2013.

risation of the Ogiek through the establishment of the Mariashoni and neighbouring settlement schemes and the receipt of allotment letters for land that was surveyed and allocated to individual beneficiaries furthermore led to an opportunity to make quick money through land sales. Considering the high demand for forest land since the mid-1990s, some Ogiek also ventured into the slippery territory of selling non-allocated forest land to 'outsiders', consolidating the assumption that material progress and possession had somewhat overtaken the priority of forest guardianship.

The amalgamation of at least three dynamics – the Government creating the settlement scheme, its commissioning of the big timber companies to cut most of the trees that used to stand on the land that was allocated and surveyed, and the politically driven in-migration of members of traditional farming communities – led to fundamental changes in Mariashoni that could not have left the Ogiek community untouched. The increase in population numbers led to the establishment of more formal educational facilities. Altogether, numerous interrelated dynamics, including exposure to formal education, exposure to other customs and practices, and continuous witnessing of the important financial gains that others made from deforestation, had permanently influenced the generation of young men who engaged in forest commodification at present ever since they were children. In the context of growing population numbers within the Ogiek community, partly because of sedentarisation and partly in pursuit of an intentional 'Ogiek survival' strategy, which further compounded the complex realities in the Easter Mau, many of the young boys opted out of 'traditional' income-generating activities and livelihoods. Beyond this complexity, it was visible that habit had become another powerful force, which somewhat attributed normative power to everyday acts. Through everyday observation and participation in deforestation, it seemed that many Ogiek simply got used to the commodification of their natural environment. Exchanging trees for money thus became first imaginable and then desirable for many locals, particularly the younger generation.

Billy Kahora, a famous Kenyan intellectual and novelist, in 'How to Eat a Forest' commented on the schism within the Ogiek community in the Mau Forest and the tension 'between the Ogiek as a conservationist and the Ogiek as land broker'. He called out the traditional Ogiek leaderships' continuous 'invention of tradition', in line with Hobsbawm and Rangers' (1983) conceptualisation, as being exclusively 'environmentally friendly' by virtue of belonging to an indigenous hunter-gatherer group, while the community on the ground manifested 'the forest-dwelling, hunting and gathering aspects of their culture, but also this kind of perverse modernisation' (Kahora, 2015). This tension challenged one of the foundations of community conservation orthodoxy (Berkes, Colding, & Folke, 2000; Gadgil, Berkes, & Folke, 1993; Gadgil & Rao, 1994) and also the Government's decision to define the Ogiek by virtue of 'ethnicity' as the 'only legitimate inhabitants of the Mau Forest' (Human Rights Council, 2010), since both were based on a supposed absolute validity and appropriateness of externally ascribed indigenous or traditional ecological knowledge, and thus neglected the other socio-cultural forces at play in highly politicised environmental crises. The self-representation and 'external' recognition of the Ogiek as a somewhat homogenous social group with shared norms that would somewhat lead to optimal outcomes, in line with common 'community' representations (Agrawal & Gibson, 1999; Gibson & Koontz, 1998), clearly led to an 'ethnicisation of community' (Gibson & Koontz, 1998) in the Eastern Mau. This representation also stood in stark contrast to the portrayal of the Ogiek among many residents of the Eastern Mau, particularly among *wageni*. The discursive connection that many of them made between the supposed inability of the Ogiek to adapt to changed living conditions in Mariashoni because they supposedly were bad farmers and not interested in improving their farming methods can be understood as part of a potentially powerful narrative according to which the Ogiek were not able to take care of their lives and their environment, which came close to the influential colonial narrative of the 'caricature of the African as destroyer of the environment' (Bassett & Crummey, 2003, p. 17). This caricature had far-reaching consequences for the socio-spatial organisation of environments that were supposedly under threat, mainly through the set-up of exclusionist national parks; only that this time it was the 'caricature of the Ogiek, the unable and lazy farmer, as the destroyer of the environment'. This common discourse among *wageni* was embedded in and evoked images of a history of discursive degradation and defamation. In that vein, an Ogiek resident explained that members of other Kalenjin groups, especially the 'big Kipsigis leaders', had attempted to publicly defame the Ogiek in the media by treating them as backward forest dwellers 'who give dogs as dowry' [3/063] ever since the tension between the host and in-migrant communities started in the 1990s.

Furthermore, the contribution of some members of the Ogiek community to active forest degradation and destruction was closely related to land having been de facto privatised within the Mariashoni settlement scheme. The relationship between land tenure and/or land ownership, particularly Private Land ownership and environmental conservation, continued to be discussed controversially in the literature. However, beyond the official land status question, de facto, land use was a major contributor to the political ecology of the Mau crisis. Concerning the factors that influenced land use, the size of land seemed to have played a crucial role in how the land was used. On the 'lower side' of Mariashoni, the land had primarily been allocated to 'big men' in big chunks, mostly converted to medium- to large-scale agricultural crop plantations, from which trees were cut entirely (see Map 4 in Chapter 2). In the 'middle zone', where land had been parcelled by the Government and given out to individual beneficiaries, the Government had cut most of the trees. These plots were typically much smaller and mostly contained both a homestead and some small-scale agricultural production. There was little evidence of individual initiative to reforest Private Land parcels among these landholders. In the third 'upper zone', which had not been parcelled and allocated to individual beneficiaries but where individual homesteads were built by encroaching into the forest reserve behind the 'cut line', realities were more complex. Some homesteads were built right into the remaining trees, while others cut some trees around their homesteads, and very few residents cut all the trees on 'their' land. While it might be argued that secure tenure of supposedly privatised land might have contributed to more-sustainable land-use practices, this might realistically only apply to the smallholders among the land beneficiaries since land-use modalities among the 'big players' with large parcels of land were unlikely to have changed due to a legal regime change. Among the smallholders, one can reasonably argue that land uncertainty generally, and specifically since the onset of the 'Save the Mau' initiative, might have contributed to practices strongly oriented towards short-term gains rather than potentially more sustainable long-term goals. On top of land size, uncertainty was also caused by the way the land had been obtained, and hence by whether individual beneficiaries expected to lose their land, and if they did, whether they would lose it with or without compensation. On the other hand, the 'big men' and the locally connected elites displayed a certain degree of certainty that their 'rights' would not be violated by the state and ensured vocal backing among political representatives, even if the land was to be returned to the state. Yet, many local Ogiek disputed the idea that secured private property rights might have led to the uptake of more sustainable practices; particularly because land privatisation directly led to the impossibility of pursuing livelihoods and engaging in practices based on existing and context-specific ecological knowledge, while many Ogiek arguably lacked the agricultural skills to farm more sustainably. Based on observed social differentiation on the ground, one might reasonably argue that both 'developmentalist' Ogiek and *wageni* might potentially have been interested in engaging in agricultural practices with a longer-term perspective, potentially including sustainable soil and land management practices such as agroforestry, if their land tenure was secured. On the other hand, among several residents, particularly the 'traditionalist' Ogiek, practices of 'everyday resistance' to the imposition of a sedentary lifestyle and a sometimes almost defiant opposition to engaging in practices that might have been represented as endorsing this imposition – in line with Scott's (1985) argument – were visible as well. This can also be related to the opposition between exogenous and endogenous heritage ascription processes proposed by Cormier-Salem and Basset (2007), which contribute to the controversial acceptance of propositions made. These might not be changed, even if land tenure was secured, since the subdivision and individual allocation, as well as the inequity in the allocation of the forest land in the Eastern Mau, was the founding 'momentum' for their opposition, and the construction and consolidation of their 'identity'. Land use depended rather on the identities, experiences, and interests of individuals and groups that had obtained the land than on the legal status of the land. In this context, it is important to note that 'communities' that are primarily ethnically defined are neither homogeneous nor do their members necessarily share norms and values or engage in uniform behaviours leading to social outcomes that can be anticipated and planned for, but that 'communities' comprise complex sets of actors whose differences are defined by several factors.

Social differentiation – including characteristics such as wealth, gender, age, and ethnicity (Chomba et al., 2015; Leach, Mearns, & Scoones, 1999), which can 'be mapped onto existing perceptions of inequality' (Martin, 2005) and hence intersect with experience and historicity, including resident status (indigenous vs immigrant; indigenous vs stranger) and temporality of residence (early vs late comer) (Mbembe, 2000; Hulme & Murphree, 2001b; Bassett, Blanc-Pamard, & Boutrais, 2007), as well as objective exposure to and subjective representations of marginalisation, dispossession, and displacement (Lusigi, 1981; Nixon, 2010) – strongly influenced individual and group positionalities and hence different 'environmentalisms' (Rahmato, 2003) in the Eastern Mau. Altogether, historicity, shared experience, and temporality played a much more important role in self-identifying and relations between communities than did ethnic affiliation.

Concerning the contribution of land privatisation to the environmental crisis in the Eastern Mau, it is furthermore essential to consider that the attempted land privatisation was at no point introduced with the objective of engendering sustainable livelihood practices and conserving the forest land, but it was exclusively driven by the will to provide access and tenure of fertile land to various groups of persons, predominantly in a patronage logic, in line with Bayart (1989), Klopp & Sang (2011), and Wrong (2009). Furthermore, the 'mental' separation between farm and forest land, between the 'here' and the 'there', was apparent, as were the implications in terms of attitudes towards adequate behaviour: farmland was represented as being explicitly reserved for farming, while conservation mainly mattered 'there'. The existing spatial subdivision of the area in the 'here' and 'there' seemed to have contributed to residents not feeling responsible for deforestation and forest degradation or the conservation of the forest since 'here' was not considered to be part of the forest that needed to be rehabilitated [5/115, 5/209]. This was particularly true in the context of residents being uncertain about their future. If land privatisation had been accompanied by clear conservational narratives and targeted support for sustainable land-use and management practices, the outcomes might potentially have been very different. They might also have contributed to meaningful self-mobilisation of 'landowners' to establish community-driven and sustainable environmental and livelihood development initiatives.

The social changes witnessed in the Mariashoni area contributed to a lot of tension and confrontation. The 'environmental conflict' literature, inspired by Homer-Dixon (1994, 1995, 1999), is commonly invoked when discussing conflicts that occur in an overall context of environmental stress, while a range of academics (Hauge & Ellingsen, 1998; Martin, 2005; Timura, 2001) caution against over-simplified and causal explanation patterns between environmental crises and conflict. While conflicts experienced in the Mau Forest were undoubtedly influenced by environmental changes and the resulting reduction of available natural resources, most of these conflicts were more clearly determined by competition over access to and use of forest land, in line with the political ecology premise that the environmental is political, as well as by competition about a presumed legitimacy to live in and benefit from forest resources – hence the politics of inclusion and exclusion – than about the degradation of the resources as such. In line with Martin's (2005) argument, the actors defining this presumed legitimacy hence socially constructed resource-use competition, which, in turn, manifested as resource-use conflict. It could even be argued that the Government pursued an active strategy of keeping the Ogiek busy with land and natural resource-use claims to divert their attention from the socio-cultural effects of their sedentarisation that seemed to have led to an important degree of 'deculturation' of the Ogiek community. The accumulation of different conflict-enhancing determinants clearly demonstrated the interconnectedness of socio-economic and environmental tensions and their relevance for local and national security debates, even though it might not be warranted to define the latter as a *direct* trigger for conflict.

Overall, land access and ownership regulations were fundamental for land and natural resource use and management in the Mau Forest. Beyond the regulations, actual land allocation practices and tenure arrangements, as well as the social consequences and representations engendered by these practices, determined the Mau settlers' behaviour towards the forest and imposed conservation and restoration measures. Beyond this first layer related to land access and use, various interconnected socio-economic and socio-cultural dynamics contributed to the behaviours of different individuals and groups. As with the overall environmental crisis, and concerning each of the individual actors' contribution to that crisis, the status quo experienced in the Eastern Mau was the outcome of political interests, and struggled and illustrated the ways and forms in which powerful actors seek control over other actors' environments, how less powerful actors develop and employ their agency through the creation of counter-narratives, and by using 'hidden transcripts', as well as the manifestation and translations of these power relations in the physical landscape. Indeed, how the crisis was framed, and which linguistic repertoires were used fundamentally influenced where various actors localised blame, the types of solutions proposed, the actors to be included, and ultimately how to navigate the crisis in line with Hulme (2009).

Conclusions

This book has analysed the drivers of the Mau Forest environmental crisis that are critical to understanding the destruction and dynamics preventing its restoration, which is widely appreciated as extraordinarily important for the country, the wider East African region and beyond. Its continuous degradation and destruction defy understanding. This book represents an attempt to analyse what has gone wrong and deconstruct the dynamics of non-protection. This final chapter draws together conclusions about responsibility for the destruction of the forest, local, national, and beyond, and suggests how its findings might point towards a better and more equitable solution to the depletion of habitat and livelihoods.

The sheer size of the Mau Forest and its location in the fertile and politically as well as economically critical Rift Valley region mean it is hardly possible to address the complexity of drivers of the 'Mau crisis' in totality. However, it is possible to make evidence-based assumptions based on my analysis of a specific area of the Mau Forest, which can contribute to understanding how the current 'environmental crisis' might be addressed. The empirical evidence generated in the Eastern Mau Forest underpins the analysis of the dynamics of non-protection of Kenya's most important forest.

The failure to 'Save the Mau' and the political ecology of its environmental crisis

Common approaches to explaining forest degradation and destruction often invoke people's poverty and their subsistence practices on the one hand, and some variation of agricultural expansion and/or unsustainable forest harvesting rates and hence some degree of 'institutional failure' on the other hand. While both explanations involve aspects influenced by the interests and actions of powerful actors, these approaches typically remain entirely apolitical. Despite several factors related to power dynamics being included in the FAO (2016) list of factors contributing to forest loss, for instance, their political nature is omitted by the way they are classified. Examples include *agriculture*, as well as *encroachment and land grabbing* being classified as *agriculture-related*; *insecure tenure of forest land* and *unsustainable harvesting rates* being classified as *wood and forest-related*; or *settlement and industrial development*, as well as *poverty*, being classified as *social and governance-related*. Hence, both the underlying political dynamics behind these supposed drivers and the implication that the political dimension of these factors has for possible solutions are neglected. Such apolitical framings have an important bearing on the conceptualisation and the implementation of rehabilitation programmes to environmental crises in the Mau Forest and beyond, and hence on the solutions found to address the destruction of habitats and livelihoods.

The root cause analysis presented by the Kenyan government was aligned with these general explanation patterns for environmental degradation and destruction. Forest-dwellers and forest-adjacent communities were defined as 'destroyers of the Mau Forest' given their presumed poverty, in line with the 'Poverty-Environment Nexus'. The second aspect that was addressed in the Task Force Report, but much less taken up in the Government discourse, was 'institutional failure' in both 'securing' public forests against forest dwellers accessing and using the forest as an 'open-access' resource, as well as weak enforcement of existing laws and weak management capacities. The latter had supposedly led to irregular and ill-planned settlements, encroachment into the primary forest, uncontrolled and illegal forest resource extraction, and conversion of forest to agricultural land.

In response to both those 'problems', the Kenyan government followed the recommendations of the Mau Task Force and adopted a programme to 'Save the Mau', the Mau Forest Rehabilitation Programme (GoK, 2010c) that contained four main components and various short- and long-term tasks under each of them. The first component, 'restoration, management and rehabilitation', targeted forest boundary solidification, reforestation, and reinstatement of forest production provisions and sites, including forest plantations. The second component, 'livelihoods and employment creation', targeted both community-based forest management (CBFM) and farm forestry development, while the third component, 'relocation and resettlement', focused on forest land reclamation that had been illegally excised. The fourth component, 'institutional arrangements', considered various institutional reforms and legal and judicial processes for improved forest rehabilitation and restoration coordination.

While the Task Force made rather sophisticated recommendations for the implementation of the programme, and although the Government endorsed the Task Force Report as a framework for the Mau Restoration programme (2009e), the five-phase spatial-temporal plan that was adopted to implement the recommendations focused primarily on the short-term measures, and revolved mainly around securing the forest boundary and reclaiming forest land. Beyond the fact that the five-phase plan did not directly involve the longer-term measures recommended by the Task Force, its implementation came to an early stop in Phase III, and with it, most of the pursued measures. Content-wise, government-driven forest rehabilitation was halted after non-occupied forest land in the Eastern Mau and land that mainly had been occupied by smallholder farmers in the South-Western Mau was reclaimed, and after a few reforestation drives were completed. Largely uncoordinated non-government actors continued being allowed to implement livelihood-centred projects, while the Kenya Water Towers Agency (KWTA) was created as a regulatory body, however, without being adequately capacitated through the allocation of sufficient funds.

The analysis of the political ecology of the Mau Forest destruction, non-protection and failed recovery allows drawing various conclusions. The first conclusion is that the initial problem statement by the Task Force and the Kenyan Government was insufficient since it left out crucial drivers of destruction and non-protection of the forest. The second is that despite the relatively complexity-embracing Task Forest Report recommendations, the Government limited its activities on the ground to those recommendations that involved 'quick-fix' technical and policy solutions and did not challenge the interests of the powerful political and economic actors, including large-scale landowners and major timber-producing companies. The third is that despite proposing a rich analysis and a wide-ranging list of recommendations, the Report and the Government failed to comprehensively address the most pressing issues in the analysis and recommendations on the one hand and on the ground on the other.

In line with general political-ecological thinking, this study proposes to understand the failed approach to 'Save the Mau' as the result of powerful actors' interests and powers at various highly interconnected scales, whose agency allowed them to stop important measures that were part of the initial four-pronged forest rehabilitation plan by attracting negative attention to the fact that the plan involved 'creating' new IDPs. Hence, these powerful actors were able to directly prevent activities that would potentially have interfered with their interests while retaining systemic features that had maintained the structural causes of the 'Mau crisis' and were produced by the 'politicised environment' of natural resource management in Kenya, in the first place (see Figure 4).

Furthermore, the empirical analysis of the dynamics of non-protection addressed showed that the livelihood-centred approaches implemented on the ground, in combination with the continuous emphasis on forest management for the benefit of commercial production, meant that the state continued prioritising its 'developer' role over its 'steward'

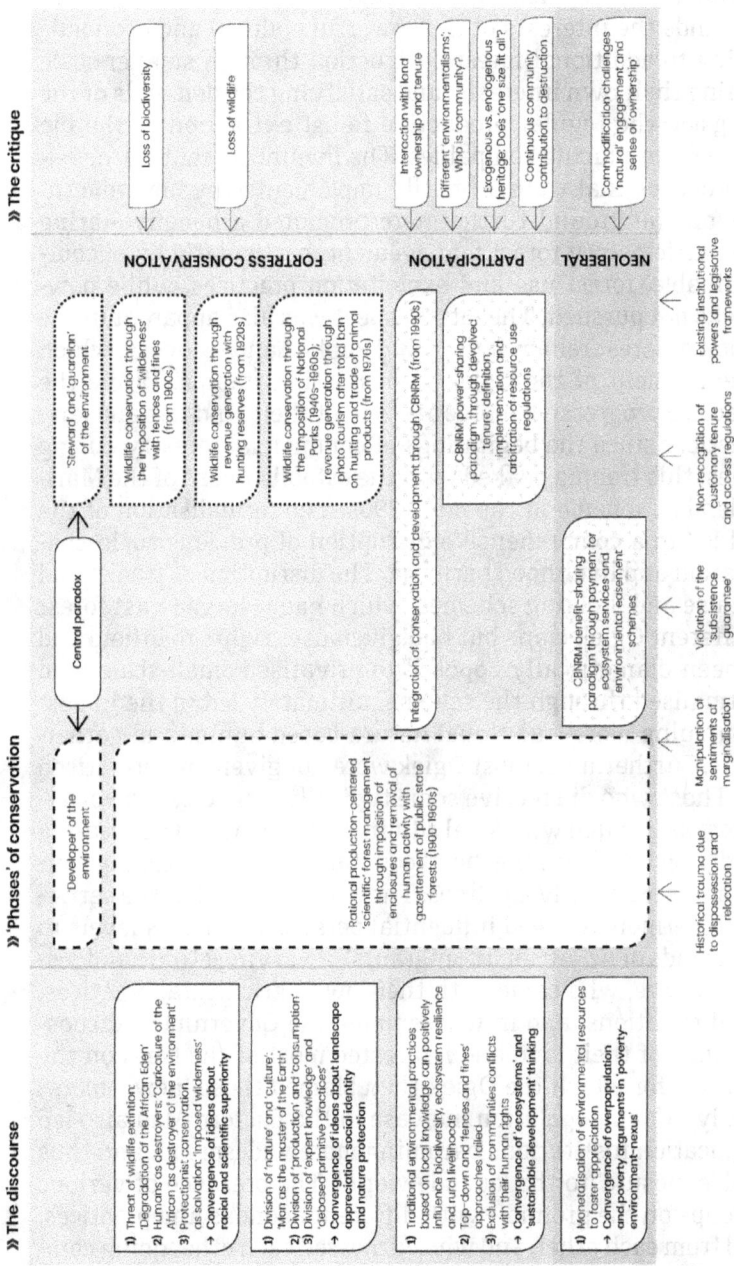

Figure 4 The 'politicised environment' of natural resource governance and management in Kenya.

Source: Author composition based on various referenced sources. Note: Aspects related to the different components of the politicised environment are represented through different outline styles (read from left to right): 1) Forest production aspects are indicated with dash, 2) forest conservation focus with square dots, and 3) various combinations of production and conservation concerns for sustainable forest management with solid line and light dots.

role. The Mau crisis was embedded in the colonial legacy of defining forests predominantly as commodified natural resources for commercial forest production. In pursuing its 'developer' role, the state furthermore foregrounds the interests of the powerful political and economic actors, leading to additional forest destruction through smaller-scale actors pursuing their own interests, and satisfying the demands of the people, alongside the regular productive forest extraction of the big timber and wood-producing companies. The livelihood-centred 'development' approaches that were primarily implemented by non-government actors on the ground furthermore promoted a benefit-sharing approach to participatory forest management, particularly by encouraging 'sustainable' forest use and exploitation practices, while power-sharing was not pursued. The latter aspect was also apparent in the amalgamation of forest rehabilitation and Public Land recovery, which led to a re-enactment of the Ogiek dispossession trauma. While the Ogiek had faced a progressive reorganisation of their land-use and governance practices since the beginnings of commercial forestry during colonial times, this trauma peaked with the establishment of the Mariashoni settlement scheme in the mid-1990s. The formalisation of the scheme had led to a comprehensive disruption of previous socio-spatial organisation and livelihood patterns. The disruption of traditional shared land-use and -holding schemes, which had reserved vast forest tracts for different Ogiek clans but had given user rights to others and had hence been diametrically opposed to privatised small-scale land holdings formalised through the scheme, ultimately led to the impossibility of pursuing more traditional nature-based hunter-and-gatherer livelihoods. Furthermore, most Ogiek were not given any privatised land either. Those who did receive some typically were close to powerful local actors associated with local administration officials, revealing underlying divisions within the 'host' community along patronage but also gender and particularly age lines. The establishment of the settlement had furthermore allowed influential persons at various levels to bring in thousands of *wageni* or 'in-migrants' of varying ethnic and residential provenance, who came with their own agricultural practices, customs, and traditions, and in whose name the Government dispossessed the Ogiek of their land and harvested most of the trees on the settlement land, for which the Ogiek then blamed those 'newcomers'. The politically driven population increase in the Eastern Mau also led to formal education institutions becoming more widespread, and thus to increased 'exposure' to the 'outside world'. The presence of various different groups on the ground – with different agendas and practices, who learned from each other, and who witnessed each other doing comparatively well – led to a lot of confusion about who benefited because of which presumed patronage relationship, about whose presence was supposedly legitimate, and about who allegedly was able and held the right to use and benefit from the forest, as well as who should be responsible for its management and restoration. In a context of being everyday witnesses of those associated with powerful actors across scales benefiting from forest destruction in a relatively unchallenged manner, and given the increased uncertainty about the future after the onset of the 'Save the Mau' campaign – which, again, re-enacted fears of being evicted from the forest altogether – many 'non-traditional' community actors, particularly the Ogiek youth, started engaging in destructive forest exploitation practices as well. Further 'exposure' to the life outside of the forest through nightly business visits to forest-adjacent towns also transformed the local community by sweeping in a lot of cash for the participating young men, leading to young families being formed, and broken, due to their livelihoods being relatively unstable in the 'fast cash' economy, and because of bringing in fatal diseases from these nightly ventures. While the magnitude of the local youth's engagement in terms of deforestation might have been negligible, this engagement contributed further to deepening the rift between those segments of the local Ogiek community who continued defending a more 'traditional' version of their distinct cultural identity, including their self-identification as 'guardians of the Mau Forest', and those who just wanted to be 'like other normal Kenyans' and have 'development' and 'a good life'.

Underlying the described dynamics was an apparent lack of political will to analyse and tackle the complexity of issues perpetuating the Mau crisis, or rather a presence of political will not to investigate and address the dynamics of non-protection of the Mau. This political will manifested at various, highly interconnected levels and scales, including:

1) in the continuous acceptance of bribes by Kenya Forest Service (KFS) officers in exchange for non-sanction of illegal small- and medium-scale forest extraction;

2) in the prevention of the set-up of a joint forest management agreement between the KFS and the Community Forest Association (CFA), which might have contributed to more power sharing in the management and governance of the forest;

3) in the continuous promotion of biased benefit-sharing approaches to CBFM, including by the KFS colluding with CFA officials to benefit more from their engagement in forest plantation establishment and harvesting than other CFA members, leading to a complete distortion of the CFA vehicle, and general dissatisfaction and abandonment of the same;

4) in the KFS forester's refusal to implement a plantation establishment and livelihood improvement scheme (PELIS), which might have contributed to benefit sharing and more sustainable thinking

and practices on the ground beyond the community's engagement in extractive forestry ventures;

5) in the complete absence of government promotion of environmentally sustainable thinking and practices on the ground;

6) in the continuation of powerful land holders subdividing land and giving it to new in-migrants with the local administration's blessings despite the 'Save the Mau' initiative;

7) in the local administration's role in perpetuating the looming dissatisfaction within the local community by not apprehending claims about irregular land occupation and take-over;

8) in the local administration's decision not to address inter-community conflict on the ground that it kept people busy and shielded the authorities from being blamed;

9) in the manipulation of local political processes to ensure continuation by keeping the same elites in charge despite changing administrative order etc.

Altogether, a complex picture of the political ecology of the environmental crisis in the Eastern Mau Forest can be drawn (see Figure 5), in which various features of the 'politicised environment' within which the crisis unfolded are highly interconnected and interdependent. While attributing relative weight to separate dynamics in terms of their contribution to the political ecology of the Mau crisis is complex, some of them seemed to have had a more substantial influence than others. The state prioritising extraction-based forest management for commercial forest production through major politically connected timber-producing companies appeared to be a significant contributor. The parallel deforestation of settlement land by medium and small-scale sawmillers, and the 'cutting craze' that engulfed both the big timber companies and the sawmillers after the onset of the 'Save the Mau' initiative, were further major contributors. Parallel to the state prioritising its 'developer' function by focusing on commercial forest production, various state and politically connected actors also actively fought to preserve the political economy of land attribution and distribution. Being able to access, redistribute and withdraw land provided for direct benefits, including income from large-scale agricultural production, as well as indirect benefits of political and economic nature. The continuous political will to maintain the status quo in these regards played a major role in the Mau crisis.

These 'local dynamics' were embedded, and often perpetuated, by parallel manifestations of maintaining the Mau crisis at higher governance levels, for example:

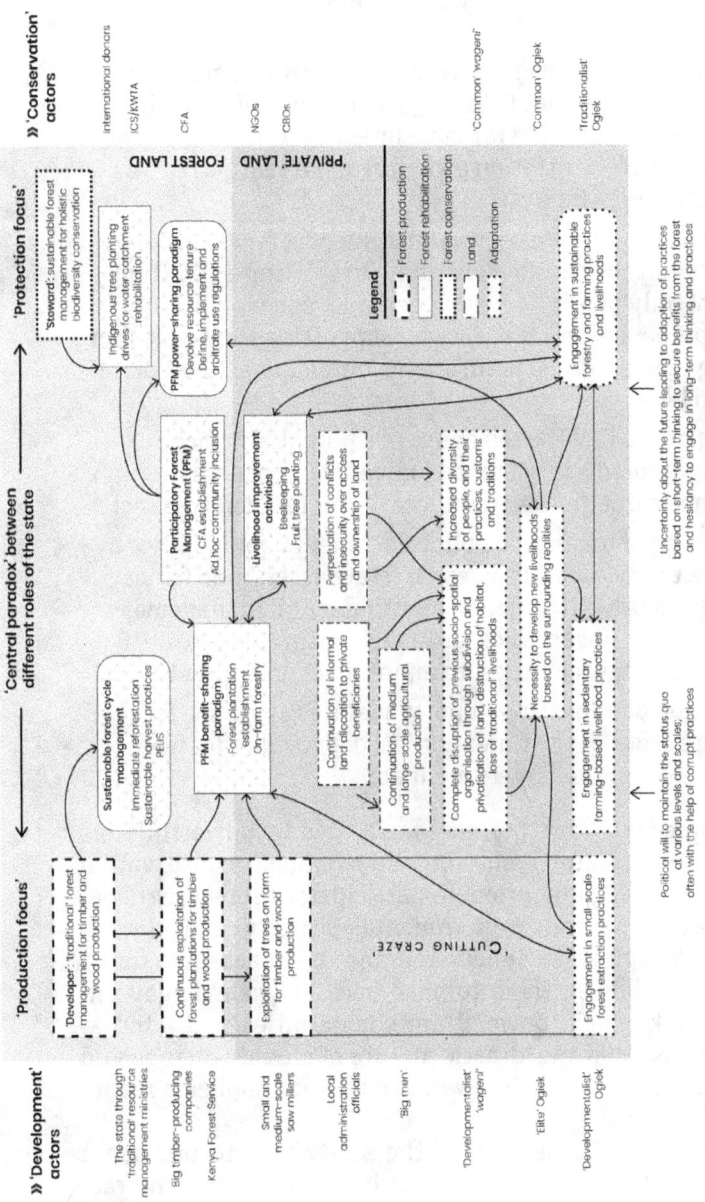

Figure 5   The political ecology of the 'environmental crisis' in the Eastern Mau Forest.

Source: Author composition based on discussed empirical evidence. Note: This figure summarises the core arguments of the book and places them in the context of the central paradox that defines the 'politicised environment' of natural resource governance. Aspects related to the different components of that politicised environment are represented through different outline styles (read from left to right, and top to bottom): 1) Forest production aspects are indicated with thick dashes, 2) forest rehabilitation and conservation aid with thin solid line and light dots, 3) forest conservation ideals with square dots, 4) land matters with long and short dashes, and 5) socio-cultural adaptation with small round dots. Round borders indicate missed opportunities related to these components.

1) in the continuous leeway given to big timber-producing companies by the Government to use and benefit from forest plantations located on primary forest land during and after the logging ban and despite the 'Save the Mau' initiative being pursued in the very same area;

2) in the Government and the KFS continuing to turn a 'blind eye' to those powerful companies not fulfilling their responsibilities in the implementation of more sustainable forest cycle management, including immediate reforestation after forest harvesting, as foreseen since the 2005 Forests Act;

3) in the Government not providing financial support for provisions in the 2005 Forests Act that might contribute to shifting away from the Government only playing a 'developer' role, and would allow for more holistic approaches, for instance by supporting the set-up and by empowering viable CFA structures and joint management plans at forest station level;

4) in the disabling of the KWTA and hence of a potentially more holistic and coordinated approach to biodiversity conservation and forest governance through the non-allocation of financial means;

5) in the undermining of important policy documents, for instance by redefining the country's water towers as 'state assets' and hence undermining the decentralisation of environmental management to subsidiary levels of governance, provided for through the 2010 Constitution via the new counties, to maintain control over them;

6) in the continuation of allocating important state functions, for instance the core office of the Chief Justice, to persons that were presumed to be loyal to the Government etc.

These local dynamics were furthermore facilitated by powerful state actors' ability to appropriate themselves international conservation discourses and hence allegedly promote participatory forest management (PFM) while using the environmental scarcity and climate change narratives to legitimise 'fences and fines approaches' to forest management, which allowed them to push back polycentric governance models and 'take back' power from communities and alternative actors – justifying that the 'drastic' nature of climate change and deforestation required a 'drastic' answer, even if that implied a reduction of democratic spaces.

While the most critical objective of the study was to propose a method to conceptualise complexity resulting from power interactions and interrelations at the local, national, and global scales as well as resulting from combined political, economic, and identity dynamics, the application of a political ecology lens to the study of the failed approach to the rehabilitate the Mau Forest furthermore allowed the identification of several relevant aspects connecting political ecology, policy, and practice in an overall 'development' context. Consequently, the lessons learned can be used to inform recommendations for how to address the Mau crisis more comprehensively. Both the findings and lessons learned are relevant for similar environmental crises elsewhere, in Africa and beyond, and could make an important contribution to reframing both the crises themselves and proposed solutions.

How to 'Save the Mau': Lessons learned and evidence-based recommendations

Beyond management, forest governance is essential to rehabilitate the Mau Forest comprehensively. Yet, both are complex and prone to conflicting agendas, as illustrated throughout the analysis. Generally, the forestry sector is becoming increasingly globalised, and decentralised management systems are increasingly common, leading to multi-actor, multi-level decision-making and governance.

Taking the complex dynamics of the political ecology of the Mau crisis into account, while considering the applicable regulatory frameworks, what could sustainable forest conservation and management look like? Combining opinions raised by Mariashoni residents and external experts on how such sustainability could be achieved based on evidence found on the ground with the analyses conducted throughout the empirical chapters of this study – and given political ecology theory and ulterior empirical research – five separate but interdependent recommendations are made. Each of the five main recommendations includes various specific recommendations. The first four main recommendations are loosely structured in line with this book's Introduction and four core empirical chapters, while the fifth is broader and more conceptual. (The section numbering below follows that in Figure 6.)

1) Provide a regulatory and institutional framework that promotes sustainability

Much of the invoked 'institutional failure' to protect the Mau Forest might mainly be attributed to what Bryant and Bailey (1997) call the 'central paradox' between the state's role as developer and as protector or steward of the natural environment. The tension between these two roles typically manifests in conflicts between different state ministries and agencies, both in policy and in practice on the ground, pitting those responsible for sustainable environmental conservation against those that traditionally manage resources, including ministries for agriculture and forestry (Bryant & Bailey, 1997). While competition between different state agencies can be productive, counter incentives to sustainable forestry must be addressed comprehensively if the dynamics of non-protection of the Mau are to be reversed. This first main recommendation addresses the broader politicised environment of environmental and forest conservation (see Introduction).

Enact regulatory frameworks that address sustainable forest production and forest conservation holistically

The enactment of the 2005 Forest Act and the subsequent creation of the KFS in 2007 led to important changes because the KFS started managing forests based on forestry principles and relatively autonomously without significant political or government interference – although the Director of the KFS, as all directors of the country's parastatals, continued being appointed by the President. The abolition of the logging ban in October 2011 furthermore allowed the KFS to take up proper forest cycle management again. The 2005 Forest Act also includes provisions which involve important changes in forest management, hence addressing most of the critical aspects that had contributed to previous forest mismanagement. These changes target both environmental and socio-economic sustainability. Relevant factors include provisions on compulsory revegetation of harvested areas; provisions for co-management of the forest and its natural resources with the forest-dwelling and/or forest-adjacent communities through the establishment of joint management plans between the local KFS representatives and CFAs and hence introducing PFM; and the re-introduction of the previously abolished *'shamba'* system under the PELIS label with better checks-and-balances that aim to contain the destruction of young trees that had previously been witnessed in forest plantations, by establishing community responsibility and liability mechanisms for the land portions allocated to individuals and ultimately aim to combine conservation and livelihood concerns.

However, the enactment of the existing provisions and the punishment for violations through disciplinary action were problematic in the Eastern Mau. Specifically, compulsory afforestation remained sketchy, while the KFS provided little support for CBFM on the ground. While no joint management plan was signed between the local Kiptunga CFA and the forester, and PELIS had hence not commenced in Mariashoni during the research for this book, the Mariashoni forester criticised the system as 'untimely', arguing that among the local residents, the necessary 'change of attitude is yet to come' [3/069], publicly supporting an alternative approach according to which it would be more useful to empower forest dwellers to make the most of their forest resources from their farmland, and to encourage various agroforestry or on-farm forestry practices actively, and not to let them interfere with official forests located on forest land. These approaches imply very weak community participation in actual forestry. They hence are neither captured by any 'stage' of the classification that lists conservation as 'for', 'with' or 'through' the people (Murphree, 2000), nor in Alden Wily and Mbaya's (2001) differentiation between benefit-sharing and pow-er-sharing CBFM paradigms.

Despite important progress made through the 2005 and 2016 Forest Acts, existing regulations remained incomplete. Experiences from other countries illustrate that forest production can be pursued while minimising potentially adverse environmental impacts much more decisively. Various tree-harvesting practices can, for instance, be pursued, including (among many others):

1) the selective removal of individual and valuable trees and tree species rather than clear-cutting entire forest;
2) logging at sustainable rates so that regrowth matches removals;
3) cutting smaller areas in mature forest plantations so that remaining trees can contribute to natural regeneration of the cut area;
4) individual replanting of trees.

Such practices can fall under broader frameworks for sound and sustain-able forest management, for instance, defined by the international NGO Forest Stewardship Council (FSC), which has successfully promoted sustainable forest production by mobilising consumers to insist on specifically certified forest products.

The FSC list for sustainable forest production includes ten detailed criteria that encompass important principles, including:

1) harvesting trees at a rate that can be sustained indefinitely, with the growth of new trees adequate to replace felled trees;
2) sparing of forests of exceptional conservation value, such as old-growth forests, which should not be converted into homoge-neous tree plantations;
3) long-term preservation of biodiversity, nutrient recycling, soil integrity, and other forest ecosystem functions;
4) protection of watersheds, and maintenance of adequately wide riparian zones along streams and lakes;
5) a long-term management plan;
6) acceptable off-site disposal of chemicals and waste;
7) compliance with prevailing laws;
8) acknowledgement of the rights of local indigenous communities and forest workers (Diamond, 2005).

In the context of the enactment of the Forest Law Enforcement, Govern-ance and Trade (FLEGT) Action Plan, Cerutti, Putzel, Pacheco, and Baxter (2015), however, point out that such frameworks often leave out small-scale loggers and hence fail to account for their negative impact on forests. The authors argue that certification of forest products should target all forest products produced within a given country, including those traded in local and domestic markets that often find their way to the international markets after all. They add that a scalar instead of a blanket compliance approach should be pursued that considers differences between large and small-scale forest enterprises to avoid excluding and criminalising the least powerful actors.

Beyond that, following the decentralisation of numerous competencies as part of the devolution process engendered by the 2010 constitutional reform, the central Government found itself compelled to share matters of natural resource management with county governments. This added an additional layer of complexity to the set-up of meaningful framework institutions to oversee the Mau Forest rehabilitation. Kenya's territorial reorganisation and the devolution and decentralisation of state functions to the counties were initially expected to have another significant impact on water tower management overall, particularly on Saving the Mau. Some of the complexity stemmed from the fact that Public Land, which included gazetted forests such as the Mau Forest, continued 'belonging' to the central Government, while natural resource management overall was supposed to be led by the counties. A 2015 Land Development and Governance Institute report suggests that the results of decentralising decision-making on land were mixed (Klopp & Lumumba, 2016), and many observers said the central state had been hesitant to devolve natural resource resource management to the counties. According to the Interim Coordinating Secretariat (ICS) and KWTA forestry specialist, the Government's hesitancy involved a fear that counties would act selfishly and manage their resources for their exclusive benefit, while some areas of operation required a national perspective since they were related to national interests [1/040]. In that vein, infrastructure considered critical for national interest, including power generation plants, ports, oil infrastructure, airports, and all water towers, including the Mau Forest, were later declared national assets. The eighteen recognised water towers were defined as being under government ownership by law, while some provisions for the counties' involvement in their management were made (Republic of Kenya, 2012c). Since forestry and wildlife, alongside education, roads, and health, remained county prerogatives, wrangles during the transition were to be expected, the forestry specialist insisted, especially in terms of licensing sawmills. At the same time, foresters, and all other Provincial Administration officials, who were relics of the old central state order, were supposed to be phased out [1/022]. While the transition from central to county control at the regional level seemed to progress well initially, the strong opposition of the Provincial Administration to their looming redundancy[1] de facto led to the superimposing of the old onto the new structures and specifically of provincial and county officials at the local level. At the national level, considerable opposition could be witnessed as well, which for example, manifested in the fact that the Government declared seventy new areas as 'water towers' in 2018.[2] What at first seemed to be an expression of increased political will to implement environmental policies and protect vital environments however also disguised that the 'water tower' declaration allowed the central state to take back control over these 'important areas' from the counties.

Land legislation had changed considerably since the mid-2000. Most of the legal provisions, which had previously allowed for much of the manipulation in land allocation and distribution, were addressed in these reforms. However, the comprehensive enactment of these reforms was staunchly opposed, and their implementation was sabotaged at various levels, rendering the reform process incomplete.

Targeted and comprehensive regulations that align objectives related to both roles of the state in forest management, and as developer and protector, at various levels of governance, and hence commercial forest production and forest protection and conservation, are important to overcoming the competition between both roles that had contributed considerably to the non-protection of the forest.

Enable and empower institutions responsible for implementing sustainable forestry frameworks

In the context of pursuing increased polycentrality in natural resource governance, and specifically in the management of the water towers, including the Mau Forest, both national and international interested parties placed much hope in the creation of a parastatal institution by which to coordinate forest land recovery and forest rehabilitation activities in the Mau Forest. While the creation of the KWTA marked a significant formal achievement, its importance remained far behind these parties' hopes and expectations.

However, the evolution of the creation of the KWTA provides important insights into its limited powers to 'Save the Mau'. The establishment of the ICS and subsequently of the KWTA can be understood as institutional adaptation, in line with what seemed to be a trend in Kenya of a reconstruction of the state through agencies that focus on specific areas, sectors or activities; creating a 'patchwork of state responsibility' [1/035]. In the case of the Mau Forest, two different

---

[1]   Nation Team, 'Chiefs threaten to sabotage polls', *Daily Nation*, 24 October 2012.
[2]   Apollo, S., 'Agency to gazette 70 more water towers in race to save forests', *Daily Nation*, 13 March 2018.

approaches to setting up an institution to support the Mau rehabilitation were pursued at different times. First, an institution was set up
that was organised along geographical lines, the ICS, and the initially
planned Mau Forests Complex Authority, which hence focused explicitly on the Mau Forest. Later, this localised approach was overturned,
and an institution was created that was responsible for a specific type
of territory, and the KWTA was put in charge of all areas defined as
water towers.

While state institutions specialising in a specific area or on a particular type of territory are likely to be more professionalised and potentially more holistic in their approach to managing these areas than sectoral
management approaches, such 'landscape-level' arrangements entail
several risks. One risk can be that different sets of regulations co-exist
in neighbouring areas, which might subject bordering regions and their
residents to unclear rules, potentially leaving them unresponsive. This
is further amplified in case these landscape-level institutions are not
neatly aligned with the extent or the type of territory, in this case the
Mau Forest ecosystem. Such cross-border arrangements also need the
buy-in of administrative and political structures across these borders
within the landscape, and between different institutions within each
of the administrative zones, for instance, different ministries that were
previously in charge of specific sectors related to such an area (Fuchs,
Njuguna, Robinson, et al., 2018; Nagendra & Ostrom, 2012).

The inability of the ICS and the KWTA to fulfil their mandate of
bringing about a more holistic approach to forest management based
on a change in focus on biodiversity conservation can be interpreted
at different levels. While some observers attributed the administrative
and institutional weakness of the KWTA to the fact that the institution was young and was understood as a 'small brother' to other pre-existing institutions, mainly the KFS and the KWS, others invoked more
complex explanations.

According to the former national coordinator of the KFWG, much
of the initial opposition to the ICS was based on the ICS having been
housed under the former Prime Minister's office. He added that the creation of the KWTA was an important step in the depoliticisation of forest
rehabilitation in general and in attempting to 'Save the Mau' particularly [1/030]. Several other experts, including various representatives
of the ICS/KWTA [1/042, 1/258], expressed the view that the Government was not sufficiently interested in having a strong KWTA. On the
one hand, in line with its historical mandate and objective to maintain
national wood and timber production (GoK, 2009e), there was strong
government interest in maintaining the KFS in charge, whose mandate
traditionally prioritised commercial forest production of forest commodities rather than forest or biodiversity conservation. Furthermore,
the various natural resource managing ministries and their different

directories, as well as the parastatals KFS and KWS, were historically 'strong', which rendered their coordination difficult [1/010]. On the other hand, disabling the ICS was supposedly both personal, to safeguard interests in Mau Forest, and political, since most of the international credit for successfully conducting the 'Save the Mau' initiative had been attributed to the opposition [1/005]. Some said that lacking government support for the KWTA manifested clearly in the fact that very little money was allocated to the KWTA, which, as a result, remained unable to fulfil its mandate [1/258]. Creating structures but not funding them was a popular approach to incapacitating organisations whose mandates were uncomfortable, in Kenya as elsewhere. One observer said that the KWTA became even more severely under-funded than it had been when Uhuru Kenyatta was Finance Minister after the political change of 2013 [1/042].

Consequently, due to lacking budget allocations, the KWTA largely remained a shell institution, despite the elaboration and publication of a five-year strategic plan, the launch of the Water Towers Atlas in February 2016 and the nomination of four directors in 2015 (Republic of Kenya, 2016c). Since early 2012, the development and adoption of a strategic management plan (SMP) for the Mau had become a priority for the ICS, which was supposed to be an inclusive and integrated plan providing for assessments and integrated planning in all sectors, including water, wildlife, forest, fisheries, hydro- and geothermal power production, agriculture, and related socio-economic systems [1/022, 1/040]. The plan was to have the SMP gazetted and placed under the 1999 Environmental Management and Co-ordination Act (EMCA) but above the Forest, Water, and Wildlife Acts, making the National Environmental Management Authority (Nema) from whom, as the custodian of the SMP, extractive businesses must obtain prior approval. Through this arrangement, all other organisations would have to follow the SMP, even if the mandate of the KWTA ran out or even if it was incapacitated [1/042]. Such an SMP was not adopted.

The ICS/KWTA forestry specialist suggested that the new land legislation and the 2010 Constitution could contribute to solving some of the issues preventing the KWTA from fulfilling its mandate, hence helping the rehabilitation of the Mau Forest. Acknowledging that the amalgamation of the Mau rehabilitation agenda and land recovery had hampered previous progress, he further suggested that once the regulations and provisions related to land were settled on, and clear solutions on land proposed, the KWTA might be freed of the political deadlock, which could, in turn, allow the agency to concentrate on conservation matters [1/040]. He also said that the development of the National Land Commission (NLC), officially created in 2012, was of primary importance since issues related to illegal land allocation were to be addressed through this controversial institution [1/040].

The NLC had been hampered by various political manoeuvres since its creation, including in its attempt to resettle members of the Ogiek community in the Eastern Mau, but had also achieved some critical successes (Klopp & Lumumba, 2016). Since the necessary documentation about illegal land allocation had been produced, including through the 2004 Ndung'u Report, the 2009 Mau Task Force Report and a few other highly contested reports, processing land questions should also become easier. Meaningful enactment of the new land legislation had also become more realistic, according to the specialist, since the Senate and the National Assembly had become more independent through the 2010 Constitution and because ministers were no longer allowed to be Members of Parliament and could hence no longer influence legislation as much as they used to [1/022]. He drew further optimism from the fact that the KWTA was a 'political' entity and 'not just a group of civil servants', so it was able to log formal complaints and could push the Government to make decisions [1/040].

The neglect of the institutional structure supposed to supervise, support, and monitor integrated and holistic forest and biodiversity management needs to be placed in a broader understanding that pre-existing forest management structures and institutions concentrated primarily on forest production, not forest conservation. In that vein, the KFS's primary mandate, in the tradition of the previous colonial and post-colonial Forest Departments, was to produce forest commodities. Rather than operating within the same guiding principles as the KWTA, the KFS's mandate was to develop and sustain the forestry sector. For the KWTA to be effective, a vision that emphasises sustainable forest production and combines forest production with environmental conservation might be required. Furthermore, a more empowered KWTA might also require much more political unity and will among those in power.

In 2014, the administration of Uhuru Kenyatta declared the intention to merge the existing 246 parastatals into thirty-five, and then later into eight and eventually five to tackle the country's wage bill problem. Through this merger, the four parastatals implicated in forest management and rehabilitation were to be transformed into one super-parastatal. To that effect, the KWTA, the KWS, the KFS and the Nyayo Tea Zones Development Corporation were to be merged into a proposed Kenya Forests and Wildlife Service (KFWS).[3] The service was to have only one chief executive officer (CEO) and four deputy directors, a significant reduction from the previous four CEOs and twenty-one deputy directors [1/042]. These plans were, however, not concluded.[4]

---

[3]   Omondi, G., '42 parastatals to be dissolved under new reforms plan', *Business Daily Africa*, 12 November 2013; Mobile Nation, 'The proposed parastatal mergers', *Daily Nation* online, 5 October 2013.

[4]   Kemei, K., 'Parastatals' planned merger stalls', *The Standard*, 15 April 2014;

On the ground, part of the KWTA's insignificance stemmed from its difficult cohabitation with the KFS, which had its feet firmly grounded in the country's forests and wielded considerably more influence. Since the KFS' primary mandate remained forest production, KFS foresters were primarily interested in planting and selling as many exotic trees as possible, further incentivised by the prospect of promotions if they did well [5/200] and avoided sharing management responsibilities and benefits with the community members as much as possible [3/069]. Aligning incentive structures among relevant state organisations towards creating co-benefits is important if the state is interested in sustainable forestry. In the same vein, despite indigenous trees not contributing directly to commercial forestry, the forestry service should be mandated with a decisive approach to planting indigenous trees instead of focusing solely on developing and planting forest plantations with exotic trees for forest production [5/220].

The study of the KWTA furthermore illustrated that the mere existence of regulations and institutions tasked with their implementation is largely irrelevant without the enactment of rules and the empowerment of the implementing institutions. Here again, a clear regulatory framework that contains relevant and realistic provisions, which unite commercial forest production and forest conservation and foster the creation of co-benefits instead of pitting these two priorities against each other, and their decisive enactment, are indispensable.

Identify reliable funding mechanisms

Insufficient funds were one of the leading causes of the KWTA's relative insignificance, which contributed to the extraversion (Bayart, 1999) of the 'Save the Mau' campaign that was representative of the overall dependence on donor funds for environmental conservation initiatives and priorities in Kenya. Monetary valuations of crucial environmental assets were discussed at various levels as a potential solution to address problems of under-funding and empowering important institutions. While contributing to overcoming budget-related issues, these valuations might also help illustrate the importance of the conservation of such assets by proposing numbers for the losses incurred and potentially contributing to producing political consensus.

Pursuing a monetary valuation for the Mau Forest Complex, UNEP, KWS, KFWG, & ENSDA (2008) estimate the direct and indirect revenues from the Maasai Mara National Reserve and Lake Nakuru National Park alone at approximately KES 5 billion ($50 million) for 2007. The market value of the hydropower potential of 508 MW of the Mau Complex is estimated at about KES 5.3 billion ($53 million) per year,

---

Omondi, G., 'Job cuts loom in State firms merger plan', *Business Daily Africa*, 28 May 2015; Koech, G., 'Parastatals should be merged – CS', *The Star*, 27 May 2017.

while the market value for tea produced in the Kericho and Nandi high-lands near the Mau Complex is estimated at KES 8 billion ($80 million) (UNEP, KFS, & KFWG, 2005; UNEP, 2008). Using a different model that includes various 'identifiable benefits' from the Mau ecosystem, including large-scale agricultural production, subsistence agriculture, energy, tourism, climate regulation, recreational and cultural value, genetic resources, and various ecosystem services, Kipkoech, Mogaka, Cheboiywo, and Kimaro (2011) estimate the total annual economic value of the Maasai Mau, Trans Mara, and Eastern Mau Forest blocks of the wider Mau ecosystem at KES 17 billion ($170 million).

More recent publications propose approaches to monetary valuations of Kenya's water towers, specifically the UNEP report on The Role and Contribution of Montane Forests and Related Ecosystem Services to the Kenyan Economy (2012). This report – co-authored by UNEP-REDD, the Republic of Kenya, and the KFS – proposed an improved model for the economic valuation of Kenya's water towers, in line with ongoing efforts by the Government, since 'measuring and understanding the economic value of forests is important for decision-making processes including planning and budgetary allocations' (UNEP, 2012, p. 4), according to then-UNEP Executive Director Achim Steiner and then-KFS Executive Director David Mbugua. The 2002 UN Conference on Sustainable Development (Rio+10) also contributed to an understanding according to which natural capital and critical ecosystems should be captured through 'new systems of environmental and economic accounts' to put an end to systemic undervaluation or even exclusion of the contribution of the value added by environmental services and particularly by forest services (UNEP, 2012). Beyond the ecosystem services that have explicit prices or that are traded in markets, these systems should consider various timber- and non-timber forest products, but also a range of regulating ecosystem services, as well as 'secondary' or 'indirect multiplier effects' associated with the direct economic value of such systems (UNEP, 2012). The economic benefits of the water towers are based on the water towers providing intermediate products and services for the industries downstream, as well as goods for household consumption. A so-called 'insurance value', called 'regulating services' by the Millennium Ecosystem Assessment (2005), is furthermore attributed to montane forests since they 'maintain economic resilience to seasonal environmental and economic changes but also long-term economic hazards, such as climate change' (UNEP, 2012, Summary). According to the Millennium Ecosystem Assessment, regulating services are part of the broader ecosystem services, alongside provisioning services and cultural services. Regulating services include local climate regulation, water regulation, erosion regulation, water purification, natural hazard regulation and disease regulation, among others, while provisioning services cover the renewable resources that are mostly directly consumed. Cultural services include 'non-use' services, such as spiritual, religious, aesthetic, and inspirational (UNEP, 2012).

While the Government had not officially adopted any of the proposed methodologies or results, the Cabinet Secretary in charge of the Ministry of Environment and National Resources, Professor Judi Wakhungu, announced in 2016 that the Government was to conduct an economic valuation of the country's water towers.[5] The hitherto absence of such valuations had previously been described as one major underlying problem for the recovery and rehabilitation of the Mau Forest since budget allocations by the Kenyan treasury supposedly were based on estimations of the worth of these objects. Not knowing the value of Kenya's water towers meant that the money allocated to the institution that was supposed to manage these water towers, in evidence, the KWTA, was insufficient [1/258].

Some observers said that this absence of monetary valuations of the country's forests had historical roots. Undervaluing forests in the books supposedly used to help those responsible for forest production to make illegal money. By registering undervalued timber sales, those forest officers could keep the difference between the fictive and the selling price of timber. Consequently, former forest valuations only counted 'standing timber', and forest resources were undervalued, while there were no attempts to conduct a comprehensive valuation of forests at the national level [1/259]. In the same vein, a high official of the ICS/ KWTA claimed that the main objective of the pursued SMP had been to promote the same economic rationale and to base natural resource management on monetary valuation since, as he said, 'only this can save the Mau' [1/042]. Some argued that valuations of the ecosystem services that the Mau Forest provided to the broader region could meaningfully inform PES schemes, including zoning and payment for conservation activities [1/026]; others doubted whether monetary valuations of the forests could render PES schemes meaningful [1/042]. Proper monetary valuation could potentially serve as a relevant basis for any type of benefit-sharing agreement, notably through joint management plans between the KFS and CFAs, and improve forest-dwelling communities' access to resources and the benefits drawn from these resources. By refusing to produce appropriate figures about their 'wealth' in terms of 'standing timber' and indicating how much revenue was made from the sale of trees, the KFS had hitherto refused to share control and benefits with the communities [1/034]. In line with the benefit-sharing paradigm, Mogaka et al. (2001) also argue that communities' willingness and financial ability to engage in sustainable forest management (SFM) depends on the benefits of conservation being greater than the

---

5 Xinhua News Agency, 'Kenya to conduct economic valuation of water towers', *Xinhua News*, 5 February 2016.

benefits of degradation, which requires opportunity costs incurred because of that engagement to be counter-balanced and hence calls for precise economic valuation of conservation. The active pursuit of realistic monetary valuations for the country's water towers through the Ministry of the Environment and Natural Resources, in accordance with general evolutions at the global scale, supported by UNEP and international donors, manifests that much hope is placed in such valuations. Whether they can indeed be a silver bullet remains to be seen.

While the connection between the valuation of environmental assets and fundraising for their conservation is imperfect, raising awareness about the economic impact of forest destruction can undoubtedly go a long way in increasing direct and indirect national budgetary allocations, which could in turn address some of the critiques related to the extraversion of the environmental conservation sector. At the same time, financial valuations can also help to access the much sought-after 'green climate funds', which have become a primary avenue of international development funding in a context in which climate change adaptation has become the global development paradigm. Access to such funding sources might, in turn, empower the relevant institutions, notably the KWTA, to pursue its objectives with more zeal than it had previously been able to. In line with criticism related to continuous extraversion of conservation enterprises and market-centric conservation approaches (Bushley, 2014), also conceptualised in terms of 'neoliberal conservation' (Büscher, 2013; Vaccaro, Beltran, & Paquet, 2013), the current popular paradigms such as ecosystem services, wetland credits, and species banking are based on the assumption that capitalism and conservation are not only compatible but that their connection is desirable. While these concepts postulate sustainable accumulation under capitalism, Büscher (2013) terms such approaches 'fictitious conservation' (p. 20), in line with Fairhead, Leach, and Scoones's (2012) critique of the 'valuation, commodification and markets for pieces and aspects of nature' (p. 237) allegedly engendered by such 'green grabbing'.

2) Coordinate sustainable and context-specific approaches to forest rehabilitation

Without a strong and financially empowered government body able to engage, coordinate, and guide activities implemented to 'Save the Mau' on the ground, all projects, apart from the initial tree-planting drives and forest evictions, were implemented by externally funded NGOs. These NGOs typically operated within their own terms of reference outside supervision or accountability mechanisms. An enabled institution that defines and coordinates context-specific approaches to forest rehabilitation could make an important contribution. The Mariashoni residents made many suggestions about the active definition of an own

vision, an agenda, and specific activities to achieve greater sustainability of forest rehabilitation activities. These suggestions are structured along the axes of activities that were implemented in the Eastern
Mau: reforestation, the 'development' of livelihoods, and participatory
forest management. This second main recommendation focuses on the
politics of conservation aid (see Chapter 1).

Promote sustainable and context-specific reforestation

The public emphasis on mitigation activities at the beginning of the
'Save the Mau' initiative, particularly on planting trees as a response
to forest destruction, reveals that forest rehabilitation was initially
framed as a linear reversal process, in which the destruction and
removal of trees were countered with the substitution of trees. While
this approach conceals important conceptual challenges related to
defining forests and forest health in primarily biophysical terms, the
potential positive impact of tree-planting drives was also hampered by
insufficient considerations of suitability at several levels. At the very
least, those engaged in climate change mitigation, and hence in tree-
planting activities, should plant tree species appropriate for the local
ecology and promote sustainable tree management practices instead
of just planting random tree seedlings without putting appropriate
management arrangements in place [5/200]. Reforestation efforts
should explicitly promote native and threatened species. Successes
of externally driven conservation efforts also might be tremendously
improved if activities were implemented in areas where forest destruction had been most intense, or where targeted activities could be most
successful, and not only target conveniently located areas along major
roads [5/167]. Both aspects highlighted by the residents, tree species,
and management suitability for a given context align with the options
by context paradigm (Coe, Sinclair, & Barrios, 2014; Smith-Dumont,
Bonhomme, Pagella, & Sinclair, 2017).

Take forest dweller-driven approaches to development

A core aspect of more comprehensive approaches to 'developing' local
livelihoods concerns the comprehensive inclusion of different groups of
forest dwellers in all activities related to 'development' projects carried
out by both government and non-government bodies. Since community
buy-in and 'ownership' are important for the eventual success of such
projects (Fuchs, Peters, & Neufeldt, 2019; Maathai, 2010; Martin, 2005),
conscious community inclusion in the design, planning and implementation is important (Agrawal & Gibson, 1999; Leach, Mearns, & Scoones,
1999; Peluso, Turner, & Fortmann, 1994).

While the four projects that were implemented in Mariashoni at the
time of the research were considerate of context-specificity and exist-

ing 'traditional' ecological knowledge, in line with the assumption that both can contribute meaningfully to biodiversity conservation and sustainable resource use (Berkes, Colding, & Folke, 2000; Gadgil, Berkes, & Folke, 1993; Gadgil & Rao, 1994) and hence focused on bee-keeping, the design and implementation of the projects displayed that these priorities were set externally through what Cormier-Salem and Bassett (2007) call 'exogenous heritage' claims, and imposed through top-down mechanisms. Community engagement and inclusion in the self-identification of identities, interests, and preferences, and the definition of community action plans based on these, could have contributed to a wider inclusion of existing knowledge of various segments of the community in interaction with rational choices and individual tastes of these community members, and might hence have led to a broader range of more diversified activities being supported by those projects, which could ultimately have contributed to both uptake of proposed activities and actual livelihood improvement, as shown by Fuchs, Peters, and Neufeldt (2019).

Specifically, members of non-Ogiek communities complained about being excluded from externally supported projects, which had prevented them from obtaining enough knowledge about environmental conservation, arguing that 'you can't know the forest if you don't come from here' [5/204]. Beyond the inclusion of members of various ethnic communities, external actors should specifically target the youth and encourage them to plant trees and support them in developing alternative sources of income to prevent them from cutting trees for a living, another resident opined [5/202]. Inclusion is hence also important across gender and age categories. A third aspect mentioned by various residents concerned the risk of project knowledge, means, and opportunities being captured by elites [1/027, 5/148, 5/229]. Specifically, they identified the exclusion of those represented as 'foreigners' and those represented as 'opposition' by the established elites, which is in line with the observations made by Hulme and Murphree (2001a). Sensible community involvement needs to be based on intra-community stakes, stakeholders, and power relations, which consider various intersectional characteristics and attributes, and a clear sense of differences in and between stakeholder interests, particularly in highly heterogeneous communities (Barrow, Clarke, Grundy, Jones, & Tessema, 2002).

Foster community ownership and participatory forest management

While natural resource management was likely to evolve in the direction of somewhat shared management responsibilities, in line with the 2005 and 2016 Forests and Environmental Management Acts, support of community forestry (CF) through the inclusion of communities into the management and benefit sharing from exotic tree plantations bears important challenges. These, for example, revolve around forests becoming further commodified since forest plantations are neither the subject nor the concern of culturally inspired traditional knowledge and might hence not attract attitudes involving responsibility and care among community members. The inclusion of indigenous communities into 'thinking' forest commodification furthermore contains the risk of encouraging a commodified view of all trees and forests, including primary forests whose trees arguably are of considerable monetary value. The proximity of primary and secondary forests in general, and, as in the Mau Forest, the destruction of primary forest and the establishment of secondary forest plantations containing exotic tree species whose exclusive purpose was timber and wood production, should hence be problematised. In that vein, the existing CFA was mainly considered as being concerned with exotic trees and narrow income generation for its privileged members, while their environmental ambitions were understood as secondary [2/048, 3/070, 5/200]. The existing CFA hence 'failed' in two fundamental aspects that, according to Gibson and Koontz (1998), render community conservation successful: the CFA members did not develop shared values regarding the resource on the one hand. They did not set up the CFA as an institution that translates such values into rules that members could have followed, which could have defended these values, on the other hand.

Payment for environmental/ecosystem services (PES), a popular vehicle for benefit-sharing approaches to managing forested or reforested areas, was widely supported among Mariashoni residents. Many others cautioned that payments might only be useful if they went to individuals and not groups since the money could easily end up in the hands of a few in case it was given to community groups [5/228]. Furthermore, many residents expressed doubts about the existing community groups' ability to bring about sustainable change due to widespread experiences related to elite capture of knowledge and funds [5/148, 5/229]. Yet, numerous authors insist that PES resembles wage-labour relationships that can threaten community 'ownership' and commitment and hence bias the communities' vision about the role they have to play in their environments for conservation to be sustainable (Maathai, 2010; Martin, 2005). However, especially among the Mariashoni youth, there was considerable support for the idea that residents should be able to gain financially from engaging in conservation [5/257], exposing, once more, the schism within the local community, which, once again, highlights the importance of considering and comprehensively addressing community dynamics and 'environmentalisms' (Rahmato, 2003) in the institutional set-up of resource governance organs and programmes (Coe et al., 2014; Fuchs, Peters, & Neufeldt, 2019; Nagendra & Ostrom, 2012; Smith-Dumont et al., 2017).

Power-sharing was challenged by the KFS personnel's resistance to setting up joint management plans on the ground, despite existing provisions since the 2005 Forest Act. The Participatory Forest Management Plan was finally signed between the Kiptunga CFA and the KFS in early 2016. Yet, it ignored important provisions such as PELIS (Sonkoyo, 2016) and is unlikely to have led to meaningful changes to the status quo. In line with Alden Wily and Mbaya's (2001) suggestion, customary tenure regimes should be considered in locally based forest management proposals. The authors also related missing community interest in SFM with lacking consideration of customary socio-spatial organisation patterns. Given that many Mariashoni residents indeed decried non-recognition of customary land and spatial management regimes, forest rehabilitation measures might be more successful if they were based on those customary set-ups, inspired by various forms of local ecological knowledge rather than being entirely driven by externally defined community participation principles. Such consideration could also stimulate longer-term visions and interest pursuit, which are more likely to devolve from genuine power-sharing than from benefit-sharing paradigms (Alden Wily & Mbaya, 2001). A combination of both through a spatial separation of production and conservation sites, and the set-up of distinct governance structures and mechanisms, might hence allow benefiting from the advantages of both extremes on the participatory management continuum while consciously addressing related challenges. This is in line with Ojha, Ford, Keenan, Race, et al. (2016), who aptly summarise that open and exploratory approaches are required to facilitate context-specific spaces and expressions of local democracy 'with diverse, flexible and networked models of community participation' (p. 14), alongside a clear recognition of rights and responsibilities.

Develop a context-specific, locally driven and independent agenda to 'Save the Mau'

Related to the identification and sustainable use of reliable funding mechanisms, some of the complications in streamlining rehabilitation activities on the ground stem from the Government relying on the aid industry for most of their environmental docket. Southern countries' active pursuit, perpetuation and participation in the creation and maintenance of their dependent position within the global system is aptly captured by Bayart's (1999) 'extraversion' concept. Consequently, Northern donors and transnational NGOs are regularly accused of 'green imperialism' (Grove, 1996, title) through which problem identification, concepts, and approaches are imposed. While some argue that this external interference potentially compromises the economic development of countries in the Global South (Weiner, 2005), others criticise that 'environmental crises provide the necessary pretext for outside intervention' (Bassett, Blanc-Pamard, & Boutrais, 2003, p. 71) and instrumentalise these crises to advance alternative agendas. In the context of a climate-change-related resurge of protectionism (Dressler, Büscher, Schoon, Brockington, et al., 2010), Fairhead et al. (2012) describe what they term 'green grabbing' as 'an emerging process of deep and growing significance' (p. 238). They differentiate between two modes of land appropriation for environmental ends. First, green credentials are called upon to justify land grabbing, for instance, when land is appropriated for food or fuel production in an apparent effort to increase the efficiency of farming, alongside food security, and also to alleviate pressure on forests. Furthermore, green grabs result from environmental green agendas, which include biodiversity conservation, biocarbon sequestration, biofuel production, ecosystem services, ecotourism, and 'offsets' related to all mentioned. Both can involve either complete alienation of the concerned land or restructuring access, use, and management rules and authorities. The authors further argue that while being ostensibly in line with colonial and neo-colonial resource alienation for conservation purposes, the 'valuation, commodification and markets for pieces and aspects of nature' (Fairhead et al., 2012, p. 237) was novel. A further challenge is posed by the fact that, despite community involvement having become the new orthodoxy of development and conservation actors, this involvement is often more pragmatic than programmatic in that there are 'blueprints' for community conservation projects and initiatives (Weisser, Doevenspeck, Müller-Mahn, & Bollig, 2011; Weisser, Bollig, Doevenspeck, & Müller-Mahn, 2013). Such blueprints often come in the form of 'best practices'. Yet, the idea that 'right practices' or 'right policies' might be identified and generalised is a 'historic artefact', according to Adams and Hulme (2001, p. 22).

Dressler et al. (2010) identified a clear standardisation of community-based natural resource-management (CBNRM) programmes, policies, and practices in a comparative study, which led to programmes being misaligned with local realities. Analysing the influence of conservation 'blueprints' on outcomes in terms of visible improvements in the environment in Bhutan, Siebert and Belsky (2014) associate the fact that most environmental analyses and conservation programmes continued ignoring complex historical dynamics and hold local producers and communities responsible for environmental changes and destruction with the adoption of internationally inspired 'one-size-fits-all' conservation models. The impossibility of defining universally applicable 'best practices' emphasises that sound analyses of a given context remain essential for conceptualising successful, efficient, and sustainable projects (Coe et al., 2014; Smith-Dumont et al., 2017). Finding a solution, however 'clumsy' it may be, to overcome the tension between imposing blueprints and genuine bottom-up planning, which, specifically, is flexible enough to allow for the inclusion of pre-existing social institutions, is, however, not easy when setting up guidelines for participatory initiatives, particularly if they are implemented over a broad geographical scale (Martin, 2005). Various authors nonetheless insist (Coe et al., 2014; Dressler et al., 2010) that the more general political and economic dynamics that constrain and negatively influence CBNRM spaces, and hence 'context', need to be analysed, understood, and strategically addressed to have a chance at achieving the dual objective of environmental conservation and livelihood enhancement.

In response to the extraversion and 'green imperialism' paradox, intellectuals such as Professor Wangari Maathai have long called upon African countries to develop a shared vision, a joint African agenda, to emancipate conservation policies from donor funds and external influence. Specifically, Maathai insisted that African countries, including Kenya, should implement environmental conservation measures that do not require much money, and promote tree planting, rainwater harvesting, soil erosion prevention, and wetland protection 'instead of just looking up to the West for aid'.[6] Maathai's arguments are important because they highlight that conservation does not need to be expensive and that conservation priorities can and should be, defined 'at home'. Her argument also alludes to the fact that challenges, such as the environmental crisis in the Mau Forest, need to be addressed intentionally and deliberately to effect change. As long as priorities and activities are funded and designed by external actors, it will remain possible and sometimes legitimate to criticise the objectives and strategies of these activities; whereas conservation actors might face fewer challenges and less opposition on the ground if they were designed and funded by some of 'their own'. Demonstrated political will through manifested agency could contribute to increased local appropriateness, inclusion, and 'ownership' and be more mindful of the tension between different sets of traditional ecological knowledge and different 'conservationisms'.

Since the ICS/KWTA tasked with implementing the 'Save the Mau' initiative almost exclusively depended on donor funds, this was vulnerable to strings attached to the money provided by external donors [1/010]. These strings involved conditionalities at various levels. This external influence was evident in the very institutional set-up of the water towers' managing agency, institutionalised in the KWTA. The European Union (EU) had supposedly signalled interest in investing more in Kenya's water towers to combat climate change, but only if long-term measures were taken, which required the KWTA be created first [1/022]. The external influence was also obvious in the approach taken to address the water tower crises, which focused on the promotion of livelihoods-based activities in response to a problem definition

6   Ndegwa, A., 'Maathai: Why overdepend on donor funds?', *The Standard*, 14 October 2009, p. 10.

along the lines of the Poverty-Environment Nexus. In that vein, external actors rather supported on-farm forestry for wealth creation, following the principle that 'people who make money forget about government forests' [1/021] than focusing on the slippery territory of benefit sharing through 'real' participatory forest management; and effectively drove the 'Save the Mau' initiative however they wanted, independently from the initial evictions. The external influence was also visible in the precise trees and crops to promote, for instance, the European Commission's Euro 300 million ($350 million) project promoting bamboo in the northern parts of the Mau Forest. According to the ICS/KWTA forestry specialist, the EU's interests defined the environmental management docket in Kenya the most [1/022], despite the USA's leadership in the coordination and implementation of activities of external actors in the forest and wildlife sectors during the period of 2007–2012, according to the Kenya Joint Assistance Strategy (KJAS). This was discontinued after 2012, and other aid effectiveness arrangements were pursued through the Government's Second Medium Term Plan towards achieving its Vision 2030, covering 2013 to 2017 (Asuna, 2014).

In the absence of a robust independent agenda based on strong policies and enabled implementing institutions, external actors remained free to implement activities however they liked, with very few requirements regarding accountability for project approaches and contents. While it might be unrealistic that the Government will entirely reject donor funds and activities in the environmental field any time soon, more decisive guidance and coordination, and the creation and implementation of mechanisms that hold actors accountable, could go a long way in ensuring increased sustainability of activities implemented on the ground. Such activities should promote the development of local livelihoods that is conscious of future climate and builds on nature and ecosystem services.

3) Spatially separate commercial forest development from forest conservation sites

In discussions about the Mau crisis, observers questioned and speculated about why the protection of other environmental hotspots, specifically other water towers, was relatively more successful than the rehabilitation of the Mau Forest, despite the regional importance and the advanced state of destruction of the latter. The main difference between the Mau and most of the other water towers, for instance, the Aberdare Forest and the Mount Kenya, was that these latter had been subjected to the national park regime since the 1950s, while the Mau Forest was 'merely' a gazetted public forest. This difference in legal status was accompanied by vast disparities in management structures and mechanisms, which also illustrated the difference in the primary roles attributed to them over time. This third main recommendation addresses the commercial forestry industry (see Chapter 2).

Attribute and enact differential legal statuses for different forest areas

Due to their placement under the national park regime, the forest in the Aberdares and Mount Kenya regions, for instance, had been relatively well conserved, and both areas had largely maintained their water tower functions over time. It could be argued that the primary indigenous forest they contained played an important role in maintaining the ecological balance required for the wildlife and scenery of these parks, and thus for the continuation of tourism ventures in the area, which might have 'saved' them from being deforested. The protection of these forests hence paid tribute to the legacy of historical approaches to environmental conservation in Kenya, which had focused on wildlife rather than wider biodiversity or forest conservation since colonial times. The organisations behind the total fencing of the Aberdare National Park, credited as the main drivers of environmental conservation in the area, were prominent conservation organisations whose primary interest remained wildlife, exemplified even in the leading NGO's name, Rhino Arc. Overall, as everywhere in the country, this National Park's management was assumed by the KWS, and the KFS had no stakes in the forests therein. The difference in legal status was an expression of the state taking a 'developer' role in the Mau and a 'protector' role in the other water towers.

Based on this difference in legal status, the state implemented vastly different management practices in the Mau Forest and the two other major water towers on the ground. Fundamentally, commercial forest production through the continuous development and exploitation of forest plantations only existed within the Mau Forest. Here, the establishment and management of commercial forest plantations with exotic tree species had overridden the preservation of primary forests since the 1930s and accelerated tremendously in the 1990s. Commercial forest production continued being spearheaded by the KFS, which had taken over the Forest Department's role in 2007. The destruction of the primary forest in the Mau did not have any immediate economic consequences since commercial forest production was guaranteed through forest plantations and because there were no direct implications for tourism. Its deforestation, on the contrary, provided short-term benefits to the elites with access to these forest resources, specifically through land speculation and crop farming. On the other hand, the national park status of the Aberdare and Mount Kenya had kept the massive land grabbing and forest encroachment that could be witnessed in the Mau Forest to a minimum.

Due to the difference in legal status, the role attributed to the forest differed considerably. Access to land for ordinary people and larger-scale investors was also fundamentally different, and management was assumed by different authorities and followed different sets of priorities. While the restrictive national park regime came with its challenges, the differences between the crisis in the Mau and challenges experienced in other water towers, or important biodiversity hotspots, were impossible to overlook.

The case of the Mau Forest, altogether, shows that forest production is questionable when achieved through forest plantations composed of exotic tree species that are developed and located on land that initially held primary forest and whose ecological importance goes beyond the value of the harvested trees. Removing forest plantations from primary forest land and establishing sustainable forest plantations on alternative land might be the only solution to addressing other drivers of non-protection, including socio-cultural ones.

In that vein, while most Mariashoni residents insisted on wanting to continue living in Mariashoni, several community members argued that, in the first instance, different 'zones' should be defined within the area to overcome confusion about the official boundaries between Public Forest Land and Private Land. At present, most residents did not define the area they lived in, the 'here' around them, as forest, but only the 'there', where the intact forest cover remained. De facto, the Mariashoni area was subdivided into three zones. The first zone included the area of the 'settlement' scheme that was initially surveyed, demarcated, and individual plots allocated in 1997. The second zone was the 'transition' zone, into which the settlement had been expanded beyond the surveyed area and in which a de facto settlement zone was created. It was here as well that the highest degrees of forest destruction were observed [1/030]. The third zone was the 'forest' zone with remaining government forest, including primary forest patches and forest plantations. While both the indigenous and the plantation forests were defined as one 'zone', these could also be defined as two different zones.

Define context-specific land and governance regimes for different forest areas

The spatial separation of forest production and conservation sites could also be accompanied by different land and governance regimes since lacking security of tenure was an essential contributor to unsustainable land-use practices among Mariashoni dwellers. However, since 'fences and fines approaches' had neither led to ecological nor social sustainability, including communities in forest management would be a moral and practical necessity. Since the communities' sense of lacking tenure security was a significant crisis contributor, this tenure will have to be considered comprehensively, albeit it should not automatically be equated with securing tenure through individual private property rights alone. Clearer land rights, and zoning of the land, could help to prevent the 'cut and run' attitude that had engulfed the area, which was also related to the fact that residents were not sure whether they might eventually be evicted from the area altogether [5/221]. According to this argument, increased security of tenure would encourage longer-term thinking and further investment in the sustainable use of the land. Many residents equated secured tenure with being given title deeds, which would foster a sense of 'being home' and hence encourage people to take care of their home [5/222, 5/224]; provided, however, that private property documents would not be used to allocate forest land to people from outside the forest. While land tenure is recognised as a central factor that influences land use and conservation, including in the community conservation literature, research has shown that land property rights regimes do not necessarily determine the success or failure of specific natural resource-management initiatives (Feeny, Berkes, McCay, & Acheson, 1990). However, due to the historical sensitisation of Mariashoni residents to the land question, many Ogiek residents specifed secure tenure as a precondition for engagement in long-term conservation measures.

Such security of tenure might, for instance, be envisaged by establishing two different legal regimes for the spatially differentiated production and conservation sites. Conservation sites could be registered as 'core catchment areas' in which the nature and extent of human activity are clearly regulated. It could be possible to define permitted land use in line with 'traditional' hunter-gatherer livelihood activities. Yet, legitimacy of presence and land use, and hence 'belonging', could be less defined by ethnicity and ancestry, as attempted by the Ogiek register (GoK, 2010a, 2010d) and the referral to a community's 'traditional' identity in line with colonial ethno-spatial ascriptions (Barrow, Gichohi, & Infield, 2001), but by adopting a practice-driven definition of what a hunter-gatherer identity entails. In practice, those who adhere to 'traditional' non-harmful ways of living and who would want to live and dwell within these spaces could do so. In terms of governance, it might be possible to set these areas up as 'core catchment conservancies', in which largely 'traditional' socio-spatial patterns of land use and governance could be maintained, including common land tenure. However, such adoption would have to be defined by a conscious process to ensure that 'tradition' is defined in a way that avoids elite capture and ontological traps. Several residents supported the idea of maintaining a 'forest' zone that could be fenced off to the general public and whose access should be regulated, while various user rights could be granted through one single authority's office [5/210]. Others proposed a further subdivision of the 'forest' zone into two zones, one that should remain relatively freely accessible for those who qualified as legitimate stakeholders that could be used to hang beehives and to graze cows, and one in which water sources would be closed off entirely for exclusive biodiversity conservation [5/245]. In these areas, explicit and planned forest succession should include sustainable phasing out of exotic trees and reforestation with native and threatened species, and support for natural regeneration of indigenous trees.

On the other hand, more 'development'-oriented community members could be relocated to downstream areas where they could pursue more sedentary lifestyles. In their case, the definition of 'community' would neither be 'identitary' nor necessarily practice-based, but largely interest-based. The latter could also be supported to engage in sustainable forest production activities, including on-farm forestry, PELIS, and forest plantation establishment within the ecologically less crucial downstream areas. Such zoning would be largely in line with the Government's attempt to define and differentiate non-critical areas within the Mau Forest from the 'critical water catchment areas' in which 'prescribed farming' could be maintained, which was described as one of the KWTA's main objectives for Phase IV [1/040]. Several residents made specific suggestions about how they could practically contribute to forest rehabilitation. One suggestion was that individual landowners could contribute to improving the environment within the zone defined as 'settlement' by being obliged to plant trees [5/228]. Tree planting on private farms, or on-farm forestry, had supposedly been low due to insecurities about the future, leading residents to cut and sell their trees without considering replanting [5/213]. If the 'settlement' area was clearly defined, such hesitance could be overcome. Furthermore, beyond only obliging residents to plant trees, tree quotas could be imposed for Private Land holdings, which could revolve around the 10% tree cover stipulated in Kenya's Vision 2030. One local KFS officer proposed that 10% tree cover could be achieved by planting sixty-four trees per acre, which, he said, was easy to achieve [5/123]. To improve the impact of such on-farm forestry on the overall forest cover, trees could be planted in rows that connect various individual plots to form long continuous forest tracks, one resident suggested [5/199]. Tree removal from farms could also be regulated, and permits could be allocated only if the removed trees were replaced by a pre-defined number of new trees, perhaps three, suggested another resident [5/255]. Better regulation of agricultural practices could also be important, including restricted use of chemical farm inputs and restrictions on cultivation close to the river and in swampy areas [5/173]. However, such regulations would need to be realistic about the changes that the forest-dwelling communities had experienced, including the adoption of small-scale cultivation as primary income-generating activity, and not recommend that people return to 'how life was before', one person cautioned [5/224]. Another person said the *shamba* system continued to be a useful instrument combining food security, income generation, and forest conservation [5/236]. Peru's experience with agroforestry concessions is interesting in this regard. This innovative legal provision anchored in the country's forest law grants farmers at the agricultural frontier specific land-use rights, while observing compliance with the maintenance of tree cover, the adoption of context-specific agroforestry, as well as soil and water conservation practices (Robiglio & Reyes, 2016).

While Kenya's 2010 Constitution legally recognised hunter-gatherer communities' rights to land, which was further addressed in the 2016 Community Land Act, Manji (2014) proposes that the 'neoliberal global land policy' agenda pursued by the World Bank and bilateral donors focused more on 'superficial redistribution' based on compulsory land registration, rather than on equitable land redistribution, and emphasised individualisation of land tenure, while 'embedding in law a presumption against customary tenure' (p. 126). Alden Wily and Mbaya (2001) also hypothesised that this non-recognition of customary tenure regimes by the state law might have led to other PFM propositions not having been taken up as viable options by the concerned communities. If a spatial separation of forest production and conservation sites was to be pursued, and community members were to be included both through physical presence and participation in governance, governance models of these spaces could be different. A conservancy-type group tenure security based on context-specific historical socio-spatial organisation patterns, however, without individual private property rights to land, might be a possible solution for the forest conservation sites. In contrast, the more commodified production sites could either remain under Public Land status, with secure land-use and tenure rights being guaranteed, or be privatised altogether, but on the condition that certain sustainable production practices and targets be observed.

While the current laws do not explicitly exclude such 'partial' solutions, more guidance is required in law and from decision-makers on how to navigate potential solutions to the 'Mau question' and on how to anticipate and prevent clashes with state interests in maintaining forest tenure and ownership by creating co-benefits.

4) Find sustainable solutions for land and land-use claims

The scramble for land was one of the main drivers of the scramble for the Mau Forest, and the absence of a political consensus on how to solve land claims contributed considerably to the failure to 'Save the Mau'. Yet, beyond looking at the overall spatial reorganisation and separation of production and conservation sites, decisive decisions must be made on individual persons' and groups' land claims, including both the 'Ogiek question' and the overall compensation question. This fourth main recommendation addresses the political economy of land and the politics of belonging and exclusion (see Chapters 3 and 4).

Identify a solution to the Ogiek land claims

Deciding how to go about the forest dwellers' land claims is, first, a matter of defining human activity about their environment, and hence whether the conceptualisation of nature that underlies the forest reha- bilitation effort emphasises an exclusionist or inclusionist approach to biodiversity conservation (Neumann, 1998; Proctor, 1998; Sills, 1975; Southgate & Hulme, 2000; Weiner, 2005; Woodhouse, Bernstein, & Hulme, 2000). Considering that considerable blame for forest destruc- tion was discursively put on the forest dwellers and that conserva- tion practices in Kenya historically tended towards 'fences and fines approaches', the Mau Forest Rehabilitation Programme initially pursued a total removal of forest dwellers. Given the considerable back- lash to this approach at the national level and rallying of support for the Ogiek cause, citing human rights arguments, but also in line with conceptual and political evolutions recognising the traditional ecolog- ical knowledge of forest-dwelling communities and the inevitability of including both their knowledge and their interests through their active inclusion in community-based natural resource management (CBNRM), and particularly CFM, the Government later announced that the Ogiek had a categorical right to their ancestral homeland. This association between an 'ethnic' group and specific territory goes back to the establishment of ethnic reserves under colonial rule (Barrow et al., 2001). This acknowledgement, however, engendered the compli- cated task of defining who was Ogiek and who was not, and hence who was a legitimate forest dweller and who was not, and who among those who had been evicted from the forest had been displaced 'legitimately' and should be left to their fate, and who, on the other hand, deserved to be resettled since forest evictions illegitimately made them IDPs.

Despite the ICS' strong opposition to labelling forest evictees as IDPs [1/018], a label that amalgamated various groups of people in Kenya displaced for various reasons and whose situation had remained a thorn in every government's foot, the public push and pull between the ICS and then-Prime Minister Raila Odinga on the one hand and political opponents surrounding then-Minister for Agriculture William Ruto on the other hand, Raila effectively became the 'face of the evic- tions' [1/008]. In response, Raila attempted to gather support for their resettlement. In that vein, a 'Committee on the resettlement of the Mau IDPs' was appointed in September 2011. The Committee – which included powerful politicians including Kipkelion MP Labosso Koness, as well as Bifwoli Wakoli and James Orengo, under the leadership of

Franklin Bett[7] – was tasked to identify suitable land for the resettlement of the evictees in the proximity of the Mau, including in Nakuru,
Kericho, Bomet, and Kuresoi. Identifying suitable resettlement land
proved complex since only Public Land could be allocated for resettlement by transforming it into Community or Private Land. Yet, the
Government encountered challenges in identifying suitable land since
land used for resettlement needed to be free of claims, especially ancestral claims, since such claims could engender more court cases [1/018].
Attempts to allocate land to the Mau IDPs on a 30,000-acre piece of land
in Mau Narok in 2011 and 2012 failed because the local Maasai community claimed ownership of the land that had previously been taken
by the colonial government and consecutively been grabbed by various
government elites. After that, the land was given out to multiple contenders, particularly members of the Kipsigis community, in exchange
for political support in favour of family members of the powerful Paramount Chief Ole Ntutu [1/005, 1/009]. The deal hence fell through.
Another attempt by the NLC to allocate land to the Ogiek in the Eastern
Mau failed in 2016 due to claims to the land by various individuals and
groups that had previously been given land in the area. The NLC was
stopped through an injunction from a Nakuru court, where more than
4,900 residents of Nessuit had sued the NLC for infringement on their
land rights in case the commission allocated the land to the Ogiek. The
plaintiffs also requested to be given title deeds for the land they occupied instead of issuing title deeds to the Ogiek.[8]

Hence, members of the Ogiek community continued facing land-
lessness, either because they had been left out during the initial land
allocations in 1997 or because they had sold the land they had initially
been given and because they had moved deeper into the forest reserves.
In the Mau rehabilitation exercise context, discussions about moving
the Ogiek out of the critical water catchment area in Mariashoni and
resettling them elsewhere or evicting them altogether if they failed to
prove their 'Ogiek-ness' contributed to increasing the overall vulnerability of the Ogiek. Following the argument of Mariashoni's famous
Ogiek leader, there were only two solutions to the 'Ogiek question'.
The first option would be to confirm the legality of the settlement of
those Ogiek who already obtained land in 1997 and settle the ones who
had not received land within formally and legally agreed settlement
boundaries. The second option would be to relocate the Ogiek outside

---

[7]   The Government initially wanted to appoint Gideon Moi, son of former
President Daniel arap Moi, as chairman of the committee but his nomination
was withdrawn after Raila Odinga's staunch opposition [1/031].
[8]   Openda, J., 'Court stops NLC from settling Ogieks on disputed Mau Forest
land', *Daily Nation*, 3 March 2017.

the Mariashoni settlement scheme. Either way, he emphasised, people would need to be given ownership documents [3/056].

Both options are interesting, considering the Ogiek leader's influence on the current status quo in the late 2010s. He was at the forefront of the group of 'traditionalists' who opposed land privatisation and the subdivision in 1997. His charisma and leadership contributed to the mobilisation of legal and political support for the court case that eventually led to an injunction on land allocation during the settlement creation in 1997. It also allowed him to attract international attention to the plight of the Ogiek. The first option he mentioned is particularly interesting because it represents a departure from the initial insistence on a communal land title that would subsequently allow the community members to give out differentiated user rights to individual clans and households to retain traditional Ogiek socio-spatial organisation in an altered environment. The first option that the Ogiek leader proposed hence basically implies support for what had initially been proposed in 1997: the individual allocation of land to individual Ogiek households, as long as individual land allocation was not used as a vehicle to bring in members of other communities. The second option, a relocation of the Mariashoni Ogiek to another area altogether, is also interesting since it is in line with government suggestions to take the Ogiek settlement out of the biodiversity hotspots, specifically the critical water catchment areas, and to relocate the community further downstream. However, such exercises bear many risks and require in-depth agro-ecological analyses to confirm the suitability of various proposed areas. Such suitability would have to straddle different sets of realities since members of the Ogiek community had largely diversified from the traditional hunter-gatherer lifestyle into more sedentarised small-scale agricultural livelihoods. Since many members of the Ogiek community maintained some aspects of their traditional lifestyles – and often a considerable attachment to the cold and montane environment – and continued using tree products and forest areas for spiritual practices, access to these places would have to be guaranteed as well. A third option, which Mariashoni's Ogiek leader did not mention, would be to pursue a PES in which the Ogiek would be allowed to remain in the Mariashoni area but under strict and specific conditions related to acceptable practices in the area. At the same time, it might be impossible to improve and ensure such conditions due to the important changes in the overall community, especially if commercial forestry continues to be permitted in the forest. It is also important to consider that compliance and satisfaction among the members of the Ogiek would not automatically be assured, considering changes in lifestyles and livelihood strategies witnessed in the area and the considerable generational divide among the Mariashoni Ogiek, even if the Ogiek land question was addressed in a manner that satisfies the 'traditional' Ogiek leadership. Altogether, the proposed differential land and governance regimes for *here* and *there* could be explored in response to the 'Ogiek question' as well.

Either option of land redistribution in favour of members of the Ogiek community in Mariashoni would require a previous decision from the High Court in the 1997 Ogiek land case, which had seemed attainable under Chief Justice Willy Mutunga, who had been appointed in June 2011, but less so since his resignation and the appointment of David Maraga as Chief Justice in September 2016.[9]

Identify a solution to other stakeholders' land claims

Apart from defining which place human activity should have in overall biodiversity conservation and how to identify those whose active inclusion in the management of the resource can be considered as being aligned with conservation objectives, and after that identifying land that could indeed be given to them, the difficulty of resettling forest evictees was also related to the fate of those who fell into the category of 'the others'. The question of 'the others' also included questions about potential compensation for those who were not part of the 'local community' but who held lands within the Mau, including big and small land beneficiaries. While the Government initially announced that no compensation would be paid at all and later that compensation would only be paid to third-party land purchasers, the compensation discussion opened a Pandora's box since it necessitated an analysis of the modes of land acquisition in the first place.

This book addresses various instances in which people were brought into the forest, either without paying for their land or who had been encouraged to exchange their land outside of the forest for bigger pieces of land inside the forest, who might legitimately be called 'third-party purchasers', and who hence might be absolved from the responsibility and consequences for occupying forest land illegally. At the same time, discussions about forest evictions and resettlements also brought about 'fake IDPs' [1/005], which added an extra layer of complexity to the definition of legitimacy in the forest. In the South-West Mau, for instance, evictions were carried out in November 2009, during which approximately 4,000 households were evicted. Consequently, ten IDP camps were set up close to the new forest boundary, in which those forest dwellers who could not relocate elsewhere found refuge. At the same time, two 'fake camps' came up as well, where people from the surrounding areas had built shelters, hoping to benefit from relief aid [2/046]. While the Government claimed to have evicted around 3,000

---

9   Maraga is commonly portrayed as being close to President Kenyatta; an allegation he refutes after the President alluded to the same; Muthoni, K., 'Chief Justice Maraga tells President Uhuru Kenyatta he is not his project', *The Standard*, 11 April 2017.

households from the South-West Mau, William Ruto and his allies claimed the figure was closer to 10,000 households; displaying the discrepancy between potential beneficiary numbers for compensation and resettlement, and powerfully illustrating the implications that such differences in estimates can potentially have [1/008]. In 2009, the Land Audit Committee of the Prime Minister's Taskforce on the Mau advised the Government that for the eastern parts of the Mau Forest alone, which included areas in Sigotik, Nessuit, Baraget, Ngongongeri, Sururu, Teret, Likia and Likia Extension, Mariashoni, and Kapsita Elburgon settlement schemes, approximately KES 38 billion ($380 million) would be required if the one hundred thousand households identified by then were to be compensated.[10] By inflating beneficiary lists, politicians practised 'political sabotage' of the conservation agenda 'because people have learned to use politics and flooded in camps as soon as registers for possible compensation schemes were to be completed' [1/002], whose costs hence became impossible to shoulder. The compensation question was crucial for those who had obtained land illegally and had been fighting hard not to lose their privileges, even at the price of derailing the entire Mau rehabilitation exercise [1/005].[11] In sum, solutions will have to be found for these other forest dwellers, both the big and the small land beneficiaries. These solutions will have to be enacted comprehensively to avoid simply shifting people, and their interests and problems, from one area within the forest to another.

Beyond that, fraudulent privatisation and allocation of forest land to individual beneficiaries had already become more complex during the 2010s. On the one hand, important changes were introduced in land regulation and management, primarily through the enactment of the 2009 National Land Policy and the 2010 Constitution, as well as the enactment of various land Acts and the set-up of the NLC, which rendered new conversion of Public Forest Land to Private Land almost impossible. Beyond that, these changes can potentially affect the recovery of previously converted and misallocated land. Provisions on minimum and maximum land holdings, for instance, might potentially convince large landowners to sell their land. Furthermore, Chapter 6 of the Constitution, also called the Integrity Chapter, already encouraged some 'former crooks' to surrender some of their illegally obtained land during the transition phase due to the increased focus on the Mau Forest [1/022] and could continue to do so.

Despite these significant changes, the Government at large and individual government actors continued using the Mau Forest, particularly

---

[10] Ochami, D., 'How land audit advised State on Mau', *The Standard*, 3 August 2009.

[11] See also: Munyeki, J., 'Rift Valley MPs oppose phase three Mau evictions', *The Standard*, 27 March 2010.

secure access to land, as a prime political resource. For instance, rhetoric about giving out land and promising title deeds to forest dwellers
was witnessed in the Mau during the 2013 and 2017 general election
campaigns. In March 2016, for example, Cabinet supposedly approved
the excision of 17,000 ha of land in the Mau Forest, a move vehement-
ly opposed by various civil society actors.[12] Later, in mid-2017, both
Deputy President William Ruto and President Uhuru Kenyatta supposedly promised compensation to those evicted from the Maasai Mau and
announced 'no-one will evict them again'; again staunchly opposed by
civil society and local elders.[13] Similar announcements on the lifting
of the caveat on the Mau Forest, and hence on the ban on transactions
of land imposed in 2008, had been made by government officials in
2013 and 2016; which had attracted widespread criticism in the media
as well.[14]

Altogether, solving the environmental crisis in the Mau Forest will
require staunch action from the Government about land, which will
necessarily involve taking a stand about whether settlers will have
to evacuate the area, whether the Ogiek will be given preferential
treatment, whether this preferential treatment will include a right to
remain within the Mau Forest, and most of all whether those who own
or occupy land will be compensated. While reasonable arguments can
be made in favour and against compensation, decisions must be made.

After the political change in 2013, discussions about the recovery
of Public Land within the Mau Forest, alongside discussions about the
rehabilitation of the forest itself, largely subsided. The question at the
core of the land problem failed to be addressed as well.

5) Re-frame the crisis, embrace complexity and address it holistically

There were two main 'themes' in popular and government explanations
for the destruction of the Mau Forest: On the one hand, forest-dwelling
and forest-adjacent communities were blamed for resource over-use
and poverty-related environmental destruction, and on the other hand
'institutional failure' was held responsible for laws and provisions
not having been implemented that should have saved the forest from

---

[12] Editorial, 'Stop latest plot to kill the Mau Forest', *Daily Nation*, 24 March
2016; Mutambo, A., 'Rights group oppose 'proposed' 17,000ha Mau Forest allocations', *Daily Nation*, 22 March 2016; Kiplagat, R., 'Maasai community oppose
excision of forest', *The Standard*, 25 March 2016.
[13] Mbula, R., 'Don't use Mau Forest to woo voters, elders warn politicians',
Daily Nation, 16 July 2017.
[14] Nation correspondent, 'Governor wants caveats on Mau forest land lifted',
Daily Nation, 15 October 2013; Kirui, K. 'Mau Forest land caveat will soon be
lifted, Tunai promises', *The Star*, 17 August 2016.

being destroyed. The question about which institutions arguably failed at which levels was hardly addressed. As previously discussed, the Mau crisis was attributed to both supposed causes in relatively simple one-liners without embracing much complexity.

This book, however, has shown that a complex interaction of factors contributed to the political ecology of the Mau Forest and hence the destruction and the perpetuation of environmental degradation in the Mau Forest, and that a multitude of factors need to be considered when attempting to 'Save the Mau'. Fundamentally, the complexity and the multiplicity of identities, interests, and preferences between and within groups and individual stakeholders must be recognised and addressed comprehensively. These identities, interests, and preferences, with all their internal tensions and deliberations, determine the structures, mechanisms, and outcomes of the decision-making processes of those individuals and groups. They also allow explanations of why it is possible at the same time to criticise the role that the Government, timber companies, and 'big men' play in land grabbing, land-use change, forest destruction, and deforestation, while somewhat peacefully engaging in their small-scale timber businesses. The various rationalities at play effectively act as alternative narratives of forest life and illustrate that different 'conservationisms' can co-exist in the same area, among the same groups of people, and even in the same individual persons.

A solution to this complex interaction between various push-and-pull factors will require decisive political will and a manifestation and translation of that political will into enabled institutions and relevant activities on the ground. Several issues will remain particularly critical. It will, for instance, continue to be challenging to encourage forest dwellers, whether members of indigenous communities or not, to conserve the forest and appreciate 'the honey rather than the money' from trees until commercial forest production is taken out of primary forests that are the guarantors of the ecosystem services that are associated with water towers. Forest-based livelihood activities can be very well in line with forest conservation and rehabilitation, but areas under imminent natural regeneration must be managed carefully to protect them from accidental disturbance. Such livelihoods can, however, only be sustainable if engagement in short-dated income-generating strategies that involve the destruction rather than the valorisation of the forest and the trees is not more attractive than more sustainable livelihood set-ups and if the social acceptability of engaging in such ephemeral practices is maintained at and/or reduced to a minimal level. While evictions and resettlements of forest dwellers might not be achievable, for various reasons, there are other ways of phasing out undesirable activity, for instance, by restricting inheritance of land leading to a natural reduction of population numbers on the land.

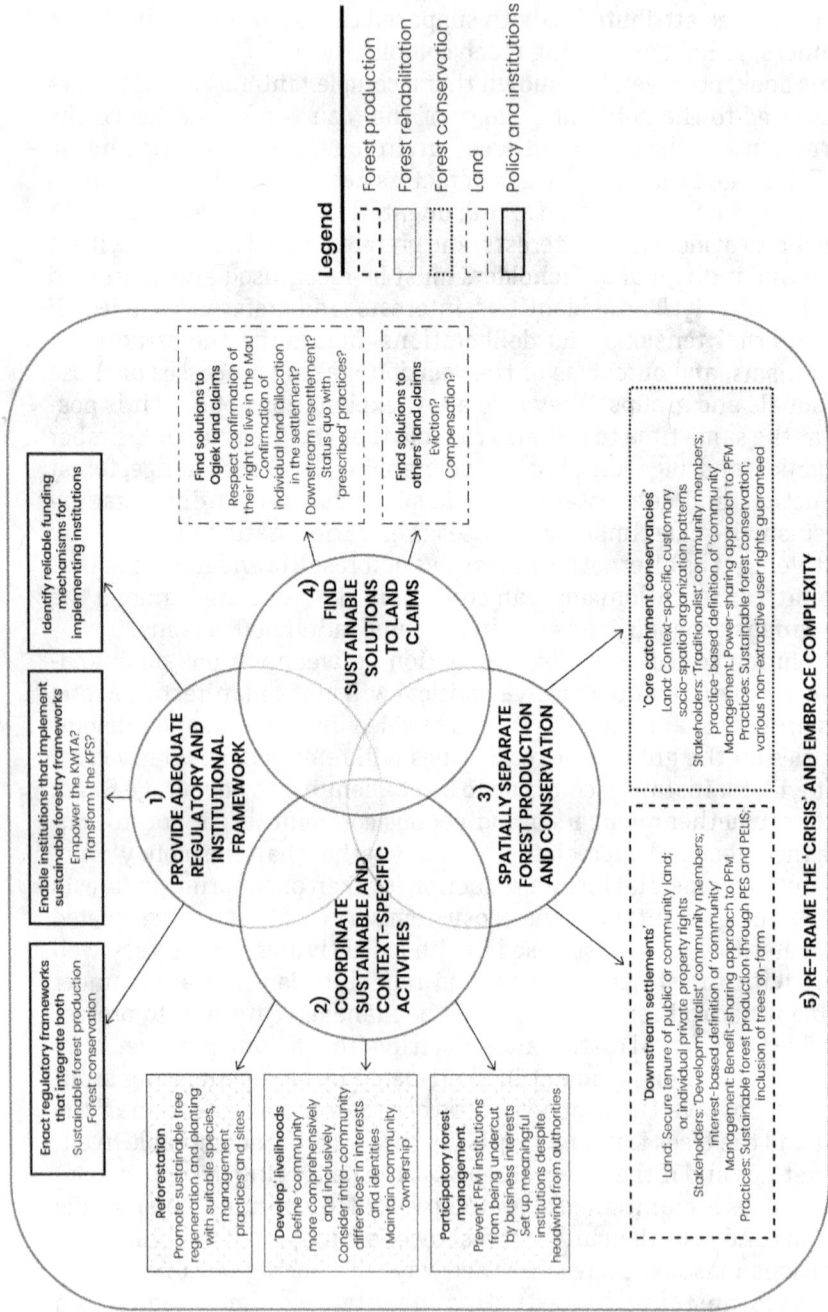

Legend

- Forest production
- Forest rehabilitation
- Forest conservation
- Land
- Policy and institutions

1) PROVIDE ADEQUATE REGULATORY AND INSTITUTIONAL FRAMEWORK

Enact regulatory frameworks that integrate both
- Sustainable forest production
- Forest conservation

Enable institutions that implement sustainable forestry frameworks
- Empower the KWTA?
- Transform the KFS?

Identify reliable funding mechanisms for implementing institutions

2) COORDINATE SUSTAINABLE AND CONTEXT-SPECIFIC ACTIVITIES

Reforestation
- Promote sustainable tree regeneration and planting with suitable species, management practices and sites

'Develop' livelihoods
- Define 'community' more comprehensively and inclusively
- Consider intra-community differences in interests and identities
- Maintain community 'ownership'

Participatory forest management
- Prevent PFM institutions from being undercut by business interests
- Set up meaningful institutions despite headwind from authorities

3) SPATIALLY SEPARATE FOREST PRODUCTION AND CONSERVATION

'Downstream settlements'
- Land: Secure tenure of public or community land; or individual private property rights
- Stakeholders: 'Developmentalist' community members; interest-based definition of 'community'
- Management: Benefit-sharing approach to PFM
- Practices: Sustainable forest production through PES and PELIS; inclusion of trees on-farm

'Core catchment conservancies'
- Land: Context-specific customary socio-spatial organization patterns
- Stakeholders: 'Traditionalist' community members; practice-based definition of 'community'
- Management: Power-sharing approach to PFM
- Practices: Sustainable forest conservation; various non-extractive user rights guaranteed

4) FIND SUSTAINABLE SOLUTIONS TO LAND CLAIMS

Find solutions to Ogiek land claims
- Respect confirmation of their right to live in the Mau
- Confirmation of individual land allocation in the settlement?
- Downstream resettlement?
- Status quo with 'prescribed practices'?

Find solutions to others' land claims
- Eviction?
- Compensation?

5) RE-FRAME THE 'CRISIS' AND EMBRACE COMPLEXITY

Figure 6 Overview of recommendations on how to 'Save the Mau'.

Source: Author composition based on discussed observations.

Complex solutions for complex problems: A political-ecological
approach to sustainable forest management of the Mau Forest

Altogether, the difference between the results from the political ecology
analysis of the 'politicised environment' within which the 'Save the
Mau' initiative evolved and the conclusions made with regards to the
suitability of the initiative itself, as well as the recommendations
derived, are fundamentally different from what was previously known,
or publicly shared about both the Mau crisis and potential avenues for
'Saving the Mau'.

Hence, the failure of the Mau Forest Rehabilitation Programme can
largely be attributed to the skewed problem analysis upon which the
elaboration of the plan was based, which failed to identify and address
the underlying dynamics of non-protection holistically. Hence, these
complex dynamics were either left unaddressed or approached in a
way that led to the witnessed political gridlock, eventually leading to
a total standstill in the Mau restoration initiative. Given the analysis
presented, deconstructing the Mau crisis might first require shifting
away from the Poverty-Environment Nexus, where poverty is directly
equated with destructive environmental behaviours, to a perspective
where social reality is understood as a function of what *is* rather than
of what *is not*. This shift in focus could liberate forest dwellers from the
patronising and disempowering framing as faceless men and women
whose lives can primarily be defined by what they lack, and could place
them at the centre of a complex mix of actions and interactions that are
inspired by who they are, what they want and what they like. The same
applies to the identified 'institutional failure', which rather simplisti-
cally implies that existing institutions weakly enforced existing laws
rather than identifying the alternative agendas that they, and those in
power of enabling or dis-enabling them, pursued apart from sustainable forest management. The problem is not whether poverty as a driver
of deforestation is realistic or whether failing institutions are an issue.
What is problematic is that the narrative of the destitute forest dwellers who cannot help themselves but to destroy the very environment
that supports, even enables, and conditions their lives, alongside the
narrative of institutions that simply are not able, is incomplete, since
it fundamentally negates the various stakeholders' agency in making
and perpetuating the Mau crisis.

In line with Blaikie's (2012) critique, which called political ecology
out for being 'mostly rooted in academia', the analysis of the dynamics of non-protection and the recommendations formulated to address
these dynamics comprehensively contribute to those works within the
political ecology school of thought that attempt to be explicit about
political goals and that provide strategies to achieve those goals in
pursuit of rendering the produced knowledge accessible, socially rel-

evant and hence 'useful and engaged' (p. 231) beyond university settings. Using a political ecology lens to identify the dynamics of the scramble, and therefore the non-protection of the Mau Forest, allowed defining an alternative narrative of the Mau crisis that might eventually contribute to an improved approach to 'Saving the Mau' after all.

Altogether, this book recognises that the 'Mau Forest Saga',[15] like many so-called environmental crises, involves 'detailed uncertainties that are legitimate subjects for debate' (Diamond, 2005, p. 503). The Mau crisis further displays that beyond being 'boundary objects' (Fujimura, 1992, p. 168) that 'pull together multiple research communities, each with their own institutional involvement, objectives, and, at times, epistemologies' (Timura, 2001, p. 105), environmental crises are intrinsically 'wicked problems' (Rittel & Webber, 1973) that defy rational and optimal solutions. Since such situations involve uncertainty and unpredictability, a plurality of perspectives and interests, complex problems of scale and scientific uncertainty (Gunningham, 2011), solutions are difficult to discern because of the complex interdependencies in the affected systems. In these contexts, solutions to some aspects can reveal and create other, often more complex, problems requiring further solutions (Hulme, 2009).

In that vein, the Mau Forest 'saga' comes close to what Hulme (2009) describes in his book *Why we Disagree about Climate Change*: 'A mega-problem awaiting, demanding, a mega-solution [by constructing it as the] "mother of all problems" – "the (greatest/defining/most serious)* long-term (problem/challenge/threat)*"' (p. 333).[16] In the Mau Forest context, this 'mother of all problems' characteristic involves all kinds of individual issues, including climate change, deforestation, forest destruction, the drying up of vital ecosystems with tremendous economic value, the reduction in rainfall and its effects on the agricultural sector, competition about land and legitimacy, identity crises, corruption, the redefinition of the state, underdevelopment, and so many more which were amalgamated in the 'meta-narrative' (p. 333) of the 'Mau Forest crisis'. Hulme cautions that in doing so, 'a political log-jam of gigantic proportions [was created], one that is not only insoluble, but one that is perhaps beyond our comprehension' (p. 333). He also warns that this amalgamation leads us to 'overestimate the abilities of economics, politics and technologies to tame and master [the problem at hand, and] rely too heavily on either rational choice theory in economics, regime theory in politics, social coercion in behaviour management, or control engineering in

---

[15] See: Mkawale, S., 'The return of Mau Forest politics', *The Standard*, 18 August 2013; Sayagie, G., 'Mau Forest saga returns to haunt DP Ruto, Jubilee', *Daily Nation*, 30 December 2015.
[16] The original has a footnote which explains that the asterisk signifies that terms can be 'deleted as desired'.

the implementation of technology' (p. 336), while underestimating the 'wickedness' of environmental crises. The only solution to this 'wicked problem' is to embrace 'clumsy solutions', which requires that 'multiple values, multiple frameworks and multiple voices be harnessed together – clumsily, contradictorily – in ... response' (p. 338), which, by definition, 'are not only suboptimal in design, they are suboptimal in outcome and their metrics are incommensurable' (p. 339). Following Klooster's (2009) argument, such 'clumsy solutions' require

> flexible integration of local knowledge, scientific forestry, and appro-
> priate institutional parameters to modulate human needs and goals
> with the discordant harmonies of inhabited and heavily used forests
> in a constant state of flux under processes of succession, disturbance,
> and spatial variation (p. 43)

to overcome the 'faulty models, limited and socially inappropriate goals, and incomplete information on basic parameters' (p. 44) that have characterised conventional approaches to resource management.

While the Government's attempt to 'Save the Mau' had hitherto failed, a fundamental shift in the representation of the Mau Forest took place that might potentially contribute to wide-reaching transforma-tions in the future. The Mau Forest used to be primarily understood as a commodity, a place that allowed for the extraction of valuable but replaceable natural resources, and not as a natural environment that required protection and conservation. The limelight surrounding the initiative to 'Save the Mau' contributed to a considerably transformed narrative about the Forest, so that it started to be represented as one of Kenya's most vital natural environments, and not exclusively an exploitable forest, and hence became part of the 'imaginary landscapes' of conservationists, government institutions and the general public, after numerous previous attempts of the local indigenous Ogiek com-munity to attract attention to the degradation of their ancestral home had remained unsuccessful. While the effects of the 'Save the Mau' ini-tiative had remained far behind hopes and expectations, and while it had failed to address and overcome the powerful dynamics of non-pro-tection discussed, at the very least it achieved one considerable change: it forced all stakeholders to consider that a natural environment which had been subjected to commodification and resource exploitation for decades continued being fundamentally a natural environment worthy and also in dire need of protection. It thereby contributed to a consid-erable volte-face in the public acceptance of unsustainable natural resource use and the accompanying commodification of nature. The Mau Forest crisis also mobilised the attention and passion of many who had traditionally not engaged in environmental conservation discus-sions and activities. Environmental protection in terms of wildlife con-servation had traditionally been dominated by the 'old conservation establishment', which somewhat failed to involve younger generations. The Mau Forest crisis, with all its underlying issues and connections to water, climate change, clean air, cool landscapes, food security, and right to life, sparked the interest of the youth and rallied their voices in the call to save it. Consequently, tree-planting drives became social happenings attended by all segments of the Kenyan society.[17] These evolutions resembled what Nixon (2010), who analysed the role played by environmental activists in attracting attention and bringing about change in situations of environmental crises, identified as success factors for Wangari Maathai and her Green Belt Movement (GBM). First, tree planting, beyond serving to increase tree cover, was used to create a symbolic hub for political resistance and to attract media attention to a rather amorphous issue. Second, environmental degradation was powerfully associated with historically founded violent land loss, and the GBM succeeded in fostering debate about the connection between land allocation and environmental crises. Third, the GBM made use of what Nixon (2010) calls 'intersectional environmentalism', in which various other civil rights issues were taken up alongside environmental campaigns, which led to the creation of a narrative that illustrated the political in the environmental.

Even contemporary pop culture seized the momentum and contributed to environmental awareness, including by defining conservation as an issue that affects the youth. In the same vein, knowledgeable observers of the situation opined that 'the youth in this country need to step up to save Kenya's legacy'[18] and that an aware and active youth might hence contribute to finding new ways of addressing climate change and of 'saving the Mau'. Kenyan Poet TearDrops, in his widely performed spoken word piece '7 Billion Dreams, 7 Billion Heartbeats per Second', uses his wit and language to raise the awareness and interest of the young people for the Mau crisis and environmental conservation, combining Swahili and English in poetry in motion. Sarabi, a Kenyan band that made headlines with controversial social-critical lyrics, even sang about the Mau Forest in their song '(Fuata) Sheria' (Follow the Law), in which the band decries widespread corruption in the country. Alluding to the political drivers of the Mau Forest, lead singer Mandela sings *'nani aliuza Mau, na wako wapi Mau Mau'* (who sold the Mau Forest, and where are the Mau Mau).[19] By alluding to the Mau Mau, the rebel group

---

[17] For Environment Day in June 2017, various organisations organised a tree planting drive in the Mau Forest and promoted the activity using the 'hashtag' #TwendeMau.

[18] Mbaria, J., 'Mau is not about settlement of the landless, it's about greed', *Daily Nation*, 2 April 2009.

[19] This highly controversial statement was cut out of the shorter official 'single' version: Sarabi, '(Fuata) Sheria', www.youtube.com/watch?v=8QGx _6lMjGI (published 12 December 2013, accessed 7 August 2017); but can, for

that brought the colonial government to its knees, eventually leading to Kenya's Independence in 1963, Sarabi furthermore frames the Mau Forest issue as one of national importance that requires that all people 'stand up' and take responsibility both for individual behavioural change, and fighting for systemic change.

---

instance, be heard at minute 5:20 in Sarabi 'Sheria' Live at Roskilde Festival 2015, www.youtube.com/watch?v=KBfqRHOwyMU (published 28 October 2015, accessed 7 August 2017).

Appendix 1: Medicinal plants used and inventoried by survey respondents in the Eastern Mau in 2012–2013

Plant names and uses of indigenous trees: '*miti kienyeji*' (indigenous trees), '*miti ya mungu*' (God's trees), '*miti ya dawa*' (medicinal trees).

Indigenous name of plant	Latin name	Common name	Uses	Comments
Aonet / Aounet	*Polyscias fulva* or *Polyscias kikuyensis*		Timber is used on ceiling boards and plywoods. For shade and firewood.	Kipsigis name
Bondet	*Hagea abyssinica*	African redwood, East African Rosewood	Mouth rash. Chest pains. Ribs, joint aches.	Leaves are burned and taken as herbs for babies and adults to treat mouth rash, chest pains and ribs and joint aches.

Local name	Scientific name	Common name	Uses	Notes
Botkawet / Chepkawet	*Phytolacca dodecandra*		For small children's diseases. Skin rashes, acne, pimples, jaundice. Stretchmarks. Asthma, pneumonia, cough. Ringworm. Backache. Inflammation, painful swellings.	It is a poisonous plant and handled with care. Juice from the leaves used for treatment of skin rashes, acne, pimples, stretchmarks. Leaves are burned to ashes and used to treat chronic asthma, pneumonia, backache, cough, ringworm, jaundice, inflammation, and painful swellings.
Busaret / Busarek	*Thunbergia alata*	Black-eyed Susan vine	Chest, stomach.	Burned ash to treat stomach ulcers and oral thrush. Ash is alkaline and neutralises acid in stomach, and changes the pH, killing off most pathogens.
Chebobut			Medicine and for honey.	
Chelumbut / Chelmbut / Chelembut / also Tinet / Chinet	*Schefflera volkensii*		Cold, cough, chest problems. Headache. Pneumonia. For honey. Forage.	Leaves, bark, stem, sap.
Chelwanda	*Amaranthus dubius*	Amaranth	Vegetable, food.	Terere (Swahili).
Chepkimun / Chepkomon	*Caesalpina decapetala*	Mauritius thorn	Rashes. Common cold, tonsilitis.	Leaves are chewed to heal common cold and tonsils. Kipsigis name.

(Appendix 1 continued)

Indigenous name of plant	Latin name	Common name	Uses	Comments
Chepkolokoliot	*Rhamnus prinoides*		Malaria, cold, diarrhoea, for cows; give strength back to weak legs.	Most commonly named for malaria. Powder, mixed with honey, taken before meal, will make someone vomit for hours – after that, the malaria is gone. Mukarakinya or mukarakinga (Kikuyu).
Chepkowet / Chepkawet	*Trimeria grandiflora*		Small kids' sicknesses. Coughs, chest pains. Boost libido in men. Joint pain. Firewood. Landscaping, shades, fencing, home gardens.	Most commonly named for cold. Roots are boiled and taken for coughs, chest pains, libido, joint pains. Leaves are burned and taken as herbs for babies and adults to treat joint and rib aches.
Chepndorwet / Chepindorwet / Chepdorio	*Toddalia asiatica*	Orange climber or Cockspur orange	Cough, cold, malaria, pneumonia, chest. All sicknesses. For cows.	Most commonly named for cough and cold Roots are boiled and taken for chest and leg pains. Fruits are edible and treats common cold and flu. Leaves are burned or boiled for treatment of whooping cough.
Chepsagitiet / Chepsagitiot	*Hoslundia opposita*		Stomach. Used to treat mouth thrush in babies.	Ogiek name.

Chigoweit / Chigowet / Sigowet / Sigogoveit / Sosoireit / Sighoguat / Sigoguet / Sighoweit	*Solanum aculeastrum*	Chest. Tongue problems. Bones, ribs, joints. Cold (for children). Fencing.	Roots are boiled and taken against arthritis due to weakening of bones, joints, coughs, and severe tonsils. Fruits are used to make boils burst, and for injuries from caterpillar stings. Leaves are burned and consumed as herbs for treatment of rib pains and other diseases. Thorns are used to prick out other thorns from those who walk barefoot.
Chorwet	*Pavetta gardeniifolia*	Firewood. Charcoal. Medicine.	Kipsigis name.
Emitiot	*Olea europeana*	Firewood. Fencing.	
Emulliloi		Construction.	Maa name?
Gogogola		Multipurpose, including malaria.	Maa name?
Guluma		Malaria.	Roots.
Indreme / Inderemiat (sing.) / Inderemek (plural) / Nderemiat	*Basella alba*	Cold. Eaten as vegetable.	Leaves are boiled and good source of iron.
Ithuithia		Teeth.	Kikuyu name?

(Appendix 1 continued)

Indigenous name of plant	Latin name	Common name	Uses	Comments
Itet / Eitet	*Senna didimobotrya*		Skin rashes. Ringworm. Insect bites. Cleansing of blood.	Sap from leaves is used to treat skin rashes, ringworm and insect bites. Charcoal from dry branch is used to prepare fermented milk. Roots are used for cleansing of blood. Kipsigis and Ogiek name.
Kamnyalilet / Chepnyaliliet	*Acacia kirkii*		Medicine and for honey. Roots boiled and taken as contraceptive.	
Kanunga (Kikuyu)	*Acacia melanoxylon*	Blackwood	Construction, wood, firewood, charcoal. Stomach. Pollinator bees.	Indigenous tree that used to be common before forest plantations.
Karabwet			For honey.	
Katet	*Dichrostachys cinerea*		Medicine for children.	Kipsigis name.
Kasisidwet / Kesisitiet / Kesiengit			Cold, malaria, running nose and sicknesses of children. For cultural practices.	Considered important and mostly planted in the homesteads.
Ketegan			Cold, cough, lungs.	Powder put in tea.

Names	Scientific name	Uses	Notes
Kibarinyat / Kibranyat / Kiripanyan / Kepranyat / Giparnyat / Gerbanyat / Girbanyat		Joint pain. Beekeeping. Heals the whole body. Cough. Stomach. Washes kidneys.	Used to mix with other herbal medicines to reduce their bitter taste. Boiled in soup.
Kigorwet / Gigorwet		For soup. When cows or kids have chest problems. Thorns are used for body piercings.	Invasive species.
Kimanue		Stomach.	Tugen name?
Kipkoboriet		Beekeeping.	
Korabariat / Korapariat / Gorbariat / Gorapariat / Giribanyeit	*Baddeia polystachya*	Cough, malaria. Stomach, liver, deworming.	
Korobosi / Korombosi / Mkorombosi	*Cornus volkensii*	Chest (cough), malaria. Bees for honey, beehives. Firewood, construction.	Mukorombothi (Kikuyu). Good for charcoal.
Kosisitu / Kosisito / Kosisitiet / Ekosisito / Gosisito	*Rhamnus prinoides* or *Rhamnus staddo*	Splits fatty meat. Joint pain. Stomach. Chest, malaria, cough, cold. Allergy.	Kipsigis name.

(Appendix 1 continued)

Indigenous name of plant	Latin name	Common name	Uses	Comments
Kuriot / Koriot	*Teclea nobilis*	Teclea	Many sicknesses. Roots are used to treat heart diseases and high blood pressure. Good for landscaping.	
Laktanet / Laktanot			When the baby has a cold.	
Langabarra / Langaba Marais			Multipurpose. Malaria. Masala.	Maa name?
Leketetyet	*Akokanthera oppositifolia* or *Akokanthera schimperi*		All sicknesses.	Olmoroijoi (Maa), Kipsigis name.
Lelnet / Leinet / Leldet	*Acacia abyssinica Acacia seyal var. fistula*		Stomach. Cold, mouth rash and pneumonia. Treat born and unborn babies.	Bark is boiled and used to wash, and given babies against cold, mouth rash, and pneumonia. Used by pregnant mothers to treat infections on the foetus.
Makiparinyat			Stomach.	
Manarariat	*Helichrysum schimperi*		Stomach.	
Maraisit			For honey.	

Local name	Scientific name	Common name	Uses	Notes
Masaita	*Olea capensis* subsp. *macrocarpa* or *Olea hochstetteri*	East African Olive / Elgon olive	Malaria. Circumcision (girls). Mouth infection. Joint pain. For livestock. Skin. Beehives.	Might also be called Chorwet. Mucarage / Msharage (Kikuyu).
Mianzi	*Bambusa vulgaries*	Bamboo	Firewood, fencing.	Swahili name.
Mkarasit			Liver.	
Monduleliot			For children.	
Moronget			Stomach upset of children. Malaria. Rashes. Massage oil for soft tissue injuries.	Leaves are used as tissue paper. Leaves are boiled for steaming of the body against skin rashes. Roots can be added to mix of Tendwet, Arorwet against malaria.
Mororta			Lungs. Bee forage. For cultural purposes.	
Mondoyet / Mondoywet	*Phragmanthera rufescens*	Epiphyte	Brings luck.	Put on top of the house for luck.
Muindeiyet / Mindeiywet	*Rumex usambarensis*		Cleans blood. Food.	Leaves are vegetables and are cooked as sour and bitter vegetables to replace tomatoes. Roots are medicinal.
Mindililwet	*Dovyalis abyssinica*		For women.	Mukambura (Kikuyu). Kipsigis.
	Buddleia polystachia		For women.	Muthimbari (Kikuyu)

(Appendix 1 continued)

Indigenous name of plant	Latin name	Common name	Uses	Comments
Mutereriet	*Ehretia cymosa*		Urinary tract infections. Chest, cough. Rashes. Shade. Firewood, fencing.	Bark is used to treat urinary tract infections. Leaves are burned and used to treat common diseases like chest pains, coughs, and skin rashes.
Mwaarubaini	*Azadirachta indica*	Neem	Many diseases. Fencing. Home gardening and shades.	One of the most common medicinal trees said to cure forty diseases. Mwarubaini (Swahili).
Nerubat/ Narubat			Heart problems; cold (children).	Bush.
Ngonyet / Ng'ononyet / Ng'egeonyet / Ng'onoiyet / Ng'onoiyeit / Ng'onoiyet / Ngongyilet/ Chemng'ororiet / Ngonoyoik / Ng'onoiyek	*Pappea capensis*		Chest. Stomach. Malaria. Worms. Heals the whole body. Cold. Knees.	Kipsigis name.
Nukiat / Nukia / Nukiu/ Nukiot / Lukia / Lukiat	*Dovyalis abyssinica*		Coughs, chest pains, and tonsils. Stomach aches. Cleans blood. Home garden and fencing. Firewood. Fruits are edible and nutritious. Malaria.	Roots are boiled and taken for coughs, chest pains, and tonsils, also for stomach ache.

Name	Scientific name	Other name	Uses	Notes
Olgogoloit			Washes blood.	
Olgolnjet			Multipurpose, including malaria.	Maa name?
Olkokola	*Rhamnus staddo*		Multipurpose, including malaria.	Maa name?
Ororwet / Ororuet	*Ekebergia capensis*		Cold. Malaria. For children. Watershed trees that protect and purify water and keep the watertable high.	Barks are boiled with those of prunus to treat malaria.
Pisinda / Pisindat			Poles for construction	
Pisinela			Cold	
Poinda / Puindat / Poindat / Pondet	*Engleromyces goetzei*		Malaria. Stomach, worms. Cold. For cows.	
Pomolet			Spice.	Bark used as spice in tea.
Sabtet	*Podocarpus Africana* or *Podocarpus falcatus*	Podo, Pondo	Weddings and ceremonies. For tea. Cold for children. To hang beehives. Lungs. Worms. Malaria. Teething pain. Construction, charcoal.	Distinguished look with green leaves and hanging flowers, red wood. Old men sniff the powder against cold. Commonly mentioned.

(Appendix 1 continued)

Indigenous name of plant	Latin name	Common name	Uses	Comments
Sagawaita	*Faurea saligna*		Chest, cough, tonsils, pneumonia.	Soft leaves are chewed to treat chest pains, coughs and tonsils. Wax is edible and treats pneumonia. Bark is either boiled or chewed raw to treat chest pains, coughs, tonsils, and pneumonia.
Seet	*Albizia lebbeck*		Shade. Parkland system practices. Forage. Fuelwood, timber for ceiling boards, plywood, fencing. Rashes.	Barks and leaves can be boiled to steam body with rashes, and to treat acne.
Seretuet / Senetwet	*Faidherbia albida* or *Acacia abyssinica*		Malaria.	Nandi name.
Silibwet / Silibuet	*Dombeya goetzenii* or *Dombeya torrida*		Children's stomach upset. Allergies (wind/cold). Malaria. Construction, firewood. For honey, to **hang beehives**. Back pain. Cow cough and stomach problems. Pneumonia. Ulcers, stomach.	Most commonly named for hanging beehives. Mix with honey. Roots for stomach upset. Kipsigis name. Mukeu (Kikuyu).

Simotwet	*Ficus thoningii*	Fig tree	For cultural and religious rites. Herb for casting out witchcraft and treating of inflammation. Firewood. Fencing. Shade.	
Sinendeit / Sinendet / Seneteit	*Periploca linearifolia*		Rituals and ceremonies. Fungal infections, cleans the stomach, inflammation. For children. Chest. Venereal diseases. Warts. Pneumonia. Cancer. Diarrhoea. Fertility.	Commonly mentioned, especially for rituals and ceremonies. Liquid milky substance used to treat inflammation.
Siryat	*Rhus vulgaris*	Muthigio (Kikuyu)	Soup.	
Situtwa / Sitotwet	*Myrsine melanophloeos*		Cold.	Nandi/Kipsigis name.
Siwot / Isiek		Stinging nettle	Cold. Increases and cleans blood. Worms. For livestock.	Thabai (Kikuyu).
Smeito/ Simieito/ Simeito	*Cucumis ficifolius*		Addresses all problems, from stomach to nose. Malaria.	

(Appendix 1 continued)

Indigenous name of plant	Latin name	Common name	Uses	Comments
Socholeit			Deworming.	
Soget / Sogheet / Sogeit / Sogheit / Sorghet / Sogheit	*Warburgia ugandensis*	Ugandan greenheart	Malaria. Cough, chest, flu, cold. Lungs. Many sicknesses. Family planning. Joints. Fencing, shade. Used in parkland system.	Commonly mentioned, especially for cough, chest, flu, cold. Bark is chewed as contraceptive. Leaves are chewed to treat coughs and chest pains. Bark is boiled and taken in small quantities to treat joint aches.
Sosuriet	*Ehsente vetricosum*	Wild banana	Edible fruits. Landscaping and beautification of the compound. Lightening arrester.	Fruits are edible and consumed by people and wild animals. Leaves are burned and consumed with goat milk to treat ulcers.
Sumeita			Malaria.	Maa name?
Tangaratwet	*Aloe kedongensis Reynolds*	Aloe vera	Washes kidneys, Treatment of wounds, swellings, and reduces pains. Treatment of skin infections, and deworming in human beings. Feed for chickens.	Mostly grown for landscaping. Leaves and roots are prepared as infusions for external/internal use. Typhoid, skin diseases, malaria, colds, ear problems, wounds, coccidiosis.

Tebeng'wet	*Vernonia auriculifera*		Ropes. Tissue paper. Cough. Joint pain. Stops bleeding.	Leaves are used to make ring to balance water and firewood on the head when carrying, to avoid being hurt. Leaves used as soft tissue paper. Roots are used to treat chest pains, coughs, and joint pains. Juicy bark applied on the wounds; also stops excessive bleeding. Kipsigis name.
Tegat	*Arundinaria alpina*	Bamboo	Construction. Circumcision rites. Cultural practice to keep wild animals away.	
Tekelteit/ Tegetetiet/ Tekitetiet / Tiegelitit			Cold. Stomach. For children.	
Tendwet / Tenetwet	*Prunus Africana*	African cherry	Good against meat allergy, arthritis. When babies' teeth are growing. Kidney problems, prostate cancer. Stomach upsets. Fencing, firewood. Malaria. Lungs.	Boiled with Ororwet against Malaria. Kipsigis name. Muuiri /muiiri (Kikuyu). Commonly mentioned.

(Appendix 1 continued)

Indigenous name of plant	Latin name	Common name	Uses	Comments
Tepesweit / Tebesuet	*Croton macrostachyus*		For beehives. Timber, fencing, firewood. Cold, cough. Acne. Stops bleeding.	Barks are boiled and taken for colds. Roots are also boiled to treat coughs and acne. The juicy part is applied on wounds and enables instant stoppage from excessive bleeding. Kipsigis name.
Tongotwet / Tongotuet / Tongotwelt	*Ilex mitis*		Honey; beekeeping.	
Torokwet	*Juniperus procera* (perhaps also *Bersama abyssinica*)	East African cedar / Pencil cedar	Construction, firewood, charcoal. Charcoal also used as alternative steel wool. For honey, mainly used to build indigenous beehives.	Commonly mentioned, especially for construction and firewood.. One of the favourite species for charcoal and construction. Kipsigis name. Mutarakwa (Kikuyu). Teek.(Ogiek).
Visindah			Cough, cold.	
Vuinda			Removes all problems.	
Yemdit / Yemdeit/ Yembit/ Yimet	*Olea africana* or *Olea europaea* subsp. *cuspidata*	African wild olive	Malaria. **Firewood**, construction, charcoal. Honey. Eye problems. Cold, cough (children), lungs. Joint pains. Many sicknesses.	Commonly mentioned, especially for firewood. Mutamayiu / Mitamayo (Kikuyu).

Plant names and uses of exotic trees: *'miti ya wazungu'* (white peoples' trees), *'miti ya biashara'* (trees for business), *'zile zingine'* (those other ones)

Indigenous name of tree	Latin name	Common name	Uses	Comments
Blue gum	Eucalyptus species	Eucalyptus	Construction, firewood, furniture, fencing, electricity poles.	
Cypress	*Cypressus lusitanica*	Cypress	Construction, firewood, furniture, fencing.	
Pine	*Pinus patchula, Pinus radiator*	Pine	Construction, firewood, fencing.	

Note. The local names and uses indicated were exclusively provided by survey respondents. Latin and some of the common names were retrieved from literature (Muchemi & Ehrensperger, 2011; Maundu & Tengnäs, 2005). Knowledgeable colleagues supported the identification of species. This list is neither exhaustive nor comprehensive and depicts an incomplete picture of the existing traditional ecological knowledge among forest dwellers in the Eastern Mau Forest. In cases in which numerous respondents cited a specific use, this use was noted as 'commonly mentioned'.

Appendix 2: Full overview of interview partners

Expert interviews

Code	Date	Description	Place	Type
1/001	17/02/2011	Journalist with *The Standard*	Nakuru	Expert
1/002	18/02/2011	IDP coordinator, later with the Internal Displacement Policy and Advocacy Centre (IDPAC)	Nakuru	Expert
1/003	18/02/2011	IDP Network coordinator	Nakuru	Expert
1/004	23/02/2011	ProMara communications specialist	Nakuru	Expert
1/005	25/02/2011	*Daily Nation* journalist based in Molo	Molo	Expert
1/006	11/04/2011	ICS/KWTA Forestry Specialist	Nairobi	Expert
1/007	03/05/2011	ICS/KWTA Forestry Specialist	Nairobi	Expert
1/008	10/11/2011	*Daily Nation* journalist	Narok	Expert
1/009	10/11/2011	Maasai Community Partnership Project coordinator	Narok	Expert
1/010	01/12/2011	ICS/KWTA Forestry Specialist	Nairobi	Expert
1/011	02/12/2011	Lecturer at the University of Pau, France	Nairobi	Expert

1/012	06/12/2011	Dean of School of Environmental Studies, Kenyatta University	Nairobi	Expert
1/013	01/02/2012	Program Support Manager, NRC Kenya & Somalia	Molo	Expert
1/014	06/02/2012	ProMara Conflict Management Specialist	Nakuru	Expert
1/015	09/02/2012	Nakuru Coordinator for the Youth Congress	Nakuru	Expert
1/016	09/02/2012	ProMara Gender Equality specialist	Nakuru	Expert
1/017	09/02/2012	ProMara Conflict Management Specialist	Nakuru	Expert
1/018	22/02/2012	ProMara Chief of Party	Nakuru	Expert
1/019	22/02/2012	Lecturer at the Department of Peace, Security and Social Studies, Egerton University	Nakuru	Expert
1/020	24/02/2012	ProMara Mau Outreach Centre Assistant	Olenguruone	Expert
1/021	01/03/2012	Executive officer of FoMaWa (Friends of Mau Watershed)	Rongai	Expert
1/022	17/04/2012	ICS/KWTA Forestry Specialist	Nairobi	Expert
1/023	02/05/2012	KAPP (Kenya Agricultural Productivity Project) Monitoring and Evaluation Officer	Nakuru	Expert
1/024	03/05/2012	Deputy Principal of Baraka Agricultural College	Molo	Expert
1/025	08/05/2012	GIZ Programme Manager	Nairobi	Expert
1/026	09/05/2012	Founder and Executive Director of IREN (Inter Region Economic Network)	Nairobi	Expert
1/027	17/05/2012	Country coordinator of the Network for Eco-farming (Necofa) Kenya, Molo	Molo	Expert
1/028	19/07/2012	Lawyer at Kituo Cha Sheria, The Centre for Legal Empowerment	Nairobi	Expert
1/029	10/08/2012	Formerly responsible for NRM aspect in ProMara	Nakuru	Expert
1/030	14/08/2012	National coordinator of the Kenya Forest Working Group (KFWG)	Nairobi	Expert
1/031	14/08/2012	ProMara Conflict Management Specialist	Nairobi	Expert
1/032	08/11/2012	Dean of School of Environmental Studies, Kenyatta University	Nairobi	Expert

Code	Date	Description	Place	Type
1/033	12/11/2012	Director of the Forest Action Network (FAN)	Njoro	Expert
1/034	15/11/2012	National Alliance for Community Forest Associations (NACOFA), Accountant and Programme Assistant	Nakuru	Expert
1/035	07/12/2011	Professor for Geography, Université Bordeaux III	Nairobi	Expert
1/036	07/12/2012	Project manager at MEFoCo (Mau East Forest Conservation Group)	Nakuru	Expert
1/037	19/12/2012	Returning Officer and Constituency Elections Coordinator, IEBC	Molo	Expert
1/038	21/01/2013	Necofa project manager in Mariashoni	Mariashoni	Expert
1/039	17/03/2013	Copenhagen Business School, Associate Professor of Globalisation & Sustainability	Nairobi	Expert
1/040	04/04/2013	ICS/KWTA Forestry Specialist	Nairobi	Expert
1/041	31/08/2013	Copenhagen Business School, Associate Professor of Globalisation & Sustainability	Nairobi	Expert
1/042	19/05/2014	CEO of the ICS, and later of the KWTA	Nakuru	Expert

Local external stakeholder interviews

Code	Date	Description	Place	Type
2/043	26/02/2011	Chairman of Kirbangat Governmental IDP Camp	Kirbangat, Mau Forest	Local external
2/044	26/02/2011	Chairman of Kipkongur Governmental IDP Camp	Kirbangat, Mau Forest	Local external
2/045	27/02/2011	Local political representative in the Eastern Mau	Mauche, Mau Forest	Local external
2/046	28/02/2011	KFS officer affected to Chematich Camp for KFS officers; camp next to watch tower	Chematich Camp, Mau Forest	Local external

2/047	08/08/2012	KFS Molo District Forest Officer and Assistant Zonal Manager in charge of the Eastern Mau	Molo	Local external
2/048	09/08/2012	Chairman of the Timber Millers' Association (TMA)	Nakuru	Local external
2/049	12/12/2012	'Backshwara' carrier from Elburgon	Mariashoni	Local external
2/050	17/12/2012	IEBC clerk in Mariashoni Primary School polling station	Mariashoni Primary School	Local external
2/051	17/12/2012	IEBC coordinator of Mariashoni Ward	Mariashoni Primary School	Local external
2/052	23/02/2013	Nakuru-based sawmiller	Njoro	Local external
2/053	27/02/2013	Nakuru-based sawmiller	Nakuru	Local external

Mariashoni official stakeholder interviews

Code	Date	Description	Place	Type
3/054	27/02/2011	Chief of Mariashoni Location	Mauche	Official
3/055	27/12/2011	Chairman of Ogiek Council of Elders (ICS) and Ogiek Welfare Council (OWC)	Kapcholola area in Mariashoni	Official
3/056	05/01/2012	Chairman of Ogiek Council of Elders and OWC	Nakuru	Official

3/057	14/04/2012	ProMara community facilitator; Jubilee candidate; since 2013 Mariashoni MCA	Mariashoni Centre	Official
3/058	14/03/2012	Chief of Mariashoni Location	Mariashoni Centre	Official
3/059	15/03/2012	Division representative of the Forest Conservation Committee (MEFoCo)	Mariashoni	Official
3/060	17/03/2012	Chairman of Ogiek Council of Elders and OWC	Nakuru	Official
3/061	28/03/2012	Assistant Chief of Mariashoni sub-location	Mariashoni Centre	Official
3/062	03/04/2012	KFS Forester, Mariashoni Forest Station	Mariashoni Centre	Official
3/063	13/04/2012	Headteacher, Mariashoni Primary School	Mariashoni Primary School	Official
3/064	13/04/2012	Teacher and animator of the environmental club, Mariashoni Primary School	Mariashoni Primary School	Official
3/065	04/05/2012	Division representative of MEFoCo	Molo	Official
3/066	16/05/2012	KFS tree nursery worker at Mariashoni Forest Station	Mariashoni	Official
3/067	17/05/2012	ProMara community facilitator, Necofa field officer	Mariashoni Centre	Resident
3/068	28/09/2012	Necofa field officer	Mariashoni	Official
3/069	08/08/2012	KFS Forester, Mariashoni Forest Station	Molo	Official
3/070	24/01/2013	Headteacher, Kaprop Primary School	Kaprop, Mariashoni	Official

3/071	12/02/2013	Town clerk, Mariashoni	Mariashoni Centre	Official
3/072	14/02/2013	ProMara community facilitator; Jubilee candidate; since 2013 Mariashoni MCA	Mariashoni	Official
3/073	14/02/2013	KFS officer affected to Mariashoni Forest Station	Mariashoni	Official
3/074	14/02/2013	ProMara community facilitator, Necofa field officer	Mariashoni Centre	Official
3/075	14/02/2013	KFS officer, Mariashoni Forest Station, and chairman of MaCoDev	Mariashoni	Official
3/076	23/02/2013	Mariashoni ODM representatives	Elburgon	Official
3/077	25/02/2013	KFS officer affected to Mariashoni Forest Station	Mariashoni	Official
3/078	25/02/2013,	Nurse, Clinic Mariashoni	Mariashoni Centre	Official
3/079	25/02/2013	KANU candidate for the 2013 MCA elections	Mariashoni Centre	Official
3/080	25/02/2013	UDF candidate for the 2013 MCA elections	Mariashoni Centre	Official
3/081	26/02/2013	ProMara community facilitator; Jubilee candidate; from 2013 Mariashoni MCA	Mariashoni Centre	Official
3/082	27/02/2013	Necofa field officer	Mariashoni	Official
3/083	27/02/2013	KANU candidate for the 2013 MCA elections		Official
3/084	27/02/2013	Necofa field officer in Mariashoni	Mariashoni Centre	Official
3/085	27/02/2013	Chief of Mariashoni Location	Mariashoni Centre	Official

3/086	21/05/2013	Town clerk, Mariashoni	Mariashoni Centre	Official
3/087	21/05/2013	KFS officer, Mariashoni Forest Station, and chairman of MaCoDev	Mariashoni Centre	Official
3/088	21/05/2013	Doctor, Clinic Mariashoni	Mariashoni Centre	Official

Mariashoni residents free interviews

Code	Date	Description	Place	Type
4/089	04/04/2012	Middle-aged Ogiek man, former Councillor	Mariashoni Centre	Resident
4/090	17/05/2012	Young Ogiek man	Mariashoni Centre	Resident
4/091	10/10/2012	Middle-aged Ogiek man	Mariashoni Centre	Resident
4/092	10/10/2012	Motorcycle taxi rider from Elburgon to Mariashoni	Mariashoni Centre	Resident
4/093	28/11/2012	Young Ogiek men	Mariashoni Centre	Residents
4/094	20/12/2012	Elderly man	Chai Moto	Resident
4/095	12/02/2013	Elderly Ogiek man	Mariashoni	Resident
4/096	12/02/2013	Young Mariashoni men	Mariashoni	Resident
4/097	14/02/2013	Focus group discussion with old men on Mariashoni's past	Mariashoni Centre	Resident

Code	Date				Place	Type
4/098	23/02/2013	Motorcycle taxi rider from Elburgon to Mariashoni			Mariashoni Centre	Resident
4/099	25/02/2013	Last Kikuyu resident of Mariashoni			Mariashoni Centre	Resident
4/100	21/05/2013	Last Kikuyu resident of Mariashoni			Mariashoni Centre	Resident

Mariashoni survey interviews

Code	Date	Gender	Age	'Community'	Place	Type	Survey interview number
5/101	27/09/2012	male	25–45	Tugen	Mariashoni	Survey	001
5/102	27/09/2012	female	18–25	'Dorobo'	Mariashoni	Survey	002
5/103	27/09/2012	male	45–70	Ogiek	Mariashoni	Survey	003
5/104	27/09/2012	female	25–45	'Dorobo'	Mariashoni	Survey	004
5/105	28/09/2012	female	25–45	Ogiek	Mariashoni	Survey	005
5/106	28/09/2012	female	under 18	Ogiek	Mariashoni	Survey	006
5/107	02/10/2012	female	over 70	Ogiek	Mariashoni	Survey	007
5/108	02/10/2012	male	45–70	Ogiek	Mariashoni	Survey	008
5/109	02/10/2012	female	45–70	Ogiek	Mariashoni	Survey	009
5/110	02/10/2012	male	45–70	Kisii	Mariashoni	Survey	010
5/111	02/10/2012	male	18–25	Ogiek	Mariashoni	Survey	011
5/112	03/10/2012	male	18–25	Ogiek	Mariashoni	Survey	012

5/113	03/10/2012	female	25–45	Ogiek	Mariashoni	Survey	013
5/114	03/10/2012	female	25–45	Ogiek	Mariashoni	Survey	014
5/115	04/10/2012	male	45–70	Ogiek	Mariashoni	Survey	015
5/116	10/10/2012	female	25–45	Ogiek	Mariashoni	Survey	016
5/117	10/10/2012	female	25–45	Ogiek	Mariashoni	Survey	017
5/118	10/10/2012	female	25–45	Ogiek	Mariashoni	Survey	018
5/119	13/10/2012	female	25–45	Ogiek	Mariashoni	Survey	019
5/120	13/10/2012	male	25–45	Ogiek	Mariashoni	Survey	020
5/121	13/10/2012	male	25–45	Ogiek	Mariashoni	Survey	021
5/122	13/10/2012	female	25–45	Ogiek	Mariashoni	Survey	022
5/123	22/10/2012	male	18–25	Ogiek	Mariashoni	Survey	023
5/124	22/10/2012	female	25–45	Ogiek	Mariashoni	Survey	024
5/125	22/10/2012	female	18–25	Maasai	Mariashoni	Survey	025
5/126	23/10/2012	female	18–25	Ogiek	Mariashoni	Survey	026
5/127	23/10/2012	male	under 18	Ogiek	Mariashoni	Survey	027
5/128	24/10/2012	male	45–70	Ogiek	Mariashoni	Survey	028
5/129	24/10/2012	female	45–70	Ogiek	Mariashoni	Survey	029
5/130	25/10/2012	female	18–25	Ogiek	Mariashoni	Survey	030
5/131	25/10/2012	male	25–45	Ogiek	Mariashoni	Survey	031
5/132	25/10/2012	female	25–45	Ogiek	Mariashoni	Survey	032
5/133	25/10/2012	female	25–45	Ogiek	Bondeni, Mariashoni	Survey	033

5/134	25/10/2012	female	25–45	Kisii, Ogiek spouse	Quarry, Mariashoni	Survey	034
5/136	08/11/2012	female	45–70	Ogiek	Mowlem, Mariashoni	Survey	035
5/137	08/11/2012	male	25–45	Ogiek	Quarry, Mariashoni	Survey	036
5/138	08/11/2012	female	25–45		Tilatliet, Mariashoni	Survey	156
5/139	09/11/2012	female	25–45	Ogiek	Kapcholola, Mariashoni	Survey	037
5/140	09/11/2012	female	25–45	Ogiek	Kapcholola, Mariashoni	Survey	038
5/141	10/11/2012	male	18–25	Ogiek	Kapcholola, Mariashoni	Survey	039
5/142	10/11/2012	female	18–25	Ogiek	Quarry, Mariashoni	Survey	040
5/143	10/11/2012	female	25–45	Ogiek	Quarry, Mariashoni	Survey	041
5/144	13/11/2012	female	under 18	Ogiek	Quarry, Mariashoni	Survey	042
5/145	13/11/2012	male	18–25	Ogiek	Quarry, Mariashoni	Survey	043
5/146	13/11/2012	male	25–45	Ogiek	Quarry, Mariashoni	Survey	044

5/147	14/11/2012	male	25–45	Ogiek	Tilatiliet, Mariashoni	Survey	045
5/148	14/11/2012	male	25–45	Ogiek	Tafaita Tilatiliet, Mariashoni	Survey	046
5/149	14/11/2012	male	25–45	Luo	Tilatiliet, Mariashoni	Survey	047
5/150	15/11/2012	female	25–45	Ogiek	Quarry, Mariashoni	Survey	048
5/151	15/11/2012	male	25–45	Ogiek	Kamawe, Mariashoni	Survey	049
5/152	15/11/2012	male	45–70	Ogiek	Kamawe, Mariashoni	Survey	050
5/153	16/11/2012	female	25–45	Ogiek	Kapcholola, Mariashoni	Survey	051
5/154	16/11/2012	female	25–45	Ogiek	Kapcholola, Mariashoni	Survey	052
5/155	20/11/2012	female	25–45	Ogiek	Mariashoni, Mariashoni	Survey	053
5/156	20/11/2012	male	45–70	Nandi	Mariashoni, Mariashoni	Survey	054
5/157	20/11/2012	female	45–70	Ogiek	Kapcholola, Mariashoni	Survey	055
5/158	21/11/2012	male	25–45	Tugen	Mariashoni, Mariashoni	Survey	056

5/159	21/11/2012	female	25–45	Ogiek	Mariashoni, Mariashoni	Survey	057
5/160	21/11/2012	female	over 70	Ogiek	Kitiro, Mariashoni	Survey	058
5/161	22/11/2012	female	25–45	Ogiek	Kitiro	Survey	059
5/162	22/11/2012	male	18–25	Ogiek	Kitiro	Survey	060
5/163	22/11/2012	female	18–25	Kipsigis	Quarry	Survey	061
5/164	23/11/2012	male	18–25	Ogiek	Kitiro	Survey	062
5/165	23/11/2012	female	18–25	Ogiek	Kanunga	Survey	063
5/166	23/11/2012	female	25–45	Kipsigis, Ogiek spouse	Kitiro, Kanunga	Survey	064
5/167	23/11/2012	male	45–70	Ogiek	Kitiro, Kanunga	Survey	065
5/168	27/11/2012	female	45–70	Ogiek	Mariashoni	Survey	066
5/169	27/11/2012	male	45–70	Kipsigis	Quarry	Survey	067
5/170	27/11/2012	male	45–70	Tugen	Mariashoni	Survey	068
5/171	28/11/2012	female	18–25	Kipsigis	Mariashoni	Survey	069
5/172	28/11/2012	male	18–25	Ogiek	Mariashoni	Survey	070
5/173	28/11/2012	female	45–70	Ogiek	Mariashoni	Survey	071
5/174	29/11/2012	male	18–25	Ogiek	Mboroti	Survey	072
5/175	29/11/2012	male	25–45	Kipsigis	Mariashoni	Survey	073
5/176	29/11/2012	male	25–45	Kipsigis	Mboroti	Survey	074

5/177	04/12/2012	female	18–25	Kipsigis	Kitiro, Mboroti	Survey	075
5/178	04/12/2012	male	25–45	Ogiek	Kitiro, Mboroti	Survey	076
5/179	04/12/2012	male	18–25	Ogiek	Kitiro, Mboroti	Survey	077
5/180	05/12/2012	female	45–70	Kipsigis, Ogiek spouse	Kitiro, Mboroti	Survey	078
5/181	05/12/2012	female	25–45	Ogiek	Kitiro, Mboroti	Survey	079
5/182	05/12/2012	male	25–45	Kipsigis	Mboroti	Survey	080
5/183	05/12/2012	male	18–25	Kipsigis	Kitiro, Mboroti	Survey	081
5/184	10/12/2012	male	18–25	Ogiek	Mariashoni	Survey	082
5/185	10/12/2012	male	18–25	Kipsigis	Mariashoni	Survey	083
5/186	10/12/2012	male	25–45	Ogiek	Kitiro, Buruburu	Survey	084
5/187	10/12/2012	male	25–45	Kipsigis	Mariashoni	Survey	085
5/188	11/12/2012	female	25–45	Kipsigis, Ogiek spouse	Kitiro, Bondeni	Survey	086
5/189	11/12/2012	female	45–70	Ogiek	Kitiro, Bondeni	Survey	087
5/190	11/12/2012	female	25–45	Ogiek	Kitiro, Bondeni	Survey	088

ID	Date	Gender	Age	Ethnicity	Location	Type	No.
5/191	12/12/2012	female	45–70	Ogiek	Kitiro, Bondeni	Survey	089
5/192	12/12/2012	male	over 70	Ogiek	Kitiro, Kapcholola	Survey	090
5/193	12/12/2012	male	25–45	Turkana	Kitiro, Buruburu	Survey	091
5/194	17/12/2012	female	25–45	Ogiek	Quarry	Survey	092
5/195	20/12/2012	female	18–25	Tugen	Segut, Chai Moto, Mariashoni	Survey	093
5/196	20/12/2012	male	over 70	Maasai	Chai Moto, Mariashoni	Survey	094
5/197	20/12/2012	male	45–70	Luhya	Chai Moto, Mariashoni	Survey	095
5/198	22/12/2012	female	25–45	Kipsigis	Chai Moto, Mariashoni	Survey	096
5/199	22/12/2012	male	25–45	Tugen	Chai Moto, Mariashoni	Survey	097
5/200	21/01/2013	male	25–45	Ogiek	Mariashoni Centre	Survey	098
5/201	22/01/2013	male	25–45	Maasai, Kipsigis	Mariashoni	Survey	099
5/202	22/01/2013	male	25–45	Kipsigis	Chai Moto	Survey	100
5/203	22/01/2013	male	25–45	Tugen	Chai Moto	Survey	101

5/204	22/01/2013	male	25–45	Tugen	Chai Moto	Survey	102
5/205	23/01/2013	female	18–25	Kisii	Mariashoni	Survey	103
5/206	23/01/2013	female	18–25	Ogiek	Mariashoni	Survey	104
5/207	24/01/2013	male	25–45	Ogiek	Kitiro, Kaprop	Survey	105
5/208	24/01/2013	female	18–25	Ogiek	Kaprop	Survey	106
5/209	24/01/2013	male	25–45	Ogiek	Kaprop	Survey	107
5/210	25/01/2013	male	18–25	Ogiek	Mariashoni	Survey	108
5/211	25/01/2013	male	25–45	Kipsigis	Mariashoni	Survey	109
5/212	25/01/2013	male	25–45	Luo, Ogiek	Mariashoni	Survey	110
5/213	29/01/2013	male	25–45	Kipsigis	Mariashoni	Survey	111
5/214	29/01/2013	male	45–70	Luo	Mariashoni	Survey	112
5/215	29/01/2013	female	45–70	Ogiek	Mariashoni	Survey	113
5/216	05/02/2013	male	25–45	Luo	Mariashoni Centre	Survey	114
5/217	05/02/2013	male	18–25	Ogiek	Mariashoni Centre	Survey	115
5/218	05/02/2013	male	25–45	Kikuyu, Kalenjin	Mariashoni Centre	Survey	116
5/219	06/02/2013	male	18–25	Ogiek	Mariashoni Centre	Survey	117
5/220	06/02/2013	male	under 18	Kipsigis	Mariashoni Centre	Survey	118
5/221	06/02/2013	male	18–25	Ogiek	Mariashoni Centre	Survey	119

ID	Date	Sex	Age	Ethnicity	Location	Type	No.
5/222	07/02/2013	male	25–45	Ogiek, Kipsigis	Kitiro, Mboroti	Survey	120
5/223	07/02/2013	female	25–45	Ogiek	Kitiro, Mboroti	Survey	121
5/224	07/02/2013	female	25–45	Ogiek	Kitiro, Mboroti	Survey	122
5/225	08/02/2013	male	over 70	Ogiek	Mariashoni	Survey	123
5/226	08/02/2013	male	45–70	Ogiek	Mariashoni	Survey	124
5/227	08/02/2013	female	25–45	Ogiek	Mariashoni	Survey	125
5/228	09/02/2013	male	25–45	Kipsigis	Mariashoni Primary School	Survey	126
5/229	09/02/2013	male	25–45	Kipsigis (?)	Mariashoni Primary School	Survey	127
5/230	09/02/2013	female	25–45	Kipsigis	Mariashoni Primary School	Survey	128
5/231	09/02/2013	female	25–45	Ogiek	Mariashoni	Survey	129
5/232	11/02/2013	male	25–45	Ogiek	Mariashoni	Survey	130
5/233	11/02/2013	male	25–45	Kikuyu	Mariashoni	Survey	131
5/234	11/02/2013	male	45–70	Ogiek	Mariashoni	Survey	132
5/235	11/02/2013	female	45–70	Ogiek	Mariashoni	Survey	133
5/236	12/02/2013	male	45–70	Kikuyu	Mariashoni	Survey	134

ID	Date	Gender	Age	Ethnicity	Location	Type	Number
5/237	12/02/2013	male	25–45	Ogiek	Mariashoni	Survey	135
5/238	23/02/2013	female	25–45	'Dorobo'	Mariashoni	Survey	136
5/239	13/02/2013	female	over 70	Ogiek	Mariashoni	Survey	137
5/240	13/02/2013	male	25–45	Ogiek	Mariashoni	Survey	138
5/241	13/02/2013	male	25–45	Ogiek	Mariashoni	Survey	139
5/242	13/02/2013	male	45–70	Kipsigis	Mariashoni	Survey	140
5/243	14/02/2013	male	45–70	Ogiek	Mariashoni	Survey	141
5/244	15/02/2013	female	25–45	Ogiek	Mariashoni	Survey	142
5/245	15/02/2013	male	45–70	Ogiek	Mariashoni	Survey	143
5/246	15/02/2013	female	45–70	Kipsigis	Mariashoni	Survey	144
5/247	15/02/2013	female	45–70	Kipsigis	Mariashoni	Survey	145
5/248	15/02/2013	female	25–45	Kikuyu	Mariashoni	Survey	146
5/249	22/02/2013	female	25–45	Ogiek	Mariashoni	Survey	147
5/250	22/02/2013	female	18–25	Ogiek	Mariashoni	Survey	148
5/251	22/02/2013	male	25–45	Ogiek	Mariashoni	Survey	149
5/252	22/02/2013	male	25–45	Ogiek	Mariashoni	Survey	150
5/253	23/02/2013	male	45–70	Embu	Kapcholola	Survey	151
5/254	23/02/2013	male	25–45	Ogiek	Kapcholola	Survey	152
5/255	25/02/2013	female	25–45	Kikuyu	Mariashoni	Survey	153
5/256	25/02/2013	male	25–45	Nandi	Mariashoni	Survey	154
5/257	26/02/2013	male	18–25	Ogiek	Mariashoni Centre	Survey	155

Additional interviews (across categories)

Code	Date	Description	Place	Type
1/258	24/11/2016	Director of the KTWA	Nairobi	Expert discussion contribution
1/259	24/11/2016	Chairman of Karura CFA and Executive Director of the Centre for Environmental Action	Nairobi	Expert
4/260	28/01/2012	Ogiek elder	Mariashoni	Resident
1/261	07/12/2012	MeFoCo accounting assistant and Chemusus CFA member	Nakuru	Expert
2/262	02/03/2012	Ogiek elder	Saino, South-Western Mau	Local external stakeholder
1/263	01/09/2019	Kenya Land Alliance	Nairobi	Expert
4/264	30/03/2012	Outspoken Tugen man	Mariashoni	Resident
4/265	18/05/2012	Mariashoni resident	Mariashoni	Resident
2/266	03/02/2012	KFS officers, Timboroa Forest Station	Timboroa,	Local external stakeholder
1/267	17/06/2013	CEO of the ICS/KWTA	Nairobi	Expert
1/268	29/07/2010	President of the Kenya Landowners' Association	Nairobi	Expert discussion contribution
1/269	22/06/2016	Acting Programmes Coordinator of the Kenya Institute for Public Policy Research and Analysis	Nairobi	Expert discussion contribution

Bibliography

Primary sources

University research papers

Bore, N.C. (2014). A struggle between livelihoods and forest conservation: A case of Mau forest in Kenya (Master's thesis). University of Nairobi.

Connan, D. (2007). 'No politics please...?' Conditions et dynamiques de l'échange politique autour du Parc National Kenyan d'Amboseli (Master's thesis). Université Paris I-Panthéon Sorbonne.

Kweyu, R.M. (2015). Linking the social and the spatial in forest related conflicts: The case of Eastern Mau Forest adjacent communities, Kenya (Doctoral Dissertation). University of Nairobi. http://erepository.uonbi.ac.ke/handle/11295/90674.

Omvvoyo, S.M. (2000). The agricultural changes in the Kipsigis land, c. 1894–1963: An historical inquiry (Doctoral Dissertation). Kenyatta University. https://halshs.archives-ouvertes.fr/tel-01236648.

Oruya-Oginga, J.C. (2015). Environmental diplomacy and conflict resolution: A case study of Mau forest (Master's Thesis). University of Nairobi.

Soi, J.K. (2015). Politics and conservation of the Mau forest in Kenya (Master's thesis). University of Nairobi.

Spruyt, C. (2011). Changing concepts of nature and conservation regarding Eastern Mau Forest: A case study of the Mariashoni Ogiek (Master's Thesis). Universiteit Gent.

Kenya government records and reports

DRSRS, & KFWG (2006). *Changes in forest cover in Kenya's five 'Water Towers' 2003–2005* (November).

ENSDA (Ewaso Nyiro South Development Authority), UNEP, KFWG, & KWS (2005). *Maasai Mau Forest status report 2005*. Narok, Kenya.

GoK (2009a). *Frequently asked questions about the Mau Forests Complex: Version 1–2 November 2009*. Nairobi.

GoK (2009b). *Mau Forests Complex: Government's response*. A presentation by the Interim Coordinating Secretariat. Nairobi.

GoK (2009c). *Mau Forests Complex: Threats and way forward* (November).

GoK (2009d). *Rehabilitation of the Mau Forest ecosystem: A Project concept prepared by the Interim Coordinating Secretariat, Office of the Prime Minister, on behalf of the Government of Kenya* (September). Nairobi.

GoK (2009e). *Report of the Prime Minister's Task Force on the conservation of the Mau Forests Complex* (March). Nairobi.

GoK (2010a). *Brief on the rehabilitation of the Mau Forests Complex* (7, December). Nairobi, Kenya.

GoK (2010b). *Coordinating multiple stakeholders in the restoration of the Mau Forests Complex, Kenya: Challenges and lessons learnt* (April).

GoK (2010c). *Rehabilitation of the Mau forest ecosystem: Executive summary* (April).

GoK (2010d). *Update on rehabilitation of the Mau Forests Complex.* Nairobi, Kenya.

GoK (2018). *Press Statement: Extension of the moratorium on logging activities in public and community forests* (November).

IEBC Dispute Resolution Committee (2013a). *Amended allocation of nominees to County Assembly special seats.*

IEBC Dispute Resolution Committee (2013b). *Amendments made to the nomination list following the complaints and the decision of the IEBC Committee.*

KFS (2009). *Mau Forests Complex Map.* Nairobi, Kenya.

KFS & KFWG (2009). *Manual on forming and registering Community Forest Associations (CFAs).* Nairobi, Kenya.

Republic of Kenya (1970a). *Kenya National Assembly Official Record (Hansard) June 16–July 15, 1970: The Timber Bill.*

Republic of Kenya (1970b). The Timber Act (Cap. 386).

Republic of Kenya (1982). The Forests Act (Cap. 385).

Republic of Kenya (1985). The Wildlife (Conservation and Management) Act (Cap. 376). *Kenya Gazette Supplement.*

Republic of Kenya (1999). The Environmental Management and Co-ordination Act.

Republic of Kenya (2002). The Water Act.

Republic of Kenya (2003). *Kenya National Assembly Official Record (Hansard): Revoking of Gacheru and Company sawmillers license.*

Republic of Kenya (2004a). *Kenya National Assembly Official Record (Hansard): Debate on the Forests Bill.*

Republic of Kenya (2004b). *Report of the Commission of Inquiry into the Illegal/Irregular Allocation of Public Land (The Ndung'u Report).* Nairobi.

Republic of Kenya (2005). The Forests Act.

Republic of Kenya (2008a). *National Accord and Reconciliation Act.* Nairobi: Government Printer.

Republic of Kenya (2008b). *Report of the Commission of Inquiry into Post Election Violence in Kenya (CIPEV)*. Nairobi: Government Printer.

Republic of Kenya (2008c). *Kenya National Assembly Official Record (Hansard): Question No. 268; Number of IDPs settled by the Government* (November).

Republic of Kenya (2009a). Gazette Notice no. 12058; The National Accord and Reconciliation Act; Interim Coordinating Secretariat for the Mau Forest Complex. *The Kenya Gazette* 3279 (November).

Republic of Kenya (2009b). *Kenya National Assembly Official Record (Hansard): Tree Harvesting by Comply / Timsales/ Raiply Companies.*

Republic of Kenya (2009c). Sessional Paper No. 3 of 2009 on National Land Policy.

Republic of Kenya (2010a). Government Financial Management (Water Towers Conservation Funds) Regulations. *Kenya Gazette Supplement No. 47*, 461–463.

Republic of Kenya (2010b). The Constitution of the Republic of Kenya.

Republic of Kenya (2012a). *Kenya National Assembly Official Record (Hansard): Question No. 1431: Resettlement of Mau Forest Complex evictees.*

Republic of Kenya (2012b). The Kenya Water Towers Agency Order. *Kenya Gazette Supplement No. 27*, 301–305.

Republic of Kenya (2012c). State Corporations Act Kenya: Kenya Water Towers Agency: Arrangement of Orders.

Republic of Kenya (2013). The Wildlife Conservation and Management Act. *Kenya Gazette Supplement.*

Republic of Kenya (2016a). The Climate Change Act. *Kenya Gazette Supplement No. 68 (Acts No. 11)*, 179–208.

Republic of Kenya (2016b). Forest Conservation and Management Act.

Republic of Kenya (2016c). *National forest programme 2016–2030.* Nairobi.

International organisation and NGO reports

Africa Centre for Open Governance (2009). *Mission impossible? Implementing the Ndung'u Report.* Nairobi.

Asuna, M. (2014). *Country policy brief: Kenya.* Review of the development effectiveness efforts in Kenya. Nairobi: Global Partnership for Effective Development Co-operation.

Cottrel-Ghai, J., Ghai, Y., Oei, K.S., & Wanyoike, W. (2013). *Taking diversity seriously: Minorities and political participation in Kenya.* London: Minority Rights Group International.

Development Partnership Forum (2010). *Sector notes: Land note.* Nairobi: The World Bank.

FAO (1991). *FAO Yearbook Production, 1991: Vol. 45.* Rome: The *FAO Yearbook Production, 1991: Vol. 45.* Rome: Food and Agriculture Organization of the United Nations.

FAO (2006). *The Global Forest Resources Assessment 2005 (FRA 2005): Progress towards sustainable forest management.* FAO Forestry Paper 147. Rome: Food and Agriculture Organization of the United Nations (FAO).

FAO (2007). *State of the world's forests 2007.* Rome: Food and Agriculture Organization of the United Nations.

FAO (2010). *Global forest resources assessment 2010: Main report. FAO forestry paper, 0258–6150: Vol. 163.* Rome: Food and Agriculture Organization of the United Nations.

FAO (2012). *Forest resources assessment 2015: Terms and definitions.* Forest resources Assessment Working Paper 180. Rome: Food and Agriculture Organization of the United Nations.

FAO (2015). *Global forest resources assessment 2015.* Rome: Food and Agriculture Organization of the United Nations.

FAO (2016). *State of the world's forests 2016: Forests and agriculture: Land-use challenges and opportunities.* Rome: Food and Agriculture Organization of the United Nations.

Heinrich Böll Foundation (2006). *Protectors of environment: Mapping and profiling environmental organisations in Kenya.* Nairobi: Heinrich Böll Foundation.

Human Rights Council (2010). Report by the special rapporteur on the situation of human rights and fundamental freedoms of indigenous people, James Anaya. Addendum. Cases examined by the Special Rapporteur (June 2009–July 2010). Geneva: United Nations Human Rights Office of the High Commissioner.

Human Rights Watch (2008). *'All the men have gone': War crimes in Kenya's Mt. Elgon conflict.* Nairobi: Human Rights Watch (HRW).

International Crisis Group (2008). *Kenya in crisis, Africa Report No. 137.* Nairobi: International Crisis Group (ICG).

Jones, S., Nyamongo, M., & Thomson, A. (2008). *Making aid more effective through gender, rights and inclusion: Evidence from implementing the Paris declaration. Kenya case study.* Social Development Direct, Oxford Policy Management.

Kamau, J. (2000). *The Ogiek: The ongoing destruction of a minority tribe in Kenya.* Nairobi: Rights Features Service.

Kenya Land Alliance (2010). *Land in the proposed constitution of Kenya: What does it mean?*

Makoloo, M. (2005) *Kenya: Minorities, indigenous peoples and ethnic diversity.* London: Minority Rights Group International.

Millennium Ecosystem Assessment (2005). *Ecosystems and human well-being: Synthesis* (Vol. 5). Washington, DC: Island Press. https://doi.org/10.1196/annals.1439.003.

Mogaka, H., Simons, G., Turpie, J., Emerton, L., & Karanja, F. (2001). *Economic aspects of community involvement in sustainable forest manage-*

ment in Eastern and Southern Africa. Forest and social perspectives in conservation: no. 8. Nairobi: IUCN Eastern Africa Regional Office.

Ogweno, D.O., Opanga, P., & Obara, A.O. (eds) (2009). *Proceedings of the 3rd Annual Forestry Society of Kenya (FSK) Conference and Annual General Meeting held at the Sunset Hotel, Kisumu.*

Ohenjo, N. (2003). *Kenya's castaways: The Ogiek and national development processes.* London: Minority Rights Group International.

Rolnik, R. (2010). *Report of the Special Rapporteur on adequate housing as a component of the right to an adequate standard of living, and on the right to non-discrimination in this context.* Geneva: United Nations Human Rights Council.

Sang, J. (2003). Case study 3: Kenya: The Ogiek in Mau Forest. In J. Nelson & L. Hossack (eds), *From principle to practice: Indigenous peoples and protected areas in Africa.* Forest Peoples Programme, 111–138.

Towett, J.K. (2004). *Ogiek land cases and historical injustices 1902–2004.*

UNEP (2008). *Mau Complex and Marmanet forests: Environmental and economic contributions: Current state and trends.* Nairobi: United Nations Environment Programme (UNEP).

UNEP (2009). *From conflict to peacebuilding: The role of natural resources and the environment.* Nairobi: United Nations Environment Programme (UNEP).

UNEP (2012). *The role and contribution of montane forests and related ecosystem services to the Kenyan economy.* Nairobi: United Nations Environment Programme (UNEP).

UNEP, ENSDA, KFWG, KWS, & RSRS (2006). *Maasai Mau Forest: Assessments and way forward* (June). Nairobi: United Nations Environment Programme (UNEP).

UNEP, KFS, & KFWG (2005). *Mau Complex under siege: Continuous destruction of Kenya's largest forest* (June). Nairobi: United Nations Environment Programme (UNEP).

UNEP, KWS, KFWG, & ENSDA (2008). *Mau Complex under siege: Values and threats.* Nairobi: United Nations Environment Programme (UNEP).

UNEP-WCMC (2014). *United Nations list of protected areas of Kenya from the global statistics from the World Database on Protected Areas (WDPA), August 2014.* Nairobi: United Nations Environment Programme (UNEP).

World Commission on Environment and Development (1987). *Our common future.* Oxford: Oxford University Press.

World Resources Institute; Department of Resource Surveys and Remote Sensing, Ministry of Environment and Natural Resources, Kenya; Central Bureau of Statistics, Ministry of Planning and National Development, Kenya; and International Livestock Research Institute (2007). *Nature's benefits in Kenya: An atlas of ecosystems and human well-being.* Washington, DC and Nairobi: World Resources Institute.

Secondary sources

Achterbosch, T.J., van Berkum, S., & Meijerink, G.W. (2014). *Cash crops and food security: Contributions to income, livelihood risk and agricultural innovation*. LEI Report 2014–15.

Adams, W.M. (2001). *Green development: Environment and sustainability in the Third World*. London: Routledge.

Adams, W.M., & Hulme, D. (2001). Conservation and community. Changing narratives, policies and practices in African conservation. In D. Hulme & M. Murphree (eds), *African wildlife and livelihoods: The promise and performance of community conservation*, 9–23.

Adams, W.M., & Hutton, J. (2007). People, parks and poverty: Political ecology and biodiversity conservation. *Conservation and Society*, 5(2), 147–183.

Agrawal, A., Chhatre, A., & Hardin, R. (2008). Changing governance of the World's forests. *Science*, 320(5882), 1460–1462. https://doi.org/10.1126/science.1155369.

Agrawal, A., & Gibson, C.C. (1999). Enchantment and disenchantment: The role of community in natural resource conservation. *World Development*, 27(4), 629–649. https://doi.org/10.1016/S0305-750X(98)00161-2.

Agrawal, A., & Ribot, J. (1999). Accountability in decentralization: A framework with South Asian and West African cases. *Journal of Developing Areas*, 33, 473–502.

Akinnagbe, O.M., & Irohibe, I.J. (2015). Agricultural adaptation strategies to climate change impacts in Africa: A review. *Bangladesh Journal of Agricultural Research*, 39(3), 407–418. https://doi.org/10.3329/bjar.v39i3.21984.

Alden Wily, L., & Mbaya, S. (2001). *Land, people and forests in eastern and southern Africa at the beginning of the 21st century: The impact of land relations on the role of communities in forest future*. Nairobi: IUCN-EARO. http://search.ebscohost.com/login.aspx?direct=true&db=lah&AN=20033214112&site=ehost-live.

Alfredsson, G. (2005). Minorities, indigenous and tribal peoples, and peoples: Definitions of terms as a matter of international law. In N. Ghanea & A. Xanthaki (eds), *Minorities, peoples and self-determination: Essays in honour of Patrick Thornberry*, 163–172. Leiden/Boston: Martinus Nijhoff Publishers.

Alvesson, M., & Skoldberg, K. (2009). *Reflexive methodology: New vistas for qualitative research* (2nd). London: Sage.

American Anthropological Association (2012). *AAA Code of Ethics – Statement on Ethics: Principles of Professional Responsibility*.

Anderson, D. (2005). 'Yours in struggle for Majimbo'. Nationalism and the party politics of decolonization in Kenya, 1955–64.

Journal of Contemporary History, 40(3), 547–564. https://doi.org/ 10.1177/0022009405054571.

Anderson, D. (2006). *Histories of the hanged: Britain's dirty war in Kenya and the end of empire: Testimonies from the Mau Mau rebellion in Kenya.* London: Weidenfeld and Nicolson.

Anderson, J., & Ahmed, W. (2016). *Smallholder diaries: Building the evidence base with farming families in Mozambique, Tanzania, and Pakistan.* Perspectives 2. Washington, DC: CGAP.

Arendt, H. (1970). *On violence.* New York: Harcourt, Brace & World.

Bäckstrand, K., & Lövbrand, E. (2006). Planting trees to mitigate climate change: Contested discourses of ecological modernization, green governmentality and civic environmentalism. *Global Environmental Politics, 6*(1), 50–75. https://doi.org/10.1162/glep.2006.6.1.50.

Barrow, E., & Murphree, M. (2001). Community conservation. From concept to practice. In D. Hulme & M. Murphree (eds), *African Wildlife and Livelihoods. The promise and performance of community* conservation, 24–37. Oxford: James Currey.

Barrow, E., Clarke, J., Grundy, I., Jones, K.-R., & Tessema, Y. (2002). *Analysis of stakeholder power and responsibilities in community involvement in forest management in eastern and southern Africa. Forest and social perspectives in conservation*, no. 9. Nairobi, Kenya, IUCN Eastern Africa Regional Office distributor, 2002. http://rmportal. net/library/content/nrm_dg_partic/analysis-of-stakeholder-power-and-community-involvement-in-forest-management.

Barrow, E., Gichohi, H., & Infield, M. (2001). The evolution of community conservation policy and practice in East Africa. In D. Hulme & M. Murphree (eds), *African Wildlife and Livelihoods. The promise and performance of community conservation*, 59–73. Oxford: James Currey.

Bassett, T.J. (1988). The political ecology of peasant-herder conflicts in the northern Ivory Coast. *Restoration Ecology, 78*(3), 453–472. https://doi.org/10.1111/j.1467-8306.1988.tb00218.x.

Bassett, T.J., Blanc-Pamard, C., & Boutrais, J. (2007). Constructing locality: The terroir approach in West Africa. *Africa: Journal of the International African Institute, 77*(01), 104–129. https://doi.org/10.3366/ afr.2007.77.1.104.

Bassett, T.J., & Crummey, D. (2003). Contested images, contested realities: Environment & society in African savannas. In T.J. Bassett & D. Crummey (eds), *African savannas: Global narratives and local knowledge of environmental change in Africa*, 1–30. Oxford & Portsmouth, NH: James Currey & Heinemann.

Bassett, T.J., Koli Bi, Z., & Ouattara, T. (2003). Fire in the savanna: Environmental change & land reform in Northern Côte d'Ivoire. In T. J. Bassett & D. Crummey (eds), *African savannas: Global narratives and local knowledge of environmental change in Africa*, 53–71. Oxford & Portsmouth, NH: James Currey & Heinemann.

Bayart, J.-F. (1989). *L'Etat en Afrique. La politique du ventre.* Paris: Fayard.

Bayart, J.-F. (1999). L'Afrique dans le monde: Une histoire d'extraversion. *Critique internationale, 5*(1), 97–120. https://doi.org/10.3406/criti.1999.1505.

Beinart, W., & Hughes, L. (2007). *Environment and empire.* New York: Oxford University Press.

Bennett, J.W. (1976). *The ecological transition: Cultural anthropology and human adaptation.* Oxford: Pergamon.

Berkes, F., Colding, J., & Folke, C. (2000). Rediscovery of traditional ecological knowledge as adaptive management. *Ecological Applications, 10*(5), 1251–1262. https://doi.org/10.2307/2641280.

Berman, B., & Lonsdale, J. (1992a). *Unhappy valley: Conflict in Kenya and Africa.* Book one: *State and class* (Eastern African Studies). Oxford, Nairobi, & Athens: James Currey, EAEP, & Ohio University Press.

Berman, B., & Lonsdale, J. (1992b). *Unhappy valley: Conflict in Kenya and Africa.* Book two: *Violence and ethnicity* (Eastern African Studies). Oxford, Nairobi & Athens: James Currey, EAEP & Ohio University Press.

Bernard, F. (2014). What can climate-smart agricultural landscapes learn from the gestion de terroirs approach? In P.A. Minang, M. Noordwijk, O.E. Freeman, C. Mbow, J. de Leeuw, & D. Catacutan (eds), *Climate-smart landscapes: Multifunctionality in practice,* 51–60. Nairobi: World Agroforestry Centre (ICRAF).

Berntsen, J.L. (1976). The Maasai and their neighbors: Variables of interaction. *African Economic History, 2*(2), 1–11. https://doi.org/10.2307/3601509.

Bhabha, H.K. (1994). *The location of culture.* London: Routledge.

Bixler, R.P., Dell'Angelo, J., Mfune, O., & Roba, H. (2015). The political ecology of participatory conservation: Institutions and discourse. *Journal of Political Ecology, 22,* 164–182. https://doi.org/10.2458/v22i1.21083.

Blackburn, R.H. (1970). *A preliminary report of research on the Ogiek tribe of Kenya.* Nairobi.

Blackburn, R.H. (1974). The Okiek and their history. *Azania: Archaeological Research in Africa, 9*(1), 139–157. https://doi.org/10.1080/00672707409511720.

Blackburn, R.H. (1986). Okiek resource tenure and territoriality as mechanisms for social control and allocation of resources. *Sprache und Geschichte in Afrika, 7*(1), 61–82.

Blaikie, P. (1985). *The political economy of soil erosion in developing countries.* London: Longman.

Blaikie, P. (2006). Is small really beautiful? Community-based natural resource management in Malawi and Botswana. *World Development, 34*(11), 1942–1957. https://doi.org/10.1016/j.worlddev.2005.11.023.

Blaikie, P. (2012). Should some political ecology be useful? The inaugural lecture for the cultural and political ecology specialty group, annual meeting of the association of American geographers, April 2010. *Geoforum*, *43*(2), 231–239. https://doi.org/10.1016/j.geoforum.2011.08.010.

Blaikie, P., & Brookfield, H. (eds) (1987). *Land degradation and society*. London: Methuen.

Bongers, F., & Tennigkeit, T. (2010). Degraded forest in Eastern Africa: Introduction. In F. Bongers & T. Tennigkeit (eds), *Degraded forests in eastern Africa: Management and restoration*, 1–18. Washington, DC: Earthscan.

Bosselmann, K. (2008). The way forward: Governance for ecological integrity. In L. Westra, K. Bosselmann, & R. Westra (eds), *Reconciling Human Existence with Ecological Integrity: Science, Ethics, Economics and Law*, 319–332. London and Sterling, VA: Earthscan.

Bourdieu, P., & Wacquant, L. (1992). *The practice of reflexive sociology*. Chicago, IL and London: University of Chicago Press. https://doi.org/10.1080/1369183X.2010.489382.

Branch, D. (2011). *Kenya: Between hope and despair, 1963–2011*. New Haven, CT: Yale University Press.

Bray, Z. (2016). Reconciling development and natural beauty: The promise and dilemma of conservation easements. *Harvard Environmental Law Review*, *34*, 120–137.

Brewer, J.D. (2000). *Ethnography: Understanding social research*. Buckingham and Philadelphia: Open University Press. https://doi.org/10.1007/SpringerReference_300852

Brown, K. (2003). 'Trees, forests and communities': Some historiographical approaches to environmental history on Africa. *Area*, *35*(4), 343–356.

Brown, S. (2001). Authoritarian leaders and multiparty elections in Africa: How foreign donors help to keep Kenya's Daniel arap Moi in power. *Third World Quarterly*, *22*(5), 725–739. https://doi.org/10.1080/01436590120084575.

Brown, S. (2009). Donor responses to the 2008 Kenyan crisis: Finally getting it right? *Journal of Contemporary African Studies*, *27*(3), 389–406. https://doi.org/10.1080/02589000903118847.

Brown, S. (2013). The national accord, impunity and the fragile peace in Kenya. In C.L. Sriram, J. García-Godos, J. Herman, & O. Martin-Ortega (eds), *Transitional justice and peacebuilding on the ground: Victims and ex-combatants*, 238–254. London: Routledge.

Bryant, R.L., & Bailey, S. (1997). *Third World political ecology*. London and New York: Routledge.

Bunker, S.G. (1985). *Underdeveloping the Amazon: Extraction, unequal exchange, and the failure of the modern state*. Urbana: University of Illinois Press.

Büscher, B. (2013). Nature on the move I: The value and circulation of liquid nature and the emergence of fictitious conservation. *New Proposals: Journal of Marxism and Interdisciplinary Inquiry, 6*(1–2), 20–36.

Bushley, B.R. (2014). REDD+ policy making in Nepal: Toward state-centric, polycentric, or market-oriented governance? *Ecology and Society, 19*(3). https://doi.org/10.5751/ES-06853-190334.

Calas, B. (1998). Des contrastes spatiaux aux inégalités territoriales. Géographie d'un « modèle » de développement fatigué. In F. Grignon & G. Prunier (eds), *Le Kenya contemporain*, 13–51. Paris and Nairobi: Karthala and IFRA.

Carneiro da Cunha, M., & de Almeida, M.W.B. (2000). Indigenous people, traditional people, and conservation in the Amazon. *Daedalus, 129*(2), 315–338.

Cavanagh, C.J. (2017). Anthropos into humanitas: Civilizing violence, scientific forestry, and the 'Dorobo question' in eastern Africa. *Environment and Planning D: Society and Space, 35*(4), 694–713. https://doi.org/10.1177/0263775816678620.

Cerutti, P.O., Putzel, L., Pacheco, P., & Baxter, J. (2015). Tackling illegal logging in the tropics: From good intentions to smart policies. *Biores, 9*(4), 10–11.

Chambers, R. (1993). *Challenging the professions: Frontiers for rural development*. London: Intermediate Technology Publications.

Chapin, S.F., Matson, P.A., & Mooney, H.A. (2002). *Principles of terrestrial ecosystem ecology* (2nd edn). New York: Springer. https://doi.org/10.1007/978-1-4419-9504-9.

Charnley, S., & Poe, M.R. (2007). Community forestry in theory and practice: Where are we now? *Annual Review of Anthropology, 36*(1), 301–336. https://doi.org/10.1146/annurev.anthro.35.081705.123143.

Chaudhry, S. (2015). The impact of climate change on human security: The case of the Mau Forest complex. *Development, 58*(2–3), 390–398. https://doi.org/10.1057/s41301-016-0022-4.

Cheeseman, N. (2006). Introduction: Political linkage and political space in the era of decolonization. *Africa Today, 53*(2), 3–24. https://doi.org/10.1353/at.2006.0071.

Chomba, S.W., Nathan, I., Minang, P.A., & Sinclair, F. (2015). Illusions of empowerment? Questioning policy and practice of community forestry in Kenya. *Ecology and Society, 20*(3). https://doi.org/10.5751/ES-07741-200302.

Cliffe, L., & Moorsom, R. (1979). Rural class formation and ecological collapse in Botswana. *Review of African Political Economy, 6*(15–16), 35–52. https://doi.org/10.1080/03056247908703395.

Clifford, J., & Marcus, G.E. (eds) (1986). *Writing culture: The poetics and politics of ethnography*. Berkeley and Los Angeles, CA: University of California Press.

Coe, R., Sinclair, F., & Barrios, E. (2014). Scaling up agroforestry requires research 'in' rather than 'for' development. *Current Opinion in Environmental Sustainability, 6*(1), 73–77. https://doi.org/10.1016/j. cosust.2013.10.013.

Collett, D. (1987). Pastoralists and wildlife: Image and reality in Kenya Maasailand. In D. Anderson & R. Grove (eds), *Conservation in Africa: People, policies, and* practice, 129–148. Cambridge: Cambridge University Press.

Collins, D., Morduch, J., & Rutherford, S. (2009). *Portfolios of the Poor: How the World's Poor Live on $2 a Day*. Princeton, NJ and Oxford: Princeton University Press.

Compagnon, D. (2000). Impératifs et contraintes de la gestion communautaire. In D. Compagnon & F. Constantin (eds), *Administrer l'environnement en Afrique. Gestion communautaire, conservation et développement durable*, 13–35. Paris and Nairobi: Karthala and IFRA.

Connan, D. (2005). Identités ethniques, identité nationale et émergence d'une conscience d'appartenance régionale au Kenya. *Les Cahiers d'Afrique de l'Est, 30.*

Constantin, F. (1994). L'Homme et la Nature: 'Une gestion à réinventer'. *Politique Africaine, 53*(3), 3–10.

Cormier-Salem, M.-C., & Bassett, T.J. (2007). Nature as local heritage in Africa: Longstanding concerns, new challenges. *Africa: Journal of the International African Institute, 77*(01), 1–17. https://doi.org/10.3366/ afr.2007.77.1.1.

Cresswell, J.W., Plano-Clark, V.L., Gutmann, M.L., & Hanson, W.E. (2003). Advanced mixed methods research designs. In A. Tashakkori & C. Teddlie (eds), *Handbook of mixed methods in social and behavioral research*, 209–240. Thousand Oaks, CA: Sage. https://doi. org/10.1017/CBO9781107415324.004.

Cronon, W. (1996). The trouble with wilderness: Or, getting back to the wrong nature. *Environmental History, 1*(1), 7–26. https://doi. org/10.2307/3985059.

de Lame, D. (2006). Gris Nairobi: Esquisse de sociabilités urbaines. In H. Charton-Bigot & D. Rodriguez-Torres (eds), *Nairobi contemporain: Les paradoxes d'une ville fragmentée*, 221–283. Paris and Nairobi: Karthala and IFRA.

de Smedt, J. (2009). 'No Raila, No Peace!' Big man politics and election violence at the Kibera grassroots. *African Affairs, 108*(433), 581–598. https://doi.org/10.1093/afraf/adp043.

Diamond, J. (2005). *Collapse: How societies choose to fail or succeed.* Revised edition. New York: Penguin.

Distefano, J.A. (1990). Hunters or hunted? Towards a history of the Okiek of Kenya. *History in Africa, 17*, 41–57. https://doi. org/10.2307/3171805.

Dove, M.R. (1985). *Swidden agriculture in Indonesia: The subsistence strategies of the Kalimantan Kantu*. New York: Mouton.

Dressler, W., Büscher, B., Schoon, M., Brockington, D., Hayes, T., Kull, C.A., McCarthy, J., & Shrestha, K. (2010). From hope to crisis and back again? A critical history of the global CBNRM narrative. *Environmental Conservation, 37*(1), 5–15. https://doi.org/10.1017/S0376892910000044.

D'Silva, M.U., Smith, S., Della, L.J., Potter, D.A., Rajack-Talley, T.A., & Best, L. (2016). Reflexivity and positionality in researching African-American communities: Lessons from the field. *Intercultural Communication Studies, 25*(1), 94–109.

Duffy, R. (1997). The environmental challenge to the nation-state: Superparks and national parks policy in Zimbabwe. *Journal of Southern African Studies, 23*(3), 441–451. https://doi.org/10.1080/03057079708708549.

Duguma, L., Minang, P., Aynekulu, E., Carsan, S., Nzyoka, J., Bah, A., Jamnadass, R. 2020. From tree planting to tree growing: Rethinking ecosystem restoration through trees. ICRAF Working Paper No. 304. Nairobi: World Agroforestry (ICRAF). http://dx.doi.org/10.5716/WP20001.PDF.

Ehrlich, P.R. (1968). *The population bomb*. London: Ballantine.

Ellen, R.F. (1982). *Environment, subsistence and system: The ecology of small-scale social formations*. Cambridge: Cambridge University Press.

England, K.V.L. (1994). Getting personal: Reflexivity, positionality, and feminist research. *The Professional Geographer, 46*(1), 80–89. https://doi.org/10.1111/j.0033-0124.1994.00080.x.

Escobar, A. (1995). *Encountering development: The making and unmaking of the Third World*. Princeton, NJ: Princeton University Press.

Escobar, A. (1999). After nature: Steps to an antiessentialist political ecology. *Current Anthropology, 40*(1), 1–30. https://doi.org/10.1086/515799.

Fairhead, J., & Leach, M. (1994a). Représentations culturelles africaines et gestion de l'environnement. *Politique Africaine, 53*, 11–25.

Fairhead, J., & Leach, M. (1994b). Whose forest? Modern conservation and historical land use in Guinea's Ziama reserve. *Rural Development Forestry Network Paper, 18*(c), 24.

Fairhead, J., & Leach, M. (1995). False forest history, complicit social analysis: Rethinking some West African environmental narratives. *World Development, 23*(6), 1023–1035. https://doi.org/10.1016/0305-750X(95)00026-9.

Fairhead, J., & Leach, M. (1996). Enriching the landscape: Social history and the management of transition ecology in the forest-savanna mosaic of the Republic of Guinea. *Africa: Journal of the International African Institute, 66*(01), 14–36. https://doi.org/10.2307/1161509.

Fairhead, J., Leach, M., & Scoones, I. (2012). Green grabbing: A new appropriation of nature? *Journal of Peasant Studies, 39*(2), 237–261. https://doi.org/10.1080/03066150.2012.671770.

Feeny, D., Berkes, F., McCay, B.J., & Acheson, J.M. (1990). The tragedy of the commons: Twenty-two years later. *Human Ecology, 18*(1), 1–19. https://doi.org/10.1007/BF00889070.

Feierman, S. (1990). *Peasant intellectuals: Anthropology and history in Tanzania*. Madison: University of Wisconsin Press. http://hdl.handle.net/2027/heb.02591.0001.001.

Finnegan, R. (1991). Tradition, but what tradition and for whom? *Oral Tradition, 6*(1), 104–124.

Folke, C. (1996). Conservation, driving forces, and institutions. Review of the article 'Principles for the conservation of wild living resources' by M. Mangel et al. *Ecological Applications, 6*(2), 370–372.

Fortmann, L. (1995). Talking claims: Discursive strategies in contesting property. *World Development, 23*(6), 1053–1063. https://doi.org/10.1016/0305-750X(95)00024-7.

Foucault, M. (1991). Governmentality. In G. Burchell, C. Gordon, & P. Miller (eds), *The Foucault effect: Studies in governmentality*, 87–104. Chicago, IL: University of Chicago Press.

Fuchs, L. (2014). Political integration of minority communities: The Ogiek of Eastern Mau Forest in the 2013 elections. In C. Thibon, M.-A. Fouéré, M. Ndeda, & S. Mwangi (eds), *Kenya's past as prologue: Voters, violence and the 2013 general election*, 77–95. Nairobi: Twaweza Communications.

Fuchs, L., Njuguna, L., Robinson, L., Zampaligre, N., Coulibaly, J., Crane, T., et al. (2018). Characterizing local adaptive capacity at various scales: A framework for adaptation planning. LGACC Policy Brief No. 2. Nairobi: World Agroforestry Centre (ICRAF).

Fuchs, L., Orero, L., Namoi, N., & Neufeldt, H. (2019). How to effectively enhance sustainable livelihoods in smallholder systems: A comparative study from Western Kenya. *Sustainability, 11*(6), 1564. https://doi.org/10.3390/su11061564.

Fuchs, L., Peters, B., & Neufeldt, H. (2019). Identities, interests, and preferences matter: Fostering sustainable community development by building assets and agency in Western Kenya. *Sustainable Development*, 1–9. https://doi.org/10.1002/sd.1934.

Fujimura, J.H. (1992). Crafting science: Standardized packages, boundary objects and 'translation'. In A. Pickering (ed.), *Science as Practice and Culture*, 168–211. Chicago, IL: University of Chicago Press.

Gadgil, M., & Rao, P.R.S. (1994). A system of positive incentives to conserve biodiversity. *Economic and Political Weekly, 29*(32), 2103–2107.

Gadgil, M., Berkes, F., & Folke, C. (1993). Indigenous knowledge for biodiversity conservation. *Ambio, 22*(2/3), 151–156. https://doi.org/10.2307/4314060.

Geertz, C. (1973). *The interpretation of cultures.* New York: Basic Books.

Geertz, C. (1983). *Local Knowledge: Further essays in interpretative anthropology.* New York: Basic Books.

Gibson, C.C., & Koontz, T. (1998). When 'community' is not enough: Institutions and values in community-based forest management in southern Indiana. *Human Ecology, 26*(4), 621–647. https://doi.org/10.1023/A:1018701525978.

Gibson, C.C., Lehoucq, F.E., & Williams, J. (2002). Does privatization protect natural resources? Property rights and forests in Guatemala. *Social Science Quarterly, 83*(1), 206–225.

Glasmeier, A.K., & Farrigan, T. (2005). Understanding community forestry: A qualitative meta-study of the concept, the process, and its potential for poverty alleviation in the United States case. *The Geographical Journal, 171*(1), 56–69. https://doi.org/10.1111/j.1475-4959.2005.00149.x.

Gouldner, A.W. (1970). *The coming crisis of western sociology.* London: Heinemann.

Green, K.E. (2016). A political ecology of scaling: Struggles over power, land and authority. *Geoforum, 74,* 88–97. https://doi.org/10.1016/j.geoforum.2016.05.007.

Gregory, D., Johnston, R., Pratt, G., Watts, M., & Whatmore, S. (eds) (2009). *The dictionary of human geography* (5th edn). Chichester: Wiley-Blackwell.

Grove, R.H. (1996). *Green imperialism: Colonial expansion, tropical island Edens and the origins of environmentalism.* Cambridge: Cambridge University Press.

Guha, R. (1989). *The unquiet woods: Ecological change and peasant resistance in the Himalaya.* Delhi: Oxford University Press.

Gunningham, N. (2011). Governance, wicked problems and water. In S. Russell, B. Frame, & J. Lennox (eds), *Old problems new solutions: Integrative research supporting natural resource governance,* 13–21. Lincoln, NZ: Manaaki Whenua Press.

Guyer, J., & Richards, P. (1996). The invention of biodiversity: Social perspectives on the management of biological variety in Africa. *Africa: Journal of the International African Institute, 66*(01), 1–13. https://doi.org/10.2307/1161508.

Hardesty, D.L. (1977). *Ecological anthropology.* New York: Wiley.

Hardin, G. (1968). The tragedy of the commons. *Science, 162*(3859), 1243–1248. https://doi.org/10.1126/science.162.3859.1243.

Hassan, R., & Nhemachena, C. (2008). Determinants of African farmers' strategies for adapting to climate change: Multinomial choice analysis. *African Journal of Agricultural and Resource Economics (AfJARE), 2*(1), 83–104.

Hauge, W., & Ellingsen, T. (1998). Beyond environmental scarcity: Causal pathways to conflict. *Journal of Peace Research, 35*(3), 299–317. https://doi.org/10.1177/0022343398035003003.

Hawkes, J. (2001). *The fourth pillar of sustainability: Culture's essential role in public planning.* Melbourne: Common Ground Publishing in association with the Cultural Development Network.

Hecht, S. (1985). Environment, development and politics: Capital accumulation and the livestock sector in Eastern Amazonia. *World Development, 13*(6), 663–684. https://doi.org/10.1016/0305-750X(85)90114-7.

Hecht, S., & Cockburn, A. (1989). *The fate of the forests: Developers, destroyers and defenders of the Amazon.* London: Verso.

Hedlund, H. (1979). Contradictions in the peripheralization of a pastoral society: The Maasai. *Review of African Political Economy, 6*(15–16), 15–34. https://doi.org/10.1080/03056247908703394.

Heilbroner, R. (1974). *An inquiry into the human prospect.* New York: W.W. Norton.

Henrard, K. (2001). Devising an adequate system of minority protection. *Global Review of Ethnopolitics, 1*(1).

Hicks, R.L., Parks, B.C., Roberts, J.T., & Tierney, M.J. (2008). *Greening aid? Understanding the environmental impact of development assistance.* Oxford: Oxford University Press.

Hobley, C.W. (1903). Notes concerning the Eldorobo of the Mau, British East Africa. *Man, 3,* 33–34.

Hobsbawm, E.J., & Ranger, T.O. (eds) (1983). *The invention of tradition.* Cambridge: Cambridge University Press. https://doi.org/10.2307/25142744.

Hohenthal, J., & Minoia, P. (2018). Political ecology of asymmetric ecological knowledges: Diverging views on the eucalyptus-water nexus in the Taita Hills Kenya. *Journal of Political Ecology, 25,* 1–19. https://doi.org/10.2458/v25i1.22005.

Homer-Dixon, T. (1994). Environmental scarcities and violent conflict: Evidence from cases. *International Security, 19*(1), 5–40. https://doi.org/10.2307/2539147.

Homer-Dixon, T. (1995). Environmental scarcities, state capacity, and civil violence. *Bulletin of the American Academy of Arts and Sciences, 48*(7), 26–33. https://doi.org/10.2307/3824330.

Homer-Dixon, T. (1999). *Environment, scarcity, and violence.* Princeton, NJ: Princeton University Press.

Homewood, K., Coast, E., & Thompson, M. (2004). In-migrants and exclusion in East African rangelands: Access, tenure and conflict. *Africa: Journal of the International African Institute, 74*(04), 567–610. https://doi.org/10.3366/afr.2004.74.4.567.

Hornsby, C. (2013). *Kenya: A history since independence.* London and New York: I.B. Tauris.

Hornsby, C., & Throup, D. (1998). *Multi-party politics in Kenya: The Kenyatta & Moi states & the triumph of the system in the 1992 election.* Oxford: James Currey.

Howden, S.M., Soussana, J.-F., Tubiello, F.N., Chhetri, N., Dunlop, M., & Meinke, H. (2007). Adapting agriculture to climate change. *Proceedings of the National Academy of Sciences, 104*(50), 19691–19696. https://doi.org/10.1073/pnas.0701890104.

Hughes, L. (2006). *Moving the Maasai: A colonial misadventure* (Vol. 107). Basingstoke and New York: Palgrave Macmillan.

Hulme, D. (2009). *Why we disagree about climate change: Understanding controversy, inaction and opportunity.* Cambridge: Cambridge University Press.

Hulme, D., & Murphree, M. (2001a). Community conservation as policy: Promise and performance. In D. Hulme & M. Murphree (eds), *African Wildlife and Livelihoods: The promise and performance of community conservation,* 280–297. Oxford: James Currey.

Hulme, D., & Murphree, M. (2001b). Community conservation in Africa. An introduction. In D. Hulme & M. Murphree (eds), *African Wildlife and Livelihoods: The promise and performance of community conservation,* 1–8. Oxford: James Currey.

Huntingford, G.W.B. (1929). Modern hunters: Some account of the Kamelilo-Kapchepkendi Dorobo (Okiek) of Kenya colony. *The Journal of the Royal Anthropological Institute of Great Britain and Ireland, 59,* 333–378. https://doi.org/10.2307/2843890.

Huntingford, G.W.B. (1931). Free hunters, serf-tribes, and submerged classes in East Africa. *Man, 31,* 262–266.

Huntingford, G.W.B. (1942). The social organization of the Dorobo. *African Studies, 1*(3), 183–200. https://doi.org/10.1080/00020184208706584.

Huntingford, G.W.B. (1951). The social institutions of the Dorobo. *Anthropos, 46,* 1–48.

Huntingford, G.W.B. (1955). The economic life of the Dorobo. *Anthropos, 50*(4–6), 602–634.

ICRAF (2014). Local knowledge (including indigenous and traditional knowledge). Policy Guidelines Series. Nairobi: World Agroforestry Centre (ICRAF).

James, P. (2015). *Urban sustainability in theory and practice: Circles of sustainability.* London and New York: Routledge.

Jewitt, S. (1995). Europe's 'others'? Forestry policy and practice in colonial and postcolonial India. *Environment and Planning D: Society and Space, 13,* 67–90. https://doi.org/10.1068/d130067.

Johnson, B. (1976). International environmental conventions. *Ambio, 5*(2), 55–66.

Johnson, R., & Onwuegbuzie, A.J. (2004). Mixed methods research: A research paradigm whose time has come. *Educational Researcher, 33*(7), 14–26. https://doi.org/10.3102/0013189X033007014.

Kagwanja, P. (2010). *Fighting for the Mau forests: Land, climate change and the politics of the Kibaki succession*. African Policy Report. Nairobi: Nairobi Africa Policy Institute.

Kahora, B. (2015). How to eat a forest. In N. Edjabe (ed.), *Chimurenga Chronic*. Cape Town: Kalakuta Trust.

Kameri-Mbote, P. (2009). The land question in Kenya: Legal and ethical dimensions. In E. Gachenga, L.G. Franchesci, M. Aketch, & D.W. Lutz, *Governance, institutions and the human condition*, 219–246. Nairobi: Strathmore University and Law Africa.

Kangwana, K. (2001). Can community conservation strategies meet the conservation agenda? In D. Hulme & M. Murphree (eds), *African Wildlife and Livelihoods; The promise and performance of community conservation*, 256–266. Oxford: James Currey.

Kaufman, P. (2013). Scribo Ergo Cogito: Reflexivity through writing. *Teaching Sociology, 41*(1), 70–81. https://doi.org/10.1177/0092055X12458679.

Kellert, S.R., Mehta, J.N., Ebbin, S.A., & Lichtenfeld, L.L. (2000). Community natural resource management: Promise, rhetoric, and reality. *Society & Natural Resources, 13*(8), 705–715. https://doi.org/10.1080/089419200750035575.

Khan, M.T. (2013). Theoretical frameworks in political ecology and participatory nature/forest conservation: The necessity for a heterodox approach and the critical moment. *Journal of Political Ecology, 20* (January), 460–472. https://doi.org/10.2458/v20i1.21757.

King, J., Lalampaa, T., Craig, I., & Harrison, M. (2015). *A guide to establishing community conservancies: The NRT model* (Version 1). Isiolo, Kenya.

Kipkoech, A., Mogaka, H., Cheboiywo, J., & Kimaro, D. (2011). *The total economic value of Maasai Mau, Trans Mara and Eastern Mau forest blocks of the Mau Forest, Kenya*. Kisumu and Nairobi: Lake Victoria Basin Commission and Environmental Research and Policy Analysis (K).

Klooster, D.J. (2009). Toward adaptive community forest management: Integrating local forest knowledge with scientific forestry. *Economic Geography, 78*(1), 43–70. https://doi.org/10.1111/j.1944-8287.2002.tb00175.x.

Klopp, J.M. (2001). 'Ethnic clashes' and winning elections: The case of Kenya's electoral despotism. *Canadian Journal of African Studies / Revue canadienne des études africaines, 35*(3), 473–517. https://doi.org/10.1080/00083968.2001.10751230.

Klopp, J.M. (2002). Can moral ethnicity trump political tribalism? The struggle for land and nation in Kenya. *African Studies, 61*(2).

Klopp, J.M. (2012). Deforestation and democratization: Patronage, politics and forests in Kenya. *Journal of Eastern African Studies, 6*(2), 351–370. https://doi.org/10.1080/17531055.2012.669577.

Klopp, J.M., & Lumumba, O. (2016). The state of Kenya's land policy and law reform: A political institutional analysis. In World Bank, Land and poverty conference 2016: Scaling up responsible land governance. 14–18 March. Washington, DC.

Klopp, J.M., & Sang, J. (2011). Maps, power and the destruction of the Mau Forest in Kenya. *Georgetown Journal of International Affairs, 12*(1), 125–135.

Kratz, C.A. (1980). Are the Okiek really Masai? Or Kipsigis? Or Kikuyu? *Cahiers d'Études Africaines, 20*(79), 355–368.

Kratz, C.A. (1993). 'We've always done it like this ... except for a few details': 'Tradition' and 'innovation' in Okiek ceremonies. *Comparative Studies in Society and History, 35*(1), 30–65.

Kratz, C.A. (1996). Okiek in portraits: Mediation, interpretation a photographic exhibition. *Cahiers d'Études Africaines, 36*(141/142), 51–79.

Kratz, C.A. (1999). The Okiek of Kenya. In R.B. Lee & R. Daly (eds), *Foraging peoples: An encyclopedia of contemporary hunter-gatherers.* Cambridge University Press.

Kull, C.A., Ibrahim, C.K., & Meredith, T. (2006). Can privatization conserve the global biodiversity commons? Tropical reforestation through globalization. IASCP Conference Paper, 1–28.

Lafargue, J., & Katumanga, M. (2008). Kenya in turmoil: Post-election violence and precarious pacification. *Les Cahiers d'Afrique de l'Est, 38*, 13–32.

Landesa, L.C. (2011). *Assessment of the South Western Mau forest IDPs.*

Langat, D.K., Maranga, E.K., Aboud, A.A., & Cheboiwo, J.K. (2016). Role of forest resources to local livelihoods: The case of East Mau Forest ecosystem, Kenya. *International Journal of Forestry Research, 2016*, 1–10. https://doi.org/10.1155/2016/4537354.

Leach, M., Mearns, R., & Scoones, I. (1999). Environmental entitlements: Dynamics and institutions in community-based natural resource management. *World Development, 27*(2), 225–247. https://doi.org/10.1016/S0305-750X(98)00141-7.

Little, P., & Horowitz, M.M. (eds) (1987). *Lands at risk in the Third World: Local-level perspectives.* Boulder, CO: Westview Press.

Little, P. (2003). Rethinking interdisciplinary paradigms & the political ecology of pastoralism in East Africa. In T.J. Bassett & D. Crummey (eds), *African savannas: Global narratives and local knowledge of environmental change in Africa*, 161–177. Oxford & Portsmouth, NH: James Currey & Heinemann.

Liverman, D. (2015). Reading climate change and climate governance as political ecologies. In T. Perreault, G. Bridge, & J. McCarthy (eds), *Routledge handbook of political ecology*, 252–253. New York: Routledge.

Lonsdale, J. (1992). The political culture of Kenya. Occasional Paper No. 37. Edinburgh: Centre of African Studies, Edinburgh University.

Lonsdale, J. (1994). Moral ethnicity and political tribalism. In P. Kaarsholm & J. Hultin (eds), *Inventions and boundaries: Historical and anthropological approaches to the study of ethnicity and nationalism*, 131–150. Roskilde: Institute for Development Studies.

Lonsdale, J. (1996). Ethnicité, morale et tribalisme politique. *Politique Africaine* (61), 98–115.

Lovatt-Smith, D. (2008). *Amboseli. A miracle too far?* Nairobi: English Press.

Lozano, R. (2008). Envisioning sustainability three-dimensionally. *Journal of Cleaner Production, 16*(17), 1838–1846. https://doi.org/10.1016/j.jclepro.2008.02.008.

Ludeki, J.V., Wamukoya, G.M., & Walubengo, D. (2006). *Environmental management in Kenya: A framework for sustainable forest management in Kenya: Understanding the new forest policy and Forests Act, 2005*. Nairobi: Centre for Environmental Legal Research and Education.

Lusigi, W.J. (1981). New approaches to wildlife conservation in Kenya. *Ambio, 10*(2–3), 87–92.

Lynch, G. (2011). *I say to you: Ethnic politics and the Kalenjin in Kenya*. Chicago, IL and London: University of Chicago Press.

Maathai, W. (2010). *Replenishing the earth: Spiritual values for healing ourselves and the world*. New York: Doubleday.

Mackenzie, A.F.D. (2003). Land tenure and biodiversity: An exploration in the political ecology of Murang'a District, Kenya. *Human Organization, 62*(3), 255–266. https://doi.org/10.17730/humo.62.3.d1dfv6mlr3hevdy7.

Mackey, B. (2008). The Earth charter, ethics and global governance. In L. Westra, K. Bosselmann, & R. Westra (eds), *Reconciling Human Existence with Ecological Integrity: Science, Ethics, Economics and Law*, 61–71. London and Sterling, VA: Earthscan.

Maffi, L. (2005). Linguistic, cultural, and biological diversity. *Annual Review of Anthropology, 34*(1), 599–617. https://doi.org/10.1146/annurev.anthro.34.081804.120437.

Mallon, S. (2010). Against tradition. *The Contemporary Pacific, 22*(2), 362–381.

Manji, A. (2014). The politics of land reform in Kenya 2012. *African Studies Review, 57*(01), 115–130. https://doi.org/10.1017/asr.2014.8.

Markakis, J. (1999). Pastoralists & politicians in Kenya. *Review of African Political Economy, 26*(80), 293–296. https://doi.org/10.1080/03056249908704388.

Martin, A. (2005). Environmental conflict between refugee and host communities. *Journal of Peace Research, 42*(3), 329–346. https://doi.org/10.1177/0022343305052015.

Maundu, P. & Tengnäs, T. (eds) (2005). Useful trees and shrubs for Kenya. Technical handbook No. 35. Nairobi: World Agroforestry Centre – Eastern and Central Africa Regional Programme (ICRAF-ECA).

Mbembe, A. (2000). At the edge of the world: Boundaries, territoriality, and sovereignty in Africa. *Public Culture, 12*(1), 259–284. https://doi.org/10.1215/08992363-12-1-259.

McCann, J.C. (1999). *Green land, brown land, black land: An environmental history of Africa 1800–1990.* Oxford & Portsmouth, NH: James Currey & Heinemann.

McLain, R.J. (2001). Inclusive community forest management. *Journal of sustainable forestry, 13*(1–2), 195–203. https://doi.org/10.1300/J091v13n01_01.

Médard, C. (2008a). Elected leaders, militias and prophets: Violence in Mount Elgon (2006–2008). *Les Cahiers d'Afrique de l'Est, 38*, 339–361.

Médard, C. (2008b). Key issues in disentangling the Kenyan crisis: Evictions, autochthony and land privatisation. *Les Cahiers d'Afrique de l'Est, 38*, 365–381.

Meyer, J.W., Frank, D.J., Hironaka, A., Schofer, E., & Tuma, N.B. (1997). The structuring of a world environmental regime, 1870–1990. *International Organization, 51*(4), 623–651. https://doi.org/10.1162/002081897550474.

Michael, J.A. (2003). Efficient habitat protection with diverse landowners and fragmented landscapes. *Environmental Science & Policy, 6*(3), 243–251. https://doi.org/10.1016/S1462-9011(03)00042-X.

Mills, C.W. (1959). *The sociological imagination.* New York: Oxford University Press. Review by W.L. Kolb in *American Sociological Review, 25*(6) (December 1960), 966–969. https://doi.org/10.2307/2089989.

Morse, B. (2008). Indigenous rights as mechanism to promote environmental sustainability. In L. Westra, K. Bosselmann, & R. Westra (eds), *Reconciling human existence with ecological integrity: Science, ethics, economics and law,* 159–193. London and Sterling, VA: Earthscan.

Muchemi, J., & Ehrensperger, A. (2011). *Ogiek peoples ancestral territories atlas: Safeguarding territories, cultures and natural resources of Ogiek indigenous people in Kenya.* Volume 1: *Eastern Mau Forest.* Nairobi: ERMIS Africa and CDE.

Muchemi, J., Ehrensperger, A., & Kiteme, B. (2015). Ogiek peoples ancestral territories atlas. In A. Ehrensperger & U. Wiesmann (eds), *Eastern and Southern Africa Partnership Programme: Highlights from 15 Years of joint action for sustainable development,* 51–54. Bern: Centre for Development and Environment (CDE), University of Bern, with Bern Open Publishing (BOP).

Mugo, E., Nyandiga, C., & Gachanja, M.K. (2010). *Development of forestry in Kenya (1900–2007): Challenges and lessons learnt.* Nairobi: Kenya Forests Working Group.

Munro, W.A. (2003). Ecological crisis & resource management policy in Zimbabwe's communal lands. In T.J. Bassett & D. Crummey (eds), *African savannas: Global narratives and local knowledge of environ-*

mental change in Africa, 178–204. Oxford & Portsmouth, NH: James Currey & Heinemann.

Murphree, M. (2000). 'Ex Africa semper aliquid novi?' Pour une nouvelle approche de la conservation. In D. Compagnon & F. Constantin (eds), *Administrer l'environnement en Afrique: Gestion communautaire, conservation et développement durable*, 41–52. Paris and Nairobi: Karthala and IFRA.

Musembi, C.N., & Kameri-Mbote, P. (2013). Mobility, marginality and tenure transformation in Kenya: Explorations of community property rights in law and practice. *Nomadic Peoples, 17*(1), 5–32. https://doi.org/10.3167/np.2013.170102.

Musyoki, J.K., Mugwe, J., & Mutundu, K. (2016). Factors influencing level of participation of community forest associations in management forests in Kenya. *Journal of Sustainable Forestry, 35*(3), 205–216. https://doi.org/10.1080/10549811.2016.1142454.

Mutugi, M., & Kiiru, W. (2015). Biodiversity, local resource, national heritage, regional concern, and global impact: The case of Mau Forest, Kenya. *European Scientific Journal, 1*(October), 681–691.

Nagendra, H., & Ostrom, E. (2012). Polycentric governance of multifunctional forested landscapes. *International Journal of the Commons, 6*(2). https://doi.org/10.18352/ijc.321.

Nakhooda, S., Caravani, A., Bird, N., & Schalatek, L. (2011). *Climate finance regional briefing: Sub-Saharan Africa.* Climate Finance Fundamentals Brief No. 7. London and Washington, DC: Overseas Development Institute and Heinrich Böll Stiftung North America.

Nassali, M. (2011). Ethnic and racial minorities and movement towards political inclusion in East Africa: Cases of Kenya, Uganda and Tanzania. In H. Majamba, *Towards a rights-sensitive East African Community: The case of ethnic and racial minorities*, 1–65. Kampala: Fountain Publishers.

Neumann, R.P. (1992). Political ecology of wildlife conservation in the Mt. Meru area of Northeast Tanzania. *Land Degradation and Development, 3*(2), 85–98. https://doi.org/10.1002/ldr.3400030203.

Neumann, R.P. (1998). *Imposing wilderness: Struggles over livelihood and nature preservation in Africa.* Berkeley, Los Angeles, and London: University of California Press.

Nixon, R. (2010). Unimagined communities: Developmental refugees, megadams and monumental modernity. *New Formations, 69*(69), 62–80. https://doi.org/10.3898/NEWF.69.03.2010.

Njeru, J. (2012). Mobilization and protest: The struggle to save Karura Forest in Nairobi, Kenya. *African Geographical Review, 31*(1), 17–32. https://doi.org/10.1080/19376812.2012.681294.

Noriega, I.L., Dawson, I.K., Vernooy, R., Köhler-Rollefson, I., & Halewood, M. (2017). Agricultural diversification as an adaptation strategy. *Agriculture for Development, 30*, 25–28.

Nunan, F. (2015). *Understanding poverty and the environment: Analytical frameworks and approaches*. London and New York: Routledge. https://doi.org/10.4324/9781315886701.

Nyangena, W. (2008). Economic issues for environmental and resource management in Kenya. In C.O. Okidi, P. Kameri-Mbote, & M. Akech (eds), *Environmental governance in Kenya: Implementing the framework law*, 61–89. Nairobi, Kampala, and Dar es Salaam: East African Educational Publishers.

O'Brien, J. (1985). Sowing the seeds of famine: The political economy of food deficits in Sudan. *Review of African Political Economy, 12*(33), 23–32. https://doi.org/10.1080/03056248508703630.

Odhiambo, E.A., & Lonsdale, J. (eds) (2003). *Mau Mau and nationhood: Arms, authority, and narration*. Athens, Oxford, and Nairobi: Ohio University Press, James Currey, and EAEP.

Ohenjo, N. (2011). Participation of minorities and indigenous peoples in political decision making in Kenya. In H. Majamba, *Towards a rights-sensitive east African community: The case of ethnic and racial minorities*, 156–224. Kampala: Fountain Publishers.

Ojha, H.R., Ford, R., Keenan, R J., Race, D., Vega, D.C., Baral, H., & Sapkota, P. (2016). Delocalizing communities: Changing forms of community engagement in natural resources governance. *World Development, 87*(November), 274–290. https://doi.org/10.1016/j.worlddev.2016.06.017.

Okidi, C.O. (2008). Concept, function and structure of environmental law. In C.O. Okidi, P. Kameri-Mbote, & M. Akech (eds), *Environmental governance in Kenya: Implementing the framework law*, 3–60. Nairobi, Kampala, and Dar es Salaam: East African Educational Publishers.

Okidi, C.O., Kameri-Mbote, P., & Akech, M. (eds) (2008). *Environmental governance in Kenya: Implementing the framework law*. Nairobi, Kampala, and Dar es Salaam: East African Educational Publishers.

Okumu, B., & Muchapondwa, E. (2017a). Determinants of successful collective management of forest resources: Evidence from Kenyan community forest associations (ERSA working paper). Cape Town: Economic Research Southern Africa.

Okumu, B., & Muchapondwa, E. (2017b). Economic valuation of forest ecosystem services in Kenya: Implication for design of PES schemes and participatory forest management (ERSA working paper). Cape Town: Economic Research Southern Africa.

O'Neill, K.M. (1996). The international politics of national parks. *Human Ecology, 24*(4), 521–539. https://doi.org/10.1007/BF02168865.

Ophuls, W. (1977). *Ecology and the politics of scarcity: Prologue to a political theory of the steady state*. San Francisco: W.H. Freeman and Company.

Orlove, B.S. (1980). Ecological anthropology. *Annual Review of Anthropology, 9*(1), 235–273. https://doi.org/10.1146/annurev.an.09.100180.001315.

Ostrom, E. (1998). Coping with tragedies of the commons. Paper prepared for delivery at the 1998 Annual Meeting of the Association for Politics and the Life Sciences (APLS), Back Bay Hilton Hotel, Boston, Massachusetts.

Ostrom, E., & Gardner, R. (1993). Coping with asymmetries in the commons: Self-governing irrigation systems can work. *Journal of Economic Perspectives, 7*(4), 93–112. https://doi.org/10.1257/jep.7.4.93.

Pacheco, P., Mejía, E., Cano, W., & de Jong, W. (2016). Smallholder forestry in the Western Amazon: Outcomes from forest reforms and emerging policy perspectives. *Forests, 7*(9). https://doi.org/10.3390/f7090193.

Parker, D.P. (2004). Land trusts and the choice to conserve land with full ownership or conservation easements. *Natural Resources Journal, 44*, 483–518. https://digitalrepository.unm.edu/nrj/vol44/iss2/8.

Patel, E., Robinson, L., & Ng'ang'a, I. (2018). Multilevel dialogue and planning for improving rangelands in northern Kenya. Policy Brief No. 1. Nairobi: International Livestock Research Institute (ILRI). http://hdl.handle.net/10568/92395.

Peet, R., & Watts, M. (1996). Liberation ecology: Development, sustainability, and environment in an age of market triumphalism. In R. Peet & M. Watts (eds), *Liberation ecologies: Environment, development, social movements*, 1–45. London: Routledge.

Peluso, N.L. (1992). *Rich forests, poor people: Resource control and resistance in Java.* Berkeley: University of California Press.

Peluso, N.L., & Vandergeest, P. (2001). Genealogies of the political forest and customary rights in Indonesia, Malaysia, and Thailand. *The Journal of Asian Studies, 60*(3), 761–812. https://doi.org/10.2307/2700109.

Peluso, N.L., Turner, M., & Fortmann, L. (1994). Introducing community forestry: Annotated listing of topics and readings. Community Forestry Note 12. Rome: Food and Agriculture Organization of the United Nations.

Peters, B. (2010). Per Diems: To pay or not to pay? That is the question. *Strategies* (October), 11–14.

Poteete, A.R., & Ribot, J. (2011). Repertoires of domination: Decentralization as process in Botswana and Senegal. *World Development, 39*(3), 439–449. https://doi.org/10.1016/j.worlddev.2010.09.013.

Proctor, J.D. (1998). The social construction of nature: Relativist accusations, pragmatist and critical realist responses. *Restoration Ecology, 88*(3), 352–376. https://doi.org/10.1111/0004-5608.00105.

Rahmato, D. (2003). Littering the landscape: Environmental policy in Northeast Ethiopia. In T.J. Bassett & D. Crummey (eds), *African savannas: Global narratives and local knowledge of environmental change in Africa*, 205–224. Oxford & Portsmouth, NH: James Currey & Heinemann.

Razac, O. (2000). *Histoire politique du barbelé: La prairie, la tranchée, le camp.* Paris: La fabrique-éditions.

Redford, K. (1990). The ecologically noble savage. *Cultural Survival Quarterly, 15*(1), 46–48.

ReVelle, P., & ReVelle, C. (1992). *The global environment: Securing a sustainable future.* Boston and London: Jones and Bartlett.

Rittel, H.W.J., & Webber, M.M. (1973). Dilemmas in a general theory of planning. *Policy Sciences, 4*(2), 155–169. https://doi.org/10.1007/BF01405730.

Robiglio, V. & Reyes, M. (2016). Restoration through formalization? Assessing the potential of Peru's Agroforestry Concessions scheme to contribute to restoration in agricultural frontiers in the Amazon region. *World Development Perspectives, 3*(1), 42–46.

Ronoh, T.K. (2016). Contextualizing historical and socio-anthropological literature on indigenous education in enhancing environmental conservation: Case of Ogiek of Mau Forest, Kenya. *European Journal of Alternative Education Studies, 1*(1), 1–26. https://doi.org/10.5281/zenodo.57094.

Said, E.W. (1978). *Orientalism.* Harmondsworth: Penguin.

Scott, J.C. (1985). *Weapons of the weak: Everyday forms of peasant resistance.* New Haven, CT and London: Yale University Press.

Scott, J.C. (1990). *Domination and the Arts of Resistance: Hidden Transcripts.* New Haven, CT: Yale University Press,

Serrano Alvarez, J.A. (2014). When the enemy is the state: Common lands management in northwest Spain (1850–1936). *International Journal of the Commons, 8*(1), 107–133. https://doi.org/10.18352/ijc.389.

Siebert, S.F., & Belsky, J.M. (2014). Historic livelihoods and land uses as ecological disturbances and their role in enhancing biodiversity: An example from Bhutan. *Biological Conservation, 177*, 82–89. https://doi.org/10.1016/j.biocon.2014.06.015.

Sills, D.L. (1975). The environmental movement and its critics. *Human Ecology, 3*(1), 1–41. https://doi.org/10.1007/BF01531771.

Smith, D. (2003). Patronage, per diems and the 'workshop mentality': The practice of family planning programs in southeastern Nigeria. *World Development, 31*(4), 703–715. https://doi.org/10.1016/S0305-750X(03)00006-8.

Smith, N. (2010). *Uneven development: Nature, capital, and the production of space* (Third edn). Athens and London: University of Georgia Press.

Smith-Dumont, E., Bonhomme, S., Pagella, T.F., & Sinclair, F. (2017). Structured stakeholder engagement leads to development of more diverse and inclusive agroforestry options. *Experimental Agriculture*, 1–23. https://doi.org/10.1017/S0014479716000788.

Sonkoyo, L. (2016). Community participation in forest management. *Forester* (18), 10.

Southgate, C., & Hulme, D. (2000). Uncommon property: The scramble for wetland in Southern Kenya. In P. Woodhouse, H. Bernstein, & D. Hulme (eds), *African enclosures? The social dynamics of wetlands-in-drylands*, 73–118. Oxford: James Currey.

Stalley, P. (2003). Environmental scarcity and international conflict. *Conflict Management and Peace Science, 20*(2), 33–58. https://doi.org/10.1177/073889420302000202.

Standing, A., & Gachanja, M. (2014). The political economy of REDD+ in Kenya: Identifying and responding to corruption challenges. *U4* Issue No. 3. Bergen, Norway: U4 Anti-Corruption Resource Centre Chr. Michelsen Institute (CMI).

Steinhart, E.I. (2006). *Black poachers, white hunters: A social history of hunting in colonial Kenya* (East African studies). Oxford, Nairobi, and Athens: James Currey, EAEP, and Ohio University Press.

Taylor, R. (2001). Participatory natural resource monitoring and management: Implications for conservation. In D. Hulme & M. Murphree (eds), *African wldlife and livelihoods: The promise and performance of community conservation*, 267–279. Oxford: James Currey.

Teddlie, C., & Tashakkori, A. (2009). *Foundations of mixed methods research: Integrating quantitative and qualitative approaches in the social and behavioral sciences*. Thousand Oaks, CA: Sage.

Thenya, T., Wandago, B.O.B., Nahama, E.T., & Gachanja, M.K. (2008). *Participatory forest management experiences in Kenya (1996–2007)*. Nairobi: Kenya Forests Working Group.

Thompson, E. (1971). The moral economy of the English crowd in the eighteenth century. *Past and Present, 50*, 76–136.

Throup, D. (1987). *Economic and social origins of Mau Mau 1945–53*. London: James Currey.

Timura, C.T. (2001). 'Environmental conflict' and the social life of environmental security discourse. *Anthropological Quarterly, 74*(3), 104–113.

Tönnies, F. (1887). *Gemeinschaft und Gesellschaft: Abhandlung des Communismus und des Socialismus als empirischer Culturformen*. Leipzig: Fues.

Vaccaro, I., Beltran, O., & Paquet, P.A. (2013). Political ecology and conservation policies: Some theoretical genealogies. *Journal of Political Ecology, 20*(1). https://doi.org/10.2458/v20i1.21748.

Vale, T.R. (Ed.) (2002). *Fire, native peoples, and the natural landscape*. Washington, DC: Island Press.

van Zwanenberg, R. M. (1976). Dorobo hunting and gathering: A way of life or a mode of production? *African Economic History, 2*(2), 12. https://doi.org/10.2307/3601510.

Vian, T. (2009). Benefits and drawbacks of per diems: Do allowances distort good governance in the health sector? *U4* BRIEF No. 2.

Vian, T., Miller, C., Themba, Z., & Bukuluki, P. (2013). Perceptions of per diems in the health sector: Evidence and implications. *Health Policy and Planning*, *28*(3), 237–246. https://doi.org/10.1093/heapol/czs056.

Ville, J.-L. (1998). La conservation des ressources naturelles: De l'exclusion à la participation communautaire. In F. Grignon & G. Prunier (eds), *Le Kenya contemporain*, 231–243. Paris and Nairobi: Karthala and IFRA.

von Hellermann, P. (2007). Things Fall Apart? Management, Environment and Taungya Farming in Edo State, Southern Nigeria. *Africa*, *77*(03), 371–392. https://doi.org/10.3366/afr.2007.0052.

Walker, K. (1989). The state in environmental management: The ecological dimension. *Political Studies*, *37*(1), 25–38. https://doi.org/10.1111/j.1467-9248.1989.tb00263.x.

Wamukoya, G.M., & Ludeki, J.V. (eds) (2003). Environmental management in Kenya: Understanding environmental impact assessment process. Nairobi: CREEL Publication Series No. 3.

Watts, M. (1983). *Silent violence: Food, famine and peasantry in Northern Nigeria*. Berkeley: University of California Press.

Watts, M., & Peet, R. (1993). Environment and development, parts I and II, special issue. *Economic Geography 69*(3/4).

Weber, M. (1922). *Grundriß der Sozialökonomik. III. Abteilung: Wirtschaft und Gesellschaft*. Tübingen: J.C.B. Mohr (Paul Siebeck).

Weiner, D.R. (2005). A death-defying attempt to articulate a coherent definition of environmental history. *Environmental History*, *10*(3), 404–420.

Weisser, F., Bollig, M., Doevenspeck, M., & Müller-Mahn, D. (2013). Translating the 'adaptation to climate change' paradigm: The politics of a travelling idea in Africa. *The Geographical Journal*, *180*(2), 111–119. https://doi.org/10.1111/geoj.12037.

Weisser, F., Doevenspeck, M., Müller-Mahn, D., & Bollig, M. (2011). Translating adaptation to climate change: The politics of a travelling idea in developing countries. Draft working paper (unpublished in this form)

Westra, L. (2008). Ecological integrity: Its history, its future and the development of the global ecological integrity group. In L. Westra, K. Bosselmann, & R. Westra (eds), *Reconciling Human Existence with Ecological Integrity: Science, Ethics, Economics and Law*, 5–20. London and Sterling, VA: Earthscan.

Williams, R. (1973). *The country and the city*. New York: Oxford University Press.

Wolf, E. (1972). Ownership and political ecology. *Anthropological Quarterly*, *45*(3). https://doi.org/10.2307/3316532.

Wolfe, P. (2006). Settler colonialism and the elimination of the native. *Journal of Genocide Research, 8*(4), 387–409. https://doi.org/10.1080/14623520601056240.

Woodhouse, P. (1997). Governance & local environmental management in Africa. *Review of African Political Economy, 24*(74), 537–547. https://doi.org/10.1080/03056249708704280.

Woodhouse, P., Bernstein, H., & Hulme, D. (eds) (2000). *African enclosures? The social dynamics of wetlands-in-drylands.* Oxford: James Currey.

Wrong, M. (2009). *It's our turn to eat.* London: Fourth Estate.

Zeppel, H. (2007). *Indigenous ecotourism: Sustainable development and management* (Ecotourism). Wallingford, UK and Cambridge, MA: CABI Pubishers.

Eastern Africa Series

EASTERN AFRICAN STUDIES

These titles published in the United States and Canada by Ohio University Press

Revealing Prophets
Edited by DAVID M. ANDERSON
& DOUGLAS H. JOHNSON

*East African Expressions of
Christianity*
Edited by THOMAS SPEAR &
ISARIA N. KIMAMBO

The Poor Are Not Us
Edited by DAVID M. ANDERSON
& VIGDIS BROCH-DUE

Potent Brews
JUSTIN WILLIS

Swahili Origins
JAMES DE VERE ALLEN

Being Maasai
Edited by THOMAS SPEAR &
RICHARD WALLER

Jua Kali Kenya
KENNETH KING

*Control & Crisis in
Colonial Kenya*
BRUCE BERMAN

Unhappy Valley
Book One: State & Class
Book Two: Violence & Ethnicity
BRUCE BERMAN & JOHN
LONSDALE

Mau Mau from Below
GREET KERSHAW

The Mau Mau War in Perspective
FRANK FUREDI

*Squatters & the Roots of Mau Mau
1905–63*
TABITHA KANOGO

*Economic & Social Origins of Mau
Mau 1945–53*
DAVID W. THROUP

*Multi-Party Politics
in Kenya*
DAVID W. THROUP & CHARLES
HORNSBY

Empire State-Building
JOANNA LEWIS

*Decolonization & Independence in
Kenya 1940–93*
Edited by B.A. OGOT &
WILLIAM R. OCHIENG'

Eroding the Commons
DAVID ANDERSON

Penetration & Protest in Tanzania
ISARIA N. KIMAMBO

Custodians of the Land
Edited by GREGORY MADDOX,
JAMES L. GIBLIN & ISARIA N.
KIMAMBO

*Education in the
Development of Tanzania
1919–1990*
LENE BUCHERT

The Second Economy in Tanzania
T.L. MALIYAMKONO & M.S.D.
BAGACHWA

*Ecology Control & Economic Devel-
opment in East African History*
HELGE KJEKSHUS

Siaya
DAVID WILLIAM COHEN & E.S.
ATIENO ODHIAMBO

*Uganda Now • Changing Uganda
Developing Uganda • From Chaos
to Order • Religion & Politics in
East Africa*
Edited by HOLGER BERNT
HANSEN & MICHAEL TWADDLE

*Kakungulu & the Creation of
Uganda, 1868–1928*
MICHAEL TWADDLE

Controlling Anger
SUZETTE HEALD

Kampala Women Getting By
SANDRA WALLMAN

*Political Power in Pre-Colonial
Buganda*
RICHARD J. REID

Alice Lakwena & the Holy Spirits
HEIKE BEHREND

Slaves, Spices & Ivory in Zanzibar
ABDUL SHERIFF

Zanzibar Under Colonial Rule
Edited by ABDUL SHERIFF & ED
FERGUSON

*The History & Conservation of
Zanzibar Stone Town*
Edited by ABDUL SHERIFF

Pastimes & Politics
LAURA FAIR

*Ethnicity & Conflict in the Horn
of Africa*
Edited by KATSUYOSHI FUKUI
& JOHN MARKAKIS

*Conflict, Age & Power in North
East Africa*
Edited by EISEI KURIMOTO &
SIMON SIMONSE

*Property Rights & Political Devel-
opment in Ethiopia & Eritrea*
SANDRA FULLERTON
JOIREMAN

Revolution & Religion in Ethiopia
ØYVIND M. EIDE

Brothers at War
TEKESTE NEGASH & KJETIL
TRONVOLL

From Guerrillas to Government
DAVID POOL

Mau Mau & Nationhood
Edited by E.S. ATIENO
ODHIAMBO & JOHN LONSDALE

*A History of Modern Ethiopia,
1855–1991* (2nd edn)
BAHRU ZEWDE

Pioneers of Change in Ethiopia
BAHRU ZEWDE

Remapping Ethiopia
Edited by W. JAMES, D.
DONHAM, E. KURIMOTO
& A. TRIULZI

*Southern Marches of Imperial
Ethiopia*
Edited by DONALD L. DONHAM
& WENDY JAMES

A Modern History of the Somali
(4th edn)
I.M. LEWIS

*Islands of Intensive
Agriculture in East Africa*
Edited by MATS WIDGREN &
JOHN E.G. SUTTON

Leaf of Allah
EZEKIEL GEBISSA

*Dhows & the Colonial Economy of
Zanzibar 1860–1970*
ERIK GILBERT

*African Womanhood in Colonial
Kenya*
TABITHA KANOGO

African Underclass
ANDREW BURTON

In Search of a Nation
Edited by GREGORY H.
MADDOX & JAMES L. GIBLIN

A History of the Excluded
JAMES L. GIBLIN

Black Poachers, White Hunters
EDWARD I. STEINHART

Ethnic Federalism
DAVID TURTON

Crisis & Decline in Bunyoro
SHANE DOYLE

*Emancipation without Abolition
in German East Africa*
JAN-GEORG DEUTSCH

*Women, Work & Domestic Virtue
in Uganda 1900–2003*
GRACE BANTEBYA KYOMU-
HENDO & MARJORIE
KENISTON McINTOSH

Cultivating Success in Uganda
GRACE CARSWELL

*War in Pre-Colonial Eastern
Africa*
RICHARD REID

*Slavery in the Great Lakes Region
of East Africa*
Edited by HENRI MÉDARD &
SHANE DOYLE

The Benefits of Famine
DAVID KEEN

www.ingramcontent.com/pod-product-compliance
Lightning Source LLC
Chambersburg PA
CBHW050624280326
41932CB00015B/2514